Daniel

THE NIV
APPLICATION
COMMENTARY

From biblical text . . . to contemporary life

THE NIV APPLICATION COMMENTARY SERIES

EDITORIAL BOARD

General Editor
Terry Muck

Consulting Editors
Old Testament

Tremper Longman III *Robert Hubbard*
John H. Walton *Andrew Dearman*

Zondervan Editorial Advisors

Stanley N. Gundry
Vice President and Editor-in-Chief

Jack Kuhatschek *Verlyn Verbrugge*
Senior Acquisitions Editor Senior Editor

DANIEL

THE NIV APPLICATION COMMENTARY

From biblical text . . . to contemporary life

TREMPER LONGMAN III

GRAND RAPIDS, MICHIGAN 49530 USA

ZONDERVAN™

The NIV Application Commentary: Daniel
Copyright © 1999 by Tremper Longman III

Requests for information should be addressed to:
Zondervan, *Grand Rapids, Michigan 49530*

Library of Congress Cataloging-in-Publication Data

Longman, Tremper.
    Daniel / Tremper Longman III.
       p. cm. — (NIV application commentary)
    Includes bibliographical references and indexes.
    ISBN: 0–310–20608–1 (hardcover : alk. paper)
       1. Bible. O.T. Daniel — Commentaries.   I. Title.   II. Series.
BS 1555.3.L66 1999
224'.5077 — dc21   98–46640
                                                                                                                                                                                     CIP

This edition printed on acid-free paper.

All Scripture quotations, unless otherwise indicated, are taken from the *Holy Bible: New International Version*®. NIV®. Copyright © 1973, 1978, 1984 by International Bible Society. Used by permission of Zondervan. All rights reserved.

All rights reserved. No part of this publication may be reproduced, stored in a retrieval system, or transmitted in any form or by any means — electronic, mechanical, photocopy, recording, or any other — except for brief quotations in printed reviews, without the prior permission of the publisher.

Printed in the United States of America

02 03 04 05 06 07 08 /❖ DC/ 16 15 14 13 12 11 10 9 8 7 6

Dedication
To Alice

Contents

9
Series Introduction

13
General Editor's Preface

15
Author's Preface and Acknowledgments

16
Abbreviations

19
Introduction

30
Outline

32
Bibliography

41
Text and Commentary on Daniel

307
Scripture Index

311
Subject Index

The NIV Application Commentary Series

When complete, the NIV Application Commentary
will include the following volumes:

Old Testament Volumes
Genesis, John H. Walton
Exodus, Peter Enns
Leviticus/Numbers, Roy Gane
Deuteronomy, Daniel I. Block
Joshua, Robert Hubbard
Judges/Ruth, K. Lawson Younger
1-2 Samuel, Bill T. Arnold
1-2 Kings, Gus Konkel
1-2 Chronicles, Andrew E. Hill
Ezra/Nehemiah, Douglas J. Green
Esther, Karen H. Jobes
Job, Dennis R. Magary
Psalms Volume 1, Gerald H. Wilson
Psalms Volume 2, Gerald H. Wilson
Proverbs, Paul Koptak
Ecclesiastes/Song of Songs, Iain Provan
Isaiah, John N. Oswalt
Jeremiah/Lamentations, J. Andrew Dearman
Ezekiel, Iain M. Duguid
Daniel, Tremper Longman III
Hosea/Amos/Micah, Gary V. Smith
Jonah/Nahum/Habakkuk/Zephaniah,
  James Bruckner
Joel/Obadiah/Malachi, David W. Baker
Haggai/Zechariah, Mark J. Boda

New Testament Volumes
Matthew, Michael J. Wilkins
Mark, David E. Garland
Luke, Darrell L. Bock
John, Gary M. Burge
Acts, Ajith Fernando
Romans, Douglas J. Moo
1 Corinthians, Craig Blomberg
2 Corinthians, Scott Hafemann
Galatians, Scot McKnight
Ephesians, Klyne Snodgrass
Philippians, Frank Thielman
Colossians/Philemon, David E. Garland
1-2 Thessalonians, Michael W. Holmes
1-2 Timothy/Titus, Walter L. Liefeld
Hebrews, George H. Guthrie
James, David P. Nystrom
1 Peter, Scot McKnight
2 Peter/Jude, Douglas J. Moo
Letters of John, Gary M. Burge
Revelation, Craig S. Keener

To see which titles are available,
visit our web site at http://www.zondervan.com

NIV Application Commentary
Series Introduction

THE NIV APPLICATION COMMENTARY SERIES is unique. Most commentaries help us make the journey from the twentieth century back to the first century. They enable us to cross the barriers of time, culture, language, and geography that separate us from the biblical world. Yet they only offer a one-way ticket to the past and assume that we can somehow make the return journey on our own. Once they have explained the *original meaning* of a book or passage, these commentaries give us little or no help in exploring its *contemporary significance*. The information they offer is valuable, but the job is only half done.

Recently, a few commentaries have included some contemporary application as *one* of their goals. Yet that application is often sketchy or moralistic, and some volumes sound more like printed sermons than commentaries.

The primary goal of The NIV Application Commentary Series is to help you with the difficult but vital task of bringing an ancient message into a modern context. The series not only focuses on application as a finished product but also helps you think through the *process* of moving from the original meaning of a passage to its contemporary significance. These are commentaries, not popular expositions. They are works of reference, not devotional literature.

The format of the series is designed to achieve the goals of the series. Each passage is treated in three sections: *Original Meaning, Bridging Contexts*, and *Contemporary Significance*.

THIS SECTION HELPS you understand the meaning of the biblical text in its first-century context. All of the elements of traditional exegesis—in concise form—are discussed here. These include the historical, literary, and cultural context of the passage. The authors discuss matters related to grammar and syntax, and the meaning of biblical words. They also seek to explore the main ideas of the passage and how the biblical author develops those ideas.[1]

---

1. Please note that when the authors discuss words in the original biblical languages, the series uses the general rather than the scholarly method of transliteration. For Hebrew words, consonants are differentiated, but not long or short vowels.

Series Introduction

After reading this section, you will understand the problems, questions, and concerns of the *original audience* and how the biblical author addressed those issues. This understanding is foundational to any legitimate application of the text today.

THIS SECTION BUILDS a bridge between the world of the Bible and the world of today, between the original context and the contemporary context, by focusing on both the timely and timeless aspects of the text.

God's Word is *timely*. The authors of Scripture spoke to specific situations, problems, and questions. Paul warned the Galatians about the consequences of circumcision and the dangers of trying to be justified by law (Gal. 5:2–5). The author of Hebrews tried to convince his readers that Christ is superior to Moses, the Aaronic priests, and the Old Testament sacrifices. John urged his readers to "test the spirits" of those who taught a form of incipient Gnosticism (1 John 4:1–6). In each of these cases, the timely nature of Scripture enables us to hear God's Word in situations that were *concrete* rather than abstract.

Yet the timely nature of Scripture also creates problems. Our situations, difficulties, and questions are not always directly related to those faced by the people in the Bible. Therefore, God's word to them does not always seem relevant to us. For example, when was the last time someone urged you to be circumcised, claiming that it was a necessary part of justification? How many people today care whether Christ is superior to the Aaronic priests? And how can a "test" designed to expose incipient Gnosticism be of any value in a modern culture?

Fortunately, Scripture is not only timely but *timeless*. Just as God spoke to the original audience, so he still speaks to us through the pages of Scripture. Because we share a common humanity with the people of the Bible, we discover a *universal dimension* in the problems they faced and the solutions God gave them. The timeless nature of Scripture enables it to speak with power in every time and in every culture.

Those who fail to recognize that Scripture is both timely and timeless run into a host of problems. For example, those who are intimidated by timely books such as Hebrews or Galatians might avoid reading them because they seem meaningless today. At the other extreme, those who are convinced of the timeless nature of Scripture, but who fail to discern its timely element, may "wax eloquent" about the Melchizedekian priesthood to a sleeping congregation.

Series Introduction

The purpose of this section, therefore, is to help you discern what is timeless in the timely pages of Scripture—and what is not. For example, if Paul's primary concern is not circumcision (as he tells us in Gal. 5:6), what *is* he concerned about? If discussions about the Aaronic priesthood or Melchizedek seem irrelevant today, what is of abiding value in these passages? If people try to "test the spirits" today with a test designed for a specific first-century heresy, what other biblical test might be more appropriate?

Yet this section does not merely uncover that which is timeless in a passage but also helps you to see *how* it is uncovered. The author of the commentary seeks to take what is implicit in the text and make it explicit, to take a process that normally is intuitive and explain it in a logical, orderly fashion. How do we know that circumcision is not Paul's primary concern? What clues in the text or its context help us realize that Paul's real concern is at a deeper level?

Of course, those passages in which the historical distance between us and the original readers is greatest require a longer treatment. Conversely, those passages in which the historical distance is smaller or seemingly nonexistent require less attention.

One final clarification. Because this section prepares the way for discussing the contemporary significance of the passage, there is not always a sharp distinction or a clear break between this section and the one that follows. Yet when both sections are read together, you should have a strong sense of moving from the world of the Bible to the world of today.

THIS SECTION ALLOWS the biblical message to speak with as much power today as it did when it was first written. How can you apply what you learned about Jerusalem, Ephesus, or Corinth to our present-day needs in Chicago, Los Angeles, or London? How can you take a message originally spoken in Greek and Aramaic and communicate it clearly in our own language? How can you take the eternal truths originally spoken in a different time and culture and apply them to the similar-yet-different needs of our culture?

In order to achieve these goals, this section gives you help in several key areas.

First, it helps you identify contemporary situations, problems, or questions that are truly comparable to those faced by the original audience. Because contemporary situations are seldom identical to those faced in the first century, you must seek situations that are analogous if your applications are to be relevant.

Series Introduction

Second, this section explores a variety of contexts in which the passage might be applied today. You will look at personal applications, but you will also be encouraged to think beyond private concerns to the society and culture at large.

Third, this section will alert you to any problems or difficulties you might encounter in seeking to apply the passage. And if there are several legitimate ways to apply a passage (areas in which Christians disagree), the author will bring these to your attention and help you think through the issues involved.

In seeking to achieve these goals, the contributors to this series attempt to avoid two extremes. They avoid making such specific applications that the commentary might quickly become dated. They also avoid discussing the significance of the passage in such a general way that it fails to engage contemporary life and culture.

Above all, contributors to this series have made a diligent effort not to sound moralistic or preachy. The NIV Application Commentary Series does not seek to provide ready-made sermon materials but rather tools, ideas, and insights that will help you communicate God's Word with power. If we help you to achieve that goal, then we have fulfilled the purpose for this series.

—The Editors

General Editor's Preface

"IN SPITE OF PRESENT APPEARANCES, God is in control." That, Tremper Longman tells us over and over, is the core message of Daniel. What an appropriate message for Daniel's original hearers/readers. In exile in Babylon, it must have appeared to them that the great powers of the world—the Babylonians, the Medes, the Persians—were in control. By writing of his experiences as a captive Israelite who gained power in Babylon through his ability to interpret King Nebuchadnezzar's dreams, Daniel tells his compatriots that God, not a human king, is ultimately in control.

What an appropriate message for today also. When we look at our society and find overwhelming evidences of what William Bennet calls cultural decay and the Christian Coalition describes as the loss of a moral center, it is tempting to question whether God really is in control. Perhaps we are sophisticated enough to know that human kingdoms are not in control. The failure of Maoist China, the breakup of the Soviet Union, the steep decline in the fortunes of the United States—all impress on us daily that nations and states rise and fall. Still, we tend to see behind such misfortune powers that are anything but godlike—impersonal forces of fate, theories of deterministic science, Satan the master of evil. Can God possibly be in control?

Daniel said—and would say today were he with us—yes. In spite of present appearances, God is in control. Since this is the universal message of this book, the one that bridges the sixth century B.C. and twenty-first century A.D. contexts, it is worth our while to see how Daniel goes about convincing suffering readers of this hope-giving truth. He uses a two-pronged approach. He tells us six gripping stories of God's providence, then gives us five mystical visions, which together blast our senses with impressions of God's great power. Why this combination of literal historical stories and mystical visions?

Recently I sat by Long Lake in Mercer, Wisconsin, observing a loon feeding in the bay. At least I assume the loon was feeding. The bird would bob and float on the top of the water for some seconds, then suddenly dive, stay under water for two or three minutes, and then resurface, sometimes hundreds of feet from the diving point. My observation of the loon was of a series of lake-top appearances. But to understand fully the whole meaning of those lake-top appearances, I had to infer what the bird was doing on the long dives that filled the intervals.

The book of Daniel is doing something similar. The historical stories of how God took care of the prophet as he navigated the tricky waters of Babylonian

General Editor's Preface

court politics are necessary to show us that God really does take care of his own. God is in control. Not in some meaningless, abstract, pie-in-the-sky way, but in the here and now.

But stories like this have their limitations. God's providence does not always show itself in "success" stories. Sometimes, as the book of Job attests, God is in control in cases where his children suffer mightily. "Success" stories are necessary to give us hope, but alone they tend to reify transitory elements of the stories—Daniel succeeded because he was a vegetarian, so if we all become vegetarians, we will succeed too. Daniel succeeded because he prayed in an upper room in full view of all the people of Babylon, so if we all pray in that manner we will succeed too. Not really. These stories are not irrelevant. They teach us important lessons. But they are like the appearances of the loon on top of the lake. In order to be fully understood, we must know that a great deal is happening under the surface.

Enter the apocalyptic visions, which communicate to us that a great deal is happening "under water." God's greatness can be illustrated through everyday stories but cannot be captured by them. We need something further to show us that God encompasses the ordinary and the everyday but also goes beyond it. Daniel's visions can be understood up to a point, but cannot be completely understood in all details. They are specifically designed to communicate mystery. They leave us uncertain about specifics even though they clearly tell us that God is in control.

Daniel's message about God's control requires both the stories of the first six chapters and the visions of the last six. The stories give us comfort, the visions a sense of our finitude. Without the latter, the stories could lead us to believe in a false relationship between human works and God's grace—if we do certain things, God must provide. Without the stories, the visions could lead us to an impractical, disembodied mysticism. With both, this book offers a hopeful confidence that God is indeed in control.

—Terry C. Muck

Author's Preface and Acknowledgments

THE BOOK OF DANIEL attracted my attention very early in my Christian life. As a college student in the turbulent 1970s, I was captivated by the book's vision of a violent end to history. Calmer times led to a more sober assessment of the purpose of the book, but I have never lost the thrill of reading Daniel's dramatic word pictures of the intrusion of God into the world as warrior and judge. If anything, the impact of the book has grown on me as I now see more clearly that those "simple" stories of the first half have such startling relevance for us as we struggle to come to terms with a hostile culture.

I have many people to thank for help in the composition of this book. During the past dozen years I have taught a doctoral-level seminar on the book of Daniel. Class discussions helped me sharpen my thinking about the book. For this reason, I would like to express my thanks to the students who participated in these classes. In particular, I thank Erick Allen, Mark DiGiasomo, and Jovanni Tricerri for their invaluable help as my research assistants.

This book is not the first that I have published with Zondervan. Through the years, my respect for Zondervan has grown enormously. In regard to this project, I thank Jack Kuhatschek and Verlyn Verbrugge for their insights and professionalism. I have also received excellent and insightful feedback from Terry Muck, the general editor of the series, and from John Walton of Moody Bible Institute. This volume is much better because of their critical interaction. I must say, however, that since I did not always follow their advice, they cannot be blamed for any shortcomings.

This book is dedicated to my wife, Alice, on the occasion of our twenty-fifth wedding anniversary.

—Tremper Longman III
Westmont College

Abbreviations

AB	Anchor Bible
ANET	Ancient Near Eastern Texts, ed. J. Pritchard
AusBR	Australian Biblical Review
AUSS	Andrews University Seminary Studies
BA	Biblical Archaeologist
BAR	Biblical Archaeology Review
BASOR	Bulletin of the American School of Oriental Research
Bib	Biblica
BSac	Bibliotheca Sacra
BT	The Bible Translator
CBQ	Catholic Biblical Quarterly
CBQMS	Catholic Biblical Quarterly Monograph Series
ConBOT	Coniectanca biblica, Old Testament
CT	Christianity Today
EBC	Expositor's Bible Commentary
ETL	Ephemerides theologicae lovanienses
EvQ	Evangelical Quarterly
ExpTim	Expository Times
GTJ	Grace Theological Journal
HDR	Harvard Dissertations in Religion
HUCA	Hebrew Union College Annual
ICC	International Critical Commentary
IEJ	Israel Exploration Journal
Interp	Interpretation
IOS	Israel Oriental Society
JA	Journal asiatique
JANES	Journal of the Ancient Near Eastern Society
JAOS	Journal of the American Oriental Society
JBL	Journal of Biblical Literature
JETS	Journal of the Evangelical Theological Society
JMRS	Journal of Medieval and Renaissance Studies
JNES	Journal of Near Eastern Studies
JQR	Jewish Quarterly Review
JSJ	Journal for the Study of Judaism
JSNT	Journal for the Study of the New Testament

JSOT	*Journal for the Study of the Old Testament*
JSOTSup	Journal for the Study of the Old Testament Supplement Series
JSPSS	Journal for the Study of the Pseudepigrapha Supplement Series
JTS	*Journal of Theological Studies*
NAB	New American Bible
NAC	New American Commentary
NICOT	New International Commentary on the Old Testament
NIDOTTE	*New International Dictionary of Old Testament Theology and Exegesis*, ed. W. VanGemeren
NIV	New International Version
NJB	New Jerusalem Bible
NLT	New Living Translation
NovT	*Novum Testamentum*
NRSV	New Revised Standard Version
NTS	*New Testament Studies*
OTL	Old Testament Library
REB	Revised English Bible
SBLDS	Society of Biblical Literature Dissertation Series
ST	*Studia theologica*
TrinJ	*Trinity Journal*
TynBul	*Tyndale Bulletin*
TOTC	Tyndale Old Testament Commentaries
TZ	*Theologische Zeitschrift*
VT	*Vetus Testamentum*
WBC	Word Biblical Commentary
WO	*Die Welt des Orients*
WTJ	*Westminster Theological Journal*
ZAW	*Zeitschrift für die alttestamentliche Wissenschaft*

Introduction

DANIEL IS A BOOK OF PARADOXES. The first six chapters are deceptively simple stories of faith under pressure. Daniel and his three friends have been forced to leave their homeland, Israel, and settle in the Babylonian king's palace. They are compelled to learn foreign ways in preparation to serve the government, which has made a hostile incursion against Israel and looms dangerously over that country of their birth. Each chapter brings new challenges, and each time they rise to meet the crisis. Neither Daniel nor his three friends waver in their faith or ponder their actions. They certainly seek divine help, but they are confident in their God, even if God might not preserve their lives through a trial (cf. 3:16–18). God, however, is up to the task, demonstrating his sovereignty, his power over evil human intentions, again and again. Clear and encouraging, these six stories have spoken forcefully to many believers, including the youngest of children. Many of us who grew up in the church remember the stories of Daniel as a staple of children's Sunday school programs and vacation Bible school lessons.

Not so with the second half of the book, however! The simple division between chapters 6 and 7 masks a radical shift in genre and complexity. While children resonate with the lessons of Daniel 1–6, seasoned Bible scholars scratch their heads over Daniel 7–12 with the move from simple stories to obscure apocalyptic visions (see description and discussion of apocalyptic at the beginning of the commentary on chapter 7). The first half of the book are stories about Daniel; the second half are visions of Daniel. Even though there is a dramatic contrast in genre between the two halves of the book, however, the overall message of the book is uniform: *In spite of present appearances, God is in control.*[1]

---

1. Other features of the book, beyond the theme of divine sovereignty, unite the two halves of Daniel. These include the obvious similarities between chapters 2 and 7. Even closer study indicates a chiastic arrangement between chapters 2–7, which J. G. Baldwin, "Theology of Daniel," *NIDOTTE*, 4:499, outlines as follows:

  A. Four empires and God's coming kingdom (ch. 2)
    B. Trial by fire and God's deliverance (ch. 3)
      C. A king warned, chastised, and delivered (ch. 4)
      C'. A king warned, defiant, and deposed (ch. 5)
    B'. Trial in the lions' den and God's deliverance (ch. 6)
  A'. Four empires and God's everlasting kingdom (ch. 7)

Furthermore, the book as we have it is written in Aramaic and Hebrew, and the distribution of the two languages overlaps the distinct genres (with Aramaic in 2:4b–7:28, Hebrew in 1:1–2:4a and 8:1–12:13).

Introduction

The Sovereignty of God

THE BIBLE IS a book about God. Daniel is no exception; it too is a book about God. We emphasize this at the beginning because the focus of the camera, to use a film analogy, is often on the human characters: Daniel, the three friends, Nebuchadnezzar, Belshazzar, Darius, Cyrus. But we must not be misled; Daniel's main function is to reveal God to us, the readers.

The Bible, however, is not interested in presenting its readers with an abstract understanding of the nature of God. We have little in the Bible that resembles modern systematic theology; certainly there is no listing and description of his attributes. God reveals himself in relationship with his people. We can see this in the dominant metaphors of God in the Bible. He is king, warrior, shepherd, husband, father, and mother, assuming that his people are his subjects, his soldiers, his sheep, his wife, his children.[2] As we will see, the book of Daniel utilizes some of these metaphors of relationship in support of the overall theme of divine sovereignty, but here I wish to draw attention to the fact that his sovereignty is not described abstractly in this book, but in the midst of the historical process, in the nitty-gritty of life.

We can anticipate fuller treatments by simply mentioning the first few verses of chapter 1, where we see that it is really God, not Nebuchadnezzar, who is behind the Babylonian's assertion of power over Judah. It is God, not Nebuchadnezzar and his educational and dietary regime, who is behind the extraordinary skills of Daniel and his three friends. It is God who is behind Daniel's ability to penetrate the secret of Nebuchadnezzar's dream in chapter 2. Each chapter tells a different story, but each one is a story of divine sovereignty.

God is all-powerful, and this narration and demonstration of his power has one important purpose: the encouragement of a beleaguered people. Faithful Israelites must have suffered in exile as they remembered the good relationship that they as a people had with their God in the land of Palestine. They must have suffered as they were forced to work for the good of the nation that oppressed them. And they did suffer as they found themselves in situations where they were pressed to compromise or else face dire consequences. The message of Daniel that God is all-powerful and in control in spite of present conditions intended to present a powerful encouragement to these people.

But who were these people? Who were Daniel's original audience? And, for that matter, who was Daniel himself? These questions lead us into the midst of one of the thorniest questions of the book.

---

2. For a further explication of this point and an extended discussion of the warrior image, see T. Longman III and D. Reid, *God Is a Warrior* (Grand Rapids: Zondervan, 1995).

Introduction

Daniel and Its Original Audience

THE BOOK OF Daniel sets Daniel in the sixth century B.C. There is no doubt or dispute about that. Major figures from this time period, known from other biblical and ancient Near Eastern sources, play an important role in the book: Nebuchadnezzar, Belshazzar, Cyrus, as well as Jehoiakim. Daniel 1:1 is dated to the third year of the reign of Jehoiakim (605 B.C.) and the latest references include one to the "first year of King Cyrus" (1:21; 539 B.C.) as well as that great king's third year (10:1; 537 B.C.).

Details of this period as they relate to the text will be given at the appropriate place. However, briefly, the sixth century was a crucial moment for God's people and an interesting epoch in the history of the ancient Near East. In terms of the latter, the beginning of the book of Daniel coincides with Babylon's rise on the dust of the Assyrian empire. Nebuchadnezzar's incursions into Palestine from his command center in Riblah, Syria, coincide with Babylon's bid to push Egyptian power out of the region. Under Nebuchadnezzar, Babylon grew stronger and stronger and reached the height of its power. After his death, that power slowly dissipated, though there were interesting moments under such rulers (not named in the book of Daniel) as Neriglissar and Nabonidus (for the latter's association with Belshazzar, see comments on Dan. 5). On the horizon lurked the developing power known as Persia, beginning in the middle of the sixth century to expand its imperial pretensions. Under Cyrus Persia finally took Babylon in 539 B.C.

With this crucial date we can turn to the story of Israel, more specifically the southern kingdom of Judah, in the sixth century. The year 539 B.C. was an important one for God's people because with the ascension of Persian power came a change of policy toward subjugated peoples. While the Babylonians exiled the leaders of captured peoples like the Judeans to utilize their skills and resources at the center of the empire, the Persians felt it better to return these people to their homeland. The exile from which the Israelites returned in 539 B.C. began in earnest in 587/586 B.C., though earlier incursions are documented in 597 and, as we argue in the commentary on Daniel 1:1–3, in 605 B.C.

Of course, the setting of material like what we have in Daniel 1–6 does no more than give us the earliest date for the composition of the book. Nowhere do these chapters claim that Daniel or anyone else wrote them. There is no claim for a sixth-century date of the book. They are accounts about the sixth century, not necessarily compositions of the sixth century.

The same may be said of the last six chapters of the book, but here there is a wrinkle. As mentioned above, these chapters contain prophecies by Daniel. The prophecies are recounted in the first person, but note

Introduction

that there is a third person frame. For example, the second section begins: "In the first year of Belshazzar king of Babylon, Daniel had a dream, and visions passed through his mind as he was lying on his bed. He wrote down the substance of his dream. Daniel said..." (7:1–2a). The composition of the final form of Daniel 7–12 likewise, therefore, makes no claim on a sixth-century composition.

However, we cannot use these textual facts to escape an exegetical problem that has plagued the study of the book of Daniel for many years. Though the prophecies have a third person frame, they are delivered by Daniel in the first person and therefore make an implicit claim to originate in the sixth century. The prophecies themselves, in other words, require a sixth-century setting, and here is the problem.

The issue concerns the fact that the first six chapters, while presenting themselves as historical narrative, are surrounded by issues of historical accuracy, while the second six chapters, which are prophecy, are uncannily accurate and precise through the second century B.C., at least up to a definite point. To many, these facts appear to result from a second-century date of composition, where some of the historical persons and events of the Babylonian and Persian periods are a bit murky, while the more recent events of the Greek period are well known and clear. In other words, chapters that present the events of the third and second centuries B.C. as prophecy appear to have been written after the fact, and we can recognize the attempts at real prophecy by their failure to predict accurately (see the extended discussion in connection with the prophecy of ch. 11).

The conundrum is that faithful interpreters find themselves on two sides of the debate. On the one hand, there are those who believe it is necessary to stick to a sixth-century composition. Others feel that the text drives them to a second-century date, and if they believe that the Bible is the Word of God, they must then struggle with the theological issue of a book that, at least on the surface, attempts to deceive its audience into thinking it is prophesying future events when in reality it is casting the past into a future tense.

One attempt to get around this conundrum is to point to the well-established use of pseudonymity in the ancient Near East.[3] Indeed, such pseudonymity was well practiced and often involved no attempt at deception. The original audience knew what the author was doing.[4] However, I would argue that this approach fails when applied to the book of Daniel. The

---

3. This describes the general argument of a perceptive commentator like J. Goldingay, *Daniel* (Waco, Tex.: Word, 1989).

4. See my study of ancient Near Eastern pseudonymity with an emphasis on royal autobiography; T. Longman III, *Fictional Akkadian Autobiography* (Winona Lake, Ind.: Eisenbrauns, 1991).

Introduction

only way that Daniel's intention as demonstrated in the text can be achieved is by duping the audience. In other words, in prophecy given after the fact (*vaticinium ex eventu*) the idea was to convince the audience that the prophet was a true prophet to whom God had revealed the future. After showing that by predicting events that had already passed, then there was an attempt at a real prophecy. This is more than a literary device, and one must question whether such a textual strategy would find a place in God's Word.

This should not, however, obscure the extent of the difficulties of promoting a sixth-century date. The historical problems in the first part are real, and the solutions to some we can only speculate about (see commentary). Moreover, there are problems that need to be addressed at the end of chapter 11, when the prophecy appears to fail. We will provide another explanation than a late date at that point in the commentary, but we will not glibly push the problem under the rug.

These are difficult issues that will divide faithful interpreters for years. We must resist the temptation to turn this issue into a simple litmus test. Some argue that anyone who holds to a sixth-century date is a hopeless "fundie" who refuses to look at the evidence. Others will brand those who opt for a second-century date as "liberals" or "compromisers." I know that there will be reviewers of my work and approach who will view me as softminded or softhearted on this issue, but I argue that it is an unhelpful simplification to categorize on the basis of someone's conclusions on this matter. At the very least, we need to look at the motives and arguments behind the conclusions as well as at the treatment of the text in the light of the commentator's conclusions on the date of the book.

In view of the evidence and in spite of the difficulties, I interpret the book from the conclusion that the prophecies come from the sixth century B.C. I find the problems amenable to hypothetical solutions and the theological issues of a late date difficult to surmount. However, two brilliantly insightful commentators on the book would strongly disagree with me. J. Goldingay interprets the book as finally redacted in the second century B.C. (for a description of this century, see the commentary on Daniel 11), but at the same time he is motivated by a strong desire to follow the teaching of the text. He also clearly believes in the supernatural universe presented by the Bible and does not doubt that God can speak about the future. Furthermore, as we look below the surface of Sibley Towner's excellent contribution on Daniel,[5] we note that he understands the book to be divine self-revelation, even though he categorically denies the possibility of the type of prophecy we find in the latter part of the book. To simply rule out

---

5. W. S. Towner, *Daniel* (Atlanta: John Knox, 1984).

Introduction

these two theologically astute interpreters on the basis of their late date of the book would be a tragedy.[6]

In short, while the present commentary still finds a sixth-century date defensible, it refuses to discount all those who interpret from a second-century date. We agree with J. Baldwin, also an eminent interpreter of the book of Daniel,[7] who in one of her last publications before her death stated: "The fact that the standpoint of the writer (sixth or second century B.C.) cannot be ascertained for certain does not greatly affect the interpretation."[8]

THE ISSUES SURROUNDING the relevance and application of the Old Testament to our lives and society at the turn of the third millennium A.D. is complex and debated. How does a text that was originally addressed to an audience in the sixth century B.C. retain its significance? Many Christians have difficulty relating to the Old Testament because of its distance from our lives. I would describe the book of Daniel's distance from us in three areas:

(1) Chronological. The book of Daniel was written over two and a half millennia ago. Times change. I recently watched a television show about America in the 1950s and was struck by how different life was in my youth than it is now, and there we are only speaking about forty years.

(2) Cultural. Daniel was addressed to Israelites living in Babylonian exile. The world of Daniel was an ancient Near Eastern world. Our Western culture is completely different, and even current Middle Eastern cultures bear only the slightest resemblance to the world in which Daniel and Nebuchadnezzar lived.

(3) Redemptive-historical. Perhaps here is where Daniel and the whole Old Testament are strange to Christians. In a word, Daniel lived in the world before the coming of Christ. We live looking back on his earthly ministry, death, and resurrection. Christians find the New Testament more immediately applicable for obvious reasons.

That there is continuity between the New Testament and the Old Testament is obvious to anyone who reads the Bible. The New Testament is satu-

---

6. On the other hand, there are other interpreters who do not feel a need to struggle with this issue because they do not believe the Bible is divine revelation by any definition of the term.

7. Baldwin has also strongly and clearly advocated a sixth-century date in her commentary (*Daniel*, TOTC [Downers Grove, Ill.: InterVarsity, 1978).

8. J. Baldwin, "Theology of Daniel," *NIDOTTE*, 4:499.

Introduction

rated with Old Testament references. It builds on the foundation of the Old, and there are a number of passages that strongly assert its continuing validity. Perhaps most notable is Jesus' affirmation of the Law and Prophets (a first-century A.D. way of referring to what we know as the Old Testament):

> Do not think that I have come to abolish the Law or the Prophets; I have not come to abolish them but to fulfill them. I tell you the truth, until heaven and earth disappear, not the smallest letter, not the least stroke of a pen, will by any means disappear from the Law until everything is accomplished. Anyone who breaks one of the least of these commandments and teaches others to do the same will be called least in the kingdom of heaven, but whoever practices and teaches these commands will be called great in the kingdom of heaven. For I tell you that unless your righteousness surpasses that of the Pharisees and the teachers of the law, you will certainly not enter the kingdom of heaven. (Matt. 5:17–20)

Jesus then goes on to talk about some specific ethical issues from the Old Testament, and the amazing thing is that, while he affirms the Old Testament teaching on murder, adultery, divorce, and so forth, he subtly transforms that teaching to something more internal and demanding. Adultery is not just sleeping with a woman; it is lusting after her. Murder is not just physically killing another person; it is anger toward another. Some would argue that Jesus draws a distinction not with the Old Testament teaching, but with human tradition that had grown up around the law, but I don't think a careful reading of the Sermon on the Mount in the light of the Old Testament can sustain that analysis. As we read the New Testament, there is neither strict continuity (as theonomists would insist) nor discontinuity (as some dispensationalists would have it), but rather both continuity and discontinuity between the Old and New Testaments.[9]

Sorting out continuity and discontinuity cannot be reduced to a formula or simple principle. We have to ask questions about the transformation of culture and the movement of redemptive history. We will sort these issues out as we deal with specific passages in Daniel.[10] However, here we may introduce a couple of major issues that will affect our approach throughout.

---

9. For an excellent treatment of this issue, see B. Waltke, "Theonomy in Relation to Dispensational and Covenant Theologies," in *Theonomy: A Reformed Critique*, ed. by W. Barker and R. Godfrey (Grand Rapids: Zondervan, 1990), 59–87, and T. Longman III, "God's Law and Mosaic Punishments Today" (pp. 41–57 in the same volume).

10. My book *Reading the Bible with Heart and Mind* (Colorado Springs: NavPress, 1997) is an attempt to deal with this issue with the major genres of the Bible (history, law, wisdom, poetry, prophecy, gospel, epistle, and apocalyptic).

Introduction

Christ, the Center of Biblical Revelation

THE BIBLE IS a book about God. It is God's self-revelation, and as we have seen, the book of Daniel masterfully demonstrates God's sovereignty over his people's past, present, and future. God's sovereignty infuses his people with confidence and hope in the midst of a difficult world. When Daniel's original audience read the book, they were given a new vista on their situation and their God.

Christians need to read the Old Testament from the perspective of the original audience, to be sure. But it would be a mistake to stop there. After all, we have received further revelation, and this further revelation casts its illuminating light back on the Old Testament. Saint Augustine captured what I mean with his well-known and catchy phrase: "The New Testament is in the Old concealed, and the Old Testament is in the New revealed."

The point is that continuing revelation has not imparted new meaning to the Old Testament but has illuminated the richer meaning of many texts that were not clear to the Old Testament people of God. Though debated, I believe this is what 1 Peter 1:10–12 indicates:

> Concerning this salvation, the prophets, who spoke of the grace that was to come to you, searched intently and with the greatest care, trying to find out the time and circumstances to which the Spirit of Christ in them was pointing when he predicted the sufferings of Christ and the glories that would follow. It was revealed to them that they were not serving themselves but you, when they spoke of the things that have now been told you by those who have preached the gospel to you by the Holy Spirit sent from heaven. Even angels long to look into these things.

Perhaps most illustrative of the point I am making are two comments made by Jesus after his resurrection. His disciples were in a quandary about the events surrounding his death. They did not understand what was happening. How could their leader, in whom they had invested such hopes, end his life in such an ignominious way? Jesus chides two different groups of his followers in two different, but similar passages:

> He said to them, "How foolish you are, and how slow of heart to believe all that the prophets have spoken! Did not the Christ have to suffer these things and then enter his glory?" And beginning with Moses and all the Prophets, he explained to them what was said in all the Scriptures concerning himself. (Luke 24:25–27)

> He said to them, "This is what I told you while I was still with you: Everything must be fulfilled that is written about me in the Law of Moses, the Prophets and the Psalms."

Introduction

> Then he opened their minds so they could understand the Scriptures. (Luke 24:44–45)

Most Christians would affirm that a handful of passages in the Old Testament predict Christ's coming in a spectacular way. If asked, they would point to the promise of the virgin birth in Isaiah 7, a reference to the "Anointed One" or Messiah in Psalm 2, and a few other passages. If we looked closely at these passages, we would see that they too have an Old Testament setting and are not messianic in a narrow sense. However, the point I want to emphasize is that Jesus' words invite a much broader understanding of how the Old Testament anticipates his coming. In Luke 24 Jesus speaks in global terms ("Moses and all the Prophets," "all the Scriptures," "the Law of Moses, the Prophets, and the Psalms"). As we read the Old Testament, we can read it with the expectation that we will encounter Christ there.[11]

This principle can be and often is abused. It is wrong to take a short passage of Scripture out of context and twist it until some vague connection with Christ is seen. It is dangerous to read the Old Testament in the light of the New before first reading the Old Testament in its original context. But it is equally incorrect for a Christian to neglect to read the Old in the fuller light of the New Testament. After all, the Bible, while composed of many different writings from many different time periods, is ultimately one organic revelation, whose author is God himself. We would naturally expect that later revelation will more fully disclose the truths of earlier Scripture. We will operate with this principle in the commentary that follows. Of course, the reader will have to judge whether we have persuasively shown how Christ is anticipated in a particular passage or whether we have fallen into the trap of pressing the case too strongly.

"Go Thou and Do Likewise": Do We Follow the Example of Daniel?

AS WE STUDY the book of Daniel, we expect to hear God's story. The book is filled with human characters and actions, but God is the subtle background character. We have also just argued that the Old Testament, including Daniel, is not just a theocentric book, but also a Christocentric book. Christ is anticipated in the Old Testament and proclaimed in the New. By emphasizing what might be called the theological message of the book, we avoid a common fallacy—a purely moralistic approach to the Old Testament. Most sermons and teaching on the book err by falling into the trap of simply turning

---

11. E. P. Clowney, *Preaching and Biblical Theology* (Grand Rapids: Eerdmans, 1961), develops this idea fully.

Introduction

Old Testament characters into heroes and villains: "Be like Daniel!" or "Don't be like Belshazzar!" Such teaching removes the focus of the biblical book from the intended main point, God, and thus misses the power of the passage.[12]

There is a further pitfall for which we need to account. Daniel 1–6 is historical narrative; it tells us what happened to Daniel and his three friends in the Babylonian and Persian courts. Is it legitimate to assume that just because Daniel is a hero of the faith that his actions are presented as normative for all time? When the question is presented baldly in this manner, the answer is certainly no. Just because Daniel acted in a certain way does not mean that his actions are instructions to how we should behave today. Daniel's vegetarian diet in the first chapter certainly should not have us pushing meat away from our tables. We don't have to pray in an upstairs room or in a room with windows (6:10) to pray sincerely. We must be very careful not to fall into the trap of saying that Daniel's actions are necessarily normative for our actions.

However, neither are they totally irrelevant. The Bible is not only a theological book; it is also an ethical book. The Old Testament historical books are not just there to teach us what happened in the past or about the nature of God in the abstract, but also intend to shape our emotions and our actions.[13] God could have given us a philosophical or theological treatise if his goal was to simply inform us about his nature, but instead he gave us his Word in the form of stories and poems that evoke the whole person—will and emotions as well as intellect. That the Old Testament narratives have a didactic intention[14] is suggested by the preface to Psalm 78:

> O my people, hear my teaching;
>   listen to the words of my mouth.
> I will open my mouth in parables,
>   I will utter hidden things, things from of old—
> what we have heard and known,
>   what our fathers have told us.
> We will not hide them from their children;
>   we will tell the next generation

---

12. Following the warning given by J. H. Walton, L. D. Bailey, and C. Williford, "Bible-Based Curricula and the Crisis of Scriptural Authority," *Christian Education Journal* 13 (1993): 83–94.

13. S. Greidanus, *Sola Scriptura: Problems and Principles in Preaching Historical Texts* (Kampen: J. H. Kok, 1970) narrates a debate among Dutch interpreters and preachers that drove a wedge between moralistic preaching and "redemptive-historical" preaching. The issues and debate are instructive, but the conclusion we should reach is that it is a both/and solution, not an either/or.

14. As argued in T. Longman III, *Literary Approaches to Biblical Interpretation* (Grand Rapids: Zondervan, 1987), 70.

> the praiseworthy deeds of the LORD,
> > his power, and the wonders he has done.
> He decreed statutes for Jacob
> > and established the law in Israel,
> which he commanded our forefathers
> > to teach their children,
> so the next generation would know them,
> > even the children yet to be born,
> > and they in turn would tell their children.
> Then they would put their trust in God
> > and would not forget his deeds
> > but would keep his commands.
> They would not be like their forefathers—
> > a stubborn and rebellious generation,
> whose hearts were not loyal to God,
> > whose spirits were not faithful to him. (Ps. 78:1–8)

The "parables" that follow in Psalm 78, which have as their intention obedience, are stories from Israel's past, mostly behavior to avoid. History can have a didactic function, and Old Testament history's lessons continue in an important sense in the New Testament period as well. After reminding his readers of the crossing of the Red Sea and the desert wandering, Paul asserts: "Now these things occurred as examples to keep us from setting our hearts on evil things as they did" (1 Cor. 10:6). Throughout the New Testament, different historical episodes of the Old Testament are recited to serve as paradigms of behavior in the post-Christ period (e.g., Heb. 11:4–40; James 5:10–11, 16–18).

However, warnings about simple appropriation of the Old Testament are crucial. The chronological, cultural, and redemptive-historical distance must be taken into account as we adjudicate the application of an ancient text to a modern situation. Readers of this commentary will have to judge for themselves whether I have persuasively charted the course through the potential pitfalls, but, as discussions in the specific chapters will underline, they can be sure that I am aware of the dangers both of neglecting this important aspect of the biblical text as well as blindly assuming that the ancient text provides normative role models and principles of living for us today.

Outline

I. **Daniel and the Three Friends in Nebuchadnezzar's Court (1:1–21)**
   A. Jehoiakim Delivered Into Nebuchadnezzar's Hand (1:1–2)
   B. Training for Service (1:3–7)
   C. Avoiding Defilement (1:8–16)
   D. Success Given to Daniel and His Friends (1:17–20)
   E. The Extent of Daniel's Ministry (1:21)

II. **The God of Wisdom Reveals Nebuchadnezzar's Dream to Daniel (2:1–49)**
   A. The King and His Advisors (2:1–13)
   B. God's Revealing of the Mystery to Daniel (2:14–23)
   C. The Dream and Its Interpretation (2:24–45)
   D. The King's Response (2:46–49)

III. **God Saves the Three Friends from the Fiery Furnace (3:1–30)**
   A. Nebuchadnezzar's Image of Gold (3:1–7)
   B. The Accusation Against the Three Friends (3:8–12)
   C. The Confrontation With Nebuchadnezzar (3:13–18)
   D. The Miraculous Deliverance (3:19–27)
   E. Nebuchadnezzar Worships God (3:28–30)

IV. **Nebuchadnezzar's Pride Takes a Fall (4:1–37)**
   A. Nebuchadnezzar's Decree to Praise the Lord (4:1–3)
   B. The Dream Report and the Search for an Interpreter (4:4–18)
   C. The Dream Interpretation (4:19–27)
   D. The Fulfillment of the Dream (4:28–33)
   E. Healing and Concluding Doxology (4:34–37)

V. **The Writing on the Wall (5:1–31)**
   A. The Profanation of the Holy Vessels (5:1–4)
   B. The Enigmatic Writing on the Wall (5:5–12)
   C. Daniel's Interpretation of the Inscription (5:13–28)
   D. Reward and Punishment (5:29–31)

VI. **Daniel in the Lions' Den (6:1–28)**
   A. The Plot Against Daniel (6:1–9)
   B. The Trap and Reluctant Punishment (6:10–18)
   C. Daniel's Rescue and the Accusers' Demise (6:19–24)
   D. Darius's Decree (6:25–28)

Outline

VII. **The Vision of the Four Beasts (7:1–28)**
    A. Horror by the Sea (7:1–8)
    B. Heavenly Power (7:9–14)
    C. Divine Victory (7:15–28)
VIII. **The Ram and the Goat (8:1–27)**
    A. The Vision of a Ram and a Goat (8:1–14)
    B. The Interpretation of the Vision (8:15–27)
IX. **Daniel's Prayer of Repentance (9:1–27)**
    A. Preparation for Prayer (9:1–4a)
    B. Invocation and Confession (9:4b–10)
    C. God's Punishment (9:11–14)
    D. Appeal for Mercy (9:15–19)
    E. The Prophecy of the Seventy Weeks (9:20–27)
X. **The Vision of a Heavenly Messenger (10:1–11:1)**
    A. A Heavenly Vision (10:1–9)
    B. A Conversation With a Supernatural Being (10:10–11:1)
XI. **The Scope and End of History (11:2–12:13)**
    A. Persia and Greece (11:2–4)
    B. Struggles Between the Kings of the North and the Kings of the South (11:5–20)
    C. The Climactic King of the North (11:21–35)
    D. The King Who Will Do As He Pleases (11:36–45)
    E. The Salvation of God's People (12:1–4)
    F. Final Words (12:5–13)

Bibliography

Ackroyd, P. R. "The Temple Vessels—A Continuity Theme." Pp. 166–81 in *Studies in the Religion of Ancient Israel*. Leiden: Brill, 1972.

Adler, W. "The Apocalyptic Survey of History Adapted by Christians: Daniel's Prophecy of 70 Weeks." Pp. 201–38 in *The Jewish Apocalyptic Heritage in Early Christianity*. Ed. J. C. VanderKam and W. Adler. Assen/Minneapolis: Van Gorcum/Fortress, 1996.

Allender, D., and T. Longman III. *Bold Love*. Colorado Springs: NavPress, 1991.

———. *Cry of the Soul*. Colorado Springs: NavPress, 1993.

Amerding, C. "Russia and the King of the North." *BSac* 120 (1963): 50–55.

———. "Asleep in the Dust." *BSac* 121 (1964): 153–58.

Arnold, B. T. "Wordplay and Narrative Techniques in Daniel 5 and 6." *JBL* 112 (1993): 479–85.

Arnold, C. E. *Three Crucial Questions About Spiritual Warfare*. Grand Rapids: Baker, 1997.

Avalos, H. I. "The Comedic Function of the Enumerations of Officials and Instruments in Daniel 3." *CBQ* 53 (1991): 580–88.

Bampfylde, G. "The Prince of the Host in the Book of Daniel and the Dead Sea Scrolls." *JSJ* 14 (1983): 129–34.

Beale, G. K. "The Influence of Daniel Upon the Structure and Theology of John's Apocalypse." *JETS* 27 (1984): 413–23.

———. "The Origin of the Title 'King of Kings and Lord of Lords' in Revelation 17.14." *NTS* 31 (1985): 618–20.

———. "A Reconsideration of the Text of Daniel in the Apocalypse." *Biblica* 67 (1986): 539–43.

Becking, B. "'A Divine Spirit Is in You': Notes on the Translation of the Phrase *ruah 'elahin* in Daniel 5,14 and Related Texts." Pp. 515–19 in *The Book of Daniel in the Light of New Findings*. Ed. A. S. van der Woude. Leuven: University Press, 1993.

Bergman, B. Z. "*Han'el* in Daniel 2:25 and 6:19." *JNES* 27 (1968): 69–70.

Berquist, J. *Judaism in Persia's Shadow*. Minneapolis: Fortress, 1995.

Birkeland, H. "The Belief in the Resurrection of the Dead in the Old Testament." *ST* 3 (1950–51): 60–78.

Black, M. "The Throne-Theophany Prophetic Commission and the 'Son of Man': A Study in Tradition History." Pp. 46–75 in *Jews, Greeks and Christians: Religious Cultures in Late Antiquity*. Ed. R. Hamerton-Kelly and R. Scroggs. Leiden: Brill, 1976.

Bibliography

Bloch, A. A. "Questioning God's Omnipotence in the Bible: A Linguistic Case Study." Pp. 174–88 in *Semitic Studies in Honor of Wolf Leslau*, vol. 1. Wiesbaden: Otto Harrassowitz, 1991.

Boccaccini, G. "Daniel and the Dream Visions: The Genre of Apocalyptic and the Apocalyptic Tradition." Pp. 126–60 in *Middle Judaism: Jewish Thought, 300 B.C.E. to 200 B.C.E.* Minneapolis: Fortress, 1991.

Boogaart, T. A. "Daniel 6: A Tale of Two Empires." *The Reformed Review* 39–40 (1985–1987): 106–12.

Bork, R. H. *Slouching Towards Gomorrah.* New York: HarperCollins, 1996.

Brewer, D. I. "*Mene Mene Teqel Uparsin*: Daniel 5:25 in Cuneiform." *TynBul* 42 (1991): 311–16.

Brichto, H. D. *The Names of God: Poetic Readings in Biblical Beginnings.* Oxford: University Press, 1998.

Brueggemann, W. "At the Mercy of Babylon: A Subversive Rereading of the Empire." *JBL* 110 (1991): 3–22.

Callega, J. "The Use of Daniel 3 in the *Eclogae Propheticae* (chs. 1–9) of Clement of Alexandria." *Augustinianum* 26 (1986): 401–11.

Caragounis, C. C. "History and Supra-History: Daniel and the Four Empires." Pp. 387–97 in *The Book of Daniel in the Light of New Findings.* Ed. A. S. van der Woude. Leuven: University Press, 1993.

Carroll, R. P. "Prophecy and Dissonance: A Theoretical Approach to the Prophetic Tradition." *ZAW* 92 (1980): 108–19.

Carson, D. A., and J. D. Woodbridge. *God and Culture: Essays in Honor of Carl F. H. Henry.* Grand Rapids: Eerdmans, 1993.

Casey, M. *Son of Man: The Interpretation and Influence of Daniel 7.* London: SPCK, 1979.

Chave, P. "'But if not...'" *ExpTim* 97 (1986): 369–70.

Clifford, R. J. "History and Myth in Daniel 10–12." *BASOR* 220 (1975): 23–26.

Clowney, E. P. *Preaching and Biblical Theology.* Grand Rapids: Eerdmans, 1961.

Cohn, N. *Cosmos, Chaos and the World to Come: The Ancient Roots of Apocalyptic Faith.* New Haven: Yale Univ. Press, 1993.

Collins, J. J. "Apocalyptic Eschatology as the Transcendence of Death." *CBQ* 36 (1974): 21–43.

———. *The Apocalyptic Vision of the Book of Daniel.* Missoula, Mont.: Scholars, 1977.

———. "The Court-Tales in Daniel and the Development of Apocalyptic." *JBL* 94 (1975): 218–34.

———. "Apocalyptic Genre and Mythic Allusions in Daniel." *JSOT* 21 (1981): 83–100.

———. *Daniel; First Maccabees; Second Maccabees, With an Excursus on the Apocalyptic Genre.* Wilmington, Del.: Michael Glazier, 1981.

Bibliography

———. "Daniel and His Social World." *Interp* 39 (1985): 131–43.
———. *Daniel*. Hermeneia. Minneapolis: Fortress, 1993.
Cook. E. M. "'In the Plain of the Wall' (Dan 3:1)." *JBL* 108 (1989): 115–16.
Coppens, J. "Le Livre de Daniel et ses Problèmes." *ETL* 56 (1980): 1–9.
Coxon, P. W. "Daniel 3:17: A Linguistic and Theological Problem." *VT* 26 (1976): 400–409.
———. "Another Look at Nebuchadnezzar's Madness." Pp. 211–22 in *The Book of Daniel in the Light of New Findings*. Ed. A. S. van der Woude. Leuven: University Press, 1993.
Crenshaw, J. "Method in Determining Wisdom Influence Upon 'Historical Literature.'" *JBL* 88 (1969): 129–44.
Cross, F. M. "Fragments of the Prayer of Nabonidus." *IEJ* 34 (1984): 260–64.
Davies, P. R. "Daniel Chapter Two." *JTS* 27 (1976): 392–405.
———. "Eschatology in the Book of Daniel." *JSOT* 17 (1980): 33–53.
———. "Reading Daniel Sociologically." Pp. 345–61 in *The Book of Daniel in the Light of New Findings*. Ed. A. S. van der Woude. Leuven: University Press, 1993.
Derrett, J. D. M. "Daniel in Salvation History." Pp. 132–38 in *Studies in the New Testament*. Leiden: Brill, 1986.
Dillard, R. B., and T. Longman III. *An Introduction to the Old Testament*. Grand Rapids: Zondervan, 1994.
DiLella, A. "The One in Human Likeness and the Holy Ones of the Most High in Daniel 7." *CBQ* 39 (1977): 1–19.
Doukhan, J. B. *Daniel: The Vision of the End*. Berrien Springs, Mich.: Andrews Univ. Press, 1987.
Fertch, A. J. "Daniel 7 and Ugarit: A Reconsideration." *JBL* 99 (1980): 75–86.
Fewell, D. N. *Circle of Sovereignty: A Story of Stories in Daniel 1–6*. JSOTSup 72. Sheffield: JSOT, 1988.
Flusser, D. "The Four Empires in the Fourth Sibyl and in the Book of Daniel." *IOS* 2 (1972): 148–75.
Foster, B. R. *Before the Muses: An Anthology of Akkadian Literature*. 2 vols. Bethesda, Md.: CDL Press, 1993.
Freyne, S. "The Disciples in Mark and the *Maskilim* in Daniel: A Comparison." *JSNT* 16 (1982): 7–23.
Frolich, I. *"Time and Times and Half a Time": Historical Consciousness in the Jewish Literature of the Persian and Hellenistic Eras*. JSPSS 19. Sheffield: Sheffield Academic Press, 1996.
Gammie, J. G. "The Classification, Stages of Growth, and Changing Intentions in the Book of Daniel." *JBL* 95 (1976): 191–204.
Glasson, T. F. "'Visions of Thy Head' (Daniel 2:25): The Heart and the Head in Bible Psychology." *ExpTim* 81 (1970): 247–48.

Bibliography

Goldingay, J. E. "The Book of Daniel: Three Issues." *Themelios* 3 (1977): 45–49.
———. *Daniel.* WBC. Waco, Tex.: Word, 1989.
———. "Story, Vision, Interpretation: Literary Approaches to Daniel." Pp. 295–313 in *The Book of Daniel in the Light of New Findings.* Ed. A. S. van der Woude. Leuven: University Press, 1993.
Gowan, D. E. "The Exile in Jewish Apocalyptic." Pp. 205–23 in *Scripture in History and Theology: Essays in Honor of J. Coert Rylaarsdam.* Ed. A. L. Merril and T. W. Overholt. Pittsburgh: Pickwick, 1977.
Grabbe, L. L. "'The End of the Desolations of Jerusalem': From Jeremiah's 70 Years to Daniel's 70 Weeks of Years." Pp. 67–72 in *Early Jewish and Christian Exegesis: Studies in Memory of William Hugh Brownlee.* Ed. C. A. Evans and W. F. Stinespring. Atlanta: Scholars, 1987.
———. "The Belshazzar of Daniel and the Belshazzar of History." *AUSS* 26 (1988): 59–66.
Greidanus, S. *Sola Scriptura: Problems and Principles in Preaching Historical Texts.* Kampen: J. H. Kok, 1970.
Grelot, P. "L'Orchestre de Daniel III 5, 7, 10, 15." *VT* 29 (1979): 23–38.
Gruenthaner, M. J. "The Last King of Babylon." *CBQ* 11 (1949): 406–27.
Guglielmo, Antonine de. "Dan. 5:25—An Example of a Double Literal Sense." *CBQ* 11 (1949): 202–6.
Guinness, O. *The American Hour.* New York: Macmillan, 1993.
Gurney, R. J. M. "The Four Kingdoms of Daniel 2 and 7." *Themelios* 2 (1977): 39–45.
———. "The Seventy Weeks of Daniel 9:24–27." *EvQ* 53 (1981): 29–36.
Hartman, L. F., and A. A. DiLella. *The Book of Daniel.* Garden City, N.Y.: Doubleday, 1978.
Hasel, G. F. "The Book of Daniel: Evidences Relating to Persons and Chronology." *AUSS* 19 (1981): 37–49.
———. "The Four World Empires of Daniel 2 Against Its Near Eastern Environment." *JSOT* 12 (1979): 17–30.
———. "The First and Third Years of Belshazzar (Dan. 7:1; 8:1)." *AUSS* 15 (1976): 153ff.
Hilton, M. "Babel Reversed—Daniel Chapter 5." *JSOT* 66 (1995): 99–112.
Hoehner, H. W. "Chronological Aspects of the Life of Christ." *BSac* 132 (1975): 47–65.
Humphreys, W. Lee. "A Life-Style for Diaspora: A Study of the Tales of Esther and Daniel." *JBL* 92 (1973): 211–23.
Hunter, J. D. *Culture Wars: The Struggle to Define America.* New York: Basic Books, 1991.
Husser, J.-M. "La fin et l'origine: Consequence inattendue de l'eschatologie in Dn 2." Pp. 243–64 in *Le Dieu Qui Vient.* Ed. Raymond Kuntzman. Paris: Éditions du Cerf, 1995.

Bibliography

Kalafian, M. *The Prophecy of the Seventy Weeks of the Book of Daniel.* Lanham, Md.: Univ. Press of America, 1991.

Klein, J. "In God They Trust." *The New Yorker* (June 16, 1997), 40–48.

Kline, M. G. "The Covenant of the Seventieth Week." Pp. 452–69 in *The Law and the Prophets.* Phillipsburg, N.J.: Presbyterian and Reformed, 1974.

Knibb, M. A. "'You Are Indeed Wiser Than Daniel': Reflections on the Character of the Book of Daniel." Pp. 399–411 in *The Book of Daniel in the Light of New Findings.* Ed. A. S. van der Woude. Leuven: University Press, 1993.

Kraeling, E. G. "The Handwriting on the Wall." *JBL* 63 (1944): 11–18.

Lacocque, A. "The Liturgical Prayer in Daniel 9." *HUCA* 47 (1976): 119–42.

———. *The Book of Daniel.* Atlanta: John Knox, 1979.

———. *Daniel in His Time.* Columbia, S.C.: Univ. of South Carolina Press, 1988.

———. "The Socio-Spiritual Formative Milieu of the Daniel Apocalypse." Pp. 315–41 in *The Book of Daniel in the Light of New Findings.* Ed. A. S. van der Woude. Leuven: University Press, 1993.

Lasch, C. *The Revolt of the Elites and the Betrayal of Democracy.* New York: Norton, 1995.

Lash, N. *The Beginning and the End of "Religion."* Cambridge: Cambridge Univ. Press, 1996.

Lawson, J. "'The God Who Reveals Secrets': The Mesopotamian Background to Daniel 2.47." *JSOT* 74 (1997): 61–76.

Lindenberger, J. M. "Daniel 12:1–4." *Interp* 39 (1985): 181–86.

Long, V. Philips. *The Art of Biblical History.* Grand Rapids: Zondervan, 1994.

Longman III, T. "Psalm 98: A Divine Warrior Victory Song," *JETS* (1984): 267–74.

———. *Literary Approaches to Biblical Interpretation.* Foundations in Contemporary Hermeneutics 3. Grand Rapids: Zondervan, 1987.

———. "God's Law and Mosaic Punishments Today." Pp. 41–58 in *Theonomy: A Reformed Critique.* Ed. W. S. Barker and W. Robert Godfrey. Grand Rapids: Zondervan, 1990.

———. "What I Mean by Historical-Grammatical Exegesis—Why I Am Not a Literalist." *GTJ* 11 (1990): 41–58.

———. *Fictional Akkadian Autobiography: A Generic and Comparative Study.* Winona Lake, Ind.: Eisenbrauns, 1991.

———. *Reading the Bible with Heart and Mind.* Colorado Springs: NavPress, 1997.

———. *The Book of Ecclesiastes.* NICOT. Grand Rapids: Eerdmans, 1998.

———, and D. Reid. *God Is a Warrior.* Grand Rapids: Zondervan, 1995.

Lucas, E. C. "The Origin of Daniel's Four Empires Scheme Re-Examined." *TynBul* 40 (1989): 185–202.

Lust, J. "Daniel 7:13 and the Septuagint." *ETL* 54 (1978): 62–69.
Mastin, B. A. "Daniel 2:46 and the Hellenistic World." *ZAW* 85 (1973): 80–93.
_____. "The Reading of 1QDan^a at Daniel II 4." *VT* 38 (1988): 341–46.
_____. "The Meaning of *bᵃla'* at Daniel iv 27." *VT* 42 (1992): 234–47.
_____. "Wisdom and Daniel." Pp. 161–69 in *Wisdom in Ancient Israel: Essay in Honour of J. A. Emerton*. Ed. J. Day, R. P. Gordon, and H. G. M. Williamson. Cambridge: Cambridge Univ. Press, 1995.
McComiskey, T. E. "The Seventy 'Weeks' of Daniel Against the Background of Ancient Near Eastern Literature." *WTJ* 47 (1985): 18–45.
Meadowcroft, T. J. *Aramaic Daniel and Greek Daniel*. JSOTSup 198. Sheffield: Sheffield Academic Press, 1995.
Mercer, M. E. "Daniel 1:1 and Jehoiakim's Three Years of Servitude." *AUSS* 27 (1989): 179–92.
Millard, A. "Daniel and Belshazzar in History." *BAR* 11 (1985): 73–78.
Miller, C. J. *Repentance and Twentieth Century Man*. Fort Washington, Pa.: Christian Literature Crusade, 1975.
_____, and Barbara M. Juliani. *Come Back, Barbara*. 2d ed. Phillipsburg, N.J.: Presbyterian and Reformed, 1997.
Miller, S. R. *Daniel*. NAC. Nashville: Broadman, 1994.
Montgomery, J. S. *A Critical and Exegetical Commentary on the Book of Daniel*. Edinburgh: T. & T. Clark, 1927, 1950.
Moore, M. S. "Resurrection and Immorality: Two Motifs Navigating Confluent Theological Streams in the Old Testament (Dan 12, 1–4)." *TZ* 39 (1983): 17–34.
Mouw, R. J. *Politics and the Biblical Drama*. Grand Rapids: Eerdmans, 1976.
_____. *Uncommon Decency: Christian Civility in an Uncivil World*. Downers Grove, Ill.: InterVarsity, 1992.
Neibuhr, H. R. *Christ and Culture*. New York: Harper and Row, 1951.
Newman, R. C. "Daniel's Seventy Weeks and the Old Testament Sabbath-Year Cycle." *JETS* 16 (1973): 229–34.
Nicol, G. G. "Isaiah's Vision and the Visions of Daniel." *VT* 29 (1979): 501–5.
Niditch, S. "The Visionary." Pp. 153–79 in *Ideal Figures in Ancient Judaism*. Ed. J. J. Collins and G. W. Nickelsburg. Chicago: Scholars, 1980.
Niditch, S., and R. Doran. "The Success Story of the Wise Courtier: A Formal Approach." *JBL* 96 (1977): 179–93.
Nunez, S. *The Vision of Daniel 8: Interpretations from 1700 to 1800*. Berrien Springs, Mich.: Andrews Univ. Press, 1987.
Parker, P. "The Meaning of 'Son of Man.'" *JBL* 60 (1941): 151–57.
Patterson, R. D. "The Key Role of Daniel 7." *GTJ* 12 (1991): 245–61.
Paul, S. M. "Daniel 3:29—A Case Study of 'Neglected' Blasphemy." *JNES* 42 (1983): 291–94.

Bibliography

———. "Decoding a 'Joint' Expression in Daniel 5:6, 16." *JANES* 22 (1993): 121–27.
Pierce, R. W. "Spiritual Failure, Postponement, and Daniel 9." *TrinJ* 10 (1989): 211–22.
Plantinga, Jr., C. *Not the Way It's Supposed to Be: A Breviary of Sin*. Grand Rapids: Eerdmans, 1995.
Polak, F. "The Daniel Tales in Their Aramaic Literary Milieu." Pp. 249–65 in *The Book of Daniel in the Light of New Findings*. Ed. A. S. van der Woude. Leuven: University Press, 1993.
Porteous, N. W. *Daniel: A Commentary*. OTL. Philadelphia: Westminster, 1965.
Poythress, V. S. "The Holy Ones of the Most High and Daniel vii." *VT* 26 (1976): 208–13.
Prinsloo, G. T. M. "Two Poems in a Sea of Prose: The Content and Context of Daniel 2:20–23 and 6:27–28." *JSOT* 59 (1993): 93–108.
Quaegebeur, J. "On the Egyptian Equivalent of Biblical *hartummim*." Pp. 162–72 in *Pharaonic Egypt: The Bible and Christianity*. Ed. S. Israelit-Groll. Jerusalem: Magnes, 1985.
Rad, G. von. *Wisdom in Israel*. London: SCM, 1970.
Reeves, E. "Daniel 5 and the Assayer: Galileo Reads the Handwriting on the Wall." *JMRS* 21 (1991): 1–27.
Reid, S. B. *Enoch and Daniel: A Form Critical and Sociological Study of Historical Apocalypses*. Berkeley, Calif.: Bibal, 1989.
Reston Jr., J. *The Last Apocalypse: Europe at the Year 1000*. New York: Doubleday, 1998.
Rosenberg, R. A. "The Slain Messiah in the Old Testament." *ZAW* 99 (1987): 259–61.
Rowland, C. "A Man Clothed in Linen: Daniel 10:6ff and Jewish Angelology." *JSNT* 24 (1985): 99–110.
Ryken, L., and T. Longman III. *A Complete Literary Guide to the Bible*. Grand Rapids: Zondervan, 1995.
Sawyer, J. F. A. "'My Secret Is with Me' (Isaiah 24.16): Some Semantic Links Between Isaiah 24–27 and Daniel." Pp. 307–17 in *Understanding Poets and Prophets*. Ed. A. G. Auld. Sheffield: JSOT, 1993.
Schaeffer, F. A. *A Christian Manifesto*. Westchester, Ill.: Crossway, 1981.
Shea, W. H. "Daniel 3: Extra-Biblical Texts and the Convocation on the Plain of Dura." *AUSS* 20 (1982): 29–52.
———. "A Further Note on Daniel 6: Daniel As 'Governor.'" *AUSS* 21 (1983): 169–71.
———. "Wrestling with the Prince of Persia: A Study on Daniel 10." *AUSS* 21 (1983): 225–50.
———. "Further Literary Structures in Daniel 2–7: An Analysis of Daniel 4." *AUSS* 23 (1985): 193–202.

Bibliography

———. "Bel(te)shazzar Meets Belshazzar." *AUSS* 26 (1988): 67–88.
Smedes, L. B. *Shame and Grace: Healing the Shame We Don't Deserve.* San Francisco: HarperCollins, 1993.
Soesilo, D. "Why Did Daniel Reject the King's Delicacies? (Daniel 1:8)" *BT* 45 (1994): 441–44.
Steiner, G. *No Passion Spent.* New Haven, Conn.: Yale Univ. Press, 1996.
Steussy, M. J. *Gardens in Babylon: Narrative and Faith in the Greek Legends of Daniel.* SBLDS 141. Atlanta: Scholars, 1993.
Stone, M. "A Note on Daniel i.3." *AusBR* 7 (1959): 69–71.
Thiering, B. E. "The Three and a Half Years of Elijah." *NovT* 23 (1981): 41–55.
Towner, W. S. "The Poetic Passages of Daniel 1–6." *CBQ* 31 (1969): 317–26.
———. *Daniel.* Interpretation. Atlanta: John Knox, 1984.
———. "Daniel 1 in the Context of the Canon." Pp. 285–98 in *Canon, Theology, and Old Testament Interpretation: Essays in Honor of Brevard S. Childs.* Ed. G. M. Tucker, D. L. Petersen, and R. R. Wilson. Minneapolis: Fortress, 1988.
Trever, J. "The Book of Daniel and the Origin of the Qumran Community." *BA* 48 (1985): 89–103.
Volf, M. *Exclusion and Embrace: A Theological Exploration of Identity, Otherness, and Reconciliation.* Nashville: Abingdon, 1996.
Wagner, P. *Breaking Strongholds in Your City: How to Use Spiritual Mapping to Make Your Prayers More Strategic, Effective and Targeted.* Ventura, Calif.: Regal Books, 1993.
Walton, J. H. "The Four Kingdoms of Daniel." *JETS* 29 (1986): 25–36.
———. "The Decree of Darius the Mede in Daniel 6." *JETS* 31 (1988): 279–86.
Walton, J. H., L. D. Bailey, and C. Williford. "Bible-Based Curricula and the Crisis of Scriptural Authority." *Christian Education Journal* 13 (1993): 83–94.
Walvoord, J. F. "Is the Seventieth Week of Daniel Future?" *BSac* 101 (1944): 30–49.
Watts, J. W. "Babylonian Idolatry in the Prophets as a False Socio-Economic System." Pp. 115–22 in *Israel's Apostasy and Restoration.* Ed. A. Gileadi. Grand Rapids: Baker, 1988.
———. "Daniel's Praise (Daniel 2.20–23)." Pp. 145–54 in *Psalm and Story: Inset Hymns in Hebrew Narrative.* Sheffield: JSOT, 1992.
Wenham, D. "The Kingdom of God and Daniel." *ExpTim* 98 (1987): 132–34.
Wenham, G. J. "Daniel: The Basic Issues." *Themelios* 3 (1977): 49–51.
Wesselius, J. W. "Language and Style in Biblical Aramaic: Observations on the Unity of Daniel II-VI." *VT* 38 (1988): 194–209.
Wharton, J. A. "Daniel 3:16–18." *Interp* 39 (1985): 170–76.
Willi-Plein, I. "Ursprung und Motivation der Apokalyptik im Danielbuch." *TZ* 35 (1979): 265–74.

Bibliography

Wills, L. M. *The Jew in the Court of the Foreign King*. HDR 26. Minneapolis: Fortress, 1990.

Wilson, G. "The Prayer of Daniel 9: Reflection on Jeremiah 29." *JSOT* 48 (1990): 91–99.

Wink, W. *Naming the Powers: The Language of Power in the New Testament*. Philadelphia: Fortress, 1984.

———. *Unmasking the Powers: The Invisible Forces That Determine Human Existence*. Philadelphia: Fortress, 1986.

———. *Engaging the Powers: Discernment and Resistance in a World of Domination*. Minneapolis: Augsburg Fortress, 1992.

———. *When the Powers Fall: Reconciliation in the Healing of Nations*. Minneapolis: Augsburg Fortress, 1998.

Witstruck, T. "The Influence of Treaty Curse Imagery on the Beast Imagery of Daniel." *JBL* 97 (1978): 100–102.

Wolters, A. "The Riddle of the Scales in Daniel 5." *HUCA* 62 (1991): 155–77.

———. "Untying the King's Knots: Physiology and Wordplay in Daniel 5." *JBL* 110 (1991): 117–22.

Wood, L. J. *A Commentary on Daniel*. Grand Rapids: Zondervan, 1973.

Yamauchi, E. M. "Hermeneutical Issues in the Book of Daniel." *JETS* 23 (1980): 14–22.

———. "Daniel and Contacts Between the Aegean and the Near East Before Alexander." *EvQ* 53 (1981): 37–47.

Yancey, P. "A State of Ungrace." *CT* 41 (February 3, 1997): 30–37.

———. *What's So Amazing About Grace?* Grand Rapids: Zondervan, 1997.

Young, E. J. *The Prophecy of Daniel: A Commentary*. Grand Rapids: Eerdmans, 1949.

———. *The Messianic Prophecies of Daniel*. Grand Rapids: Eerdmans, 1954.

Zadok, R. "The Origin of the Name Shinar." *ZAW* 74 (1984): 240–44.

Zevit, Z. "The Exegetical Implications of Daniel viii 1, ix 21." *VT* 28 (1978): 488–92.

Zimmermann, F. "The Writing on the Wall: Daniel 5:25f." *JQR* 55 (1964–65): 201–7.

Daniel 1:1-21

IN THE THIRD year of the reign of Jehoiakim king of Judah, Nebuchadnezzar king of Babylon came to Jerusalem and besieged it. ²And the Lord delivered Jehoiakim king of Judah into his hand, along with some of the articles from the temple of God. These he carried off to the temple of his god in Babylonia and put in the treasure house of his god.

³Then the king ordered Ashpenaz, chief of his court officials, to bring in some of the Israelites from the royal family and the nobility—⁴young men without any physical defect, handsome, showing aptitude for every kind of learning, well informed, quick to understand, and qualified to serve in the king's palace. He was to teach them the language and literature of the Babylonians. ⁵The king assigned them a daily amount of food and wine from the king's table. They were to be trained for three years, and after that they were to enter the king's service.

⁶Among these were some from Judah: Daniel, Hananiah, Mishael and Azariah. ⁷The chief official gave them new names: to Daniel, the name Belteshazzar; to Hananiah, Shadrach; to Mishael, Meshach; and to Azariah, Abednego.

⁸But Daniel resolved not to defile himself with the royal food and wine, and he asked the chief official for permission not to defile himself this way. ⁹Now God had caused the official to show favor and sympathy to Daniel, ¹⁰but the official told Daniel, "I am afraid of my lord the king, who has assigned your food and drink. Why should he see you looking worse than the other young men your age? The king would then have my head because of you."

¹¹Daniel then said to the guard whom the chief official had appointed over Daniel, Hananiah, Mishael and Azariah, ¹²"Please test your servants for ten days: Give us nothing but vegetables to eat and water to drink. ¹³Then compare our appearance with that of the young men who eat the royal food, and treat your servants in accordance with what you see." ¹⁴So he agreed to this and tested them for ten days.

¹⁵At the end of the ten days they looked healthier and better nourished than any of the young men who ate the royal

food. ¹⁶So the guard took away their choice food and the wine they were to drink and gave them vegetables instead.

¹⁷To these four young men God gave knowledge and understanding of all kinds of literature and learning. And Daniel could understand visions and dreams of all kinds.

¹⁸At the end of the time set by the king to bring them in, the chief official presented them to Nebuchadnezzar. ¹⁹The king talked with them, and he found none equal to Daniel, Hananiah, Mishael and Azariah; so they entered the king's service. ²⁰In every matter of wisdom and understanding about which the king questioned them, he found them ten times better than all the magicians and enchanters in his whole kingdom.

²¹And Daniel remained there until the first year of King Cyrus.

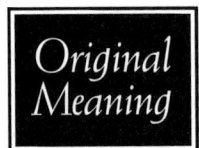

THE FIRST CHAPTER of the book of Daniel is a distinct unit. It begins and ends with a chronological marker that identifies the beginning and end of Daniel's career ("the third year of the reign of Jehoiakim" [v. 1] and "the first year of King Cyrus" [v. 21]). In terms of our dating system, this places Daniel's career from 605 to 539 B.C.[1]

Daniel 1 provides an introduction for the whole book, plunging us quickly into the action and introducing the main characters of the book. It also illustrates the overarching theme of the book: In spite of present appearances, God is in control. In keeping with the court narratives in chapters 1–6, the first chapter narrates an episode from the experience of Daniel and his three friends that models another important lesson: Though in exile, God gives his people the ability to prosper as well as to be faithful. This chapter, and the book as a whole, must have served as a tremendous encouragement to the faith of those devout exiles who felt as if their whole world had come crashing down on their heads.

This first chapter has the following outline: (1) Jehoiakim delivered into Nebuchadnezzar's hand (1:1–2); (2) training for service (1:3–7); (3) avoiding defilement (1:8–16); (4) success given to Daniel and his friends (1:17–20); and (5) the extent of Daniel's ministry (1:21).

---

1. See discussion at verse 21 for the argument that Daniel's career actually stretched beyond Cyrus's first year.

Daniel 1:1–21

Jehoiakim Delivered into Nebuchadnezzar's Hand (1:1–2)

THE NARRATOR IMMERSES us immediately into the action. Nebuchadnezzar[2] has moved against Jerusalem. As Fewell has pointed out, our story begins at the end of another story.[3] The forces that brought Nebuchadnezzar (or at least his army) to Jerusalem during the reign of Jehoiakim are hinted at elsewhere (cf. 2 Chron. 36:5–7[4]); here we are simply informed that he moved against Jerusalem, resulting in the deportation of the heroes of our book.

Before recounting the events that led up to Daniel 1:1, we must acknowledge the fact that many scholars (those who argue that Daniel 1 is written much later than the sixth century B.C.) believe that Daniel 1:1–2 is a confused historical memory,[5] based on the author's misreading of 2 Chronicles 36:6–7 in connection with 2 Kings 24:1. On this basis, Hartman and DiLella deny that Nebuchadnezzar attacked Jerusalem in 605 B.C., the date implied by our text. In addition, they argue that Nebuchadnezzar did not even become king of Babylon until the next year.[6] A surface reading of Jeremiah 25:1 ("the word came to Jeremiah concerning all the people of Judah in the fourth year of Jehoiakim son of Josiah king of Judah, which was the first year of Nebuchadnezzar king of Babylon") seems to imply that Nebuchadnezzar did not even become king until Jehoiakim's fourth year. These scholars also point out that the Babylonian Chronicle, our main native source of information for this time period, does not mention Nebuchadnezzar's siege of Jerusalem.

There are at least two possible harmonizations that permit us to accept Daniel 1:1–2 as an accurate historical memory. First, Daniel 1:1 may well refer to Nebuchadnezzar as king in an anticipatory sense. After all, it is soon after Daniel's report of a siege of Jerusalem that Nabopolassar's death would bring Nebuchadnezzar to the throne. No one doubts, based on Babylonian records

---

2. Goldingay's attempt (*Daniel*, 4), based on studies by Van Selms, to connect the Hebrew spelling of the Babylonian king's Akkadian name [*Nabu-kudurri-usur* (Nabu protects the firstborn/boundary stone)] with an insulting etymology [*Nabu-kudanu-usur* ("Nabu protects the mule")] strikes me as overly speculative.

3. D. N. Fewell, *Circle of Sovereignty: A Story of Stories in Daniel 1–6* (JSOTSup 72; Sheffield: Almond, 1988), 34.

4. Second Kings 24:1–4 narrates a later conflict between Nebuchadnezzar and Jehoiakim. After initially yielding to the Babylonians (2 Chron. 36:6–7; Dan. 1:1–3), Jehoiakim rebelled against them three years later. Before Nebuchadnezzar could respond, Jehoiakim died, leaving his young son, Jehoiachin, on the throne, to face the onslaught, being exiled himself in 598 B.C.

5. J. A. Montgomery, *The Book of Daniel* (ICC; Edinburgh: T. & T. Clark, 1927), 113, states "there is no historical corroboration of such an event in the third year of Jehoiakim."

6. See L. F. Hartman and A. A. DiLella, *The Book of Daniel* (AB; Garden City, N.Y.: Doubleday, 1978), 48.

themselves, Nebuchadnezzar's presence as crown prince and field commander of the Babylonian army in their wars against Egypt in the area of Syria-Palestine in the years before 605 B.C.

We can also harmonize the data by reminding ourselves, at the instigation of the well-known Assyriologist D. J. Wiseman, that there were two systems of dating current in the ancient Near Eastern world, both of which can be found in the Old Testament.[7] The above passages may be harmonized by assuming that Jeremiah utilized the Judaean method of chronological reckoning, which counts the first year of a king's reign as the first year, and that Daniel used the Babylonian system, which counts the first year as an "accession year." Hasel helpfully diagrammed the results:[8]

Chronology of Kings in Jeremiah and Daniel

Accession-year method	Accession year	1st year	2nd year	3rd year	Daniel 1:1
Non-accession-year method	1st year	2nd year	3rd year	4th year	Jeremiah 25:1, 9; 46:2

It is true that the Babylonian Chronicle provides ambiguous evidence in the argument for and against a Babylonian assault against Jerusalem in the period 605/604 B.C. Wiseman in 1965 argued that the Babylonian Chronicle fails to mention the siege of Jerusalem because it is preoccupied with "the major defeat of the Egyptians," but he goes on to say that "a successful incursion into Judah by the Babylonian army group which returned from the Egyptian border could be included in the claim that at that time Nebuchadnezzar conquered 'all Hatti.'"[9]

However, in 1985[10] he agreed with Grayson[11] that the relevant line of the Chronicles (BM 21946, 8) should be read as referring to Hamath and not Hatti. J. J. Collins, then, took this as decisive evidence that the Daniel account is not accurate; there was no deportation of any size this early.[12] However, he fails to report, as Wiseman goes on to say, that the next section of the Chronicle does report activity in the area of Hatti. Wiseman further reminds us that

---

7. D. J. Wiseman, et al., *Notes on Some Problems in the Book of Daniel* (London: Tyndale, 1965), 16–18.

8. G. F. Hasel, "The Book of Daniel: Evidences Relating to Persons and Chronology," *AUSS* 19 (1981): 47–49.

9. Wiseman, *Notes on Some Problems*, 18.

10. D. J. Wiseman, *Nebuchadrezzar and Babylon* (Oxford: Oxford Univ. Press, 1985), 17.

11. A. K. Grayson, *Assyrian and Babylonian Chronicles* (Toronto: Univ. of Toronto Press, 1975), 99.

12. J. J. Collins, *Daniel* (Hermeneia; Minneapolis: Fortress, 1993), 131.

Daniel 1:1–21

the phrase used in Daniel 1:1 does not necessarily mean that a formal military siege was laid against Jerusalem; it could mean no more, he says, than to "show hostility." Thus, Wiseman demonstrates how the biblical reference to the third year of Jehoiakim "could be a justifiable dating if this covered the twelve months ending in 604 B.C.,"[13] which view he indeed holds.

In spite of the difficulties, therefore, we understand Daniel 1:1–2 as an accurate memory and will now place it within the broader historical landscape as we can reconstruct it from other biblical texts as well as ancient Near Eastern texts, particularly the Babylonian Chronicle.[14]

In 609 B.C. King Nabopolassar, Nebuchadnezzar's father, attacked Haran, and this signaled a period of time when Babylon's efforts were directed toward Syria-Palestine with an eye focused on Egypt, who was an ally of the remnants of the Assyrians. Battles with Egyptian and Syrian armies continued in the next few years.

In 605 Nebuchadnezzar was now the head of the army in Syria. He defeated the Egyptians at Carchemish, a victory that opened the rest of Syria and Palestine to the Babylonian forces.[15] The Babylonian Chronicle at this point mentions in a general way that Nebuchadnezzar found success in his incursions into Syria-Palestine, and it is here that we understand that he besieged Jerusalem and compelled Jehoiakim to become an unwilling vassal. Debate surrounds 2 Chronicles 36:4–8 as to whether Jehoiakim himself was temporarily deported to Babylon or whether he was only threatened with deportation. In either case, we agree with Dillard that this deportation should be "associated with the deportation of Daniel and his friends along with articles from the temple in Jehoiakim's third year after Nebuchadnezzar defeated Neco at Carchemish" (cf. Jer. 46:2).[16]

The book of Daniel, of course, does not argue for the historical event; it narrates it. Indeed, even more, it intends to interpret the event for us. Human observation would lead to a very different understanding than that provided to us by the narrator of this book. On one level, it seems clear: Nebuchadnezzar, the leader of a powerful army, cowed Jerusalem, and, in a token of his dominance, took away some of the temple vessels and, as we will find out in the next section, a few of the noble youth. To the human eye, it appeared that Nebuchadnezzar had power; Judah did not.

---

13. Wiseman, *Nebuchadrezzar*, 22.

14. See also the convenient summary of the period provided by T. R. Hobbs, *2 Kings* (WBC; Waco, Tex.: Word, 1985), 348–49, though he passes over a siege of Jerusalem in 605, which may indicate that he does not accept Daniel 1:1–2 as reflecting historical reality.

15. Also in 605 B.C. Nabopolassar died, causing Nebuchadnezzar to quickly return to Babylon to secure the throne.

16. R. B. Dillard, *2 Chronicles* (WBC; Waco, Tex.: Word, 1987), 299.

The narrator rips away the curtain and informs his readers of the reality behind the appearance. He does so simply by saying that "the Lord delivered Jehoiakim king of Judah into his [Nebuchadnezzar's] hand." Nebuchadnezzar's might, though considerable, was not the reason why Jerusalem fell under his influence; it was the result of the will and action of God himself. This subtle phrase introduces a major theme of the book, the conflict between overweening human power and the power of God. A major concern of the book is to reinforce the belief that the sovereignty of God far surpasses the power of even the most mighty of human rulers. This theme is supported here by the use of the word "Lord" (*'adonai*) rather than "LORD" (*yhwh*) to refer to God. The former emphasizes God's ownership, his control.

It is a sign that Nebuchadnezzar's victory over Jerusalem is only the occasion for the following story that the narrator does not here even hint at the reasons why God moved against his own people in this way. As we will see later, the prayer in chapter 9 will show that Daniel himself agreed with other biblical authors (cf. the book of Kings) that the disaster took place because of the sin of the people. There he confesses on behalf of the people that they have rebelled against God and his commandments. But here again, Nebuchadnezzar's success is reported as the occasion that brought Daniel and his three friends to the Babylonian court.

Even before telling us about the human booty, however, the narrator mentions that Nebuchadnezzar took "some of the articles from the temple of God" and placed them in the temple of his god in Babylonia.[17] The specific identity of these "articles" is left unspecified.[18] In Exodus, the word "article" (*k^eli*) is a general term used to designate smaller objects used to support the cultic worship in the tabernacle (Ex. 27:19; 30:27; 31:8). In the book of Kings, we occasionally hear of the "articles," as when Asa dedicated certain gold and silver articles to temple service (1 Kings 15:15), or, in an interesting parallel to our story, when Jehoash, king of Israel, attacked Amaziah, king of Judah, robbed the temple of the "articles," and carried them back to Samaria (2 Kings 14:14). Second Chronicles 4:16 may give us an idea of the

---

17. The Hebrew text has Shinar, see NIV footnote. According to R. Zadok, "The Origin of the Name Shinar," ZA 74 (1984): 240–44, Shinar is an anachronistic reference to Babylonia. Goldingay (*Daniel*, 15), on the basis of other Old Testament usage (see particularly Genesis 11:1–9), argues that the term "suggests a place of false religion, self-will, and self-aggrandizement."

18. In an interesting article, P. R. Ackroyd, "The Temple Vessels—A Continuity Theme," in *Studies in the Religion of Ancient Israel* (Leiden: E. J. Brill, 1972), 166–79, describes the theological theme centered on the temple articles. To Ackroyd the text is not historical (esp. the reference in Dan. 1:2, cf. p. 180), but rather the removal and the restoration of the temple articles describes the continuity and discontinuity of Israel's relationship with God disrupted by the catastrophe of the Exile.

specific items included in the word *k^eli* when it lists "the pots, shovels, meat forks and all related articles." Of course, in Daniel 5 we also learn that these articles included "goblets," since Belshazzar seriously offends the Lord by using these for his banquet. Ezra 1:9–11 inventories the articles at the time of their return in consequence of Cyrus's decree, though some of these may have come from later sacks of the temple.[19]

In particular, our present passage anticipates the story in Daniel 5. Once again, from a human perspective, the plundering of the temple of the Lord, even if at this time only "some of the articles" were taken and placed in the Babylonian temple, could be seen as a great victory not only over Israel, but also over Yahweh himself. This act reflects a common ancient Near Eastern practice. A victorious army plundered the temple of the vanquished nation and placed the symbols of the defeated god in their own temple. An analogy is the placement of the ark in the temple of Dagon after the Philistines defeated the Israelites in battle during the youth of Samuel (1 Sam. 4–5). To the Philistines it appeared that Dagon had soundly whipped Yahweh, but subsequent events quickly changed their minds. The reality of the situation will take much longer to develop in Babylon, but the next time we see these "articles" in the hands of drunken Babylonians will be on the eve of their destruction (see comments in Dan. 5).

Training for Service (1:3–7)

BEGINNING WITH VERSE 3, the narrative focus begins to narrow. Nebuchadnezzar orders Ashpenaz,[20] one of his high officials, to begin the training process for the cream of the crop among the exiled youth.

We might well ask why Nebuchadnezzar would bother with the exiled youth. To answer this question we need to remember that at this time Nebuchadnezzar was trying to control Judah without actually taking it over. He has placed his puppet, Zedekiah, on the throne. His purpose with Daniel and the others was to train them in Babylonian ways for political and propaganda purposes. These members of the elite classes would become enamored with Babylonian ways and customs and either return to positions of influence at home or stay in Babylon in important positions, perhaps even serving as quasi-hostages. We can see analogies at other times in ancient Near Eastern history.[21]

---

19. See 2 Kings 24:13; 25:13–17; Jer. 52:17–23.

20. Most commentators (see A. Lacocque, *The Book of Daniel* [Atlanta: John Knox, 1979], 21) recognize the Old Persian word for "inn" in his name, thus associating his name with his work of providing for the dining and lodging of the "school of the exiles." See also, Hartman and DiLella, *The Book of Daniel*, 129.

21. For instance, Rome had the practice of taking the children of other close relatives of client states and holding them "hostage." This practice was not punishment as much as

Jon Berquist reminds us that Nebuchadnezzar's policy was fueled by other pragmatic considerations as well. The expanding empire required an expanding bureaucracy, which could not be met by the expertise of the native population. So the elite of subdued nations were pressed into service in the interest of Babylonian empire building.[22]

We refer to Daniel, his three friends, and the others implied[23] by the passage as members of the elite class of Judah for good reasons. In verse 3, for instance, they are referred to as "some ... from the royal family and the nobility." Rabbinic tradition associates this verse with Isaiah 39:7 and asserts that Daniel, Hananiah, Mishael, and Azariah were descendants of King Hezekiah.[24] Even if not direct descendants of the king, they are nobly born in Judah.

But the qualifications for admission go well beyond right of birth. The king specified physical as well as intellectual qualities. That they were to be "young men" ($y^e ladim$), though of imprecise age designation,[25] makes it hard to believe that they were over twenty and may have been much younger.[26]

Furthermore, candidates for admission to the royal school were to have impeccable physical qualifications: "without any physical defect" as well as "handsome." The latter quality is easy to understand, though the standards of masculine beauty were possibly different. We may get a clue of what those standards are when we look at the artwork of ancient Mesopotamia[27] and note the well-muscled, full-bearded, luxuriantly curled hair of the warriors and

---

security against rebellion. As these hostages lived in Rome, a high-ranking Roman family became their patron and they became acclimated to Roman ways, with the idea that they would be friends of Rome when they returned to their native lands. In the context of Daniel 11, we will note how this was also the experience of Antiochus IV and Demetrius.

22. J. L. Berquist, *Judaism in Persia's Shadow: A Social and Historical Approach* (Minneapolis: Fortress, 1995), 15–16. Berquist differentiates these urban exiles who worked in the government bureaucracy from the rural exiles, who helped in food supply.

23. Verse 6 describes Daniel and his three friends as "some" among the exiles chosen for training. We hear nothing of the others; the text focuses only on Daniel and his three friends.

24. J. Braverman, *Jerome's Commentary on Daniel: A Study of Comparative Jewish and Christian Interpretations of the Hebrew Bible* (CBQMS 7; Washington, D.C.: Catholic Biblical Association of America, 1978), 67–68.

25. Cf. V. P. Hamilton, "ילד," *NIDOTTE*, 2:457–58.

26. This is true especially in the light of the fact that Daniel lives through the entire exilic period. Many commentators cite Greek evidence that Persian education began in the early teens. L. J. Wood (*A Commentary on Daniel* [Grand Rapids: Zondervan, 1973], 33), for example, states: "Plato (*Alcibiades* 1.121) says that the education of youths in Persia began at fourteen years, and Xenophon (*Cyropaedia*, I.2) speaks of the seventeenth year as the completion"; see also J. A. Montgomery, *The Book of Daniel* (ICC; Edinburgh: T. and T. Clark, 1927), 122. Of course, this Persian evidence, if reliable, is of uncertain relevance to Babylon decades earlier.

27. Cf. J. B. Pritchard (ed.), *The Ancient Near East in Pictures Relating to the Old Testament* (Princeton: Princeton Univ. Press, 1969).

kings. Or perhaps we are to picture Daniel and his friends more like the distinguished courtiers and advisors of the court.

It is the first trait ("without any physical defect") that has drawn the most discussion. The Hebrew word here (*muʾwm*) is known from sacrificial texts, describing the appropriate type of animal that can be offered to God (Lev. 21:17, 18, 21; 22:20, etc.). But it is not unknown elsewhere as the description of the physical perfection of a human being (e.g., Absalom [2 Sam. 14:25]; the beloved [Song 4:4]).

These men are not just good-looking and well-born, but they already show intellectual aptitude. They are "showing aptitude for every kind of learning, well informed, quick to understand." The verbs and nouns used in this description are familiar to those who have read Proverbs. Of course, in the mouth of Nebuchadnezzar the words do not carry the same ethical connotations as that book, but the narrator seems to be preparing us to recognize the four, especially Daniel, as a paradigm of the wise person.

In any case, the command of the king to his chief court official, Ashpenaz, was to train these young men in "the language and literature of the Babylonians." They were to be immersed in the culture of their enemies.

Aramaic was the native language of the Chaldean tribe that was in power in Babylon at the time, and this northwest Semitic language was becoming the lingua franca of the Near East. Nonetheless, the native language of the Babylonians was Akkadian, a Semitic language like Hebrew, but with an extremely complex writing system. It was written in syllabic cuneiform, with the additional complexity that it often utilized the ancient language of the region, Sumerian, in its technical literature. It is likely that our text has Akkadian specifically in mind in terms of the special training that Daniel and his friends were about to receive. Through archaeological discovery and philological advances, we know something of the literature of the Babylonians.[28] Today we have examples of historical writings, economic tablets, religious myths, heroic epics, love poetry, and more.

However, from later descriptions of Daniel's wisdom, we should highlight the importance that mantic oracles play in the Babylonia of Daniel's time. Daniel clearly would have been trained in the arts of divination through such means as interpreting unusual terrestrial and celestial phenomena, astrology, the examination of sheep livers, and so forth. Indeed, as the footnote to the NIV text points out, the Hebrew literally reads "the literature of the Chaldeans," not "the Babylonians." It is true that Chaldea, mentioned as the tribe in control of Babylonia, is another name for Babylon. However, it

---

28. See, for instance, B. R. Foster, *Before the Muses: An Anthology of Akkadian Literature* (2 vols.; Bethesda, Md.: CDL Press, 1993).

soon[29] became a byword for "magician" or "diviner," since the culture was so closely associated with this practice.

The art of divination, or reading omens, is well-attested in ancient Mesopotamia.[30] According to William Farber, omens were the primary way by which the gods revealed their "will, intentions, or fateful decisions to people."[31] However, this type of divine revelation is different from what we know as biblical prophecy. Divination was a learned practice in that portended events were associated with certain signs (like symptoms of an illness), whether the shape of a liver, unusual births, the flight pattern of birds, the stars, or dreams.[32] Diviners used reference books to tease out the significance of the sign. Omens could be solicted or unsolicited. In the case of dreams, they could be solicited by an incubation rite, where the subject induced sleep expectant of a significant dream. But the reference books only helped diviners interpret dreams that the subject narrated to them. They did not have the tools to discover the contents of a dream if the subject chose, for whatever reason, to withhold that information.

The bottom line is that the text is telling us that Daniel was educated in the ways of Babylon, which surely included these mantic arts. As we will see, he not only took the class, he graduated summa cum laude (1:17, 20)!

Indeed, as we read closely in this section, we marvel at just how far Daniel and his friends are taken in the Babylonian acculturation program. In verses 6–7, we learn that their names were changed. On the surface, this may seem benign to those of us who live in a modern Western culture, where name and identity are only mildly associated. In the ancient Near East, however, the name, which often contained the name of the one's deity, was integrally connected with a person's identity. Thus, the Babylonians began the process of reeducation by giving their captives new names.

Daniel ("God is my judge") becomes Belteshazzar (either "May [a god] protect his life" or "Lady [a goddess], protect the king").[33] Azariah ("Yah is

---

29. J. J. Collins, *The Apocalyptic Vision of the Book of Daniel* (Missoula, Mont.: Scholars, 1977), 32 notes that Herodotus (5th century B.C.) provides the first attestation of the use of "Chaldean" in its professional sense.

30. Three of the most well-known series of omens from Mesopotamia are *Enuma Anu Enlil*, *Summa Alu*, and *Summa Izbu*.

31. Farber's article is found on pp. 1894–1906, in vol. 3 of J. Sasson (ed.), *Civilizations of the Ancient Near East* (New York: Scribers, 1995).

32. Although a learned discipline, Mesopotamian divination must be considered revelation from the divine realm according to J. Lawson, "'The God Who Reveals Secrets': The Mesopotamian Background to Daniel 2:47," *JSOT* 74 (1997): 61–76. This point will be important not only here, but especially for the next chapter.

33. See Baldwin, *Daniel*, 81, citing Millard. Also note that Dan. 4:8 connects Daniel's new name with the name of Nebuchadnezzar's god.

my help") becomes Abednego (probably a bastardized form of "servant of Nabu"). Hananiah ("Yah has been gracious") and Mishael ("Who is what God is?") becomes Shadrach and Meshach. The latter two Babylonian names are of debated etymology, though many[34] see the former as a form of the name Marduk. Though we cannot be dogmatic on the details, it appears that in their attempt to give the Judean youths a new identity and allegiance, they bestowed names that associate them with Babylonian gods. The remarkable fact is that the Hebrew youths did not choose to fight this battle.

Conceivably, the transformation may have gone further. As J. Braverman has pointed out, early rabbinic and Christian commentary on these verses concluded that Daniel and his friends literally became eunuchs at this point.[35] After all, many of those who worked closely with the Babylonian king were eunuchs, and Ashpenaz's title has been understood to literally mean "chief of the eunuchs."[36] Jerome believed that Daniel and his friends here fulfilled Isaiah 39:7, "And some of your descendants, your own flesh and blood who will be born to you, will be taken away, and they will become eunuchs in the palace of the king of Babylon."

In the final analysis, we cannot be certain. Some have argued that their description as "without defect" precludes their castration.[37] However, note that within the story the evaluation is made not by an Israelite priest but by a pagan king. To Nebuchadnezzar a eunuch in the service of the court is natural. Yet we must remember that native evidence indicates that not every male who served in the court was a eunuch. On this matter, we will have to suspend final judgment.

We have passed over the one matter in our passage that will dominate the rest of the chapter, the provision of food. During their three years of training, the king "assigned them a daily amount of food and wine from the king's table" (v. 5). Since this gift triggered a striking response from our four faithful Judeans, we will reserve discussion of the nature of this food until the next section.

Avoiding Defilement (1:8–16)

UP TO THIS point, Daniel and his three friends have provided no recorded resistance to their assimilation into Babylonian society and culture. They have received new names, submitted to a foreign educational curriculum,

---

34. Cf. Wood, *A Commentary on Daniel*, 36; Lacocque, *The Book of Daniel*, 29–30; E. J. Young, *The Prophecy of Daniel* (Grand Rapids: Eerdmans, 1949), 43.
35. Braverman, *Jerome's Commentary on Daniel*, 53–71.
36. See G. H. Johnston, "סָרִיס," *NIDOTTE*, 3:293.
37. Cf. S. R. Miller, *Daniel* (NAC; Nashville: Broadman, 1994), 59.

and perhaps even have had their gender erased. All of this makes their next move all the more startling. "Daniel resolved not to defile himself with the royal food and wine" (v. 8). What does Daniel hope to accomplish by his determined stand? Why has he chosen the area of his diet as the moral and theological line over which he refuses to step?

The question is not easy to answer with confidence. Of course, our first guess would be that Daniel is firm in his commitment to the dietary laws of the Old Testament, the laws of *kashrut* (Lev. 11; Deut. 12:23–26).[38] After all, the verb "defile" (*ga'al*) denotes religious defilement.[39] In other words, he wants to keep kosher. However, if Daniel's intention was to keep kosher, then why did he refrain from wine? The Old Testament laws do not restrict any but the Nazirite from wine (Num. 6:1–4). Further, in their threats and warnings, the preexilic prophets implied that it was impossible, by definition, to keep kosher in the land of captivity (Hos. 9:3; Amos 7:17).

If Daniel was not motivated by the dietary laws of the Old Testament, then perhaps he was concerned about the religious overtones of the food from the king's table. In a marvelously written chapter synthesizing material from various Akkadian texts, A. Leo Oppenheim informs us about the "care and feeding of the gods."[40] We learn here that sumptuous food would be offered to the gods, and, after their having time to enjoy the repast, whatever was left would be brought to the king's table. No Mesopotamian king is ever recorded as going hungry.

Perhaps Daniel would have been troubled by eating food that was first offered to idols, so that we can here locate his determination to avoid the food. However, Daniel does not avoid all the food of the palace. He does eat the vegetables, and we have no reason to think that these were not offered to the gods along with the meat and drink.

Baldwin and Fewell[41] separately argue that the motivation was more political than theological. Of course, in the ancient world these two spheres were not completely separate. In any case, these scholars point to the use of the Hebrew word *patbag* (translated "food" in v. 8; cf. also 11:26 as well as the idiom "to eat at the king's table" in 1 Sam. 20:30–34; 2 Sam. 9:9–13; 19:27–29) to argue that to eat food from the king's provision was an acceptance of his covenant/treaty overlordship. By refusing the food, Daniel refuses the relationship. But again, this view falters by virtue of the fact that Daniel did not

---

38. Wood, *A Commentary on Daniel*, 36, cites this as a major motivation for Daniel.
39. Cf. R. E. Averbeck, "גאל," *NIDOTTE*, 1:794–79; see Ezra 2:62; Neh. 7:64; Isa 59:3; Mal. 1:7, 12.
40. A. L. Oppenheim, *Ancient Mesopotamia: Portrait of a Dead Civilization* (Chicago: Univ. of Chicago Press, 1964), 183–97.
41. See Baldwin, *Daniel*, 83; Fewell, *Circle of Sovereignty*, 40.

make a public display of rejecting all the king's food. Indeed, he accepted the vegetables. On the human level, he and the three friends physically survived because the king sent food from which they selectively ate the vegetables.

Rather than these doubtful reasons, we believe that the motivation lies more closely connected to the story. Daniel and his three friends are in a process of education and preparation for service. Their minds as well as their bodies are being fed by the Babylonian court. If they prosper, then to whom should they attribute their development and success? The Babylonians. However, by refusing to eat the food of the king, they know it is not the king who is responsible for the fact that "they looked healthier and better nourished than any of the young men who ate the royal food" (1:15). Their robust appearance, usually attained by a rich fare of meats and wine, is miraculously achieved through a diet of vegetables. Only God could have done it.[42]

The diet of vegetables was a temporary regimen, as we learn from later texts that imply that Daniel at least enjoyed rich foods later in life.[43] Its purpose was to keep the four pious Judeans from believing that their physical appearance (and by consequence, perhaps, their intellectual gifts) were the gift of the Babylonian culture.

Another point, vitally important for later application, is often missed in the discussion. The diet was private, not public. As the four stood before Nebuchadnezzar and were pronounced the best in the class, the king could take pride in the products of his largesse. Only the Judean youths knew the truth.[44]

After all, observe how they achieved their goal of a substitute diet. They made no public proclamation of their intentions. They staged no food strikes. Daniel quietly approached the chief official and asked him for permission not to partake. The chief official did not agree with them and refused to participate in their plan, but he did not reject them brusquely or violently. He could presumably have caused some trouble for the four, but the text informs us that "God had caused the official to show favor and sympathy to Daniel" (v. 9). Behind this English translation we see the same verb that we encountered in v. 2, "God gave." While the Babylonians thought they were in control of the

---

42. Cf. D. Soesilo, "Why Did Daniel Reject the King's Delicacies? (Daniel 1:8)," *BT* 45 (1994): 441–44. Note K. Koch, *Daniel* (Neukirchen-Vluyn: Neukirchener Verlag, 1986), 58–69, who concludes the goal of Daniel's diet is to cause a mystical frame of mind.

43. As Calvin points out in his commentary on Daniel, *Daniel I (Chapters 1–6)* (Grand Rapids: Eerdmans, 1993), 30. This is implied by Dan. 10:3, in that the effect of the vision kept Daniel from enjoying his normal diet of choice food, meat, and wine. We should add that if Daniel's motivations in chapter 1 were to keep kosher, avoid idolatrous defilement, or political entanglement, then we should question why his eating habits changed later in life.

44. As pointed out by W. S. Towner, "Daniel 1 in the Context of the Canon," in *Canon, Theology and Old Testament Interpretation: Essays in Honor of Brevard S. Childs* (ed. G. M. Tucker, D. L. Petersen, and R. R. Wilson; Minneapolis: Fortress, 1988), 288.

Daniel 1:1–21

world and local scene, the Hebrew narrative makes it clear again that the true God is the One who orchestrates events for the good of his people.

True, the chief official declines the ruse. Daniel does not panic; he does not grow angry. He simply chooses another strategy to accomplish his goal. We see here the beginnings of a theme that will develop throughout the narratives concerning Daniel. He is the incarnation of a wise man—a man who knows how to navigate life. He knows the right action for the right situation; he knows the right word to effect a godly result.

In this case, Daniel turns to the guard whom the chief official put in charge of their diet (v. 11). He proposes this time a brief ten-day test: "Give us nothing but vegetables to eat and water to drink [and not the rich fare of the king]. Then [after ten days] compare our appearance with that of the young men who eat the royal food" (vv. 12–13). Perhaps motivated in part by the fact that he could partake of the rich fare while providing the vegetables for the four Judeans, the guard agrees; the test works; and the four eat vegetables to the glory of God for three years.

Success Given to Daniel and His Friends (1:17–20)

FOR THE THIRD time in the chapter, we read that God gave something to someone. In 1:2, he gave Jehoiakim and Jerusalem to Nebuchadnezzar. In 1:9, God gave the chief official sympathy toward Daniel and his friends. Now (v. 17) we read that God gave the four Judeans "knowledge and understanding." Of course, Nebuchadnezzar and those involved in their education would take credit for their brilliance, but Daniel and the others would know to whom the credit was due. This section anticipates the next chapter, where the plot revolves around God's granting wisdom to Daniel through revelation (cf. 2:22). After all, they had grown physically robust not because of their Babylonian diet but because of the grace of God, that is, in spite of their diet of vegetables. The effect of the theme of "God's giving" throughout the chapter is to press home who is really in control of the events of Daniel's life, not to speak of fate of the people of God in general.

For now, however, the divine origin of Daniel's success is understood only in private by the four. Nonetheless, the effect is there for all to see. Just by talking with them, Nebuchadnezzar recognizes that Daniel, Hananiah, Mishael, and Azariah (note the narrator's use of the Hebrew names) are far better[45] than the professional "magicians and enchanters" of Babylon. However, the narrative has let the readers, both ancient and modern, look in on

---

45. Literally, "ten times better" (see NIV). The number ten has the symbolic sense of "much" or "many"; cf. "Ten," in *The Dictionary of Biblical Imagery*, ed. by L. Ryken, J. Wilhoit, and T. Longman III (Downers Grove, Ill.: InterVarsity, forthcoming).

what was going on behind the scene. Thus, we might say that Daniel and his friends' actions are intended not only for themselves but as an example to all of us (see Contemporary Significance).

Commentators through the centuries have been troubled by the description of Daniel's wisdom and especially this comparison to Babylonian wisdom. In the words of Calvin,

> we must hold that Daniel had not been seduced to implicate himself completely in those impostures of Satan, for, as we shall soon see, he abstained from the royal food and drink. My opinion is, therefore, that whatever the king may have commanded, Daniel was content with the pure and genuine science of natural things.[46]

After all, the Bible makes clear that the superiority of Israelite wisdom to Babylonian mantic wisdom is not a matter of degree, it is a matter of kind. Babylonian wise men are not so much incompetent as "false." They claim to receive their wisdom from gods whom the Israelites recognize as nonexistent—or worse, from the dark side (Deut. 18:14: "The nations you will dispossess listen to those who practice sorcery or divination. But as for you, the LORD your God has not permitted you to do so"; cf. Isa. 47).

It is too facile to say that Daniel had nothing to do with this kind of wisdom. While it is true that the four are first characterized by the kind of wisdom associated with the book of Proverbs ("knowledge and understanding"), Daniel himself is associated with a kind of mantic wisdom ("Daniel could understand visions and dreams of all kinds," v. 17). Indeed, we will see that God uses Daniel's specialized knowledge as an instrument for the revelation he gives him later in the book.

The description of Daniel here and his actions later remind us of Joseph, who played a similar role in the court of the Egyptian pharaoh. God blessed him as well with the ability to interpret dreams in a style that even this pagan monarch could recognize. And who can forget the association the narrative makes between Joseph and his divination cup (Gen. 44:5)? God can utilize even the forms of pagan wisdom for his purposes.[47] As Goldingay points out, "there is no positive theology of pagan or secular learning here, but rather the assurance that it can be triumphed over."[48] The chapters that follow will show Daniel and his friends triumphing again and again over the false wisdom of the Babylonians, both through courtly wisdom (chs. 3 and 6) and

---

46. Calvin, *Daniel I*, 27.
47. In the New Testament, God's use of pagan astrology to guide the wise men to the newly born Jesus may be an analogous situation (cf. Matt. 2:1–12).
48. Goldingay, *Daniel*, 27.

Daniel 1:1–21

through mantic wisdom (chs. 2, 4, and 5 [not to speak of the second half of the book]).[49]

The Extent of Daniel's Ministry (1:21)

CHAPTER 1, AS we have seen, introduces the whole book of Daniel. Daniel is the wise man who, through God's grace, can navigate life's difficulties in the present and peer into the future. It is, therefore, fitting that we get an anticipation of the extent of his work. But the note comes with a difficulty. While the verse situates his life and career in the period between his arrival in Babylon until the first year of Cyrus, the Persian who defeated the Babylonians, Daniel 10:1 locates the concluding vision in the third year of Cyrus.

There are various ways to harmonize 1:21 and 10:1,[50] but we should not miss the intention of the verse to identify Daniel as the prophet of the Exile. He spans the entire period, and, as J. Goldingay puts it, thus "outlasts" his conquerors.[51] This message provides both encouragement and hope to those alienated from their land with the message that success without compromise was possible even in the midst of captivity.

IN THE INTRODUCTION to the chapter, we have already identified the overall theme of this chapter: In spite of present appearances, God is in control. Though the story focuses on the surface level on the actions of the human characters, the chapter primarily intends to teach us about God. He is all-powerful; in a word, he is sovereign. Powerful human figures like Nebuchadnezzar wield tremendous influence and, on one level, control the lives of many people, including Daniel. However, the opening chapter asserts a theme that runs throughout the book as a whole: Real power has a heavenly origin. People like Nebuchadnezzar simply serve his deeper, at times mysterious, purposes.

God's sovereignty displayed subtly but clearly here and elsewhere in the book has as an intended effect to comfort his people. From their limited

---

49. Cf. L. M. Wills, *The Jew in the Court of the Foreign King* (HDR; Minneapolis: Fortress, 1990), 80.

50. Perhaps the intention of the verse is simply to say that Daniel was in the Babylonian court for the rest of its days. Or perhaps Young (*The Prophecy of Daniel*, 51–52) is correct when he argues that the first year of Cyrus is mentioned because of its importance for the Judeans and in effect means "first year and beyond."

51. J. Goldingay, "Story, Vision, Interpretation: Literary Approaches to Daniel," in *The Book of Daniel in the Light of New Findings*, ed. A. S. van der Woude (Leuven: University Press, 1993), 298.

human perspective, they think they are simply pawns in the hands of hostile forces. Daniel 1 circumvents that false but understandable perception by pointing them to the reality of divine sovereignty.

The teaching on divine sovereignty is the most important lesson of the chapter, but can we go further and learn from Daniel's example of godly behavior in the midst of a hostile environment? Or are his actions so limited to a particular historical occasion that it is illegitimate to transfer anything to our lives today? We have already addressed this issue in a broad way in the introduction to the book, but this is an important place to add a few comments, since we do intend to derive lessons for our lives so many years later from the life of Daniel.

Genre identification and proper interpretation. Genre identification is crucial for proper interpretation and application. We need to know what we are reading in order to understand properly the text's message and claims (if any) on our lives.

On the surface, Daniel's opening chapters appear to inform us about the past. We hear about events that shaped the fate of a whole nation when Babylon exerted its power over Judah and exiled a number of its elite class. We get an account of the first few years of certain members of that elite class as they live in the Babylonian court. We often call such reminiscences of the past "history"—a blanket term to be sure, but one that we understand and that fits with the contents of Daniel 1. Many scholars would call our label simplistic and reductionistic, and they would be correct, but we will save our nuancing for later.

Many teachers and preachers of the historical sections of the Bible make a fundamental error at this point. In their appropriate desire to make these texts touch the lives of those to whom they are speaking, they go immediately to moral teaching of the passage as they understand it. In a moment we will see this is legitimate, though filled with pitfalls. However, we must point out that the primary purpose for these texts is not to teach us how to behave, but rather to point us to God. Daniel is first and foremost a revelation of God. Now, God does not reveal himself to us in the abstract but rather in relationship to his people and through his actions in history. From the very first verses we see that this book is not essentially about Daniel, but rather about God. It is a revelation of who he is and how he acts for our redemption.[52]

Nonetheless, neither should we ignore the didactic function of the text.[53] Several important questions arise as we consider this function. (1) We must address an issue that many Bible writers ask: How can history be normative?

---

52. See J. H. Walton, L. D. Bailey, and C. Williford, "Bible-Based Curricula and the Crisis of Scriptural Authority," *Journal of Christian Education* 13 (1993): 83–94.
53. See T. Longman III and R. B. Dillard, "Hermeneutics and Counseling," *IBC Perspective* 2 (1987): 21–30.

Daniel 1:1–21

In other words, isn't history unique? God may be working in a special way during Daniel's time, but we should not uncritically read about his actions and apply them to ourselves by saying, "Go and act like Daniel!" History is a report of past events, not a blueprint for our behavior. We can marvel at God's great acts, but we cannot presume that they have any direct relationship with us today.

As we will see throughout the first six chapters of Daniel, there is much truth to this principle. We cannot assume that God acts the same way today as he did at the time of Daniel. Nor can we simply use Daniel as a model of our behavior without asking important questions of continuity or discontinuity. Yet it is equally incorrect to say that we should never use historical narrative from the Old Testament as a guide to our faith and practice today. There is a moral force to these stories of Daniel in captivity that we ignore to our great impoverishment. After all, it is in reference to stories like this one[54] that Paul stated "these things occurred as examples" (1 Cor. 10:6).

We cannot reduce any Old Testament story to a simple historical report about the past; indeed Old Testament narrative as a whole seems to have a didactic shaping.[55] That is, they incarnate principles that intend to shape the lives of those who hear these stories.

And what appears to be true of Old Testament narrative in general is pointedly true for Daniel 1–6. Indeed, its didactic function, along with the Joseph story and Esther, have been underlined by scholars who have gone so far as to classify these prose sections as wisdom literature.[56] Wisdom literature proper (e.g., the book of Proverbs) informs its readers of the proper way to navigate life. Just as Joseph in Genesis 39 illustrates how a young man in a compromising situation should act in a way that pleases God, so Daniel and his three friends give insight and guidance to God's people as they confront oppression and the temptations of a godless life. If it is wisdom literature—and this may be doubted,[57] it guides by showing proper behavior as opposed to describing it in the manner of a proverb.

Indeed, there is no better way to learn than by a good story. We can be inspired, encouraged, and emboldened by a story like Daniel's triumph over

---

54. Though, to be sure, Paul's specific reference is to another historical account in the Old Testament, the story of wanderings in the desert.

55. Cf. T. Longman III, *Literary Approaches*, 68–71.

56. Cf. G. von Rad, *Wisdom in Israel* (London: SCM, 1970), 47, who identified Daniel 1–6 as didactic narrative and compares it to the Joseph story. Cf. H.-P. Muller, "Die weisheitliche Lehrerzahlung im Alten Testament und seiner Umwelt," *WO* 9 (1977): 77–98.

57. J. Crenshaw, "Method in Determining Wisdom Influence Upon 'Historical Literature,'" *JBL* 88 (1969): 129–42, while not addressing the issue of Daniel 1–6 directly, does raise questions about assigning these chapters to a wisdom genre per se.

Daniel 1:1–21

an impossible situation to live out our own faith with courage. After all, we are not only readers of stories; we live story.[58]

Think about it. When you tell a new friend about yourself, you tell them a story. You have a beginning, a middle, and an end (which is ongoing until your death and someone else tells the story of your life). In other words, you have a plot. Your life is peopled with characters: your parents, friends, supporters, enemies. If you are a Christian, you will give the account of your conversion and your life with Christ. Thus, it is almost impossible for us as story-bearers not to compare our story with the ones we hear, like the story of Daniel.

When we tell the story of our lives truthfully, we are recounting actual events and actual people. Nonetheless, we give it meaning and purpose from the vantage point of the present. We may now see how God had a purpose in a relationship that confused us in the past; we may see patterns in our life that we did not recognize earlier. These purposes and the situation in which we are speaking will cause us to select certain high points in our life, emphasize some more than others, and interpret them all. Our stories can be both true and shaped.

The same is true of biblical history; the accounts are true, yet shaped. They have a grander purpose than mere historical recollection, but this does not denigrate their essential historical accuracy.[59] The Daniel account is shaped so that our stories may come into contact with Daniel's story with the result that we may be changed by it.

(2) How are we changed by the story of Daniel 1? Before answering that question directly, we must acknowledge that, though these "things occurred as examples" for us (1 Cor. 10:6), there are also elements of discontinuity we must take into account, both here and in the chapters to follow. While affirming a didactic element to these chapters, we must also acknowledge that Old Testament stories do more than give us examples. They are more than just individual stories that teach us how to behave; they are part of a greater story, the story of God's redemption of his people. They are a part, to use a term common among theologians, of the history of redemption. The story of Daniel is a window on the Exile, an important event in redemptive history.

God had formed a special relationship with the descendants of Abraham and had given the patriarch a promise (Gen. 12:2–3):

> I will make you into a great nation,
>   and I will bless you;
> I will make your name great,
>   and you will be a blessing.

---

58. D. Hudson, "Come, Bring Your Story," *Mars Hill* 1 (1994): 73–86.
59. Cf. V. Philips Long, *The Art of Biblical History* (Grand Rapids: Zondervan, 1994).

Daniel 1:1–21

> I will bless those who bless you,
>> and whoever curses you I will curse;
> and all peoples on earth
>> will be blessed through you.

God later followed through on these promises. For instance, later in history Abraham's descendants had indeed become a nation, and at the time of the Exodus Moses constituted them as such. But these promises, freely given, also entailed a response of gratitude, perhaps most concretely expressed through the law later spelled out in the Ten Commandments and the case law that flowed from them. That law was accompanied by blessings and curses for obedience and disobedience. Among those curses for disobedience were some that warned of a cataclysmic judgment that could come on the people of God. Typical of these is Deuteronomy 28:64–68:

> Then the LORD will scatter you among all nations, from one end of the earth to the other. There you will worship other gods—gods of wood and stone, which neither you nor your fathers have known. Among those nations you will find no repose, no resting place for the sole of your foot. There the LORD will give you an anxious mind, eyes weary with longing, and a despairing heart. You will live in constant suspense, filled with dread both night and day, never sure of your life. In the morning you will say, "If only it were evening!" and in the evening, "If only it were morning!"—because of the terror that will fill your hearts and the sights that your eyes will see. The LORD will send you back in ships to Egypt on a journey I said you should never make again. There you will offer yourselves for sale to your enemies as male and female slaves, but no one will buy you.

The prophets of the period just before the Exile warned the people of Judah that such a cataclysm threatened them because of their disregard for their relationship with God as manifest in their disobedience to the law. The author of Lamentations understood the destruction of Jerusalem as the fulfillment of this and other curses. Daniel's personal exile was an anticipation of the national catastrophe.

In other words, the story of Daniel informs the reader that Nebuchadnezzar's intrusion into Judah was not a historical accident. God gave Jehoiakim into that pagan king's hands, after all. But without denying that the Exile was indeed an experience of God's judgment, Daniel 1 also reveals that God had not abandoned his people altogether. He was not only with the faithful in exile, but as with Joseph in the Egyptian prison, God was blessing them, allowing them to succeed in what might be considered nearly impossible situations.

Daniel 1:1–21

Continuity and discontinuity. As we will see more clearly later, Daniel 1 anticipates a theme that flows from the promise to Abraham. We begin to see what becomes explicit in the next chapter: Abraham's descendants will be a blessing to the nations.

When reading the Old Testament as history of redemption, we must be careful to read it first from the vantage point of the time of its composition. If we do not, we will easily distort its message. However, for those who read from the stance of Christian faith we must continue, because we have more of the story. Jesus himself instructed his disciples that the Old Testament had a future dimension that pointed toward himself (Luke 24:25–27, 44–49). Not that every verse or even every chapter of the Old Testament has a specific anticipation of Christ, but we must read the Old Testament, including the stories about Daniel, with an eye to the fulfillment of redemptive history in Christ.

As we read the account of Daniel in the Babylonian and, later, the Persian courts, we must acknowledge another important element of discontinuity with our moment in redemptive history. Daniel and his friends lived their lives of faith at a time when God's people were defined as an ethnic group and a distinct political entity. In a word, God's people were a nation, admittedly at the time of Daniel a nation without independent existence, but a nation nonetheless. After Christ, God's people can no longer be so identified. God's people today are the church. A much less tangible entity than a nation, the church spans ethnic, political, and national boundaries.

Unfortunately, this distinction is often lost today, especially in America, where some still think it is possible to speak of an essentially Christian nation founded on (Judeo-) Christian principles. This point is crucial for our understanding of Daniel and Daniel 1 in particular, where a fundamental issue is the relationship between faith and culture. Daniel teaches us that the struggle is not to make the culture Christian, but how a Christian can live in a hostile culture.

As we read the story of Daniel from the perspective of the New Testament and ask how we as Christians can learn from the example of Daniel, we will see how these elements of discontinuity work themselves out in such concrete instances as Daniel's bold decision not to eat the food provided by the king. Even though we have concluded that the core issue is not keeping kosher, we can learn from Acts 10 and 15, as well as 1 Corinthians 8 (cf. v. 8 " . . . food does not bring us near to God, we are no worse if we do not eat, and no better if we do") that preoccupation with a distinctive diet is a characteristic of the Old Testament people of God, not the New. However, the principle of continuity will drive us to ask ourselves where God is calling on us to make a stand of faith in the midst of our constantly changing culture, a prospect frightening as well as exciting.

 **Contemporary Significance**

DANIEL 1 THRUSTS us into an issue of contemporary significance that continues into the following chapters. For that reason, though this essay will be self-contained, we will not give an exhaustive discussion here. The reader interested in the insight that the book as a whole throws on the question of the relationship between faith and culture will have to read the commentary on the following chapters as well. Here, however, we will lay the groundwork and will refer in later chapters to the discussion found here.

God is in control. God reveals himself in the midst of the action of Daniel 1. We have seen that while on the level of human observation Nebuchadnezzar's military prowess wins the day, the Bible takes us behind the scene and shows us that God is in control. God is sovereign and he is also immanent in the world. He directs the world by his providence. This is true not only on the battlefield, but also in Daniel's classroom in the royal court. God also is the one who distributes wisdom, choosing to endow Daniel and the three friends with a special measure of it to further his purposes in history.

Relationship between faith and culture. But how does Daniel 1 address us in our everyday life? In answer, it is striking how the contemporary church finds itself in a situation similar to Daniel's. We too live in a strange land. We have seen how Daniel was taken from the shadow of the temple and forced to live in a land that worshiped idols. Babylonia under Nebuchadnezzar ultimately went further, tore down that temple in 587 B.C., and destroyed Daniel's homeland. Daniel (and the other exiles) enjoyed some measure of freedom and reputation in the land of his captivity, but he still lived in a culture that was hostile toward everything he held dear in his heart. The dichotomy between his belief and the belief of those in power is evident in this first chapter and will intensify throughout the book.

Christians today should understand that we too live in a "toxic" culture, that is, a culture that stands at odds with our faith.[60] The god of modern culture is not the God of the Bible, but is ultimately the self. This strange god demands worship that creates values different than those of Christianity. Since the individual is at the heart of the worship of secular culture, personal gratification and self-realization are prized over any sense of the other person, any sense of community, whether that community is the family, the church, the city, the nation, or the global community.

This picture, of course, is a simplification and generalization. The world does not divide neatly into Christian and secular. Especially in this day of

---

60. The term is Michael Novak's, cited by Ervin S. Duggan, "The Media and the Church Today," oral presentation at the Conference on Contemporary Issues at Westminster Theological Seminary (March 11, 1997), 3–6 in written transcripts.

Daniel 1:1–21

growing spirituality, the non-Christian world is varied. Those of us who live in big cities daily rub shoulders not only with thoroughgoing atheists and agnostics, but also with Muslims, people of Jewish faith, and those who practice a vague sort of spirituality that they refuse to put into traditional categories.

For a variety of reasons, however, the public face of our culture is predominantly secular. Since, in the United States at least, our founders thought it in the best interest of religion to keep government separate, God has become at best a buzzword in public policy and law. Moreover, because of the virtual withdrawal of Christians from the media, such things as movies, television, mainstream music, and journalism reflect the mood and opinions of those who bracket or reject God.

The lines are not always clear, but most thoughtful Christians recognize a difference between their beliefs and values and those esteemed by the culture at large. Indeed, many Christians have a sense of oppression and even hostility as they live their lives in the public square. The term *culture war* has recently been coined to describe the clash of values between people of faith and those who define what is right and wrong without reference to a higher being, more specifically the God of the Bible. In an insightful and provocative description of this conflict, James Davison Hunter of the University of Virginia has delineated the five fronts along which this war is waged: the family, education, popular media, law, and electoral politics.[61]

To highlight just one specific issue among many, note contrasting attitudes toward homosexuality. Many today believe that homosexuality is a legitimate alternative lifestyle, to be respected and treated like heterosexuality. Philadelphia, the city in which I lived until recently, has just recognized the gay partners of city employees by granting them spousal benefits. On the other side of the culture war, the place where Christians often find themselves, are those who are not ready to acknowledge homosexuality as simply an alternative to heterosexuality. In opposing what they see as a trend of "secular" culture, they believe that they protect the institution of the family, at least as traditionally defined.

The tensions are deep and more complex than I am able to describe here. Nonetheless, only the most insensitive could miss that there is a profound sense of division in our society, and Christians often find themselves out of sync with the bulk of culture.

Let me be clear at this point. I am not making a simple identification between the Christian church, or even the more narrowly defined evangelical Christian church, and the agenda of the religious right, even though the culture war in large part is defined, legitimately, as a struggle between the

---

61. J. D. Hunter, *Culture Wars: The Struggle to Define America* (New York: Basic Books, 1991).

Daniel 1:1–21

religious right and the rest of society. But no matter what their political orientation, whether conservative or liberal, Christians will find themselves at odds with the values and beliefs of the broader culture just by virtue of their ultimate allegiance to a God who is bigger than themselves.

What can the book of Daniel contribute to our own struggle and sense of identity in a modern secular world? Not only does it reflect a similar tension between God's people and the "world" (to use the language of Paul), it gives us insight into how we should interact with the world—and it does this in a surprising way, in part by undermining many of our current attitudes and practices. As we will see, the book does not simply give us a pattern of behavior as much as opens our eyes to multiple strategies for cultural engagement.

Many Christians today advocate only one stance toward culture: resistance. Ask a fairly knowledgeable passerby how the evangelical Christian church interacts with culture, and they will respond with one word: "coercion." The culture war often takes on the mantle of a holy war as Christians mobilize their forces to resist the encroachment of secularization against the family and society in schools, government, and media.

That picture cannot be blamed simply on the selective portrayal of the media, showing Christians participating in picket lines, blockades, and boycotts, with cameras focusing on faces shaking with rage screaming at those who are destroying God, country, and family. These reports may be sensationalized, but they are nonetheless in essence accurate. Most of these efforts at coercion target legislation, working through the democratic system, but with dangerously increasing frequency the coercion takes on the frightening dimensions of violence: abortion clinics in Atlanta bombed; a doctor shot in the back in Pensacola. Would that these were always the act of fringe Christians groups, but that would be a lie.[62]

This is a picture of the Christian interacting with the broader society through resistance—sometimes using the tools of the democratic system, sometimes going outside of the rules. Many, including myself, would argue that this is the predominant paradigm practiced by the evangelical Christian community today. But it is not the only one by which Christian interaction with culture can be described.

In a classic study, H. Richard Niebuhr described five different patterns,[63] and the pattern I have just described fits into the category he calls "Christ

---

62. See the intriguing "behind the scenes" study of the religious antiabortion movement in J. Risen and J. L. Thomas, *Wrath of Angels: The American Abortion War* (New York: Basic Books, 1998).

63. See H. R. Niebuhr, *Christ and Culture* (New York: Harper and Row, 1951). The five categories, only four of which I discuss here, are: (1) Christ Against Culture; (2) The Christ

Against Culture." Culture and Christianity are two different, hostile approaches to the world. As with any assault, the church has a choice of two alternatives: fight or flight.[64] Since the evangelical church has grown in recent years, it has often chosen to flex its muscles, but some Christians have nonetheless chosen withdrawal, fitting into a second paradigm of Niebuhr. This latter may be illustrated on an individual level by Frank, a friend of mine, who threw his television out a window when he caught a look at a music video his children were watching one night, and, in the extreme, by the approach of the Amish, who eschew much modern technology as represented by their use of horse-and-buggy rather than automobile. The wilderness areas of many of our Western states are populated by people whose faith has led them to leave the evil influences of our cities and towns.

Perhaps on the extreme opposite end of the spectrum are those Christians who embrace culture—"The Christ of Culture." This is not the route taken by the vast majority of evangelical Christians, but it is the conscious or unconscious strategy of many others. Niebuhr himself pointed to advocates of the social gospel in the earlier part of our century, and Yancey cites modern advocates of liberation theology, who understand their Bibles through the lens of Marxist political thought. It would be wrong to label such people as mere sycophants of culture. They are rather selective in their understanding of what the Bible teaches in terms of love, toleration of others, and the value of biblical justice. Many perhaps fall into this pattern because they are afraid to be different or maybe they just want to fit in.

Another of Niebuhr's categories is "Christ and Culture in Paradox." In this model church and society have separate, but legitimate spheres. We obey Christ in the church and the political leaders in our public, community life. After all, didn't Paul state as much in Romans 13:1–7? He begins by exhorting his readers to "obey the government" and continues by telling us to "pay your taxes." This advice seems reasonable until we realize that church and society often put opposing demands in front of us. Luther was Niebuhr's prime example of this approach, and the logic of his thought led to Christians who collaborated in the atrocities of Hitler during World War II. While the example of Christian Nazis is often taken as the end of the discussion since it is such a reprehensible recollection, we still have to deal with Paul's words in Romans. He does tell us to obey the government after all.

---

of Culture; (3) Christ Above Culture; (4) Christ and Culture in Paradox; (5) Christ the Transformer of Culture. I have also benefited from Philip Yancey's interaction with Niebuhr's material; see his "A State of Ungrace," CT 41 (February 3, 1997): 31–37. See also his *What's So Amazing about Grace* (Grand Rapids: Zondervan, 1997).

64. See D. Allender and T. Longman III, *Cry of the Soul* (Colorado Springs: NavPress, 1993), 41–53.

Daniel 1:1–21

Then there is the view most frequently associated with Calvin and his intellectual descendants, the *transformation* of culture. Working from within culture, Christians operate as agents of positive change. Here we must comment that Niebuhr's five categories are rarely found in pure form. There is often a thin line of separation between them. Yancey offers Oliver Cromwell (1599–1658) as an example of this fifth way. Cromwell was the leader of the largely Puritan Civil War against King Charles I of England. Indeed, Cromwell did transform culture from the inside. Though he was tolerant to some other religions (Quakers, for instance), the strongly Calvinist Cromwell could also be vehemently anti-Catholic and was known to deface the statuary of churches and cathedrals, considering them idolatrous.[65] Transformation can sometimes pass over into coercion.

We do not present the above categories with the intent to argue that one model is *the* biblical model. We offer them as a background on which to compare contemporary Christian strategies with Daniel's actions.

In the Original Meaning section, we observed how Daniel takes a stand and places himself against his culture. But what occasioned surprise was the extent to which he exposed himself to the pagan thinking and culture that surrounded him. Moreover, we are shocked by the great effort he took to keep his distinctiveness quiet. Daniel was no Origen, the third-century theologian, who as a young man desired to throw himself in front of the emperor's chariot and proclaim Christ so he could achieve the glory of a martyr's death. Neither was Daniel a Jerome, who fled to a monastery to avoid worldly pollution or, when feeling the unwanted arousal of sexual stimulation, would throw himself into a thorny bush.

Daniel endured much cultural assimilation, yet he knew where it was appropriate for him to draw the line of distinction. The text implies that Daniel acted in a right manner for his situation. The narrative applauds his growth in wisdom. Not only that, but as we will see in the following chapters, Daniel also had wonderful opportunities to make even bolder statements of his faith.

Once again, Daniel is not given to us as a model of the one biblical way for the believer to interact with his or her culture. Rather, when viewed in the light of the rest of Scripture, Daniel imparts the liberating, yet frightening news that there are multiple ways to be a believer in an unbelieving world. Much depends on the person and his or her specific cultural situation.

---

65. This point is not made by Yancey and indeed the extent to which Cromwell's zeal for Protestantism led to the defacing of church art is a matter of debate since royalist propoganda certainly magnified his actions. See the cautious appraisal by A. Frasier, *Cromwell: The Lord Protector* (New York: Knopf, 1974), 102–5.

Christ and our relationship with the world. After all, what is Christ's teaching on how faith acts in the world? This is a topic that deserves book-length treatment, but I would like to bring to mind two key aspects of his teaching. Jesus calls us to be "in the world, but not of it" (cf. John 17:16), but also to be as "shrewd as snakes and as innocent as doves" (Matt. 10:16).

(1) Jesus spoke a paradox when he taught that though we are "in the world" (John 17:11, 15), we are, like him, not "of it" (17:14, 16). Indeed, Jesus is the one who has sent us into the world (17:18) with the purpose that the world "may believe that you have sent me" (17:21). To use another biblical image of our involvement with the present world, we are "resident aliens" (cf. Phil 3:20).

But notice the leeway provided in Jesus' statement. It is a general principle that can be lived out in a variety of ways. What does it mean, to take a concrete example, in the area of the education of our children? All of us who have had children have struggled with the decision of how best to educate them. Schools have a huge impact on the development of our children's thinking and life direction, and there are many who will tell you that there is one, and only one, correct answer to that question. Some will say that a Christian school is the only proper choice. We want our children not only to avoid the thinking of secular humanism found in the public school system, but also to construct a positive, biblically centered understanding of the world.

Others, some because of the lack of a Christian school option and others because they believe even the Christian schools have imbibed the spirit of the age, advocate home-schooling. Occasionally a brave soul will even suggest that the public school, with all of its potential pitfalls, is the only way to go to prevent the "ghettoization" of the church, and prepare our children for "life in the real world."

Looking at this question in the light of Christ's admonition to be "in the world, but not of it" and with an eye on Daniel's success in a truly pagan educational environment does not allow us to answer this question with dogmatism. There is no single answer to this question for all people of faith at every stage of a child's development. Too much depends on the child, the school system, the parents, the church, and so much more. We can be "in the world, but not of it" in the local public school, the Christian school, or the home school.

How many of us wish that the answer was simple and clear-cut, not only in this issue but in all the issues of faith and culture that bombard us daily. What movies and television shows are appropriate for me to watch? What magazines can I read? What music can I listen to? How protective of my children should I be?

Daniel 1:1—21

Some may feel that we are advocating a kind of relativism here and in this way have imbibed the spirit of the day ourselves. We must be quick to say that there are some areas where our stand against culture should be clear and unequivocable in the light of biblical teaching. Though our culture permits it, it is not right to choose to have an abortion to avoid the embarrassment or the annoyance of an unwanted pregnancy. Though our culture permits it, it is not right to have an active sexual lifestyle outside of the institution of marriage. Though our culture permits it, it is not right to engage in homosexual acts of intimacy. But even here there are questions, not about our own behavior, but about our reactions to the behavior of others. What is the appropriate Christian response to the legalization of abortion? To the legitimization of homosexual relationships?

Once again we hear from Christians who say there is only one possible biblical response. Some advocate coercion through legislation or even violence as the only proper response. A note of urgency is heard from some of the leaders of the church that it is of the utmost necessity not only to refrain from sinful activity ourselves but make sure that no one in our country sins either. They point to the Old Testament and the law's demand on Israel, as a political entity, to be morally pure.

It is at this point that we need to remind ourselves that no modern nation, whether America, England, Korea, or whatever, is in a situation like Israel (see Bridging Contexts section). America is not a Christian nation; there is no such thing as a Christian nation. America is more like Babylon in Daniel's day or Rome in Jesus' day than Israel. We need to listen to the wise words of Martin Lloyd-Jones, who had the following insightful words for those who wanted to legislate Christian morality:

> The New Testament is never interested in conduct and behaviour in itself. I can go further and say that the New Testament does not make an appeal for good behaviour to anyone but to Christian people. The New Testament is not interested, as such, in morality of the world. It tells us quite plainly that you can expect nothing from the world but sin, and that in its fallen condition it is incapable of anything else. In Titus 3:3 Paul tells us that we were all once like that: "for we ourselves were sometimes foolish, disobedient, deceived, serving divers lusts and pleasures, living in malice and envy, hateful, and hating one another...." Thus there is nothing, according to the New Testament, that is so fatuous and so utterly futile, as to turn to such people and appeal to them to live the Christian life.... The truth is that it only has one message for people like that—the message of repentance.[66]

---

66. D. M. Lloyd-Jones, *Faith on Trial* (London: Inver-Varsity Fellowship, 1965), 63.

Lloyd-Jones gives us the healthy reminder that God is not interested in lives of external conformity to his will, but hearts that lead to thankful obedience.

(2) But this does not mean we withdraw from a dangerous and hostile world. In Matthew 10:16 Jesus calls his disciples "sheep" and the rest of the world "wolves," but he demands courage from his sheep to take the risk to live among the wolves. In the process, he gives them a strategy, using two more animal metaphors: "Therefore be as shrewd as snakes and as innocent as doves." We are to be innocent and shrewd as we live out the issues of faith in our culture. And does this not describe Daniel perfectly? Daniel certainly was innocent. He mounted no angry assault on his captors; rather, he acted quite civilly.[67] He was virtually serpent-like in his crafty strategy to remain faithful in a land antithetical to his deeply held faith. As the story continues, we will observe that Daniel not only remained faithful but exercised significant influence on the godless world around him.[68]

---

67. For a call to the church to practice civility in our interaction with others with whom we disagree, see R. J. Mouw, *Uncommon Decency: Christian Civility in an Uncivil World* (Downers Grove, InterVarsity, 1992).

68. For a stirring example of how urban churches in Boston have been agents of transformation in their community, see J. Klein; "In God They Trust," *The New Yorker* (June 16, 1997), 40–49.

Daniel 2:1–49

IN THE SECOND year of his reign, Nebuchadnezzar had dreams; his mind was troubled and he could not sleep. ²So the king summoned the magicians, enchanters, sorcerers and astrologers to tell him what he had dreamed. When they came in and stood before the king, ³he said to them, "I have had a dream that troubles me and I want to know what it means."

⁴Then the astrologers answered the king in Aramaic, "O king, live forever! Tell your servants the dream, and we will interpret it."

⁵The king replied to the astrologers, "This is what I have firmly decided: If you do not tell me what my dream was and interpret it, I will have you cut into pieces and your houses turned into piles of rubble. ⁶But if you tell me the dream and explain it, you will receive from me gifts and rewards and great honor. So tell me the dream and interpret it for me."

⁷Once more they replied, "Let the king tell his servants the dream, and we will interpret it."

⁸Then the king answered, "I am certain that you are trying to gain time, because you realize that this is what I have firmly decided: ⁹If you do not tell me the dream, there is just one penalty for you. You have conspired to tell me misleading and wicked things, hoping the situation will change. So then, tell me the dream, and I will know that you can interpret it for me."

¹⁰The astrologers answered the king, "There is not a man on earth who can do what the king asks! No king, however great and mighty, has ever asked such a thing of any magician or enchanter or astrologer. ¹¹What the king asks is too difficult. No one can reveal it to the king except the gods, and they do not live among men."

¹²This made the king so angry and furious that he ordered the execution of all the wise men of Babylon. ¹³So the decree was issued to put the wise men to death, and men were sent to look for Daniel and his friends to put them to death.

¹⁴When Arioch, the commander of the king's guard, had gone out to put to death the wise men of Babylon, Daniel spoke to him with wisdom and tact. ¹⁵He asked the king's officer, "Why did the king issue such a harsh decree?" Arioch then explained the matter to Daniel. ¹⁶At this, Daniel went in

Daniel 2:1–49

to the king and asked for time, so that he might interpret the dream for him.

¹⁷Then Daniel returned to his house and explained the matter to his friends Hananiah, Mishael and Azariah. ¹⁸He urged them to plead for mercy from the God of heaven concerning this mystery, so that he and his friends might not be executed with the rest of the wise men of Babylon. ¹⁹During the night the mystery was revealed to Daniel in a vision. Then Daniel praised the God of heaven ²⁰and said:

> "Praise be to the name of God for ever and ever;
>   wisdom and power are his.
> ²¹ He changes times and seasons;
>   he sets up kings and deposes them.
> He gives wisdom to the wise
>   and knowledge to the discerning.
> ²² He reveals deep and hidden things;
>   he knows what lies in darkness,
>   and light dwells with him.
> ²³ I thank and praise you, O God of my fathers:
>   You have given me wisdom and power,
>   you have made known to me what we asked of you,
>   you have made known to us the dream of the king."

²⁴Then Daniel went to Arioch, whom the king had appointed to execute the wise men of Babylon, and said to him, "Do not execute the wise men of Babylon. Take me to the king, and I will interpret his dream for him."

²⁵Arioch took Daniel to the king at once and said, "I have found a man among the exiles from Judah who can tell the king what his dream means."

²⁶The king asked Daniel (also called Belteshazzar), "Are you able to tell me what I saw in my dream and interpret it?"

²⁷Daniel replied, "No wise man, enchanter, magician or diviner can explain to the king the mystery he has asked about, ²⁸but there is a God in heaven who reveals mysteries. He has shown King Nebuchadnezzar what will happen in days to come. Your dream and the visions that passed through your mind as you lay on your bed are these:

²⁹"As you were lying there, O king, your mind turned to things to come, and the revealer of mysteries showed you what is going to happen. ³⁰As for me, this mystery has been revealed to me, not because I have greater wisdom than other living

Daniel 2:1–49

men, but so that you, O king, may know the interpretation and that you may understand what went through your mind.

[31]"You looked, O king, and there before you stood a large statue—an enormous, dazzling statue, awesome in appearance. [32]The head of the statue was made of pure gold, its chest and arms of silver, its belly and thighs of bronze, [33] its legs of iron, its feet partly of iron and partly of baked clay. [34]While you were watching, a rock was cut out, but not by human hands. It struck the statue on its feet of iron and clay and smashed them. [35]Then the iron, the clay, the bronze, the silver and the gold were broken to pieces at the same time and became like chaff on a threshing floor in the summer. The wind swept them away without leaving a trace. But the rock that struck the statue became a huge mountain and filled the whole earth.

[36]"This was the dream, and now we will interpret it to the king. [37]You, O king, are the king of kings. The God of heaven has given you dominion and power and might and glory; [38]in your hands he has placed mankind and the beasts of the field and the birds of the air. Wherever they live, he has made you ruler over them all. You are that head of gold.

[39]"After you, another kingdom will rise, inferior to yours. Next, a third kingdom, one of bronze, will rule over the whole earth. [40]Finally, there will be a fourth kingdom, strong as iron—for iron breaks and smashes everything—and as iron breaks things to pieces, so it will crush and break all the others. [41]Just as you saw that the feet and toes were partly of baked clay and partly of iron, so this will be a divided kingdom; yet it will have some of the strength of iron in it, even as you saw iron mixed with clay. [42]As the toes were partly iron and partly clay, so this kingdom will be partly strong and partly brittle. [43]And just as you saw the iron mixed with baked clay, so the people will be a mixture and will not remain united, any more than iron mixes with clay.

[44]"In the time of those kings, the God of heaven will set up a kingdom that will never be destroyed, nor will it be left to another people. It will crush all those kingdoms and bring them to an end, but it will itself endure forever. [45]This is the meaning of the vision of the rock cut out of a mountain, but not by human hands—a rock that broke the iron, the bronze, the clay, the silver and the gold to pieces.

"The great God has shown the king what will take place in the future. The dream is true and the interpretation is trustworthy."

⁴⁶Then King Nebuchadnezzar fell prostrate before Daniel and paid him honor and ordered that an offering and incense be presented to him. ⁴⁷The king said to Daniel, "Surely your God is the God of gods and the Lord of kings and a revealer of mysteries, for you were able to reveal this mystery."

⁴⁸Then the king placed Daniel in a high position and lavished many gifts on him. He made him ruler over the entire province of Babylon and placed him in charge of all its wise men. ⁴⁹Moreover, at Daniel's request the king appointed Shadrach, Meshach and Abednego administrators over the province of Babylon, while Daniel himself remained at the royal court.

DANIEL 2 PRESENTS a second self-contained story—a story best remembered by the bizarrely constructed (at least by modern tastes) statue that dominates Nebuchadnezzar's dream. However, we must not let our curiosity concerning God's revelation of future events distract us from the main theme of the chapter: *Only God's wisdom can reveal the mysteries of life.* In other words, it is not the content of the revelation of the future that is primary; what is most important here is the fact that it is only Daniel's God that knows that future. And God's knowledge of the future is particularly important to a people in exile and under some measure of oppression, because it implies that he controls history. Once again, therefore, we are reminded of the overall theme of this book: In spite of present appearances, God is in control.

As we read Daniel 2, the Joseph narrative in Genesis 41, which closely parallels this chapter,[1] quickly comes to mind. In Genesis a pagan king, the Egyptian pharaoh, has an anxiety-producing dream (concerning seven lean and seven fat cows). When the wise men of Egypt cannot interpret the dream for him, his cupbearer (paralleling the role of Arioch in Dan. 2) helps him discover a dream-interpreter, who turns out to be the imprisoned Joseph.

---

1. These parallels have been frequently noted by commentators: for instance Towner, *Daniel*, 29–31; Goldingay, *Daniel*, 37, 39. There is also a parallel with the Aramaic tale of Ahikar. For parallels with both the Joseph story and Ahikar, see S. Niditch and R. Doran, "The Success Story of the Wise Courtier: A Formal Approach," *JBL* 96 (1977): 179–93.

Daniel 2:1–49

Through God's help, Joseph reveals the interpretation of the dream to the pharaoh, resulting in his rise in status in the foreign court.

We thus see that Daniel is like Joseph, perhaps even better than Joseph, since he not only interprets the dream but, with God's help, actually tells the king the contents of the dream. Both Joseph and Daniel serve as models for godly behavior to God's people who live in a foreign culture (for implications see the Contemporary Significance section to Daniel 1). Goldingay nicely summarizes the lesson in regard to Daniel when he describes him as

> a model of Israelite wisdom (v 14) and a model of Israelite piety, in his prayer (v 18), his vision (v 19), his praise (vv 19–23), his witness (vv 27–28), his self-effacement (v 30), his conviction (v 45); the fruit of his work is not merely rewards and promotion (v 48) but obeisance and recognition of his God (vv 46–47).[2]

The genre of chapter 2 has been rightly identified by W. Lee Humphreys as a "court tale of contest."[3] The setting is the court, and the plot surrounds a contest of interpretation. The rivals are, on the surface of it, Daniel and the king's advisors, but more profoundly the contest is between the true God and the idols that the king's advisors worship.

The first contest is between Daniel and the king's advisors. The latter are confronted with a problem for which they are totally unprepared. They are diviners (*baru*), not seers or prophets. They deal with omens, including revelatory dreams; they do not receive revelation. In divination, the gods inform[4] humans through the diviner's interpretation of sheep livers, abnormal births, the stars, and dreams. Dreams can be solicited through incubation rites or are unsolicited—as here apparently. They can interpret dreams, and they have books that will help them do that, but there is no way they can find out the content of the dream if the king does not tell them the actual dream.[5] Daniel is also

---

2. Goldingay, *Daniel*, 36.

3. In "A Life-Style for the Diaspora: A Study of the Tales of Esther and Daniel," *JBL* 92 (1973): 211–23, though this endorsement does not imply agreement concerning his views on the historicity of the story.

4. J. Lawson, "'The God Who Reveals Secrets': The Mesopotamian Background to Daniel 2:47," *JSOT* 74 (1997): 61–76, makes the important point that Mesopotamian divination is a result of divine revelation, a point denied by many Old Testament interpreters. His article argues that "divine revelation (the revelation of 'secrets') was more commonplace in Mesopotamian culture than in Judaean, and that Daniel, rather than appearing as a Judaean wise man or prophet, appears more in the mould of a Mesopotamian mantic sage" (p. 61). This point will be important for our use of this chapter in the Contemporary Significance section.

5. Information about omens and dream interpretation in Mesopotamia is helpfully summarized in an article about divination in volume 3 of J. Sasson, *Civilizations of the Ancient Near East* (New York: Scribners, 1995).

trained in this lore, but he is able to go further, not because of his training or the reference books he shares with the Babylonian diviners, but because his God is a God who can reveal it to him. It is at this point that the contrast between Daniel's God and the gods of the Babylonian diviners comes into play.

In this regard, we can observe another Scripture text with which Daniel 2 has special association. In Isaiah 40–48, the prophet Isaiah ridicules the nations' idols. The idols are impotent to effect history (Isa. 46:6–7):

> Some pour out gold from their bags
> and weigh out silver on the scales;
> they hire a goldsmith to make it into a god,
> and they bow down and worship it.
> They lift it to their shoulders and carry it;
> they set it up in its place, and there it stands.
> From that spot it cannot move.
> Though one cries out to it, it does not answer;
> it cannot save him from his troubles.

The pagan advisors are blind to the future (47:13–14a):

> All the counsel you have received has only worn you out!
> Let your astrologers come forward,
> those stargazers who make predictions month by month,
> let them save you from what is coming upon you.
> Surely they are like stubble; the fire will burn them up.

God, by contrast, both controls history and can reveal it to his servants (46:9–10):

> Remember the former things, those of long ago;
> I am God, and there is no other;
> I am God, and there is none like me.
> I make known the end from the beginning,
> from ancient times, what is still to come.
> I say: My purpose will stand,
> and I will do all that I please.

The outline of Daniel 2 is as follows: (1) the king and his advisors (2:1–13); (2) God's revealing of the mystery to Daniel (2:14–23); (3) the dream and its interpretation (2:24–45); and (4) the king's response (2:46–49).

The King and His Advisors (2:1–13)

SIMILAR TO DANIEL 1, this second chapter begins with a chronological note that is difficult to harmonize with our general knowledge of the period. A

Daniel 2:1–49

definite answer eludes us again, though we are able to provide a possible harmonization.[6]

The first verse sets the scene in the second year of Nebuchadnezzar's reign, whereas the first chapter says that Daniel's training lasted for three years (1:5). Even assuming (as we argued in ch. 1) that the training began in Nebuchadnezzar's accession year, this is difficult to reconcile with 2:1. After all, since Daniel was included among the condemned "wise men" (2:14) and was living outside the court, the assumption is that he had already graduated.

Both Wood and Young offer different explanations to resolve the tension. The former suggests a scenario in which chapter 2 describes events that took place during Daniel's training.[7] The latter argues that if we accept that three years may include partial years, the two chronological notes can be reconciled. He provides the following chart to make his point clear:[8]

Year of Daniel's training	Nebuchadnezzar
First year	Year of Accession
Second year	First year
Third year	Second year (in which dream occurred)

We have commented on these historical conundrums because they cause close readers to stumble. The purpose of the chronological markers, however, is not primary to the story. They merely set the scene; having addressed the issue, we pass on to the message of the passage.[9]

Nebuchadnezzar had a dream that disturbed him greatly, so he called his professionals—not psychologists, of course, but the ancient equivalents, "the

---

6. All historians must grapple with the problem of gaps or apparent contradictions in their primary sources. Explanations that resolve the tension (harmonizations) are a common strategy of dealing with these issues. However, harmonizations are hypothetical constructions and are rarely certain. For an excellent treatment of harmonization as a method and a theological problem, see R. B. Dillard, "Harmonization: A Help and a Hindrance," in *Inerrancy and Hermeneutics*, ed. H. M. Conn (Grand Rapids: Baker, 1988), 151–64.

7. Wood, *A Commentary on Daniel*, 48–50. Interestingly, D. Fewell, *Circle of Sovereignty*, 55, suggests that the fact that the king needs an introduction to Daniel, though the text refers to him as Belteshazzar, indicates that the scene is set within the period of training. However, the conclusion of the story throws this in doubt since Daniel/Belteshazzar does not return to training, but is immediately promoted. Fewell herself refers to this as a "tension" that "raises the question of the narrator's reliability" (62).

8. Young, *The Prophecy of Daniel*, 56. Young bases his views on an earlier suggestion by S. R. Driver, *The Book of Daniel* (Cambridge: Cambridge Univ. Press, 1900), p. 17. This approach is rejected by J. J. Collins, *Daniel* (Hermeneia; Philadelphia: Fortress, 1993), 154–55.

9. See the interesting argument of J. H. Sims, "Daniel," in *A Complete Literary Guide to the Bible*, eds. L. Ryken and T. Longman III (Grand Rapids: Zondervan, 1995), 326–30, that Daniel's historical "'inaccuracies' are an integral part of the book's literary technique."

magicians, enchanters, sorcerers and astrologers." These professionals had dream interpretation on their list of responsibilities. Indeed, these people were the political consultants, trend spotters, and religious gurus of the day.

Babylonian religion encouraged looking for portents of the future in dreams and the fantastic occurrences of everyday life. Indications of future trends and events could be found in the skies, bizarre births, the shape of animal livers, and—as here—in dreams. It is in the latter that Babylonian religion and Daniel's faith come closest, and perhaps that is why God chose to speak to Nebuchadnezzar in this way rather than through the birth of a multiheaded ox. After all, God had spoken through dreams in the past (e.g., Gen. 28:10–22; 1 Kings 3:5), but not through other means of divination so popular in Babylonia.

The difference between these modes of revelation is profound, and in this difference we see a radical contrast between the false religion of the Babylonians and the true religion of Daniel. Biblical prophecy, which occasionally includes dreams, is the result of divine initiative and revelation; the other means of divination, practiced so strenuously by the Babylonians but condemned by the Bible (cf. Deut. 18:14), is the result of human initiation or manipulation (i.e., the pouring of oil in water). Dream interpretation is one mode of divine revelation understood by Babylonians[10] and accepted by pious Israelites.

But even with royal dreams in Babylon, there was a protocol that allowed for interpretation. It required the king to inform the professional interpreters of the content of his dream, but Nebuchadnezzar angrily refuses to satisfy the interpreters' urgent pleas to tell them the contents of his dream; this refusal puts the diviners in an awkward, even dangerous situation.

The biblical text does not clearly state why Nebuchadnezzar refuses to describe the contents of the dream to his interpreters, leading to two different understandings of his motivation.[11] Some commentators believe Nebuchadnezzar has forgotten the dream. He is disturbed, knows he has had a dream, but does not remember exactly what the dream is about.[12] Such a view, however, does not do justice to the anger of the king.[13] His reaction to the diviners' request to supply them with the content of the dream indicates that

---

10. As studied in the classic study by A. L. Oppenheim, *The Interpretation of Dreams in the Ancient Near East* (Philadelphia: American Philosophical Society, 1956). See also footnote 4.

11. Goldingay, *Daniel*, 46, is content to leave it ambiguous.

12. Baldwin, *Daniel*, 87–88. The difference arises over a debate concerning the meaning of the word *azda*, which the NIV rightly takes as "firm," based on the supposition that it is a Persian loanword, as opposed to the KJV, which takes the word as derived from a Hebrew verb that means "to go away" (cf. discussion in Miller, *Daniel*, 81).

13. Also, it renders the continual pleading of the dream interpreters meaningless.

Daniel 2:1–49

Nebuchadnezzar is testing their integrity. He realizes how easy it is to provide an interpretation of a symbolic dream and wants to assure himself of their authenticity by demanding that they also tell him something that only he himself knows, the actual contents of the dream.[14]

In spite of the reason, however, no doubt attends the divine intention that stands behind the royal stubbornness. In their exasperation, the diviners themselves utter the statement that sets up the main lesson of the chapter: "There is not a man on earth who can do what the king asks! No king, however great and mighty, has ever asked such a thing of any magician or enchanter or astrologer. What the king asks is too difficult. No one can reveal it to the king except the gods, and they do not live among men" (2:10–11). With that, the king orders all the "wise men" in Babylonia, present in the court or not, put to death. The glove is thrown to the ground; Daniel and his friends are put on the chopping block. How will God resolve this dangerous situation?

God's Revealing of the Mystery to Daniel (2:14–23)

ARIOCH, THE COMMANDER of the king's guard, has no choice but to follow through on Nebuchadnezzar's command to execute the wise men. His mission leads him to Daniel, who, being a wise man himself, is included among those scheduled for death.

Arioch's words may have shocked Daniel, but the text does not inform us that he reacts that way. As in the first chapter when his strategy for remaining faithful in a hostile court was thwarted, Daniel responds calmly and with confidence. He navigates life "with wisdom and tact" (v. 14) even when, as in this case, confronted with a threat of gargantuan proportions. Daniel is truly the paradigmatic person of wisdom.

Arioch informs Daniel on the situation that brings him to his doorstep. Daniel hears of the king's dream, the interpreters' inability to discern its contents and their impotence in interpretation. After winning some time, he returned to his house, where he meets with his three friends, here given their Hebrew names: Hananiah, Mishael, and Azariah. He knows that they have only one recourse, prayer. The Babylonian sages were only half right. While no human being could ever tell the king the contents and interpretation of his dream, God can, and, in contrast to the beliefs of the Babylonians (2:11), there is a God who lives among people: Daniel's God.

The four faithful Israelites prayed to God to reveal the "mystery" to them. In general, a mystery is something beyond human comprehension. In this context, of course, it has become painfully obvious that Nebuchadnezzar's

---

14. Young, *The Prophecy of Daniel*, 58–59.

dream is such a mystery. If Daniel and the others are to have their lives spared, God will have to tell them what to say. That night Daniel's God speaks to him and describes to him the dream and its interpretation. Before rushing off to the court, Daniel prays again—this time not a petition for help, but a thanksgiving song.[15]

In his prayer, Daniel highlights two aspects of God's character that play a pivotal role in this chapter, and indeed throughout the book. (1) God is powerful. Babylon and Nebuchadnezzar, its king, seem to have all the power on the human plane. They presume to have control over Israel and Daniel, but the prophet recognizes the truth of the matter. Nebuchadnezzar himself is a king because God is the One who "sets up kings and deposes them" (2:21).

(2) God is wise. Indeed, Daniel understands that his wisdom is derivative from God's. The revelation of the mystery has made that clear. The "wisdom and tact" that we earlier saw him display toward Ashpenaz and then Arioch might be confused with the common sense available to any sensitive human being, but the ability to describe someone else's dream can only come from a divine source. He is the One who "reveals deep and hidden things" (2:22).

Armed with this answer to prayer,[16] Daniel then sets out with Arioch to the royal court.

The Dream and Its Interpretation (2:24–45)

AFTER THANKING GOD for hearing his prayer, Daniel informs Arioch that he has the answer needed to preserve the wisdom teachers, including himself, from Nebuchadnezzar's decree of death. Calvin devotes some time to justifying Daniel's haste. After all, these wise men teach falsehood and advocate idolatry; in Calvin's opinion, they deserved to die, even if not for the reason that moves Nebuchadnezzar.[17] Calvin appeals to Daniel's sense of honesty to justify his letting the idolaters off the hook. Daniel would have preferred their death, but not for unjust reasons. Against Calvin, we would suggest that Daniel's actions here and elsewhere in the book incarnate a love for enemies (Ex. 23:4–5) that the Old Testament mandates and Jesus later advocates (Luke 6:27).

---

15. So, W. S. Towner, "The Poetic Passages of Daniel 1–6," *CBQ* 31 (1969): 317; G. T. M. Prinsloo, "Two Poems in a Sea of Prose: The Content and Context of Daniel 2:20–23 and 6:27–28," *JSOT* 59 (1993): 96, who says "the poem has much in common with traditional Israelite poetry (cf. Job 12.13; Pss. 41.14; 106.48; 113.2; Neh. 9:5; Est. 1.13) and could be described as a psalm of thanksgiving with a hymnic character."

16. Daniel's prayer of thanks comes before we, as readers, are informed of the details of the answer. Thus, in the words of J. W. Watts, "Daniel's Praise (Daniel 2.20–23)," in *Psalm and Story: Inset Hymns in Hebrew Narrative* (Sheffield: JSOT, 1992), 150, "Daniel's Praise [sic] becomes... an expression of trust that the expected deliverance will be brought to fruition."

17. Calvin, *Daniel I*, 76–77.

Daniel 2:1–49

Arioch brings Daniel into the presence of Nebuchadnezzar. The king gets right to the point: "Are you able to tell me what I saw in my dream and interpret it?"

Daniel responds in a way that puts the focus where it belongs, not on himself but directly on God. This solution has been anticipated by the inability of the Babylonian wisdom teachers, who said that the answer could only come from the divine realm (v. 11). Now Daniel bears witness to the God who speaks the life-granting answer; he is the "God in heaven who reveals mysteries" (v. 28). He then proceeds with a description of the content of the king's vision. The report of the dream is given first, followed by its interpretation. However, even within the description are indications of the interpretation. In particular, Daniel makes it clear that the vision concerns the future (vv. 28–29).

The dream is of a huge statue. As Collins points out, "apparitions of gigantic figures are characteristic of ancient Near Eastern dreams."[18] Besides its size, the statue is striking by virtue of its composition. Its head is gold; its chest and arms silver, while its belly and thighs are bronze and its legs iron. The feet are themselves composite, made of both iron and clay. While in one sense there is nothing exactly like this composite statue in ancient literature, we can note similarities. There is a tradition of recounting world history by means of metals of declining value as early as Hesiod in his *Works and Days*, composed in the eighth century B.C.[19]

The statue is not the only character in the vision. Daniel next describes a rock whose origins are mysteriously described in a negative way, made "not by human hands" (v. 34). Our first thought is that if it is not human, it must be divine, but confirmation awaits the interpretation that follows.

With two characters, we now have a plot. The rock smashes into the feet of the statue, which is obviously the weak link. This imposing figure is thus reduced to near nothingness, so that the wind can blow it away. After this, the rock becomes a huge mountain, filling the whole world.

In verse 36, Daniel moves from dream report to dream interpretation, and we begin on solid interpretive ground. Speaking to Nebuchadnezzar, Daniel says, "You are that head of gold" (v. 38). Nebuchadnezzar must have rejoiced at this news. After all, in the scheme of "things to come" he was at

---

18. Collins, *Daniel*, 162.

19. Detailed accounts may be found in G. F. Hasel, "The Four World Empires of Daniel 2 Against Its Near Eastern Environment," *JSOT* 12 (1979): 17–30; D. Flusser, "The Four Empires in the Fourth Sibyl and in the Book of Daniel," *IOS* 2 (1972): 148–75. See also E. C. Lucas, "The Origin of Daniel's Four Empires Scheme Re-Examined," *TynBul* 40 (1989): 185–202, who persuasively argues against the view that Daniel 2 derives from Persian apocalyptic imagery. Rather, he sees Daniel 2 and the Persian ideas as "independent adaptations" (201) of the earlier schema represented by Hesiod.

the top, represented by the most precious of all metals. In the light of this news, it is hard to see why some commentators wonder why Nebuchadnezzar responds so well to the dream as a whole. While the head of gold will be replaced and eventually pass away, nonetheless for the moment Nebuchadnezzar is on top. His reaction may be compared to that of Hezekiah (2 Kings 20:19) when he heard that, despite hardships to come to his descendants, his own reign would be characterized by "peace and security."

After Nebuchadnezzar, Daniel interprets the remaining metals as symbolic of nations rather than individual kings.[20] The identity of the following kingdoms has been much debated over the centuries, particularly in the past hundred years. The interpretation of the kingdoms of Daniel 2 is closely related to the interpretation of Daniel 7 (the four hybrid beasts), which in turn is related to the identity of the goat and the ram in Daniel 8. In order to get a more complete explanation of the interpretive stance we are taking in Daniel 2, the reader is encouraged to read the comments on those relevant chapters as well.

Historically, two main approaches have dominated: the Greek view and the Roman view. The latter is understood to be the traditional viewpoint and often appeals to the New Testament for support. This approach sees the following pattern:

> Head of gold = Nebuchadnezzar (Babylon)
> Arms and chest of silver = Medo-Persian empire
> Belly and thighs of bronze = Greek empire
> Legs of iron = Roman empire

This view is held by conservative scholars in the main; nonconservatives have trouble with this approach because even they, for the most part, believe Daniel 2 was written before Rome was a major player on the world scene. Since (in their view) predictive prophecy does not occur,[21] they cannot believe that the fourth kingdom is Rome. Typically, then, in the Greek view, the Medes and the Persians are treated as the second and third kingdoms respectively. The Greek kingdom is fourth. The mixed character of the toes then refers to the political situation in Egypt and the Levant after the death of Alexander, when the Ptolomies and the Seleucids vie for control of Palestine. More specifically, the attempts at mixture in verse 43 is a symbolic reference to attempts at intermarriage.[22]

---

20. However, P. R. Davies, "Daniel Chapter Two," *JTS* 27 (1976): 399, argues that the different parts of the statue represent three successors of Nebuchadnezzar: Amel-Marduk, Neriglissar, and Nabonidus, while the rock stands for Cyrus.
21. Cf. Towner, *Daniel*, 115.
22. For instance, the marriage of Berenice to Antiochus II in 252 B.C. or Cleopatra to Ptolomy Epiphanes in 193–192 B.C. (cf. Collins, *Daniel*, 170).

However, the interpretive situation is not as clear as the last paragraph might lead us to believe. It is not simply a matter of all traditional-conservative scholars holding to the Roman view and all nonconservatives arguing for the Greek view. Recently, strong evangelical arguments have been put forward for the Greek view.[23] Furthermore, there is significant disagreement among conservative interpreters concerning such details as the significance of the ten toes.[24]

In the light of this interpretive confusion, we must entertain seriously the idea that the vision of Daniel 2 does not intend to be precise as it writes its history before it occurs. In other words, though it starts in the concrete present, it is a wrong strategy to proceed through history and associate the different stages of the statue with particular empires. The vision intends to communicate something more general, but also more grand: God is sovereign; he is in control despite present conditions.

Not allowing ourselves to be distracted by the above debate, we notice some crucial theological principles in the dream.[25] We see, for instance, that the unnamed kingdoms that follow the head of gold will be inferior to Babylon. While human beings operate on the idea that we get better and stronger with time, God's vision undercuts our understanding, informing us that the opposite is true. Gold gives way to silver, which then becomes bronze, iron, and a weak mixture of clay and iron. A statue that starts out in grandeur and beauty ends in weakness. Indeed, the expression "feet of clay" has become an idiom in our language for a point of weakness in an otherwise strong person or institution.

The other important principle in this dream-vision is seen when this statue is contrasted with the object of its demise, the rock. The statue is an object made with human hands and ingenuity. The rock, however, is explicitly said not to be the result of human intention or energy. In the interpretation, Daniel identifies the rock as "God's kingdom."[26] The rock obliterates these human kingdoms. In this way, Daniel again speaks to God's oppressed people that the evil they now experience is not the end of the story. In spite

---

23. R. J. M. Gurney, "The Four Kingdoms of Daniel 2 and 7," *Themelios* 2 (1977): 39–45; J. Walton, "The Four Kingdoms of Daniel," *JETS* 29 (1986): 25–36.

24. Miller, *Daniel*, 97, 99, represents a dispensationalist approach, which takes the ten toes as "kingdoms (or nations) of unequal strength will unite to form a coalition that will rise out of the ruins of the ancient Roman Empire." Most other interpreters, myself included, note that the text itself makes no symbolic interpretation of the number of toes.

25. Our view is close to that of Goldingay, *Daniel*, 58, but we do not share his views on the late dating of the book.

26. D. Wenham, "The Kingdom of God and Daniel," *ExpTim* 98 (1987): 132–34, persuasively argues that Dan. 2 and 7 provides "the primary background for the New Testament concept of the Kingdom of God."

Daniel 2:1–49

of present appearances, God will defeat the forces that rule over them. And not only that, God's kingdom will expand and take over the world, just as the rock becomes a huge mountain. With Calvin, we affirm that "Daniel is not relating what was going to be completed in one moment; he just wants to teach that the kingdoms of the world are transient and that there is only one eternal kingdom."[27]

The King's Response (2:46–49)

DANIEL'S ABILITY TO describe and interpret his dream overwhelms the Babylonian king. He responds with worship, falling prostrate, making an offering, and burning incense. But to whom is his worship offered? In verse 46 Nebuchadnezzar bows toward Daniel and presents him with offerings and incense. One might expect Daniel to have a near heart attack and virtually grab the king and bring him to his feet, but the passage does not tell us that he objects to this treatment. Indeed, he quietly accepts the gifts and promotion mentioned in verse 48. As a matter of fact, he uses his good position to leverage his three friends to important positions as well. These new positions lead to the jealousy of native officials, which results in the conflicts in chapter 3.

No, Daniel seems quietly to accept what at least appears to be worship offered to him by Nebuchadnezzar. This behavior contrasts sharply with Paul and Barnabas in Lystra (Acts 14:8–20). After healing a lame man, the townspeople treated them as Zeus and Hermes, and the apostles reacted quickly, tearing their clothes and urgently shouting, "We too are only men!"

Appeal is often made to a speech by Alexander when he bowed before the high priest of Yahweh in Jerusalem, but when questioned stated, "It was not before him that I prostrated myself but the God of whom he has the honour to be high priest."[28] Indeed, we must understand verse 46 in the light of verse 47, where Nebuchadnezzar praises the power behind Daniel. God is "God of gods and the Lord of kings and a revealer of mysteries." Daniel is honored because of what his God has done, not because of what he has done. However, we must not be misled to think that Nebuchadnezzar is converted here. As a good polytheist, Nebuchadnezzar was more than willing to acknowledge the power of foreign deities. He could easily incorporate Yahweh into his pantheon and give him the credit due him at the moment.

Nonetheless, the parallel with Alexander does not explain Daniel's passive reception of Nebuchadnezzar's worship. Perhaps Daniel did react in the

---

27. Calvin, *Daniel I*, 97.
28. The account comes from Josephus, *Jewish Antiquities*, 11.331–35, and is quoted in B. A. Mastin, "Daniel 2:46 and the Hellenistic World," *ZAW* 85 (1973): 87.

Daniel 2:1–49

way Paul did at Lystra, but the often reticent Hebrew narrative does not inform us of this.[29] However, it is more likely to be explained by the comment that "in the world in which the author of Daniel lived a benefactor could be treated like this without impiety, and Nebuchadnezzar is simply expressing in an extravagant way his great gratitude for the very considerable service which Daniel has done him."[30]

Whatever reason we give, the concluding scene gives us a powerful picture that reinforces the theme of our book: The most powerful pagan in the world lies prostrate before an exiled Jew. Chills of excitement and the flames of hope will rise in the hearts of those who identify with Daniel and his God.

THE CHAPTER OPENS with Nebuchadnezzar's uneasiness with a dream. On a surface reading, the core issue of the story seems tightly focused on the meaning of the dream. Once Daniel describes and interprets the dream, we learn that it concerns the future rise and fall of kingdoms. What could be more fascinating to a modern reader than a divine glimpse at the future? Thus, many readers fix their rapt attention on the dream and its interpretation.

However, as we mentioned in the Original Meaning section, the core concern was not the content of the dream or even its interpretation, but on Daniel's God-given ability to interpret the dream. This is not to claim that the message of the dream is unimportant, but certainly the focus is on the context between the Babylonian wise men and Daniel. Where the "magicians, enchanters, sorcerers and astrologers" of Babylon failed, Daniel succeeded. Why? The text is structured to highlight the answer to this question, and in his prayer, Daniel articulates it well (2:23):

> I thank and praise you, O God of my fathers:
> > You have given me wisdom and power,
> you have made known to me what we asked of you,
> > you have made known to us the dream of the king.

Only God's wisdom, according to Daniel 2, can reveal the mysteries of life. Human wisdom falls short.

---

29. Noted by Calvin (*Daniel I*, 110) well before the current literary analysis: "We know many things were omitted in their narratives," which led him to suspend judgment as to Daniel's reaction.

30. Mastin, "Daniel 2:46," 85, though we are on less secure grounds arguing for this since Mastin believes the book was written in the Hellenistic period, and we are making the assumption that the practice was also current in the neo-Babylonian period.

In this way, Daniel 2 contributes to a biblical theology of wisdom that begins early in the Old Testament and continues into the New. Understanding the contours of that theology not only helps us understand chapter 2, but also permits us to see its continuing relevance to Christians today. We cannot hope to do more than scratch the surface here, though even a brief survey will prove informative.

Wisdom in the Old Testament. When we think of biblical wisdom, we normally think of the book of Proverbs. If we are not careful, however, this book can be misread and mislead us into thinking that wisdom is something that human beings attain by hard work alone. We may also be deluded into thinking that human wisdom is the key to earthly success:

> Listen, my son, to your father's instruction
>   and do not forsake your mother's teaching.
> They will be a garland to grace your head
>   and a chain to adorn your neck. (Prov. 1:8–9)

The first nine chapters of Proverbs exhort us to learn, remember, pay attention, listen well, and avoid the way of the evil fool. In chapters 10 and following we read many pithy proverbs about the wise path and its attendant rewards and about the way of the fool and its dire consequences. Proverbs 12:11 gives us a classic illustration:

> He who works his land will have abundant food,
>   but he who chases fantasies lacks judgment.

As we read the book of Proverbs, we can easily get the mistaken impression that wisdom involves the memorization and application of certain proverbs that make little direct reference to God or theology. These proverbs may ultimately be God's wisdom, but only in some distant way. An unfortunate consequence of this contemporary misreading of Proverbs is that the book is often misused as the ultimate in self-help manuals, a guide to how to be healthy and successful in a chaotic world.

Such a misunderstanding of Proverbs arises because of our modern tendency to read the book in pieces rather than as a whole. It is true that many of the proverbs in chapters 10–31 seem more like common sense based on experience, rather than the type of revealed wisdom Daniel received in answer to his prayer. But once again, we must appeal to the structure of the book of Proverbs and to the effect it has on our reading of any part of it.

The first nine chapters of Proverbs are the theological grid through which we must read each individual maxim. Running throughout chapters 1–9 is a contrast between two concepts: Wisdom and Folly. These concepts are personified at important points as two women, vying for the attention of the reader, who, in its ancient setting, is assumed to be a male. This contrast, anticipated as early as the first chapter (cf. 1:20–33), comes to a dramatic climax in chapter 9. Here, Lady Wisdom and Dame Folly appeal to men who are passing by their homes and invite them in for a meal.

The imagery is clear and powerful. The reader is asked to enter into an intimate relationship with one of two women: Wisdom or Folly. Who are these women? Their homes are located on the high point of the city. Only deities have their homes on the hill in the ancient Near East. While Folly stands for the false gods that tempt God's people, so Wisdom is Yahweh himself. In other words, the proverbs of the book are not just common sense or based on experience; they are rather the result of a relationship with God. What, after all, is the origin of wisdom according to the book of Proverbs: "The fear of the LORD is the beginning of knowledge" (Prov. 1:7).

That Proverbs was and is misread in the way we have suggested is confirmed by the presence of two other wisdom books in the Old Testament. In the first place, Job's three friends incarnate the perverse misreading of Proverbs by their mechanistic and "health-and-wealth" understanding of life. Job is in trouble; he suffers horribly. What is their proposed solution? "Get wise; you must have sinned, so get right with God."

Job is well-characterized as a wisdom debate.[31] It is not only the three friends who believe they have wisdom, but Elihu and even Job himself. They each believe they have something of a grasp on the problem; they each argue against the interpretation and solution of the others.

But the lesson comes at the end of the book. Once again, wisdom is not a concept to be learned; it is a relationship to be enjoyed (see "The New Testament and wisdom," where this will be fleshed out). Where is wisdom to be found? Not through human effort but, again, "the fear of the Lord—that is wisdom, and to shun evil is understanding" (Job 28:28). The pop quiz that God gives Job at the end has as its point that wisdom is with God and he reveals it to whom he wills.

Space does not permit a detailed treatment of the second wisdom book that serves to correct a misreading of proverbial wisdom in the Old Testament, but Ecclesiastes contributes in much the same way as Job.[32] Wisdom, says the Teacher, is not the ultimate solution. Indeed, he spent much of his life striving to be wise, and his conclusion, "Meaningless! Meaningless! ... Everything is meaningless" (12:8). At the end, a second voice is heard. This voice does not urge harder work, but once again a relationship (Eccl. 12:13–14):

---

31. See P. P. Zerafa, *The Wisdom of God in the Book of Job* (Rome: Herder, 1978); R. B. Dillard and T. Longman III, *An Introduction to the Old Testament* (Grand Rapids: Zondervan, 1994), 200–210.

32. See T. Longman III, *The Book of Ecclesiastes* (NICOT; Grand Rapids: Eerdmans, 1998).

Daniel 2:1–49

> Now all has been heard;
> > here is the conclusion of the matter:
> Fear God and keep his commandments,
> > for this is the whole duty of man.
> For God will bring every deed into judgment,
> > including every hidden thing,
> > whether it is good or evil.

Our survey of key Old Testament wisdom passages confirms what we learned from the book of Daniel. Contrary to modern misunderstandings, wisdom has a divine origin, not a human one. The minor key of books like Job and Ecclesiastes also warn us that true wisdom's reward is not always in this world, though Proverbs informs us that wisdom and success sometimes accompany one another. In the case of Daniel 2, it is the latter that is the case, for the chapter closes with Nebuchadnezzar stretched out on the floor, giving honor to God's servant. When we turn to the next chapter, however, we see that this success is short-lived. Daniel and his friends did not demand human reward for their obedience (see comments on Dan. 3).

Our survey has also taught us something implicit about wisdom in Daniel 2, but which is explicit elsewhere. The divine origin of wisdom means that at its foundation wisdom is not a lesson to be learned but a relationship to be enjoyed. Daniel's wisdom, contrary to that of the learned Babylonian astrologers, did not come from books of dream interpretation; instead, it came from a conversation, a prayer, with God himself.

The New Testament and wisdom. The apostle Paul came to understand the divine origin of wisdom. When he was young, he studied hard under Gamaliel, a well-known rabbi, and he worked hard at being a good follower of God (Acts 22:3–5). He heard about those who followed Christ, and he considered them utter fools; his mission in life was to destroy the fledgling church through his intellect and even through violence.

According to his own testimony, however, God opened his eyes, so that he saw the source of true wisdom, God himself. He knew, of course, how the world counted wisdom. It was not through revelation but through vast learning. Indeed, his later reflections in 1 Corinthians 1:18–2:16 sound like a Christian reflection on Daniel 2. First Corinthians 1:20 could be the motto: "Where is the wise man? Where is the scholar? Where is the philosopher of this age? Has not God made foolish the wisdom of the world?"

Paul realized, as Daniel did before him, that true wisdom is not the result of years of reading or even living life; rather, true wisdom is the result of a relationship, a relationship with the God who created and rules over the world. The apostle, chosen by God to testify to great acts of redemption,

Daniel 2:1–49

could speak more precisely than Daniel. If asked about the source of wisdom, he would reply: Jesus Christ. This is what he means at the crescendo of his great discourse on the difference between true wisdom and the wisdom of this world (1 Cor. 2:10b–16):

> The Spirit searches all things, even the deep things of God. For who among men knows the thoughts of a man except the man's spirit within him? In the same way no one knows the thoughts of God except the Spirit of God. We have not received the spirit of the world but the Spirit who is from God, that we may understand what God has freely given us. This is what we speak, not in words taught by human wisdom but in words taught by the Spirit, expressing spiritual truths in spiritual words. The man without the Spirit does not accept the things that come from the Spirit of God, for they are foolishness to him, and he cannot understand them, because they are spiritually discerned. The spiritual man makes judgments about all things, but he himself is not subject to any man's judgment:
>
> "For who has known the mind of the Lord
>   that he may instruct him?"
>
> But we have the mind of Christ.

We have the mind of Christ. We have a relationship with Jesus Christ, God's own divine Son, in whom "are hidden all the treasures of wisdom and knowledge" (Col. 2:3). Jesus is wisdom himself (1 Cor. 1:30). For us to be wise, we must be united with him. Understanding this is crucial to our application of the message of Daniel 2 to our lives today at the turn of the second millennium A.D.

The dream itself. Before we do so, however, we must return to the occasion that led to God's powerful and public display of his wisdom—Nebuchadnezzar's dream. While we were right to deflect the type of obsessive interest in the future that focuses on the statue's meaning as the primary meaning of Daniel 2, we would be equally wrong to ignore it altogether. As readers have long noted, Daniel 2 bears many similarities to the scheme of Daniel 7. Indeed, this chapter is unique in the first half of the book with respect to the interest in the future that it shares with the second half of the book. We will, therefore, reserve discussion of some of the key aspects of the dream for that part of the book that focuses on the future as a major concern (the interested reader should consult especially the comments on ch. 7, but also 8, 10–12).

For now, we will highlight one crucial detail of the dream. The dream of the successive world empires succumbing to the power of a rock said to represent God's "kingdom that will never be destroyed" (2:44). This dream supports the overall message of the book, repeated in different ways many times: *Though circumstances appear to favor the power of ungodly human personalities and institutions, God will overpower them.* Perhaps the most significant contribution of this vision is the note that this devastating rock was cut out of the ground "not by human hands" (2:34). The fact that God's kingdom is established apart from human efforts is an important topic as we turn to our own life situations today.

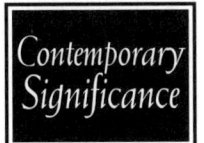

IT IS POSSIBLE to derive a formal difference between the kind of wisdom Daniel displays in chapter 2 and that which he shows in chapter 1. In chapter 1 Daniel's wisdom is similar to the kind of wisdom we find in the book of Proverbs: street smarts, knowing how to navigate life in the midst of its troubles and obstacles, based on experience and what works. Daniel ran into a roadblock in his desire to avoid the food of the king's table, so he thought of a better strategy to achieve his end, and it worked. In Daniel 2, the kind of wisdom he displayed is more striking from a human perspective. His insight into Nebuchadnezzar's dream constituted what scholars call mantic wisdom. Daniel did not know the contents and interpretation of Nebuchadnezzar's dream by virtue of looking through the prism of God's Word at past experience and applying it to a present circumstance. He knew it because God told him directly in response to a prayer.

The source of true wisdom. Today Christians debate whether such wisdom as that found in Daniel 2 is available to God's followers. On the one hand, some Christians feel a strong continuity with God's people of the biblical period and ask why we shouldn't believe that God still speaks directly and specifically to people today. How can we deny the possibility that God can speak through our dreams or reveal something in a special way to us today?[33] Other Christians, and I would include myself here (though with great respect to my brothers and sisters on the other side of the issue), note a strong connection between the giving of special revelation with the great acts of God that accomplished redemption. These acts came to a conclusion with the death and resurrection of Jesus Christ; thus, after the completion of that divinely revealed record and the interpretation of that great climactic act, God now speaks to us through his completed revelation, the Bible, rather than in sporadic dreams or prophetic utterances.

---

33. For one of the best defenses of this viewpoint, see W. Grudem, *The Gift of Prophecy in the New Testament and Today* (Westchester, Ill.: Crossway, 1988).

Daniel 2:1–49

Space does not permit an elaborate discussion of this issue,[34] but what if I am correct and God does not normally speak to us in the same way as he spoke to Daniel in chapter 2? Does that make this chapter irrelevant to us?

Not at all. I hope I have demonstrated in the Bridging Contexts section that, while it is possible to speak of a formal difference between the type of wisdom displayed in Daniel 1 and 2, substantially they are the same. It isn't as if the wisdom of Daniel in chapter 2 comes directly from God and the wisdom of chapter 1 is based on human experience apart from the divine. The latter wisdom, like the wisdom of Proverbs, is not based on common sense or experience of life; rather, it too has God as its ultimate and only source. Both types of wisdom, mantic and principial, derive from a relationship with God. For the Christian, we may state it in this manner: all wisdom comes from the One in whom "are hidden all the treasure of wisdom" (Col. 2:3), namely, Jesus Christ.

In light of these passages, even the wisdom displayed by non-Christians has to be understood as a gift of God, in what the theologians call "common grace." If we desire wisdom to live in a chaotic and confusing world, then the message of the Bible is to enrich our relationship with Christ.

We live in an increasingly complex and confusing world. With every new and improved technological advance, we are told that our lives will be simpler and easier. That's the hype, but when we buy our computer, log onto the Internet, or get our cellular phone, we find a whole host of new questions and obstacles facing us there. Where will we find the wisdom necessary to live in a world of growing complexity? Many think it is through intelligence, which we often confuse with wisdom. To get on in a world of technology, even to get a decent career, we think that knowledge, advanced degrees, and high IQs are the ticket to success and happiness in living.

Indeed, as a professor and a Ph.D. myself, I have a hard time discouraging a person's desire to gain knowledge about the Bible, about ourselves, or about our world. However, I will be the first to argue that there is no equation between one's intellect and happiness and success in life. The most intellectual people are often the worst in relationships and living a daily life. Even more, the smartest people don't always succeed in the job market either, including a heady profession like education. How often have we heard it. "My teacher is really smart but she does not know how to communicate." Or, "My boss really knows his stuff, but he certainly can't relate to his employees."

In a remarkably revealing book, Daniel Goleman counters the popular idea that a high IQ indicates a person will have the world at his or her fingertips.[35]

---

34. The interested reader is urged to look at Grudem (ibid.) and R. Gaffin, *Perspectives on Pentecost* (Grand Rapids: Baker, 1979), for opposing views on the subject.

35. D. Goleman, *Emotional Intelligence* (New York: Bantam, 1995).

His concluded that "a high IQ is no guarantee of prosperity, prestige, or happiness in life." He cites a study of college graduates with varying IQs, which showed no correlation between their Intelligence Quotient and their "salary, productivity, or status" or their "happiness with friendships, family, and romantic relationships." His conclusion is that "at best, IQ contributes about 20 percent to the factors that determine life success, which leaves 80 percent to other forces."[36]

That Goleman hit a nerve in our society was indicated that his book has enjoyed many months on the *New York Times* best-sellers list. The significance of his study for us is that he has simply stumbled across a truth stated long ago by the Bible. Biblical wisdom is more than a knowledge of facts, it is a more like a skill (a "knowing how" rather than a "knowing that") based on our relationship with Jesus Christ. Wisdom is a divinely given ability to have insight as to the best way to live life.

After his critique of IQ as the road to success, Goleman introduces the vital importance of what he calls "emotional intelligence." Again, what is striking is its uncanny similarity to biblical wisdom. Emotional intelligence goes well beyond the facts, for it "includes self-control, zeal and persistence and the ability to motivate oneself."[37] He expands this concept later in his book when he includes in emotional intelligence "abilities such as being able to motivate oneself and persist in the face of frustration; to control impulse and delay gratification; to regulate one's moods and keep distress from swamping the ability to think; to empathize and to hope."[38]

This is fine and good, but the question is, "How in the world can I do this? Regulate my moods? Control my impulses? Delay gratification? I would if I could!" Goleman gives practical suggestions for child rearing and depends heavily on the idea that once we see the benefits of our more reasonable behavior, we will conform. Most of us, however, cannot control ourselves in the way he suggests—on our own power.

Relationship with Christ. Goleman identifies the problem and points us in the right direction, but he does not provide the solution. Biblical wisdom goes much further. It points to the solution: a power greater than we are and outside of ourselves. This is a relationship with Jesus Christ.

What does this mean in practical terms? It means we live life in a troubled and confusing world in relationship with Christ. We gain our wisdom in conversation with him. And how do we converse with Christ? Through prayer and reading his Word. Through prayer we enhance our relationship

---

36. Ibid., 34–36.
37. Ibid., xii.
38. Ibid., 34.

Daniel 2:1–49

with him through praise, and we draw on his wisdom through sharing our problems and confusion. We then listen to his answer as he speaks to us through the Bible.

The Bible, however, must be understood as more than a list of principles to be memorized and then applied in a mechanical way. It takes a wise person to know the time and place to put into practice a biblical principle stated in Proverbs. A misapplied proverb can be a horrible thing (Prov. 26:7, 9):

> Like a lame man's legs that hang limp
>   is a proverb in the mouth of a fool....
> Like a thornbush in a drunkard's hand
>   is a proverb in the mouth of a fool.

But a proverb applied correctly is cause for great joy (15:23):

> A man finds joy in giving an apt reply—
>   and how good is a timely word!

Wisdom is a relationship that produces a mindset, a way of looking at the world. Indeed, it looks at life through the eyes of Christ. It does not stop with the memorization of biblical verses.

In chapter 2, God used Daniel to display his own wisdom. Though Nebuchadnezzar in his spiritual blindness (or at least serious nearsightedness) bowed before Daniel, the reader knows that God is the one who deserves the praise for the miracle of interpretation. But it is not only for the act of interpretation itself, but its content as well. The dream taught that although evil human kingdoms will dominate for a season, the ultimate victory will go to God. It is his kingdom that will be established. The rock, cut without human hands, will not only crush the statue but it will grow to mountain-like proportions.

Who is the rock? The symbolism is multifaceted, but readers of the New Testament cannot help but think of Jesus Christ as the rock who establishes God's kingdom by crushing godless nations. It is true that the tradition that identifies Jesus as the rock derives also from Psalm 118:22 (Matt. 21:42; Mark 12:10–11; Luke 20:17; 1 Peter 2:7) and Isaiah 8:14 and 28:16 (Rom. 9:33; 1 Peter 2:6, 8), but we get a clear reference to Daniel 2 in Luke 20:18. The context is the parable of the tenants (Luke 20:9–19). The parable is the story of an vineyard (often a symbol of God's kingdom)[39] rented to tenants, who then refuse to pay. The owner sends messengers to collect the rent, but they are beaten and chased off. Finally, the owner sends his son, but the tenants do the unspeakable and kill the son. At that point, the owner returns himself, kills the tenants, and gives the vineyard to others.

---

39. See L. Ryken, J. Wilhort, and T. Longman III, eds., *The Dictionary of Biblical Imagery* (Downer Grove, Ill.: InterVarsity, 1998).

Daniel 2:1–49

In a clear attempt to identify himself with the son and his listeners with the doomed tenants, Jesus quotes Psalm 118:22: "The stone the builders rejected has become the capstone," and then immediately associates this stone with the stone of Daniel 2 "Everyone who falls on that stone will be broken to pieces, but he on whom it falls will be crushed" (Luke 20:18).[40]

---

40. See Collins, *Daniel*, 171, who also points out that "the messianic interpretation is . . . found in rabbinic literature."

Daniel 3:1–30

KING NEBUCHADNEZZAR MADE an image of gold, ninety feet high and nine feet wide, and set it up on the plain of Dura in the province of Babylon. ²He then summoned the satraps, prefects, governors, advisers, treasurers, judges, magistrates and all the other provincial officials to come to the dedication of the image he had set up. ³So the satraps, prefects, governors, advisers, treasurers, judges, magistrates and all the other provincial officials assembled for the dedication of the image that King Nebuchadnezzar had set up, and they stood before it.

⁴Then the herald loudly proclaimed, "This is what you are commanded to do, O peoples, nations and men of every language: ⁵As soon as you hear the sound of the horn, flute, zither, lyre, harp, pipes and all kinds of music, you must fall down and worship the image of gold that King Nebuchadnezzar has set up. ⁶Whoever does not fall down and worship will immediately be thrown into a blazing furnace."

⁷Therefore, as soon as they heard the sound of the horn, flute, zither, lyre, harp and all kinds of music, all the peoples, nations and men of every language fell down and worshiped the image of gold that King Nebuchadnezzar had set up.

⁸At this time some astrologers came forward and denounced the Jews. ⁹They said to King Nebuchadnezzar, "O king, live forever! ¹⁰You have issued a decree, O king, that everyone who hears the sound of the horn, flute, zither, lyre, harp, pipes and all kinds of music must fall down and worship the image of gold, ¹¹and that whoever does not fall down and worship will be thrown into a blazing furnace. ¹²But there are some Jews whom you have set over the affairs of the province of Babylon—Shadrach, Meshach and Abednego—who pay no attention to you, O king. They neither serve your gods nor worship the image of gold you have set up."

¹³Furious with rage, Nebuchadnezzar summoned Shadrach, Meshach and Abednego. So these men were brought before the king, ¹⁴and Nebuchadnezzar said to them, "Is it true, Shadrach, Meshach and Abednego, that you do not serve my gods or worship the image of gold I have set up? ¹⁵Now when

Daniel 3:1–30

you hear the sound of the horn, flute, zither, lyre, harp, pipes and all kinds of music, if you are ready to fall down and worship the image I made, very good. But if you do not worship it, you will be thrown immediately into a blazing furnace. Then what god will be able to rescue you from my hand?"

[16]Shadrach, Meshach and Abednego replied to the king, "O Nebuchadnezzar, we do not need to defend ourselves before you in this matter. [17]If we are thrown into the blazing furnace, the God we serve is able to save us from it, and he will rescue us from your hand, O king. [18]But even if he does not, we want you to know, O king, that we will not serve your gods or worship the image of gold you have set up."

[19]Then Nebuchadnezzar was furious with Shadrach, Meshach and Abednego, and his attitude toward them changed. He ordered the furnace heated seven times hotter than usual [20]and commanded some of the strongest soldiers in his army to tie up Shadrach, Meshach and Abednego and throw them into the blazing furnace. [21]So these men, wearing their robes, trousers, turbans and other clothes, were bound and thrown into the blazing furnace. [22]The king's command was so urgent and the furnace so hot that the flames of the fire killed the soldiers who took up Shadrach, Meshach and Abednego, [23]and these three men, firmly tied, fell into the blazing furnace.

[24]Then King Nebuchadnezzar leaped to his feet in amazement and asked his advisers, "Weren't there three men that we tied up and threw into the fire?"

They replied, "Certainly, O king."

[25]He said, "Look! I see four men walking around in the fire, unbound and unharmed, and the fourth looks like a son of the gods."

[26]Nebuchadnezzar then approached the opening of the blazing furnace and shouted, "Shadrach, Meshach and Abednego, servants of the Most High God, come out! Come here!"

So Shadrach, Meshach and Abednego came out of the fire, [27]and the satraps, prefects, governors and royal advisers crowded around them. They saw that the fire had not harmed their bodies, nor was a hair of their heads singed; their robes were not scorched, and there was no smell of fire on them.

[28]Then Nebuchadnezzar said, "Praise be to the God of Shadrach, Meshach and Abednego, who has sent his angel and

Daniel 3:1–30

rescued his servants! They trusted in him and defied the king's command and were willing to give up their lives rather than serve or worship any god except their own God. ²⁹Therefore I decree that the people of any nation or language who say anything against the God of Shadrach, Meshach and Abednego be cut into pieces and their houses be turned into piles of rubble, for no other god can save in this way."

³⁰Then the king promoted Shadrach, Meshach and Abednego in the province of Babylon.

DANIEL 3 CONTAINS a single story with a clear beginning, middle, and end. In other words, though it fits nicely into the broader context, it has its own plot, which generates tension but moves toward resolution.

As with the first two chapters, Daniel 3 is set during the reign of King Nebuchadnezzar of Babylon. This is the first chapter, however, that does not give a more precise chronological marker. We do not know how much time has elapsed since the previous episode, but we must imagine a gap of not a few years to account for Nebuchadnezzar's shift from honoring the God of Daniel as he did at the end of chapter 2 to throwing that God's devotees into a burning furnace.[1]

The plot tension is introduced when Nebuchadnezzar made a huge golden statue and then insisted that everyone present bow down and worship it. Later we will explore the possible significance behind this command, but here we simply note that people of the time would by and large have had little difficulty with this request. After all, most people in the ancient Near East were polytheists, used to acknowledging many deities. They could easily assimilate this statue into their religious scheme, especially under the duress of capital punishment. But this was not true of the Judeans in exile. Their belief in one God prohibited participation in this ritual, and their adversaries knew it.

The text indicates that the three friends of Daniel could have gotten away with their nonconformance if it were not for certain enemies who turned them in (vv. 9–12). These informers are identified as "some astrologers" (v. 8) and probably were professional colleagues who hated to see these

---

1. The LXX felt the tension and filled in the gap by saying that this episode took place in the king's eighteenth year. This is likely an attempt to associate the ceremony with a celebration of his taking of Jerusalem (cf. Jer. 52:29) and is improbable.

gifted foreigners rise so quickly and so high in the Babylonian government. They thought they had the perfect plan to do away with them.

Thus, from a literary point of view, this account is a narrative of "court conflict."[2] This label rightly indicates that here the Judeans encounter the animosity of their enemies in a way that they have not yet experienced. This account may be the first record of specifically religious persecution, but unfortunately not the last.[3]

In chapter 2, God made known his great wisdom. Here, he will reveal his power. The story in this way will again support the overarching theme of the book of Daniel: *In spite of present appearances, God is in control.* The specific focus of this chapter is that God's power transcends even death. This stirring story intends to bolster the courage of God's people as they face what seems to be overwhelming odds.

The structure of the chapter is as follows: (1) Nebuchadnezzar's image of gold (3:1–7); the accusation against the three friends (3:8–12); the confrontation with Nebuchadnezzar (3:13–18); the miraculous deliverance (3:19–27); Nebuchadnezzar worships God (3:28–30). Catholic editions of Daniel include two additions to this chapter: a short prayer of Azariah, followed by a song sung by the three young men.[4] The prayer is one of confession and acknowledgment of God's justice, much like Daniel 9 in tone. The song (preceded by a short prose description of the furnace ordeal) is a hymn extolling God.

Nebuchadnezzar's Image of Gold (3:1–7)

THE EPISODE BEGINS with the simple statement that Nebuchadnezzar built a golden image on the plain of Dura.[5] The author of Daniel does not inform us whether the image was a god or the king himself? In one sense, this distinction does not matter. Whether deity or the divinized king, the command was to worship and bow down to this statue, to treat it or what it represented as the most important power in the universe. Such a command was impossible for a faithful follower of the true God to obey, and that is the point of the text.

---

2. A similar type of narrative occurs in ch. 6, the account of Daniel in the lion's den. In ch. 11 we read a tale of court contest.

3. J. J. Collins, *Daniel; First Maccabees; Second Maccabees, With an Excursus on the Apocalyptic Genre* (Wilmington, Del.: Michael Glazier, 1981), 41.

4. For a translation of this material, see ibid., 38–39.

5. Dura is an Akkadian word meaning "wall" or "fortress" and "is common in the geographical nomenclature of Mesopotamia" (J. S. Montgomery, *A Critical and Exegetical Commentary on the Book of Daniel* [Edinburgh: T. & T. Clark, 1950], 197; cf. *Chicago Assyrian Dictionary*, vol. 10, p. x). We cannot be dogmatic about a specific location.

Daniel 3:1–30

All we learn about the statue is its dimensions and the material out of which it was made. Like many ancient idols it was made from a precious metal, in this case gold. Analogies with other idols known from this time period suggest that the statue was gold-plated and not solid gold. The gold of this statue links the story with Nebuchadnezzar's recently described dream in which he was the head of gold. Perhaps this is a clue that the statue was indeed of the king, though rarely did Mesopotamian kings present themselves as gods, and we have no other evidence that Nebuchadnezzar broke this tradition.

The size of the image is startling: "ninety feet high and nine feet wide."[6] Commentators have grappled with what Young has called the "grotesque" shape of this statue,[7] suggesting solutions like a large dais included in the dimensions or pointing to the long, thin (though much smaller) statues of deities and worshipers recovered through archaeology.[8] Collins provides the most exhaustive list of large statues known in the ancient world, most notably mentioning the statue of Bel in Babylon as reported by Herodotus (who calls it Bel Zeus), though this statue was only eighteen feet high.[9] Other scholars mention the colossus of Rhodes, closer in height to Nebuchadnezzar's statue and built in the following Persian period.[10]

Nebuchadnezzar not only built the statue; he demanded a public demonstration of adoration. For this purpose, he issued a call for "the satraps, prefects, governors, advisers, treasurers, judges, magistrates and all the other provincial officials" to attend its dedication. With this rather imposing list of officials, we encounter a lengthy list that is repeated a number of times in the chapter. These lists appear ponderous to us, but their literary effect is to heighten the tension and the feeling of danger toward the three friends, who will soon be singled out of the group. As Fewell states it, "through repetition, the narrator creates a scenario in which conformity is normative, disobedience is unthinkable."[11] The various categories of people in the list are political officials from around the empire, which may signal that this was Nebuchadnezzar's attempt to solidify control over the diverse elements of his vast empire.

We encounter a second lengthy list as well, which is also repeated (cf. vv. 5, 7, 10, 15: "the sound of the horn, flute, zither, lyre, harp, pipes and all kinds of music"). This is a list of musical instruments at whose sound everyone was

---

6. The Aramaic text reads the measurements in cubits: sixty cubits high and six cubits wide, reflecting the sexgesimal system in use in Babylon.

7. Young, *The Prophecy of Daniel*, 84, says that all Babylonian sculpture was grotesque, an expression of personal taste not shared by the present writer.

8. Wood, *A Commentary on Daniel*, 80.

9. Collins, *Daniel*, 180.

10. Also Wood, *A Commentary on Daniel*, 80.

11. Fewell, *Circles of Sovereignty*, 66.

Daniel 3:1–30

to show their respects to the statue. This list emphasizes the "pomp"[12] surrounding the ceremony and heightens the tension, focusing on the moment of obedience or disobedience.

As reported in these first seven verses, everything seems to be proceeding according to the specifications of the king. The order was given through the musical prelude, and "all the peoples, nations and men of every language fell down and worshiped the image of gold that King Nebuchadnezzar had set up" (v. 7). Or so he thought....

The Accusation Against the Three Friends (3:8–12)

INDEED, WHEN VERSE 7 reports that everyone worshiped the image, it is probably giving Nebuchadnezzar's perspective. As his eyes scanned the plain of Dura, he apparently saw only the large crowd obeying his command to prostrate themselves before his golden statue. His contentment was shattered, however, by the report he received from a contingent of astrologers, who accused "some Jews" (v. 12) of disobedience to the king's direct command in spite of the threatened penalty of a horrible death.

We should note that this is an accusation by *some* astrologers against *some* Jews. It is not a class action against a whole people. Indeed, many aspects of this story leave us with various questions. What about the other Jewish people? Were any others present? Did they conform? And, most provocatively, where was Daniel?

We should avoid making dogmatic pronouncements when the text is silent. Wood goes over the edge when he asserts, for instance, that the three friends stood completely alone and every other Jewish person gave in.[13] Critical scholars take the silence of the text too far in a different direction when they use Daniel's absence to speak of a separate tradition that knew of the three friends but not of Daniel, and a later redaction that brought the two strands together in a kind of slipshod manner.[14]

Perhaps it is correct to treat Daniel 2:49 ("Moreover, at Daniel's request the king appointed Shadrach, Meshach and Abednego administrators over the province of Babylon, while Daniel himself remained at the royal court") as an implicit answer to the question of Daniel's absence. It certainly explains why Daniel and the three friends were not automatically together, but we cannot, again, be dogmatic.

The text is a bit more suggestive, though once again not explicit, about the motivation of the accusing astrologers. The hint comes when they

---

12. Ibid., 68.
13. Wood, *A Commentary on Daniel*, 84.
14. See Lacocque, *The Book of Daniel*, 58, fn. 1.

Daniel 3:1–30

describe the three Jews as those "whom you have set over the affairs of the province of Babylon" (v. 12). These men appear to be motivated out of professional jealousy. They beat them out for best honors in their school (ch. 1), and now they are rapidly rising in the ranks of the government—and they are foreigners to boot!

Close attention to the words of the astrologers reveal their strategy as they stir the king to action against Shadrach, Meshach, and Abednego. In a phrase, they appeal to his sense of vanity. The disobedience of the three Jews is a personal affront. After all, he was the one who issued the decree and warned of the penalty. These rebels "pay no attention to *you*, O king. They neither serve *your* gods nor worship the image of gold *you* have set up" (v. 12, italics added). With this approach, Nebuchadnezzar's reaction is predictable.

The Confrontation With Nebuchadnezzar (3:13–18)

A CASE COULD be made as early as chapter 2 that Nebuchadnezzar betrays a sense of insecurity. This sounds surprising for the most powerful human being on the face of the earth, but with power and wealth come those who want to take it away for themselves, even if it means murder. Nebuchadnezzar's insecurity is apparent in his treatment of the wisdom teachers in chapter 2 as well as in his happiness after learning that he was the head of gold.

The premise of this chapter is the enforced worship of Nebuchadnezzar's golden statue, which, whether idol or royal statue, is a way of compelling a display of loyalty. The report of disloyalty among the three friends causes an explosion of anger on his part. He immediately has them brought into his presence for a personal loyalty test.

The tension reaches fever pitch when Nebuchadnezzar orders a personal ceremony for the three, instructing the band to strike up the introit, at the end of which they are to worship the image. He climaxes his exhortation with a statement that gets at the heart of the theological teaching of the chapter: "What god will be able to rescue you from my hand" (v. 15). In chapter 2, we saw the astrologers themselves unknowingly throwing down the challenge to the Lord God as they asserted that no god had the requisite wisdom to answer the king's question (2:11). Here the king asserts his own power above all gods, and we can imagine the God of Psalm 2 raising his eyebrows and emitting a slight chuckle.

The three friends are not ready to laugh, but they stand their ground in a rather startling way. Their answer seems arrogant at first hearing: "We do not need to defend ourselves before you in this matter" (v. 16). They go on to explain in a way that strikes us as odd, but when properly understood, becomes an example of tremendous courage in the context of intense religious persecution (vv. 17–18): "If we are thrown into the blazing furnace, the God we serve is able to save us from it, and he will rescue us from your hand, O king. But even if he does not, we want you to know, O king, that we will not serve your gods or worship the image of gold you have set up."

This is no easy answer to the king's anger. They begin by acknowledging God's ability to save them, but then they envision the possibility that God may choose not to do so.[15] In other words, they answer Nebuchadnezzar in light of the possibility that they will be burned to ashes in the blazing furnace. Whichever is the case, they say, they will not worship the golden image.

In its original setting, this answer heightens the literary tension of the story (at least on first hearing). Even the faithful follower of God does not know what will happen to the three friends. Will they live or die? God may rescue them or they may die, martyrs to the cause of faith. But even those original hearers of the story who know the outcome can find great significance in this answer. Yes, the three friends survive, but they also know that some of their people have died at the hands of the persecutors. Was this because God was unable to deliver at those times? Was it because these others did not have the requisite faith? No, it was that God, in his unfathomable wisdom, did not chose to save them. No matter what the result, deliverance or death, they will not give into the evil powers of the world. They will stay faithful to God. This, of course, will have tremendous implications for how we think about suffering today (see below).

The Miraculous Deliverance (3:19–27)

THE THREE FRIENDS' speech, courageous in our ears, exasperates the king. He grows even more furious. Interestingly, the Aramaic text, which the NIV idiomatically translates as "his attitude toward them changed," may more literally be translated, "the image [*selem*] of his face changed." The one who in his pride has created an image with the purpose of assuring uniform loyalty finds his own image provoked beyond his control. He orders the furnace, apparently burning in the background of the scene, to be superheated, reflecting perhaps the heat of his own anger. Then he orders his soldiers to throw the three Jews in.

---

15. A major debate surrounds the translation of this verse from the Aramaic. It is possible on grammatical grounds to defend the translation of the NRSV ("If our God whom we serve is able to deliver us from the furnace of blazing fire and out of your hand, O king, let him deliver us"), but as many commentators have pointed out, this is unlikely from a theological perspective, and the NIV's translation is also philologically defensible (Miller, *Daniel*, 119). For a lengthy discussion of the issue, cf. P. Coxon, "Daniel 3:17: A Linguistic and Theological Problem," *VT* 26 (1976): 400–405.

Daniel 3:1–30

Our picture of this furnace is supplied by the description of the text rather than any firm archaeological knowledge. For the narrative to make sense, the furnace must be large. Some scholars have suggested that this is a furnace near the plain of Dura that was used to make the great golden image in the first place.[16] Apparently the three are thrown in from an opening at the top, but Nebuchadnezzar's ability to look into the furnace indicates that perhaps there was a window or opening at the side as well.

In any case, the soldiers obediently cast Shadrach, Meshach, and Abednego into the fire. The fire is so hot that it kills the soldiers. Loyalty to a godless and foolish king brings death, not the life one would expect. But what about those who refuse obedience when it comes to a choice between faithfulness to Nebuchadnezzar and to God himself? Is there "a god" who can rescue them from the hands of such a powerful ruler?

Nebuchadnezzar himself gives us the answer: "I see four men walking around in the fire, unbound and unharmed, and the fourth looks like a son of the gods" (v. 25). The king quickly gets the message and orders the three out, and then Nebuchadnezzar and all the others, including the accusers, witness the extent of the miracle of deliverance. Verse 21 narrated the clothing of the three when they were thrown in. They were fully dressed in "robes, trousers, turbans and other clothes," but when they emerged, "the fire had not harmed their bodies, nor was a hair of their heads singed; their robes were not scorched, and there was no smell of fire on them" (v. 27). It was as if they were not even in the fire.

In this way, God is showing Nebuchadnezzar who is in charge. Even if the image that precipitated the crisis is not of Nebuchadnezzar himself, he has certainly put himself in place of God, insisting that he is the ultimate power of the universe, from whose rage no deity could hope to save a follower. By contrast, it is only the true God who can proclaim that "no one can deliver out of my hand" (Deut. 32:39). And this great God was a proven deliverer. After all, when he rescued his people from Egypt centuries before, Moses told the Israelites that it was God who "brought you out of the iron-smelting furnace, out of Egypt, to be the people of his inheritance, as you now are" (4:20).

Nebuchadnezzar Worships God (3:28–30)

THAT GOD RESCUED the three Jews no one is in doubt, but who was that "fourth [who] looks like a son of the gods" (v. 25)? As in chapter 2, Nebuchadnezzar is moved from anger to praise toward God and his followers. In his concluding speech in the present chapter, he again mentions the mys-

---

16. For instance, Miller, *Daniel*, 115.

terious fourth person. When he first saw the figure, he labeled him a "son of the gods"; now he calls him God's "angel" (v. 28). His dual description has launched a debate that continues to the present day, which will take us into the next two sections as well as into a consideration whether our later perspective might throw even more light on the issue. But at this stage we must remember that the narrative places these two descriptions in the mouth of Nebuchadnezzar, who is not an Israelite theologian. Relying on his words, we are thrown into a quandary: Was this God himself as "a son of the gods" might lead us to believe,[17] or an angel?

In one sense, it does not make any difference. Even if the fourth figure was an angel, it was *God's* angel; God is still the redeemer. Even Nebuchadnezzar recognizes this. He further acknowledges that the three have been right to obey this God rather than a king like him.

The king then issues a command that, while not instituting worship of the true God, will not allow anyone in his kingdom to show such a powerful deity any disrespect. Furthermore, Shadrach, Meshach, and Abednego get a further promotion, thus completely thwarting the intentions of their accusers.

THE PRECIPITATING CAUSE of the action in Daniel 3 is Nebuchadnezzar's construction of a huge statue with the attendant insistence that all the leaders, indeed the "peoples, nations and men of every language" (v. 4), bow down in worship to this statue.

Near Eastern idolatry. As we have noted, it is impossible to be dogmatic concerning the identity of the statue. Is it the king himself or, as is more likely, one of the gods? And, if the latter, which one? There are two reasons to tip the scale slightly in favor of seeing the statue as that of a deity. (1) It was rare for Mesopotamian kings to be divinized, and there is no evidence that Nebuchadnezzar ever moved in this direction.

(2) If the king were divine, why would he need to build a statue-idol to receive worship when he himself was physically present?[18] An idol of a god in Mesopotamian religious conception was a way in which to make the normally invisible god present. The gods were active in the world, often as personified forces of nature, but they were not visible. An idol made a god visible. The idol was not the god, but since it represented the god, it was imbued with the god's aura. A sophisticated Mesopotamian theologian would

---

17. Young, *The Prophecy of Daniel*, 94, and most other conservative commentators argue strongly for this view.
18. I want to thank John Walton for this helpful point.

Daniel 3:1–30

have denied an equation between the physical idol and his god; but in another sense, the idol, being the physical manifestation of the god, was treated as if it were the god. We know about elaborate ceremonies of bathing and feeding statues that showed the awe with which these physical objects were approached.[19] While the theologian and other sophisticated thinkers in the society approached the idol as a symbol of the god, I suspect that many people were more crass in their identification of god and idol.[20]

Regardless of whether the idol was royal or divine, the statue was understood to represent a god or even in the minds of some identified with a god. It was a deity represented by a statue constructed from precious materials and intended to represent a deity of some sort. It was therefore the appropriate object of adoration. The three friends knew exactly what the statue stood for, and they also understood that they could not be faithful to the true God and bow the knee to the statue. They also realized that the cost was heavy indeed, namely, their lives.

They understood their God's will concerning their participation in the ritual on the plain of Dura, because God had expressed that will through the Ten Commandments centuries before and had laid the foundation with the first two commandments (Ex. 20:3–6):

> You shall have no other gods before me.
> You shall not make for yourself an idol in the form of anything in heaven above or on the earth beneath or in the waters below. You shall not bow down to them or worship them; for I, the LORD your God, am a jealous God, punishing the children for the sin of the fathers to the third and fourth generation of those who hate me, but showing love to a thousand generations of those who love me and keep my commandments.

By not worshiping this deity, Shadrach, Meshach, and Abednego became role models for God's people when faced with the seduction or the threat of the worship of deities constructed by human minds and human hands.

This occasion, of course, was not the first time where Israel felt the seduction of idol worship. Indeed, God's people during the Old Testament period lived constantly in the dangerous world of idols. Their danger was in their seductive power. All the nations around Israel worshiped them, nations more powerful and successful (in a worldly sense) than they were. Indeed, these

---

19. An excellent discussion may be found in A. L. Oppenheim, *Ancient Mesopotamia: Portrait of a Dead Civilization* (Chicago: Univ. of Chicago Press, 1964).

20. Perhaps similar to the way that icons of Mary and the saints are treated in some regions of the world.

are the nations that overpowered them. The temptation would be strong to worship the gods of their oppressors for one's own advancement and because of the apparent superiority of their culture and their military power. Daniel 3 itself illustrates how, at least in this case, the worship of idols would advance one's career, while refusing to worship this idol could result in death. Many Jewish exiles may have been tempted to worship idols because they would understand Babylon's political superiority as a reflex of the superior power of their gods.

As we read the story of Israel in the Old Testament, we observe that the people and the leaders did not always successfully resist the temptation to worship those shiny, impressive-looking statues. It is for this reason that the prophets inveigh so heavily against them. Indeed, Isaiah is at his sarcastic and rhetorical best when he ridicules the idols of the surrounding nations. He satirizes idol worship by reducing it to a fetish (Isa. 44:12–20):[21]

> The blacksmith takes a tool
> > and works with it in the coals;
> he shapes an idol with hammers,
> > he forges it with the might of his arm.
> He gets hungry and loses his strength;
> > he drinks no water and grows faint.
> The carpenter measures with a line
> > and makes an outline with a marker;
> he roughs it out with chisels
> > and marks it with compasses.
> He shapes it in the form of man,
> > of man in all his glory,
> > that it may dwell in a shrine.
> He cut down cedars,
> > or perhaps took a cypress or oak.
> He let it grow among the trees of the forest,
> > or planted a pine, and the rain made it grow.
> It is man's fuel for burning;
> > some of it he takes and warms himself,
> > he kindles a fire and bakes bread.
> But he also fashions a god and worships it;
> > he makes an idol and bows down to it.
> Half of the wood he burns in the fire;
> > over it he prepares his meal,
> > he roasts his meat and eats his fill.

---

21. Sophisticated Babylonians would not have strictly identified the idol with their god.

Daniel 3:1–30

He also warms himself and says,
    "Ah! I am warm; I see the fire."
From the rest he makes a god, his idol;
    he bows down to it and worships.
He prays to it and says,
    "Save me; you are my god."
They know nothing, they understand nothing;
    their eyes are plastered over so they cannot see,
    and their minds closed so they cannot understand.
No one stops to think,
    no one has the knowledge or understanding to say,
"Half of it I used for fuel;
    I even baked bread over its coals,
    I roasted meat and I ate.
Shall I make a detestable thing from what is left?
    Shall I bow down to a block of wood?"
He feeds on ashes, a deluded heart misleads him;
    he cannot save himself, or say,
    "Is not this thing in my right hand a lie?"

Isaiah shows in most graphic and even darkly humorous terms that the worship of an idol (in the case of Dan. 3, the statue in the plain of Dura) was a confusion of the creation with the Creator. In idol worship, a person takes a bit of created matter and says, "You are the most important thing to me in the world. You have all the power and the wisdom!"

Now, it is true that a sophisticated ancient Near Eastern theologian (as opposed to the general populace) would likely have responded to Isaiah, "Don't be ridiculous. We don't worship that wood and metal statue! That object is simply a representation of the deity, who is not restricted to the statue but is a power above human power." But even so, what do the gods of the ancient Near East themselves represent? Who are Marduk and Ishtar, or Baal and Astarte? They are personifications of bits of creation as well. Marduk, the leading god of the neo-Babylonian empire of Nebuchadnezzar, and Baal, his counterpart in Canaan, were the power of fertility, the storm, the dew. Ishtar, also from Mesopotamia, and Astarte, her counterpart in Canaan, personified sexual potency and the violence of war.

In other words, not only the statues but the deities that they represented are bits of creation raised to the level of the Creator. We can hear Paul's later words ringing in our ears (Rom. 1:21–22):

> For although they knew God, they neither glorified him as God nor gave thanks to him, but their thinking became futile and their foolish

hearts were darkened. Although they claimed to be wise, they became fools and exchanged the glory of the immortal God for images made to look like mortal man and birds and animals and reptiles.

We can see the seriousness of the challenge to the faith of Shadrach, Meshach, and Abednego. They are being told to demote their God, the one who created them, by not giving him their exclusive worship. They are also to worship a statue of a god they know does not exist. They cannot simply rationalize their actions, because the act of bowing down and worship indicates that they affirm the statue as equal to their God. By accepting this statue into the category of deity, they will inevitably reduce the ultimacy, authority, and jurisdiction of the true God and demote him in such a way that will make him out to be no more than one of the deities of the polytheistic world. Ultimately, the dilution or diminishment of deity is a denunciation of deity.[22]

As Christians in the West at the end of the twentieth century, we are not confronted with the same threat as Shadrach, Meshach, and Abednego—or are we? Certainly no one would build a statue and insist that we all bow down before it. But the threat of idolatry is much more subtle and therefore threatening to us today. To understand this, I find a concept of Paul Tillich, a German-American theologian of the mid-twentieth century, helpful, namely, that of "Ultimate Concern."[23] Tillich pointed out that a person's god is the thing or person that one is most concerned about, thinks the most about, or affects one's life the most.

If Tillich's language is a tad abstract for some, let me introduce a phrase made famous by Bill Bright and Campus Crusade. He used a catchy metaphor to get people to think about what is acting as a god in their lives by inquiring, "Who is on the throne of your life?" If it is not the true God of the Bible, he suggests, then it is an idol. In the Contemporary Significance section we will explore what permutations idolatry takes in our time.

Faithful in the face of death. But harking back to our comments on Daniel 3, we want to observe how the three friends react to Nebuchadnezzar's insistence that they worship the idol. In many ways, the problem is similar to the one encountered in chapter 1: How are God's faithful people to act in a faithless world?

In our present chapter, the dangers are heightened at least on the surface. Shadrach, Meshach, and Abednego are compelled to conform to Nebuchadnezzar's aberrant religious ceremony in a public setting under the threat

---

22. I would like to thank John Walton for his insightful comments on this topic expressed in this paragraph.
23. See the phrase used throughout P. Tillich, *Systematic Theology* (3 vols.; Chicago: Univ. of Chicago Press, 1951–1963).

Daniel 3:1–30

of death. We are first struck again by the lack of stridency exhibited by the faithful Jewish youths. Unlike the young third-century A.D. theologian Origen, who wanted to throw himself in front of the emperor's chariot and proclaim Christ, they simply quietly decide not to participate. Apparently, the king does not even notice them; it takes a group of informants who are out to get the three to bring it to the king's attention. But when they are then brought in for private interrogation, they show that their quiet rebellion earlier does not hide a heart of cowardice. They calmly and boldly proclaim their faith without a moment's hesitation.

Their courage is remarkable. They do not seek death, but neither do they shirk it. They refuse to betray their God even in the light of the real possibility that they may die for their stand.

Indeed, we must be very careful not to let the optimistic outcome of the story cloud our vision. The friends have no confidence that they will survive the ordeal ("even if he does not [save us], we want you to know, O king, that we will not serve your gods or worship the image of gold you have set up" [v. 18]). They know that that type of confidence is nothing but the most irksome of presumptions.

Their response preserves the story from devolving into a false promise that God will save every faithful person from suffering and death. Such a story would betray the faithful martyrs who have stood faithful but suffered death. Jesus himself honored God's followers who died during the Old Testament time when he spoke of "all the righteous blood that has been shed on the earth, from the blood of righteous Abel to the blood of Zechariah son of Berekiah" (Matt. 23:35). The story of church history from its beginnings under the Roman empire to the present has countless stories of faithful witnesses who have stood firm to the end.

The three friends' courage is all the more amazing when we reflect on what they may have thought concerning life after death. In a word, it is not at all clear that they had a definite idea of a judgment or reward after death, and it is extremely unlikely that, even if they did know of the resurrection of the dead, that they had an extensive picture of the blessings of heaven. They certainly do not appeal to such a hope here, and there is little explicit teaching about the resurrection of the dead, eternal life, or heaven in previous Scripture. The teaching is there implicitly, and later in the book of Daniel it becomes explicit (12:1–3), but something other than future bliss motivates the three friends and invests their potential death with meaning.

Towner at least partially captures their motivation when he states that "their deaths subverted the power of the authorities to crush integrity and to silence truth."[24] In this regard, he compares the meaningfulness of the mar-

---

24. Towner, *Daniel*, 54.

Daniel 3:1–30

tyr's death to the meaninglessness of the death of the guards, who obediently escorted the three friends to the mouth of the fiery furnace.

But a more specific answer to the question is forthcoming when we consider the actual contents of the three friends' "truth" and "integrity." They stand firm because they trust their God—no matter what, and no matter what includes death. Victor Frankl, a survivor of German death camps and no stranger to courage in the face of the danger of death himself, quotes Nietzsche's aphorism that applies to the three friends as well as to himself, "He who has a *why* to live can bear with almost any *how*."[25] But the three friends take it far beyond Nietzsche. That philosopher is well known for his statement, "That which does not kill me, makes me stronger." The three friends bear witness to the fact that even death does not defeat them.

MODERN IDOLATRY. AT first it is difficult for us as Christians living at the turn of the millennium to identify with the challenge facing the Jewish people on the plain of Dura. But we have suggested that the issue transcends the worship of a particular statue and concerns instead the constant threat to dilute the worship of the true God by elevating anything or anyone else to a comparable place of importance in our life. As John Calvin has provocatively charged, the human mind is a "factory of idols." We are constantly, even as Christians, in a struggle with this temptation.

The temptation can come from a variety of sources, not all of which seem so bad on the surface of it. Our addictions can make pleasure an idol, so that all our efforts and thoughts are directed toward where we will get our next high, whether through alcohol, drugs, sex, or some other cheap thrill. We might seek power in order to control our world or simply to have the resources of revenge toward those who have hurt us in some way. All our efforts and strength thus become directed toward amassing power and influence in society, our family, or even the church. We may make relationships, or one particular relationship, an idol. We may be gearing our life and decisions not around what we understand to be God's will, but rather the will of a spouse, a child, or a friend. Seeking knowledge or degrees, writing books, or delivering impressive sermons, these too may become idols.

The list is vast, which is why the danger is so real. The seduction is subtle, which is why we can slip so easily into idol worship.[26] But though subtle and varied, I suggest that idolatry, whether of Nebuchadnezzar's sort or

---

25. V. Frankl, *Man's Search for Meaning: An Introduction to Logotherapy* (3d ed.; New York: Simon and Schuster, 1984), 84.
26. See D. Allender and T. Longman III, *Bold Purpose* (forthcoming Tyndale House, 1998).

Daniel 3:1–30

the kind we discover in our own hearts, ultimately has one object. When the masks are ripped away, behind every idol is the *self*. Frederick Nietzsche, the late nineteenth-century philosopher whose thought has such a huge influence on contemporary postmodern culture, saw this, and in his brutal and honest atheism, advocated the killing of God and the construction of a new idol, the human self. Hear him as he preaches his new doctrine:

> Whatever in me has feeling, suffers and is in prison; but my will always comes to me as my liberator and joy-bringer. Willing liberates: that is the true teaching of will and liberty—thus Zarathustra teaches it. Willing no more and esteeming no more and creating no more—oh, that this great weariness might always remain far from me! In knowledge too I feel only my will's joy in begetting and becoming; and if there is innocence in my knowledge, it is because the will to beget is in it. Away from God and gods this will has lured me; what could one create if gods existed?
>
> But my fervent will to create impels me ever again toward man; thus is the hammer impelled toward the stone. O men, in the stone there sleeps an image, the image of my images. Alas, that it must sleep in the hardest, the ugliest stone! Now my hammer rages cruelly against its prison. Pieces of rock rain from the stone: what is that to me? I want to perfect it; for a shadow came to me—the stillest and lightest of all things once came to me. The beauty of the overman came to me as a shadow. O my brothers, what are the gods to me now?
>
> Thus spoke Zarathustra.[27]

God is dead; the self must replace it. In a sense, this might seem to be the opposite of Daniel 3, but it is not. It is not so much a ridding the world of God, but a replacing of God by another god—the self. Nietzsche attempted to kill God because he could not tolerate any but himself in that position: "But let me reveal my heart to you entirely, my friends: if there were gods, how could I endure not to be a god! Hence there are no gods."[28]

Here is the heart of modern postmodern society: In the absence of the gods we may and must create our own meaning. No longer does Christ provide meaning. No longer do we feel the existential nausea of no meaning. Now we feel the will to power and the joy in constructing our own meaning in the absence of the gods. All substitutes for God are ultimately this

---

27. F. Nietzsche, "Upon the Blessed Isles," *Thus Spoke Zarathustra, Second Part*, quoted from W. Kaufmann (ed.), *The Portable Nietzsche* (New York: Viking, 1968), 199–200.

28. *Thus Spoke Zarathustra*, 196, quoted in B. Ingraffia, *Postmodern Theory and Biblical Theology* (Cambridge: Cambridge Univ. Press, 1997), 96.

idol—the idol of self. And as the end of the twentieth century is in the process of discovering, this idol does not lead to life, but to death—cultural and individual.

As Christians, we may not bow to this idol in any of its manifestations. Our only worship is to be directed to the one and only true and full image of God, Jesus Christ, the one whom Paul called "the image of the invisible God" (Col. 1:15).[29] Ultimately, then, the second commandment, which was the heart of the three friends' resistance to the idolatry of Nebuchadnezzar, when read in the context of the canon as a whole, draws us to Jesus Christ, Word of God and Image of God. It is to this image alone that our worship is properly directed.

Resistance to the point of death. Daniel 3 teaches us that we must not only resist idolatry, but we must be prepared to resist it to the point of death. American Christians, in spite of all their complaints about the infringements on their religion, are rarely, if ever, confronted with that kind of decision. This is not true of Christians in many other parts of the twentieth-century world, where their faith and witness can lead to a prison term or a death penalty. Such Christian witness indicates to us that the courage of Shadrach, Meshach, and Abednego lives on.

But, of course, Shadrach, Meshach, and Abednego are not the only biblical role models for faithful resistance to powerful and oppressive human governments. We can think of Acts 24–26, when Paul bore witness before Felix and Agrippa, or 5:29, when Peter proclaimed before the high priest, "We must obey God rather than men!" They knew the force of Jesus' warning, "Do not be afraid of those who kill the body but cannot kill the soul. Rather, be afraid of the One who can destroy both soul and body in hell" (Matt. 10:28).[30]

Where does the Christian, starting with Peter and the apostles until today, find the moral and religious strength to make such a courageous stand? From Jesus Christ. Jesus himself was put on trial for his religious claim that he was the Messiah. Facing death himself, he refused to capitulate, dying on the cross (cf. Matt. 27:11–14).

But was Jesus at the heart of the hope of the three friends as they faced death in the furnace? It is difficult to say how specifically their hope focused on the coming Savior, the Messiah. They trusted in the saving power of God, but it is provocative to reflect on the way God chose to deliver the three from the fire. Calvin pointed out that if God wanted, he could have extinguished the

---

29. It is true we are created in the image of God, but we only reflect the glory of God in a derivative manner. For a further discussion, see D. Allender and T. Longman III, *Intimate Allies* (Wheaton, Ill.: Tyndale, 1995), 28–41.

30. I am indebted to Towner, *Daniel*, 51, for the discussion and Scripture texts quoted in this paragraph.

flames of the fire in order to save the three men. He saved them *in* the fire, not *from* the fire.[31] They were in the very jaws of death. Moreover, he could have saved them without further fanfare, simply having them walk out of the fire unscathed, but instead he chose to save them by the presence of a "fourth [who] looks like a son of the gods" (v. 25).

Was this "fourth" being Jesus, as many interpreters from the earliest Christian times have suggested? It is impossible to be dogmatic unless one insists that every incarnate appearance of God must be the second person of the Trinity. It is safer to say that what we have here is a reflection of Immanuel, "God with us." God dwelt with the three friends in the midst of the flames to preserve them from harm. In this sense, the Christian cannot help but see a prefiguration of Jesus Christ, who came to earth to dwell in a chaotic world and who even experienced death, not so that we might escape the experience of death but that we might have victory over it.

While this discussion might be an appropriate place to reflect further on the Christian hope of resurrection, we will reserve our comments until Daniel 12, which takes us even further in the book's theology of death.

---

31. Calvin, *Daniel I*, 143.

Daniel 4:1–37

KING NEBUCHADNEZZAR,

To the peoples, nations and men of every language, who live in all the world:

May you prosper greatly!

²It is my pleasure to tell you about the miraculous signs and wonders that the Most High God has performed for me.

³How great are his signs,
   how mighty his wonders!
His kingdom is an eternal kingdom;
   his dominion endures from generation to generation.

⁴I, Nebuchadnezzar, was at home in my palace, contented and prosperous. ⁵I had a dream that made me afraid. As I was lying in my bed, the images and visions that passed through my mind terrified me. ⁶So I commanded that all the wise men of Babylon be brought before me to interpret the dream for me. ⁷When the magicians, enchanters, astrologers and diviners came, I told them the dream, but they could not interpret it for me. ⁸Finally, Daniel came into my presence and I told him the dream. (He is called Belteshazzar, after the name of my god, and the spirit of the holy gods is in him.)

⁹I said, "Belteshazzar, chief of the magicians, I know that the spirit of the holy gods is in you, and no mystery is too difficult for you. Here is my dream; interpret it for me. ¹⁰These are the visions I saw while lying in my bed: I looked, and there before me stood a tree in the middle of the land. Its height was enormous. ¹¹The tree grew large and strong and its top touched the sky; it was visible to the ends of the earth. ¹²Its leaves were beautiful, its fruit abundant, and on it was food for all. Under it the beasts of the field found shelter, and the birds of the air lived in its branches; from it every creature was fed.

¹³"In the visions I saw while lying in my bed, I looked, and there before me was a messenger, a holy one, coming down from heaven. ¹⁴He called in a loud voice: 'Cut down the tree and trim off its branches; strip off its leaves and scatter its fruit. Let the animals flee from under it and the birds from its branches. ¹⁵But let the stump and its roots, bound with iron and bronze, remain in the ground, in the grass of the field.

Daniel 4:1–37

"'Let him be drenched with the dew of heaven, and let him live with the animals among the plants of the earth. ¹⁶Let his mind be changed from that of a man and let him be given the mind of an animal, till seven times pass by for him.

¹⁷ "'The decision is announced by messengers, the holy ones declare the verdict, so that the living may know that the Most High is sovereign over the kingdoms of men and gives them to anyone he wishes and sets over them the lowliest of men.'

¹⁸"This is the dream that I, King Nebuchadnezzar, had. Now, Belteshazzar, tell me what it means, for none of the wise men in my kingdom can interpret it for me. But you can, because the spirit of the holy gods is in you."

¹⁹Then Daniel (also called Belteshazzar) was greatly perplexed for a time, and his thoughts terrified him. So the king said, "Belteshazzar, do not let the dream or its meaning alarm you."

Belteshazzar answered, "My lord, if only the dream applied to your enemies and its meaning to your adversaries! ²⁰The tree you saw, which grew large and strong, with its top touching the sky, visible to the whole earth, ²¹with beautiful leaves and abundant fruit, providing food for all, giving shelter to the beasts of the field, and having nesting places in its branches for the birds of the air—²²you, O king, are that tree! You have become great and strong; your greatness has grown until it reaches the sky, and your dominion extends to distant parts of the earth.

²³"You, O king, saw a messenger, a holy one, coming down from heaven and saying, 'Cut down the tree and destroy it, but leave the stump, bound with iron and bronze, in the grass of the field, while its roots remain in the ground. Let him be drenched with the dew of heaven; let him live like the wild animals, until seven times pass by for him.'

²⁴"This is the interpretation, O king, and this is the decree the Most High has issued against my lord the king: ²⁵You will be driven away from people and will live with the wild animals; you will eat grass like cattle and be drenched with the dew of heaven. Seven times will pass by for you until you acknowledge that the Most High is sovereign over the kingdoms of men and gives them to anyone he wishes. ²⁶The command to leave the stump of the tree with its roots means that your kingdom will be restored to you when you acknowledge that Heaven rules. ²⁷Therefore, O king, be pleased to accept

Daniel 4:1–37

my advice: Renounce your sins by doing what is right, and your wickedness by being kind to the oppressed. It may be that then your prosperity will continue."

²⁸All this happened to King Nebuchadnezzar. ²⁹Twelve months later, as the king was walking on the roof of the royal palace of Babylon, ³⁰he said, "Is not this the great Babylon I have built as the royal residence, by my mighty power and for the glory of my majesty?"

³¹The words were still on his lips when a voice came from heaven, "This is what is decreed for you, King Nebuchadnezzar: Your royal authority has been taken from you. ³²You will be driven away from people and will live with the wild animals; you will eat grass like cattle. Seven times will pass by for you until you acknowledge that the Most High is sovereign over the kingdoms of men and gives them to anyone he wishes."

³³Immediately what had been said about Nebuchadnezzar was fulfilled. He was driven away from people and ate grass like cattle. His body was drenched with the dew of heaven until his hair grew like the feathers of an eagle and his nails like the claws of a bird.

³⁴At the end of that time, I, Nebuchadnezzar, raised my eyes toward heaven, and my sanity was restored. Then I praised the Most High; I honored and glorified him who lives forever.

> His dominion is an eternal dominion;
>   his kingdom endures from generation to generation.
> ³⁵All the peoples of the earth
>   are regarded as nothing.
> He does as he pleases
>   with the powers of heaven
>   and the peoples of the earth.
> No one can hold back his hand
>   or say to him: "What have you done?"

³⁶At the same time that my sanity was restored, my honor and splendor were returned to me for the glory of my kingdom. My advisers and nobles sought me out, and I was restored to my throne and became even greater than before. ³⁷Now I, Nebuchadnezzar, praise and exalt and glorify the King of heaven, because everything he does is right and all his ways are just. And those who walk in pride he is able to humble.

Daniel 4:1–37

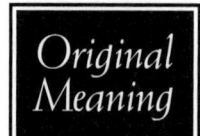 AS IN CHAPTER 2, a dream forms the center of the action in chapter 4. King Nebuchadnezzar is again the recipient of a dream he cannot interpret, and, for a second time, he calls on the services of Daniel. However, in the present account Nebuchadnezzar makes no threats, but summons Daniel immediately after the failure of his (apparently) native corps of wise men. Daniel again succeeds where the Babylonian diviners fail, proving indeed that the "spirit of the holy gods" (v. 18)[1] lives in him. However, this story does not focus or emphasize Daniel's divinely given skills as much as deals with the issue of overwhelming human pride.

As we will see in our survey of the chapter's contents, the dream properly warns Nebuchadnezzar of the dangers of his pride. This danger is extreme for Nebuchadnezzar, of course, because he is, after all, the king of Babylon, the most powerful political entity in the known world. He controls the life and death of countless human beings. He enjoys great wealth, prestige, and power. The dream and its consequences are a reminder that whatever he enjoys is at the pleasure of the true God, who, as the chapter is at pains to demonstrate, "is sovereign over the kingdoms of men and gives them to anyone he wishes" (v. 25).[2] Through the dream and its interpretation, he calls on Nebuchadnezzar to remember his subservience to a higher power, and through Nebuchadnezzar, the chapter reminds other powerful men and women of the same important truth. "Pride goes before destruction, a haughty spirit before a fall" (Prov. 16:18).

The chapter has a unique literary structure, indeed so unique that it has resulted in a discrepancy in the tradition of dividing the book into chapters. The English division is in keeping with the contours of the story and begins in verse 1 of chapter 4. Verse 1 in the English, however, is 3:31 in the Aramaic.[3] Apparently it was thought more typical to end rather than begin a story with a doxology.[4]

We should also mention the discussion about the role of Nebuchadnezzar in this chapter. In brief, the issue surrounds the fact that the story reports a period of seven years where he was unfit for royal duties, an event not

---

1. Grammatically, this expression is ambiguous and could be translated "the spirit of the (holy) God" with reference to Yahweh, but Nebuchadnezzar's use of such a phrase at this stage of the story would be strange. See B. Becking, "'A Divine Spirit Is in You': Notes on the Translation of the Phrase *ruah 'elahim* in Daniel 5,14 and Related Texts," in *The Book of Daniel in the Light of New Findings* (Leuven: University Press, 1993), 515–19.
2. N. W. Porteus, *Daniel: A Commentary* (OTL; Philadelphia: Westminster, 1965), 65, rightly argues the pivotal nature of verse 25 in the chapter.
3. Note that Dan. 2:4b–7:28 is written in Aramaic rather than in Hebrew.
4. See the discussion in Collins, *Daniel*, 221.

Daniel 4:1–37

mentioned in the extrabiblical texts. It is probably unwise to make much out of the silence of the extrabiblical texts, since the king's reign is not exhaustively documented and it is not the type of thing that Nebuchadnezzar may have wanted preserved for perpetuity in his royal inscriptions.

Nonetheless, attention has been drawn to a text discovered at Qumran called the Prayer of Nabonidus (4QPrNab), which some scholars have felt is the solution to the historical-literary conundrum.[5] The Prayer of Nabonidus is the story of an affliction of Nabonidus, the last king of Babylon and the father of Belshazzar (see Dan. 5 for more on them). In this fragmentary text Nabonidus was said to fall ill for seven years, at the end of which he was cured through the intervention of an unnamed Jewish diviner. Another extrabiblical text has also sometimes been claimed to be a "source" for Daniel 4—a text now preserved only in the writings of the church historian Eusebius.[6] It is a speech that Nebuchadnezzar gives on the roof of his palace, where he prophesies the coming of the one who will destroy Babylon (a pejorative reference to Cyrus) and wishes that that person might rather become like a beast in the field.

The surface similarities of the text, however, are overwhelmed by the differences, and in both cases it seems more reasonable to believe, if we follow a sixth-century B.C. dating of Daniel, that they were written not before but in the light of the story of Daniel 4.

This chapter has the form of a letter or written decree of Nebuchadnezzar himself. It is written predominantly in the first person, though verses 19–33 revert to the third person. The story is a tale of court contest in a subdued way, since it quietly shows Daniel succeeding where the Babylonian diviners fail. The structure is as follows—and we should especially note that Nebuchadnezzar's praise brackets the story, coming at the beginning and end of the account: (1) Nebuchadnezzar's decree to praise the Lord (4:1–3); (2) the dream report and the search for an interpreter (4:4–18); (3) the dream interpretation (4:19–27); (4) the fulfillment of the dream (4:28–33); (5) healing and concluding doxology (4:34–37).

Nebuchadnezzar's Decree to Praise the Lord (4:1–3)

THE LAST TWO chapters concluded with Nebuchadnezzar's praise of the Lord, but Daniel 4 departs from the pattern and begins (as well as ends) with Nebuchadnezzar's praise. One of the effects of this structure is to remove

---

5. A helpful discussion may be found in Collins, *Daniel*, 217–18. The Prayer of Nabonidus was first published in 1956 by J. T. Milik; cf. F. M. Cross, "Fragments of the Prayer of Nabonidus," *IEJ* 34 (1984): 260–64.

6. Eusebius refers to this as the book of Abydenus, "Concerning the Assyrians"; cf. Collins, *Daniel*, 218–19, who gives a translation of the text.

suspense concerning the nature of the outcome, but it does raise the reader's interest in discovering what leads to Nebuchadnezzar's joyful outburst. Another effect of the preface to the story, as Dana Fewell points out, is that "as an official proclamation, the piece has an air of reality, an atmosphere of authority."[7]

The outburst is more than spontaneous; it has the form of an official proclamation directed throughout the world. As a matter of fact, Nebuchadnezzar's kingdom stretched from what is today Egypt to western Iran and from modern Syria into Saudi Arabia, encompassing many different cultures and language groups.

The content of his praise is somewhat general, but it highlights God's sovereignty and the wonderful nature of his interaction with the world. The following story is the specification of the events behind the general praise.[8]

The Dream Report and the Search for an Interpreter (4:4–18)

NEBUCHADNEZZAR NOW BEARS witness to the great and supernatural experience that he underwent. He speaks in the first person, employing a form similar to neo-Babylonian royal inscriptions.[9] He begins by stating his prosperity and contentment. The chapter is not dated, but apparently comes at a time when the Babylonian kingdom experiences stability and success.

A dream, however, intrudes into the king's peaceful mind, tormenting him with doubt and fear. His first impulse is to call his professional wise men into his presence. Unlike his earlier dream he tells them the present dream's content, but they are still unable to offer a suitable interpretation. Their failure is a bit mystifying because Daniel's later interpretation is not all that surprising. Nonetheless, the wise men's failure causes the king to call Daniel.

On a psychological level, the modern reader might ask why he waited to call Daniel, considering his earlier success. The text does not give us the king's motives, but the delay does differentiate Daniel from those who used traditional dream interpretation techniques and emphasizes his superiority, who is wise only because of the gift Yahweh has given him.

That Nebuchadnezzar still really hasn't "gotten it" is indicated by the parenthetical comment at the end of verse 8. He refers to Daniel by his Babylonian name, which connects him to the king's native god. Moreover, he speaks of Daniel as the one in whom the "spirit of the holy gods" dwells. Being a polytheist, Nebuchadnezzar has the intellectual framework to subsume Yahweh into his already existing theology.

---

7. Fewell, *Circle of Sovereignty*, 89.

8. Porteous, *Daniel*, 67, points out that Nebuchadnezzar's language, particularly in v. 3, is similar to that found in the hymns of the Psalter (esp. Ps. 145:13).

9. Cf. Collins, *Daniel*, 22; Longman, *Fictional Akkadian Autobiography*.

The king then relates the contents of his dream. Its main feature is a huge tree in the middle of the land. This tree provides shade for all the animals, and its branches are the home of all the birds. The tree is the cosmic tree. It is planted in the "middle of the land," thus a kind of *axis mundi*. It is a symbol of fertility, growth, and prosperity. It is not only a symbol of life, but also a life-giver, providing sustenance and protection to the animals.

This use of the tree as an image of the life-giving nature of the king has previously been used in biblical tradition (cf. Ezek. 17:1–10; 31:3–14, both also in judgment contexts). The story also connects with the ancient Near East. There is little about a "sacred" or "cosmic" tree in the literature of Mesopotamia, but the tree occurs as a major motif in the iconography. As Parpola has pointed out, "the Tree represents the divine world order maintained by the king as the representative of the god Assur, embodied in the winged disk hovering above the tree."[10] He alerts us to the fact that sometimes the king takes the place of the tree in the iconography; "in such scenes the king is portrayed as the human personification of the Tree. Thus if the Tree symbolized the divine world order, then the king himself represented the realization of that order in man, in other words, a true image of God, the Perfect Man."[11] The implications for Daniel 4 are clear: Nebuchadnezzar's dream shows that he identifies himself with the cosmic tree; he is the keeper of the cosmos, the true image of God, the Perfect Man.

After the description of the tree, the king narrates the plot. It begins with the appearance of a "messenger" (an Aramaic word better translated "watchman" or "watcher," cf. NIV footnote). No doubt a supernatural being is meant (cf. the word's apposition with "holy one"), which reminds us of the frequent use of the word "watchers" for angels in intertestamental literature.[12]

The watcher barks orders for the dismantling of the cosmic tree. All that is to be left is the stump, and around the stump a bronze band is to be placed. The stump indicates that even though the tree is to be desolated, it is not to be killed. The roots are not touched. The band of iron and bronze that is placed around the stump is a mystery to interpreters. Perhaps it emphasizes the fact that the tree is not to be killed, since the band protects what is left. This interpretive approach would be strengthened if such a practice were known from the ancient Near East, but no such evidence is available. Others argue that the mention of the band is the first move from tree imagery to beast imagery. Indeed, the metaphors of the dream are a mixed lot, moving from

---

10. S. Parpola, "The Assyrian Tree of Life: Tracing the Origins of Jewish Monotheism and Greek Philosophy," *JNES* 52 (1993): 167.
11. Ibid., 167–68.
12. Though there it usually refers to evil or fallen angels, cf. the Book of the Watchers (I Enoch 1–36).

tree to beast; the tree becomes a beast wandering the earth for "seven times," usually understood to be years.[13]

The dream ends with the watcher's proclamation concerning the motive behind this desolation. It is clearly expressed in verse 17: "that the Most High is sovereign over the kingdoms of men and gives them to anyone he wishes and sets over them the lowliest of men."

With his account of the dream concluded, Nebuchadnezzar turns with confidence to Daniel in order to hear its interpretation.

The Dream Interpretation (4:19–27)

THE CHAPTER UP to this point has been a first-person testimony of the king. The narrative has the ring of a royal inscription, but now the first-person address is displaced by a third-person narrator, who describes the interpretation and the fulfillment of the dream.

Daniel hesitates to give the interpretation. He knows what it means, but its message is so horrifying that he takes no pleasure in relating it to Nebuchadnezzar. The dynamic between Daniel and the king is a remarkable one, considering that this is the king who destroyed Jerusalem, but God's prophet shows concern for the well-being of the king, not vindictiveness.

After receiving encouragement from the king, Daniel reveals the referent of the tree symbol. It is Nebuchadnezzar himself, whose person is the center of the Babylonian world empire, which provides protection and sustenance to the people who inhabit that empire's vast boundaries. Since Nebuchadnezzar is the tree, he is also the subject of the coming judgment. As the tree will be desolated, so he will be desolated. As the subject of the dream will be reduced to an animal-like state, so Nebuchadnezzar will be reduced from his humanity and become beast-like.

This is the message of judgment that confronts Nebuchadnezzar, but it is a conditional message. Daniel's advice is to avoid sin and be kind. In other words, he should not fall prey to the temptation to think himself a god. In spite of his greatness, he must retain his humility.

The Fulfillment of the Dream (4:28–33)

THE NARRATIVE DOES not let Daniel's hope live long. Verse 28 reports in a summarizing fashion, "All this happened to King Nebuchadnezzar." The next few verses report the details of the tragedy.

---

13. A helpful discussion may be found in P. Coxon, "The Great Tree of Daniel 4," in *A Word in Season*, J. D. Martin and P. R. Davies, eds. (Sheffield: JSOT, 1986), for the argument that the seven periods are symbolic rather than indicative of any specific time indicator (94), and for the assertion that the bands are of cultic significance (105).

Daniel 4:1–37

While the narrative gives an immediate report of Nebuchadnezzar's fall, we learn from verse 29 that a period of twelve months passed before the crucial moment. We are perhaps to understand that the dream and its interpretation frightened Nebuchadnezzar into a temporary compliance. Or perhaps he pretty much continued his sinful (v. 27) course, but God waited until this moment of monumental pride to exercise his judgment. We cannot be sure.

In any case, a year after the dream experience, Nebuchadnezzar was taking a walk on the roof of his palace in Babylon. It is not unusual that he was on the roof of his house, since roofs were flat in the ancient Near East and therefore provided living space. From this obviously high point, he got a good view of the city, and he marveled at its grandeur. As we learn from ancient texts and the results of archaeology, the Babylon of Nebuchadnezzar was grand indeed. According to Michael Roaf,

> Babylon contained two of the Seven Wonders of the Ancient World, the Hanging Gardens and the city walls. The location of the Hanging Gardens is in doubt but the walls have been traced. The outer wall stretched for more than 8 kilometers and, according to Herodotus, had enough space on top to enable a four-horse chariot to turn around.[14]

Nebuchadnezzar had much to do with the greatness of Babylon. From biblical and ancient Near Eastern records contemporary with his reign, we know he had great wealth and was an accomplished builder. He gave the orders and paid the bills. However, his power and accomplishments led to a pride that blinded him from broader realities. He lost sight of the fact that he could only do these things as God gave him the power and ability. His pride led him to make unthinkable claims, especially in the light of the vivid warning he received a year before: "Is not this the great Babylon *I* have built as the royal residence, by *my* mighty power and for the glory of *my* majesty?" (v. 30, italics added).

While God gave him time after his first warning, no time elapses ("the words were still on his lips," v. 31) before a heavenly voice decrees his doom. From being the most powerful man in the world, he is reduced to roaming the steppe like an animal. As Calvin points out, this description does not mean that he thought himself an animal.[15] His insanity[16] drives him to the

---

14. M. Roaf, *Cultural Atlas of Mesopotamia and the Ancient Near East* (New York: Facts on File, 1990), 192–93. Of course, Herodotus's report would be a century after Nebuchadnezzar, but the city's opulence was at its height under Nebuchadnezzar. Indeed, he built the Hanging Gardens for his Median queen since she was used to hilly forests, not the flat plain on which Babylon was built.

15. Calvin, *Daniel I*, 189–90.

16. Many scholars (cf. Young, *The Prophecy of Daniel*, 112; Baldwin, *Daniel*, 109) diagnose Nebuchadnezzar's illness as boathronpy or lycanthropy, where a human being thinks

Daniel 4:1–37

open spaces, where he acts like an animal, and his neglect of hygiene leads to an animal-like appearance. The appropriateness of the affliction is noted by Fewell, who states: "A man who thinks he is like a god must become a beast to learn that he is only a human being."[17]

Healing and Concluding Doxology (4:34–37)

WE GET LITTLE insight into Nebuchadnezzar's mental processes. But we are told that the divine prescription works. At the appointed time (the end of the "seven times," cf. v. 25) Nebuchadnezzar "raised [his] eyes toward heaven, and [his] sanity was restored" (v. 34). The action of looking toward heaven is obviously meant as an acknowledgment of God's ultimate superiority. Nebuchadnezzar now understands his place in the scheme of things. He may indeed be powerful relative to the rest of humanity, but he is far from the most powerful being in the universe. Even more important, he understands, at least momentarily, that whatever power he does enjoy is as a gift from God. If it is foolish to say to a human king "What are you doing?" (Eccl. 8:4), how much more foolish is it for a human king to say to the divine king, "What have you done?" (Dan. 4:35). He is the "King of heaven" (v. 37).

Thus, Nebuchadnezzar is restored to sanity and to his relative grandeur as great king of Babylon. The lesson is learned and the moral of the story is the last word: "Those who walk in pride he is able to humble" (v. 37).

Bridging Contexts

WHO IS IN control? As we turn our attention to the relevance of Daniel 4 today, we are tempted to pick up quickly on verse 37b. That God humbles the proud is a message as clearly relevant to today as it was at the time of Nebuchadnezzar. However, to move directly to this important moral lesson bypasses the overarching concern of the chapter, which is that God protects his faithful people in spite of the odds. The purpose of the story is to encourage their confidence in the light of their helplessness before a seemingly all-powerful human ruler.

---

himself or herself as an ox, dog, or wolf. According to Baldwin, it is rarely seen today because the mentally ill are less likely to be allowed to roam the countryside.

John Walton in a personal communication has drawn my attention to the fact that the description of Nebuchadnezzar's "symptoms" is not very different from common Mesopotamian descriptions of those who are outside of civilization. Enkidu in the Gilgamesh Epic, Ahiqar in exile, the citizens of destroyed cities in city laments, Lugalbanda when abandoned by his companions—all are described in beast-like terms. Nebuchadnezzar considered himself the founder of Babylonian civilization, and he was driven out of it.

17. Fewell, *Circle of Sovereignty*, 101.

After all, while most people are not bound in chains and forced into slave labor, Nebuchadnezzar controls their fate, at least seemingly. This account of his dream and madness rips away the facade and shows the reality of who is in control—not Nebuchadnezzar, but God, who calls the shots. Again, fitting in with a major theme of the book, this chapter teaches that God is sovereign (see Introduction). He uses Nebuchadnezzar as he uses all human powers, even those hostile to his name, for his own purposes. Nebuchadnezzar is Yahweh's tool. The king wins victories only when God gives them to him (Dan. 1:1–2); he understands his dreams only when God reveals their meaning through Daniel, his servant (chs. 2 and 4). Nebuchadnezzar cannot harm a hair on the head of one of God's people (ch. 3). The book of Daniel reveals that the Babylonian king is powerless in his own right.

Nebuchadnezzar himself has a hard time seeing it this way. After all, he leads the army, and his treasuries pay for the tremendous building efforts that take place during his reign. As he looks at other men and women around him, he obviously is the most powerful. Not only can he make and break other individuals, but whole nations bow before him. He sits on his throne and people cower because they know he has the power of life and death over them.

The book of Daniel, however, does not portray Nebuchadnezzar as an unsympathetic figure. Daniel appears to care about him and seems honestly chagrined when a difficult fate is decreed for him. As readers, we feel the same ambivalence. The doxological introduction to this chapter in particular makes us feel that Nebuchadnezzar is on our side again, and throughout the chapter there is no harmful move against God's people. Indeed, after another failure of his native band of dream interpreters to come through for him, he quickly sends for Daniel, whom he compliments from his pagan perspective as having the "spirit of the holy gods" in him.

However, even if we, along with Daniel, want Nebuchadnezzar to avoid his terrifying fate, the text does not allow our hopes to blossom. Although chronologically there is a gap of twelve months between the warning (v. 27) and the fulfillment of its threat, narratively there is no time, for the very next verse (v. 28) quickly tells us "all this happened to King Nebuchadnezzar."

The danger of pride. When we turn to the warning and its consequences, the account becomes a story of the danger of pride. Pride, in the negative sense, is a conception of one's self-worth that exceeds the bounds of propriety. In the Bible, as we will see in the next section, those bounds are clearly associated with seeing our every achievement, status, and possession as gifts from God.

In our present story, Nebuchadnezzar's vision of his accomplishments focuses solely on himself. As he looks out on the great city of Babylon, he

Daniel 4:1–37

sees the work of his own hands alone. Thus, God gives him a traumatic lesson to teach him the source of all his abilities and capacities by removing even his reason. Let Nebuchadnezzar glory in himself now as he roams the wilderness with the other animals, ripping grass from the ground with his teeth.

His reason, his exalted position, his wealth, and his power are ultimately returned to him, but only after he acknowledges God's ultimate sovereignty. His restoration begins with the simple gesture of looking to heaven—a cry for help and the recognition of a superior power. It culminates in the praises delivered at the beginning and end of the chapter. God took this prideful, self-centered man and humbled him. Once he acknowledged that "all the peoples of the earth [including himself] are regarded as nothing" (v. 35), God makes him something again.

Is this a lesson for all of us? Again we are faced with the question of the relevance for us of a historical account that could have a unique, time-bound significance. After all, we are speaking of someone who played a special role in the history of God's redemption. In one sense, none of us is like Nebuchadnezzar. But we have already seen that the historical narratives, particularly those in the first part of Daniel, have a broader purpose than simply historical remembrance. Earlier we quoted 1 Corinthians 10:6 to that effect; here let me cite Romans 15:4: "For everything that was written in the past was written to teach us, so that through endurance and the encouragement of the Scriptures we might have hope."

Nonetheless, we must also reckon with another source of discontinuity. Nebuchadnezzar was no ordinary human in another sense; he was king of the most powerful political entity in the world. In a sense, his power far exceeded that of any individual living today. The president of the United States has been called the most powerful individual alive, but unlike Nebuchadnezzar he is a temporary and elected official with restricted powers. On a human level, Nebuchadnezzar had none of those restrictions.

But even though Nebuchadnezzar may be an extreme example, pride potentially resides in all human beings. But does all pride get the same dramatic treatment as Nebuchadnezzar, or was the psalmist right when he said in Psalm 73:3–12:

> I envied the arrogant
> > when I saw the prosperity of the wicked.
> They have no struggles;
> > their bodies are healthy and strong.
> They are free from the burdens common to man;
> > they are not plagued by human ills.
> Therefore pride is their necklace;
> > they clothe themselves with violence.

Daniel 4:1–37

> From their callous hearts comes iniquity;
> > the evil conceits of their minds know no limits.
> They scoff, and speak with malice;
> > in their arrogance they threaten oppression.
> Their mouths lay claim to heaven,
> > and their tongues take possession of the earth.
> Therefore their people turn to them
> > and drink up waters in abundance.
> They say, "How can God know?
> > Does the Most High have knowledge?"
> This is what the wicked are like—
> > always carefree, they increase in wealth.

This we will explore in the next section.

The example of Jesus. But before we turn to Contemporary Significance, we need to introduce one more perspective on the passage that will also be more fully developed in the next section. We have already recognized that Jesus himself indicates that there are many passages of the Old Testament that pertain to his coming (Luke 24:25–27, 44–49).[18] As Augustine said so well, "the New Testament in the Old is concealed, the Old is in the New revealed."

Even without Jesus' invitation and Augustine's catchy motto, how could those of us who read the New Testament fail to think of Christ in the light of Nebuchadnezzar's pride and shame? After all, Nebuchadnezzar was a mere man who glorified himself as if he were a god. Paul sings the following praise concerning Jesus (Phil. 2:6–11):

> Who, being in the very nature God,
> > did not consider equality with God something to be grasped,
> but made himself nothing,
> > taking the very nature of a servant,
> > being made in human likeness.
> And being found in appearance as a man,
> > he humbled himself
> > and became obedient to death—even death on a cross!
> Therefore God exalted him to the highest place
> > and gave him the name that is above every name,
> that at the name of Jesus every knee should bow,
> > in heaven and on earth and under the earth,
> and every tongue confess that Jesus Christ is Lord,
> > to the glory of God the Father.

---

18. See above, pp. 26–27.

Daniel 4:1–37

What can we make of the truly glorious one, God himself, who voluntarily humbles himself to take on the flesh of humankind in the light of a mortal who takes on divine airs?

TAKING COMFORT IN **knowing God is in control.** As mentioned above, the overarching message of this chapter repeats an already common theme in the book. No matter what the odds, God is in control. Fate, or even intentional evil, may seem to have the upper hand against us, but the reality is that God is in control. In the present chapter, we observe this as God effortlessly reduces the most powerful man in the most sophisticated city in the world to a beast-like state in the wilderness.

God's people are called to take comfort in this truth, whether they lived at the time of Nebuchadnezzar, at a later time of persecution, or even today. Today Christians in certain parts of the world feel the chain of persecution and oppression because of their faith. Just within the past few months of the time of the writing of this commentary, the media has reported incredible instances of Christian persecution at the hands of government authorities. A recent issue of *Christianity Today* contains reports of execution by beheading of two Filipino Christians in Saudi Arabia, of government officials who interfere with the spreading of the gospel in Serbia, and of attacks on the house churches of China.[19]

We as Christians in America and England, though chafing at occasional restrictions of the exercise of our religion, do not really experience true religious persecution at the hands of the state. Nonetheless, all Christians, including those of us who have unprecedented freedom to exercise religion, understand the feeling of facing an obstacle that seems insuperable. We all encounter an enemy over which we seem to have no power, whether that foe is a crippling disability, a psychological disorder, a terminal disease, an abusive spouse, or the like. In this sense, the message of Daniel is for all of us, not just the politically oppressed. No one escapes the frustrations and chaos of a world suffering from the effects of the Fall (Rom. 8:18–27).

God humbles the proud. But is the message of Daniel 4 true? Is God able to humble those who walk in pride (v. 37)? Is God able to defeat those who harm us and overcome the obstacles to life and faith that threaten to engulf us? Or is Daniel 4 just a thrilling story with little connection to reality?

(1) We have seen above that the composer of Psalm 73 had his doubts. It seemed to him that the arrogant had no problems. The Teacher in the

---

19. *Christianity Today* 41 (September 1, 1997): 70–71, 86–87.

book of Ecclesiastes struggled as well. His faith taught that the godly would prosper and arrogant and evil people would languish, but that is not what he saw in the world. Not only that, but he saw death as the ultimate victor over life, rendering all the good deeds and achievements of life meaningless. Even in death, the wicked were honored: "There is a time when a man lords it over others to his own hurt. Then too, I saw the wicked buried—those who used to come and go from the holy place and receive praise in the city where they did this" (Eccl. 8:9b–10).

Isn't this also our experience? Who are the famous, the powerful, the wealthy, the tanned and smiling faces we see out there? Are they the faces of the saints? Occasionally, but more often than not they are the faces of those who sneer at religion and serve to undermine it.

But if we look more closely at the Bible, we do see that God humbles the proud. It began in the Garden of Eden. Adam and Eve enjoyed a close and intimate relationship with their Creator in the Garden. As the well-known story continues, however, their trust in God diminished, and they came, at the prompting of the serpent, to trust their own judgment. In a word, pride instigated them to break the one commandment that their friend and God told them to observe. As a result, their idyllic life in the Garden was transformed to a life of hard work and drudgery "under the sun." They exchanged their glory for shame and ended up being humbled.[20]

Another story with notable connections to Daniel 4 is the account of the Tower of Babel in Genesis 11. Again, pride led to rebellion, even an assault on heaven itself. Human beings presumed to be godlike by building a staircase to heaven. God, however, intervened, reducing the arrogant to humility and scattering them over the face of the earth.

The humble faithful can find comfort in these accounts of the reversal of pride into shame. Indeed, the psalmist of Psalm 73 finally came to his senses (vv. 17–22). He was like a "brute beast" before God until he "entered the sanctuary of God" and "understood [the] final destiny" of the arrogant and prosperous people, who ignored or attacked God. In other words, his vision was expanded beyond immediate circumstances. While the proud ultimately will be "swept away by terrors" (v. 19), he proclaims as one of the oppressed faithful (vv. 23–24):

> Yet I am always with you;
> > you hold me by my right hand.
> You guide me with your counsel,
> > and afterward you will take me into glory.

---

20. See P. Coxon, "Another Look at Nebuchadnezzar's Madness," in *The Book of Daniel in the Light of New Findings*, ed. A. S. van der Woude (Leuven: University Press, 1993), 211–21.

Certainly, I would agree that the passage cannot be read as a certain affirmation of life after death. However, I think it is wrong to attribute to this psalmist, struggling with the fact that proper rewards and punishments do not seem to be handed out in this life, a naive idea that "it's all going to turn out all right after all in this life."

And apart from Old Testament anticipation, the New Testament makes it even more clear that God is in control. He has won a victory over an enemy even more powerful than Nebuchadnezzar, over a kingdom even more deadly and oppressive than the Babylonian empire. He has defeated Satan and death itself. The book of Revelation, often likening the powers of evil to Babylon of old, shows God's ultimate victory on behalf of his faithful people.[21]

(2) But before we pass on, we cannot neglect a warning. While Daniel 4 demonstrates God's ability to humble the arrogant leader of a foreign oppressive empire—an enemy "out there," so to speak—we must be careful concerning the pride that can infect our own lives. Christians are not immune from a pride that removes our eyes from God and places them squarely on ourselves. Indeed, it is precisely in situations like ours in the West, where we do not face active persecution, that this danger is most obvious.

After all, Christians have succeeded in business, in sports, in media, and in religion. We run large companies, score touchdowns in the NFL, write popular books, and pastor megachurches. The danger is there as we watch the thousands (or even the tens of thousands) of people who flock into our church to feel confident about the attractiveness of our preaching. The danger is there to feel satisfaction in the number of books we have sold or awards we have won. We have the same tendencies that Adam had as he walked intimately with God, but then trusted his own judgment more than God.

In other words, the message that God humbles the proud is not only a comfort; it is a warning to us all. With the psalmist (and unlike Nebuchadnezzar) we must remember Psalm 127:1:

> Unless the LORD builds the house,
>   its builders labor in vain.
> Unless the LORD watches over the city,
>   the watchmen stand guard in vain.

---

21. We will reserve further discussion of this topic until the later chapters of Daniel, as the book's focus turns from the stories centered in foreign courts to an account of Daniel's vision of the future. G. K. Beale's point that Christ's title in Rev. 17:14 has its origin in Daniel 4:37 is relevant here. He argues that "by the application of this title to Christ, the author may view God's sovereign humbling of the King of Babylon in Dan 4 as a typological prophecy of Christ's sovereign defeat of the end-time foe who is closely associated with eschatological Babylon" (see "The Origin of the Title 'King of Kings and Lord of Lords' in Revelation 17.14," *NTS* 31 (1985): 620.

Daniel 4:1–37

With Paul, rather than praising ourselves for our accomplishments, we must remember to boast only in the Lord (1 Cor. 1:29, 31; 2 Cor. 10:17).

Redemptive shame. This message is an important one to remember in our present day and age, where self-esteem is in and guilt and shame are out. Many people think that shame is inherently evil and that we must foster a strong sense of self-worth in ourselves and in others.

Don't get me wrong. There is such a thing as a false sense of shame. Indeed, we must help people recognize when their shame is based on an incorrect perception or a false standard of success.[22] But there is also a true and redemptive sense of shame that we should not hide under the carpet. A true shame is a shame engendered as a result of our rebellion and sin before God. It is when our sin is exposed before God and, at times, before other people, that our embarrassment can propel us into the arms of God.

This redemptive shame is the shame experienced by Nebuchadnezzar. His overweening pride was rightfully exposed, and he was shown to be a brute beast on his own power; even his sanity was a gift from God. His humiliating experience compelled him to look at God again, and he was restored to his former dignity.

Again, several psalms illustrate this dynamic. Psalm 30 embeds the story of someone whom God blessed so that he prospered greatly. However, he forgot that his success was a gift and began to focus his eyes on himself. At that point, God turned his back on the psalmist and let him feel the shame of powerlessness (Ps. 30:6–7):

> When I felt secure, I said,
> "I will never be shaken."
> O LORD, when you favored me,
> you made my mountain stand firm;
> but when you hid your face,
> I was dismayed.

This psalm, however, is not a lament; it is a psalm of thanksgiving. The shame that the author experienced caused him to flee to God again. The result is clear: "You turned my wailing into dancing; you removed my sackcloth and clothed me with joy" (v. 11).

Our God is a God who turns shame into rejoicing. But he does not do this by some sort of magical fiat. The gospel story is the story of God himself experiencing shame on our behalf. He subjected himself to the humiliation of the cross. Christ felt shame, but he underwent the experience in order to

---

22. For a helpful examination of false shame, see L. B. Smedes, *Shame and Grace: Healing the Shame We Don't Deserve* (San Francisco: HarperSanFrancisco, 1993).

free us from shame and invite us to the glory of the resurrection. "Let us fix our eyes on Jesus, the author and perfecter of our faith, who for the joy set before him endured the cross, scorning its shame, and sat down at the right hand of the throne of God" (Heb. 12:2).

Jesus endured the shame of the cross because of joy—joy in glorifying his Father, and joy in redeeming his brothers and sisters (see Heb. 12:11–12). We are invited to bear his disgrace and offer ourselves as a sacrifice of praise to God's glory and goodness.[23]

---

23. The quote from Heb. 12:2 and the concluding paragraph are taken from D. B. Allender and T. Longman III, *Cry of the Soul* (Colorado Springs: NavPress, 1993), 209; see chapters 14 and 15 for a more extensive discussion of the destructive power and redeeming possibilities of shame.

Daniel 5:1-31

KING BELSHAZZAR GAVE a great banquet for a thousand of his nobles and drank wine with them. ²While Belshazzar was drinking his wine, he gave orders to bring in the gold and silver goblets that Nebuchadnezzar his father had taken from the temple in Jerusalem, so that the king and his nobles, his wives and his concubines might drink from them. ³So they brought in the gold goblets that had been taken from the temple of God in Jerusalem, and the king and his nobles, his wives and his concubines drank from them. ⁴As they drank the wine, they praised the gods of gold and silver, of bronze, iron, wood and stone.

⁵Suddenly the fingers of a human hand appeared and wrote on the plaster of the wall, near the lampstand in the royal palace. The king watched the hand as it wrote. ⁶His face turned pale and he was so frightened that his knees knocked together and his legs gave way.

⁷The king called out for the enchanters, astrologers and diviners to be brought and said to these wise men of Babylon, "Whoever reads this writing and tells me what it means will be clothed in purple and have a gold chain placed around his neck, and he will be made the third highest ruler in the kingdom."

⁸Then all the king's wise men came in, but they could not read the writing or tell the king what it meant. ⁹So King Belshazzar became even more terrified and his face grew more pale. His nobles were baffled.

¹⁰The queen, hearing the voices of the king and his nobles, came into the banquet hall. "O king, live forever!" she said. "Don't be alarmed! Don't look so pale! ¹¹There is a man in your kingdom who has the spirit of the holy gods in him. In the time of your father he was found to have insight and intelligence and wisdom like that of the gods. King Nebuchadnezzar your father—your father the king, I say—appointed him chief of the magicians, enchanters, astrologers and diviners. ¹²This man Daniel, whom the king called Belteshazzar, was found to have a keen mind and knowledge and understanding, and also the ability to interpret dreams, explain riddles and solve difficult problems. Call for Daniel, and he will tell you what the writing means."

Daniel 5:1—31

¹³So Daniel was brought before the king, and the king said to him, "Are you Daniel, one of the exiles my father the king brought from Judah? ¹⁴I have heard that the spirit of the gods is in you and that you have insight, intelligence and outstanding wisdom. ¹⁵The wise men and enchanters were brought before me to read this writing and tell me what it means, but they could not explain it. ¹⁶Now I have heard that you are able to give interpretations and to solve difficult problems. If you can read this writing and tell me what it means, you will be clothed in purple and have a gold chain placed around your neck, and you will be made the third highest ruler in the kingdom."

¹⁷Then Daniel answered the king, "You may keep your gifts for yourself and give your rewards to someone else. Nevertheless, I will read the writing for the king and tell him what it means.

¹⁸"O king, the Most High God gave your father Nebuchadnezzar sovereignty and greatness and glory and splendor. ¹⁹Because of the high position he gave him, all the peoples and nations and men of every language dreaded and feared him. Those the king wanted to put to death, he put to death; those he wanted to spare, he spared; those he wanted to promote, he promoted; and those he wanted to humble, he humbled. ²⁰But when his heart became arrogant and hardened with pride, he was deposed from his royal throne and stripped of his glory. ²¹He was driven away from people and given the mind of an animal; he lived with the wild donkeys and ate grass like cattle; and his body was drenched with the dew of heaven, until he acknowledged that the Most High God is sovereign over the kingdoms of men and sets over them anyone he wishes.

²²"But you his son, O Belshazzar, have not humbled yourself, though you knew all this. ²³Instead, you have set yourself up against the Lord of heaven. You had the goblets from his temple brought to you, and you and your nobles, your wives and your concubines drank wine from them. You praised the gods of silver and gold, of bronze, iron, wood and stone, which cannot see or hear or understand. But you did not honor the God who holds in his hand your life and all your ways. ²⁴Therefore he sent the hand that wrote the inscription.

²⁵"This is the inscription that was written:

MENE, MENE, TEKEL, PARSIN

Daniel 5:1–31

²⁶"This is what these words mean:

> Mene: God has numbered the days of your reign and brought it to an end.
> ²⁷ Tekel: You have been weighed on the scales and found wanting.
> ²⁸ Peres: Your kingdom is divided and given to the Medes and Persians."

²⁹Then at Belshazzar's command, Daniel was clothed in purple, a gold chain was placed around his neck, and he was proclaimed the third highest ruler in the kingdom.

³⁰That very night Belshazzar, king of the Babylonians, was slain, ³¹and Darius the Mede took over the kingdom, at the age of sixty-two.

AS WE READ Daniel 5, we begin to get a sense of *déjà vu*. Though many of the faces are different, the genre, the plot, the sins, the props, and the themes of this chapter echo from earlier ones. To begin a partial list of similarities, we once again have a court narrative. Daniel 5 gives us an account of Daniel the wise man and prophet in the court of a foreign king. Further, as in Daniel 1, 2, and 4 we witness a court contest (as opposed to a court conflict, as in chs. 3 and 6). Unlike Daniel 2, however, the focus is not on the conflict between the Babylonian wise men and Daniel, though this is an important element of the story.

As in chapters 2 and 4, Daniel can interpret an enigmatic dream or vision where the native Babylonian wisdom teachers fail. Like Daniel 4, the king demonstrates incredible arrogance and is put in his place by God. Furthermore, the account of the conquest of Jerusalem in chapter 1 paid special attention to the theft of the temple vessels (1:2), and these play an important role in the present chapter.

Dana Fewell argues for a connection between the setting of Daniel 3 and that of chapter 5. In both, the king (Nebuchadnezzar in ch. 3 and Belshazzar, "his son," in ch. 5) convenes the important people of his empire. In chapter 3, the assembly is for the dedication of a statue, while here it is for a banquet. Fewell argues, though the text is not explicit on the point, that both events were public displays of loyalty toward the king. Perhaps she is correct, but the reticence of the text will keep us from developing this theme at length.[1]

---

1. See her discussion in Fewell, *Circle of Sovereignty*, 114–16, 138–39.

Daniel 5:1—31

Nonetheless, as we proceed with our section-by-section interpretation of this chapter, we will also notice new emphases. Most notably, we observe a different attitude expressed by Daniel toward the foreign king. Prior to this moment, Daniel had been favorably disposed toward the king. Though responsible for the downfall of the Judean people, Daniel cared for Nebuchadnezzar and did not rejoice in his downfall. The king had shown himself someone quick to learn from his mistakes. Here, however, Daniel has little time or concern for Belshazzar. He seems only too happy to tell him of his dire fate. We will be exploring this matter further.

Because of the similarity between Daniel 4 and 5, we are not surprised that the theme of the chapters may be formulated in a similar way. Daniel 4 focused on Nebuchadnezzar's pride, Daniel 5 on Belshazzar's. The latter's pride will be expressed in the context of idolatry in a way that Nebuchadnezzar's was not (though see comments on ch. 3). The major difference between chapters 4 and 5 is in the response of the king. In Daniel 4, Nebuchadnezzar ultimately repents of his arrogance and is restored to his former position. In Daniel 5, Belshazzar does not repent and is destroyed.

Thus, the theme of Daniel 5 fits into the theme of the whole book: *In spite of present appearances, God is in control.* This theme is important in the context of the oppression of God's people at the hands of arrogant pagan rulers like Nebuchadnezzar and Belshazzar. In the case of the former, God shows how he can overcome the pride of a powerful ruler by humbling him into repentance. In the case of the latter, God shows what he does with one who remains unrepentant. In either case, God shows himself to be more powerful than these hostile yet powerful kings, thus again giving comfort to his faithful, suffering people.

The main character of Daniel 5 is Belshazzar, a king whom we have not yet met and whose presence in the narrative raises interesting and difficult historical questions. The transition from Daniel 4 to 5 is an abrupt one, and Belshazzar is thrust on the stage with no indication of the passage of time or the death of Nebuchadnezzar. This information is unnecessary for the purposes of the narrative, but it does raise questions in our mind, particularly since the rather full extrabiblical accounts of the lineage of neo-Babylonian kings make no mention of a king called Belshazzar. After the death of Nebuchadnezzar in 562 B.C., he was succeeded by his son Amel-Marduk (the Evil-Merodach of 2 Kings 25:27) for a short period of time (562–560 B.C.). He was executed, probably at the behest of his successor, Neriglissar, who ruled only a few years himself (560–556 B.C.). Neriglissar was succeeded by his son Labashi-Marduk, who reigned for only a few months before he was executed by the party that brought Nabonidus to the throne. Nabonidus is recorded as the last king of the Babylonians, since he ruled until the time Cyrus entered Babylon and brought his kingdom to an end (539 B.C.).

Daniel 5:1–31

So what about Belshazzar? Until recently Belshazzar was thought to be one of those errors in the Bible's understanding of history that led many to doubt its accuracy. However, after the discovery and decipherment of cuneiform tablets began in the nineteenth century, we began to learn more and more about the period in question. As a result, Belshazzar emerged from the shadows as a definite historical character. Today we have abundant textual witness to the fact that he was the son of Nabonidus. More than that, Belshazzar was coregent and actually in charge of Babylon during his father's ten-year absence from the capital city, thus explaining the reference to him as king.[2]

The story of Nabonidus's absence from Babylon is an intriguing one, but we will only give the mere outline of the story.[3] In short, Nabonidus was a devotee of the moon god Sin, the chief god of his ancestral homeland Haran. While not a monotheist, he was interested in promoting the interests of Sin, which apparently angered the powerful Marduk priesthood. Evidence exists that his son, Belshazzar, did not share his devotion to Sin and may even have led a party that, while not forcing Nabonidus to abdicate, did result in his abandonment of the capital to take up residence at a site called Teima, located at an oasis in what is today Saudi Arabia.

But much of the story is clouded in obscurity, and other motivations may have been important for the move. Teima was the location of an important trade route and Nabonidus was protecting this trade route. It seems likely, however, that the religious tensions played an important role in his decision.

This information explains, at least in broad terms, the presence of Belshazzar as ruler in Babylon even though he is not listed as one of the kings of Babylon. While not all the questions have been answered, we have moved a long way from the days when Belshazzar was considered a figment of a later writer's imagination. We should remember this when we encounter similar problems, and indeed we will as early as the end of our chapter and the next as we meet a new figure, Darius the Mede.

Daniel 5 may be outlined as follows: (1) the profanation of the holy vessels (5:1–4); (2) the enigmatic writing on the wall (5:5–12); (3) Daniel's interpretation of the inscription (5:13–28); (4) reward and punishment (5:29–31).

---

2. Though doubt is still entertained by some concerning the way Belshazzar is described in Dan. 5, cf. J. J. Collins, *Daniel With an Introduction to Apocalyptic Literature* (Grand Rapids: Eerdmans, 1984), 68.

3. For more on the story as well as the actual documentation concerning Belshazzar's role, see the excellent book by P.-A. Beaulieu, *The Reign of Nabonidus, King of Babylon 556–539 B.C.* (New Haven, Conn.: Yale Univ. Press, 1989). An earlier helpful treatment from an apologetic point of view is M. J. Gruenthaner, "The Last King of Babylon," *CBQ* 11 (1949): 406–25. For a more popular treatment, see A. Millard, "Daniel and Belshazzar in History," *BAR* 11 (1985): 73–78.

Daniel 5:1–31

The Profanation of the Holy Vessels (5:1–4)

KING BELSHAZZAR MAKES a sudden and unanticipated appearance in the narrative. He is not introduced; he springs into the action. No one today doubts that the last king of Babylon had a son named Belshazzar, who ruled as coregent during the last days of the empire. Skepticism remains,[4] however, on some of the details, most notably the narrative's description of Nebuchadnezzar as his "father" (v. 2). Indeed, though not impossible, it is unlikely that Belshazzar was the son of Nebuchadnezzar in the narrow, biological sense. Historical records indicate that Nabonidus, himself not a biological descendant of Nebuchadnezzar, was Belshazzar's father. It is more likely that "father" is used here in the sense of "predecessor."[5]

In the story itself, we learn little about Belshazzar from straightforward description; his character is revealed through his actions and speeches. He throws a huge banquet for one thousand of his nobles. The description of this boisterous party reminds us of the opening of the book of Esther, where Xerxes' banquet provided the setting for the first story of that book. That banquet, according to Karen Jobes[6] and others, was intended to unite the leaders of the empire on the eve of Xerxes' attempted conquest of Greece. The broader textual and historical setting of Daniel 5 suggests that a similar political-military purpose was at work in Belshazzar's mind.

In a word, the Persians are knocking at the door of the Babylonian empire. Indeed, as the end of the story indicates, they will take the city of Babylon the very next day. Extrabiblical sources, both cuneiform and Greek (Herodotus and Xenophon), give us more information about the events leading up to the fall of Babylon on October 12, 539 B.C.[7]

The final victory may have been a surprise attack on Babylon. Indeed, Herodotus and Xenophon indicate that the final raid on Babylon took place during a nighttime banquet. But even if the final raid was sudden, it could not have been unanticipated. The Babylonian Chronicle indicates that just a couple of days earlier, Cyrus the Persian had defeated Nabonidus and the Babylonian army near Sippar (approximately fifty miles from Babylon). Nabonidus had fled the scene, though not to the capital.

Belshazzar must have known that an attack would come sooner or later. It was in this context that the banquet described in our chapter took place. Was it to rally and encourage the leaders? To give them a diversion in the face of the onslaught? To feast today for tomorrow we die? Perhaps a bit of all

---

4. See for instance, Collins, *Daniel With an Introduction to Apocalyptic Literature*, 68.
5. For a comprehensive discussion of his issue, consult Miller, *Daniel*, 149–50.
6. See K. Jobes, *Esther* (Grand Rapids: Zondervan, forthcoming).
7. Goldingay, *Daniel*, 106–7.

three, but we are safe to assume that tension permeated the air in the Babylonian capital at this time.

Wine flowed abundantly at the banquet. The king and his nobles drank deeply together. The text does not emphasize the drinking, however, to provide a moral lesson on the dangers of thinking under the influence of alcohol. No, the focus shifts to the holy goblets that Nebuchadnezzar had removed from the temple. These precious temple vessels are about to be profaned by being pressed into common use. We do not know much about how they were used in the rituals of the temple, but we do know that they were not intended for a raucous party. Belshazzar's impiety portends dire consequences.

We cannot be certain what was going on in Belshazzar's mind at this time. But surely he did not just run out of his everyday goblets and called for the spares. He surely had a particular propaganda purpose in mind. But what? He may have been making claims to power by comparing himself to his "father" Nebuchadnezzar.[8] He trifles with Nebuchadnezzar's war booty, a booty that Nebuchadnezzar himself apparently thought too precious actually to use.[9] Perhaps in the midst of the present crisis Belshazzar is claiming more power than Nebuchadnezzar, a boast vain enough in itself.

But the challenge Belshazzar presents goes even further in his mind. Perhaps the challenge is leveled against Yahweh himself. Miller points out that Daniel had predicted the Persian victory over Babylonia during Belshazzar's reign (8:1–4, 15–20), and already by the time of Isaiah God's prophets were indicating such an end to the one-time oppressors (Isa. 44:28; 45:1); but how likely is it that Belshazzar is familiar with Isaiah's prophecy?[10] While some scholars argue that Belshazzar probably offended many foreign religious cults that night, our text indicates that Yahweh is the sole focus. In the final analysis, it does not matter what was going on in Belshazzar's mind; his very act is like spitting in the eye of God.

But Belshazzar goes even further in his sacrilege. He is not only committing blasphemy, he combines it with idolatry. Here is where his profanation surpasses that of Nebuchadnezzar. He uses God's holy goblets to toast the lifeless idols of his own religion. He spits in God's eye, as it were, and then he goes over to a statue that he himself has created (v. 4) and expects that lifeless hunk to protect him from what is to come.

The manner in which the narrative describes Belshazzar's affirmation of idolatry shows how ridiculous it is. Belshazzar's gods are of the same material

---

8. So Fewell, *Circle of Sovereignty*, 124.
9. Though by having them removed from the temple and allowing nonpriestly hands touch them, he was guilty of profaning them himself.
10. Miller, *Daniel*, 154, makes this point and believes it is possible.

Daniel 5:1–31

as the goblets from Yahweh's temple. The latter are important, holy, and precious, but they are not God himself. Those objects made out of precious metals are not objects of worship, but Belshazzar's perverted religion puts their material cousins at the heart of his confidence and hope for the future.

The Enigmatic Writing on the Wall (5:5–12)

THE ACTION OF this chapter moves quickly and with sudden surprises. Just as Belshazzar has appeared without introduction, so a hand suddenly appears without explanation. Of course, a disembodied hand writing a message on the wall of the palace needs no explanation to recognize a supernatural occurrence.

This hand is surely the hand of God. The faithful reader of the past and present has no doubts who is behind the writing, though to be sure, Belshazzar has no clue. As a polytheist, he could have seen the hand as controlled by any of a number of different divinities. Immediately, however, he suspects that the enigmatic writing has a message that intends calamity toward him. His reaction is shock and utter fright. He is in extreme distress, perhaps even implying by the last clause that he has lost control of his most basic bodily functions, which has undermined his posture of composure.[11]

The reference to the "fingers" of God should not surprise us. Though God has no body, his actions are frequently described metaphorically as the acts of his hand. Indeed, in three other notable Scripture references, God's finger is at work. In response to the plagues, the Egyptian magicians remarked, "This is the finger of God" (Ex. 8:19). Exodus also describes the commandments as written by God's finger on the stone tablets (31:18). Finally, the heavens themselves are "the work of [his] fingers" (Ps. 8:3).

The throne room of the kings of Babylon was excavated by Koldewey in 1899.[12] Of course, the message recorded here has not been found, nor are the walls intact, but enough is left to show that the walls were coated with white gypsum, which means that the writing would be clear on the wall, especially considering the text's note that the writing took place "near the lampstand." The public nature of the writing as well as the fact that the wise men and finally Daniel also read the writing belie the idea that this is some sort of private vision or drunken hallucination.[13]

Belshazzar cannot make head nor tails of the writing, so he calls for the wise men. By now the reader of the book of Daniel cannot help but picture

---

11. So A. Wolters, "Untying the King's Knots: Physiology and Wordplay in Daniel 5," *JBL* 110 (1991): 117–22.

12. See Miller, *Daniel*, 155, citing R. Koldewey, *The Excavations at Babylon* (London: Macmillan, 1914).

13. So Lacocque, *The Book of Daniel*, 94.

these men as incompetent fools, and they don't disappoint our expectations. The king entices them with the promise of great reward, virtually offering them royalty. To be third in the kingdom means to rank only after himself and his father, Nabonidus.[14] That a coregency is intended is underlined by the purple garment and the necklace, which surely denoted royal authority.

In spite of the reward, the wise men are baffled by the inscription. This means at the very least that they cannot interpret the significance of the inscription. It may also imply that it was written in some kind of code, because it has been written in Aramaic, the common language of the day. Their inability cannot be the result of a simple inability to read the script, if it were written out in a normal manner. The text ultimately does not let us know.

At this point, the queen whisks onto the stage without detailed introduction or explanation, again leading to speculation. Who is the queen? She has not been attending the party, but she enters at the moment of crisis, acting with authority and dignified confidence. We know that Belshazzar's wives and concubines are already in attendance (v. 3). All the circumstantial evidence points to the queen mother, a figure of importance in many ancient Near Eastern societies. Ever since Josephus the queen here has been identified as the queen mother.

But whose mother? If Belshazzar's mother, we do not know her name. If the mother of his father Nabonidus, then it is the venerated Adad-guppi, who lived to the ripe old age of 104; she may be the one who brought Nabonidus and his son to the throne.[15] However, we know from historical sources that she died a few years before this moment. The queen therefore may have been Nebuchadnezzar's wife, Nitocris, still exerting her influence more than two decades later. Herodotus, the Greek historian, celebrates her wisdom.[16]

Whoever she is, she has the solution to Belshazzar's problem: "Get Daniel." Daniel has come through in the past in similar situations. She chides Belshazzar for his panic, unbefitting a king, and for his ignorance of Daniel, who had played an important role in Nebuchadnezzar's court. We can detect irritation in her voice concerning his demeaning of his illustrious royal predecessor. Indeed, Fewell argues that Daniel is not called immediately more out of disdain for his past association with Nebuchadnezzar than because of his age (around eighty at the time) and because of the twenty-three years that

---

14. Though Gruenthaner, "The Last King of Babylon," 421, argues that the expression really means a high official, not specifically the third most powerful.
15. See Longman, *Fictional Akkadian Autobiography*, 158–61; also see Beaulieu, *The Reign of Nabonidus*, 68–79.
16. See Collins, *Daniel*, 248.

have passed since Nebuchadnezzar's death.[17] Whatever the explanation, the scene is set for Daniel's grand entrance onto the scene.

Daniel's Interpretation of the Inscription (5:13–28)

SO FAR, MOST of the main characters—Belshazzar, the hand of God, the queen—have appeared suddenly and without introduction. In contrast, the author prepares us for Daniel's entrance. This is the third time that Daniel intervenes and succeeds where the Babylonian wise men fail (cf. Dan. 2 and 4). But when Daniel comes this time, he manifests a new attitude.

First the king speaks. A close reading of the text reveals a condescending attitude by Belshazzar toward this man who played such a significant role in Nebuchadnezzar's life, a role concerning which he is fully aware (cf. v. 22). The king first identifies him as one of the captives: "Are you Daniel, one of the exiles my father the king brought from Judah?" (v. 13). Such an address intends to remind Daniel of his place before Belshazzar. Belshazzar is king; Daniel is his captive. Calvin understood the tone of the king's speech when he states that "the king does not acknowledge his negligence but interrogates Daniel without shame—and interrogates him as if he were a prisoner."[18]

Belshazzar then launches off a series of honorifics that cite Daniel's abilities and character, but again a close reading of the speech shows that the king himself does not endorse the reports. Twice he begins his words with "I have heard," once when speaking of Daniel's endowment with the divine spirit, insight, intelligence, and wisdom (v. 14), and again when saying that Daniel is one who can give interpretations and solve difficult problems (v. 16). Contrast this with what Nebuchadnezzar had earlier simply asserted: "I know that the spirit of the holy gods is in you, and no mystery is too difficult for you. Here is my dream; interpret it for me" (4:9). Belshazzar's flattery is more provisional and his request for interpretation, accordingly, is conditional: "If you can read this writing and tell me what it means ..." (v. 16).

Belshazzar's speech reveals that his expectations are not high, but he holds out the same reward of royal status to the aged Israelite wise man standing before him as he earlier did to the hapless Babylonian wise men (v. 16).

Daniel has not missed the slight. The abruptness and the content of the king's lengthy speech indicates the prophet's annoyance and dislike for this second-rate monarch. In earlier chapters, when he spoke to Nebuchadnezzar, he used respect and concern. Again, Calvin has caught the flavor of the speech: "I have no doubt that he meant to speak roughly to the ungodly Belshazzar, a man beyond hope; but because there had been still some

---

17. Fewell, *Circle of Sovereignty*, 124.
18. Calvin, *Daniel I*, 222.

Daniel 5:1–31

uprightness left in King Nebuchadnezzar and he had good hopes in him, he had treated him more gently."[19]

Daniel begins by refusing the gift. He will interpret the writing on the wall free of charge. We will return to this topic again in the next section, because as it turns out Daniel will accept the reward. However, for now he alerts the king that his primary motivation is not worldly reward. Indeed, perhaps having read the inscription already, Daniel knows that the reward means nothing. The king has nothing really to give.

But before actually giving the interpretation, Daniel delivers a stinging rebuke to the king. Beginning with Samuel in his relation with Saul (cf. 1 Sam. 13, 15), a major role of the prophet has been to serve as the conscience of the king. True, this role was primarily directed toward the Israelite king. Whenever the latter fell to the temptation of power and forgot who the ultimate king was, the prophet was there to remind him (cf. also Nathan's relationship with David [2 Sam. 12], Elijah's with Ahab [1 Kings 18], and Jeremiah's with Jehoiakim [Jer. 36]). Now Belshazzar hears Daniel. He uses Nebuchadnezzar, Belshazzar's predecessor and by far superior, to redress the upstart, who is not only probably young and really the second in command to his father Nabonidus, but is also on the brink of disaster. Nebuchadnezzar was great, but when God confronted him, he ultimately acknowledged his subservience.

Belshazzar did not learn the lesson. He should have known better, thanks to the example of Nebuchadnezzar. Nonetheless, far from acknowledging his subservience to a greater power, Belshazzar went far beyond the sins of his predecessor by directly assaulting Yahweh through the profane and idolatrous use of the holy vessels of the temple. This admonition explains the presence of the hand and its inscription. The time is ripe for its interpretation.

For the first time, then, we as readers hear the words: "MENE, MENE, TEKEL, PARSIN." As presented in the text, these are three different nouns, the first repeated for emphasis. As nouns, they are units of money and may be translated: "Mina, mina, shekel, and a half." The half could be either half a mina or half a shekel. Though in other contexts it appears to be the former, the context here seems to indicate a half shekel. Nonetheless, Daniel's interpretation takes these nouns and interprets them as verbal forms, passive participles to be exact. The three verbal roots in order may be translated "numbered," "weighed," and "divided."

Different rationales have been offered for the apparent discrepancy between the grammatical form of the words and Daniel's interpretation.[20]

---

19. Ibid., 223.
20. See Miller, *Daniel*, 165, where he argues, I think unnecessarily and unpersuasively, that they really are verbs, not nouns, and the strange forms may be explained by accents

Daniel 5:1–31

However, we must remember that Daniel is in the position of the divinely inspired interpreter and his answer is rightly explained by Towner as

> based upon folk etymologies of the three words, each turning on a pun. The three nouns listed in verse 25 are treated as three passive verbs by Daniel in verses 26–28: MENE is related to the verb m-n-h "numbered"; TEKEL is related to the verb t-q-l, "weighed"; and PERES is construed as the verb p-r-s, "divided."[21]

As Goldingay has stated it, "Daniel uses [the writing] to make the statement refer to Belshazzar's being appointed, evaluated, and punished."[22] In the interpretation, *parsin* is given in the singular form *peres*, and both are reminiscent of the name *Persia*, the nation that is about to devour the once mighty empire of Babylonia.

In an insightful recent article, Al Wolters argues that the Babylonian wise men stumbled because the inscription was written in scripta continua and without vocalization: *mn'tqlprs*. He goes on to say that "the interpretation given by Daniel divides this series into three words of three letters, each with three levels of meaning, depending on the vocalization chosen."[23] The first two levels of meaning are as above—the letters divided and vocalized as nouns and then as passive participles, though he interprets the third verb as "assessed" rather than "divided." The third level of interpretation, based on yet a third vocalization (*menah, tiqqal, paras*), indicates the consequences of God's judgment on Babylonia: "He has paid out, you are too light [pe'al of *qll*], Persia!" Wolters continues by arguing that the image of scales that weigh permeate all three levels and "gains further significance when we realize that the annual rising of Libra took place on the eve of Babylon's fall to the Persians."[24]

Wolters's insightful interpretation may be supplemented by an article by Rabbi Dr. Michael Hilton, who points out the connections of the tower of Babel story in Genesis 11:1–9, which associates the beginning of Babylonia with a confusion of language, with Daniel 5, which associates its end with a confusion.[25]

That Belshazzar has ruled at all—indeed, that Babylon has achieved ascendancy as the major power of the world—has been at God's sovereign deter-

---

(see Collins, *Daniel*, 250–52; Goldingay, *Daniel*, 110–11, who both cite an earlier study by C. Clermont-Ganneau, "Mane, thecel, phares et le festin de Balthasar," *JA* 8 [1886]: 36–67, and argue that the oracle had an earlier form and meaning, though Goldingay places the importance on the interpretation offered in the book by Daniel himself).

21. Towner, *Daniel*, 76.
22. Goldingay, *Daniel*, p. 111.
23. A. Wolters, "The Riddle of the Scales in Daniel 5," *HUCA* 62 (1991): 155.
24. Ibid.
25. M. Hilton, "Babel Revisited—Daniel Chapter 5," *JSOT* 66 (1995): 99–112.

Daniel 5:1–31

mination, but it was a temporary period now at an end. Belshazzar and the Babylonians have not measured up, and so now another power will come to the throne, one dominated by Persia, which includes the Medes. No further explanation is needed from Daniel; the message is clear, and it spells doom.

Reward and Punishment (5:29–31)

GOD'S JUDGMENT IS double-edged. As he punishes his enemies, so he frees and rewards his people. Here, two individuals represent the dual fates of the godly and the ungodly.

(1) Belshazzar bestows the purple garments, the gold chain, and high political status on godly Daniel. Commentators have expressed much consternation as they try to figure out what is going on in the mind of Daniel. After all, earlier he had treated the possibility of reward with disdain, but now he accepts them without recorded objection. Perhaps Daniel waited until after the interpretation to accept reward in order not to have his ministry polluted by the promise of worldly reward, but the text does not say that. Perhaps he accepted the reward because he knew that within hours it would be meaningless, but the text does not say that either.

While the text does not give us a window to Daniel's motivation, the scene does communicate that his interpretation is true and that its truth is even admitted by Belshazzar, the king. It also shows us that the godly ultimately receive their reward even from hostile and reluctant oppressors. Indeed, we might go further to point out that Belshazzar's downfall and Darius the Medes' ascendancy is a boon to the people of God as a whole. Though not narrated by the book of Daniel, the Persian-Median rise to power leads quickly to the Decree of Cyrus (Ezra 1:1–4), which allowed the return of the Jewish people to Palestine.

(2) The chapter ends by narrating the consequences of Belshazzar's ungodly acts. "That very night Belshazzar, king of the Babylonians, was slain, and Darius the Mede took over the kingdom, at the age of sixty-two" (5:30–31). We will reserve our discussion of the mysterious Darius the Mede until the next chapter, which is set during his reign. It appears that he was Cyrus's general, who made the final raid on Babylon and killed Belshazzar in the process. Thus, we witness the reward granted to insolence, idolatry, and blasphemy.

Bridging Contexts

DANIEL 5 SHARES the same basic genre as the preceding four chapters (see comments on Dan. 1). It is history with a theological and didactic purpose and so our description can be nuanced by referring to it as theological (or prophetic) history or didactic history. The

Daniel 5:1–31

latter term would indicate that this is a history that illustrates certain important moral lessons. We have earlier commented on the wisdom-like nature of these opening chapters of Daniel, thus justifying our use of this material as a guide to our behavior.

We have also seen that these chapters dealing with history have the feel of a story rather than, say, a documentary. The latter would focus on a disclosure of the facts, an emphasis on what really happened; the former tells the account in a literarily satisfying manner. It selects events and shapes its presentation to support an important theological and/or ethical message. We are caught up in the intrigue, the suspense, the drama of the scene. We are drawn to change our beliefs, our attitudes, and our actions. History and story are not mutually exclusive categories.[26] True, a substance of a story can be make-believe, but it can also be from real life.

Our point is that Daniel 5 is properly described as history, but it is more than brute fact history. Indeed, it is the genre of text that compels us to understand this chapter as more than a simple report of what happened in the past. A proper reception of the story invites us to look for important theological and ethical principles that are still relevant for today (see below). As we take these principles and consider their appropriateness for today, we will do so through the prism of the New Testament, noting that there is always the possibility of discontinuity between the Old Testament story and our own situation.

The reticent narrator. Daniel 5 illustrates clearly an important characteristic that runs throughout the theological history of the Old Testament. Old Testament history with infrequent exceptions (e.g., Ezra 7–10; Neh. 1–7; 11–13) tells its story through the eyes of an unnamed narrator. In literary studies, this style is called third-person omniscient narration. That is, the narrator describes the action, reports speech, and interprets the significance of the events to us, the readers. He is a storyteller, who can move from one side of a battle to another, from the internal workings of one mind to another. In some Old Testament stories, he even tells us what passes through the mind of God.

Daniel 5 is not given to us from the perspective of Daniel, the character, but rather through the eyes of this unnamed narrator. While this form of narration is common in literature, literary scholars have pointed out that in the Bible it gives us the impression that we receive the story from a divine perspective.[27] Thus, this form of narration gives us a high level of confidence in the story. We trust this narrator.

---

26. See V. Philips Long, *The Art of Biblical History* (Grand Rapids: Zondervan, 1994).
27. R. Alter, *The Art of Biblical Narrative* (New York: Basic Books, 1981), 114–30; A. Berlin, *Poetics and Interpretation of Biblical Narrative* (Sheffield: Almond, 1983), 99–101.

We may further characterize our narrator in a way that helps us interpret the story and also gives us guidelines as we seek to bridge the horizon from the ancient world to the modern. In a word, the narrator of biblical stories is reticent. That is, he is spare in his commentary. As we read Daniel 5, we do not get much background description or explicit statement of motivations. We are thus left with a number of questions, as we have noted above: Why is Belshazzar holding a banquet? Who is the queen? Why couldn't the Babylonian wise men read the inscription? Why is Daniel upset with Belshazzar in a way that he was not with Nebuchadnezzar?

The reticence of the narrator invites our involvement as readers. It peaks our interest and gets us thinking deeply about what is going on. It is not that the story does not give us any clues. The narrator shows us rather than explicitly tells us important information about the plot and characters. He describes the action and, in this chapter, narrates the characters' speeches in a way to shape our reaction.

As interpreters, it is our task to read between the lines without reading into the story elements that are not there—a fine line to walk, to be sure. However, our reading in the gaps must be justified by what is presented in the text itself; otherwise, our interpretation should be discounted as just so much eisegesis.

Déjà vu all over again. As we turn our attention to chapter 5 for principles that remain relevant for our contemporary situation, we again are struck by the repetition of themes from earlier chapters. Belshazzar's first and final episode in the stories of Daniel is marked by his arrogance, blasphemy, and idolatry.

(1) *Arrogance.* Pride was an issue in the preceding chapters, especially chapter 4. There we observed how Nebuchadnezzar, even though warned, succumbed to a promotion of himself, even above God. He looked at Babylon and gave himself the praise. As a result, God humbled him by reducing him to an animal-like state until he acknowledged God's superiority, at which time he was reinstated to his former human glory.

Belshazzar has not learned from his predecessor's example. He too exalts himself above God. The story illustrates his attitude by narrating his misuse of the holy temple vessels, and Daniel articulates this divine evaluation in his prophetic rebuke (vv. 22–23) even before lowering the boom of judgment on him. God humbles Belshazzar as well, but in this case there is no restoration. He is killed for his sin.

(2) *Blasphemy.* While repeating his predecessor's sin of arrogance, Belshazzar takes it to a new level of offense against Yahweh. He expresses his superiority not by taking inordinate pride in his own achievements, but by profaning the things associated with God. True, by virtue of their theft from

the temple and their being handled by nonpriestly, non-Israelite hands, the vessels have already been profaned; but because of the use Belshazzar makes of them, he supersedes previous denigration of God's holy objects.

As we commented above, we do not know Belshazzar's motivation in bringing out the up-to-this-point unused temple vessels. On the level of conscious intention, was he tweaking the memory of his great royal predecessor or was he directly and knowingly attacking God himself? Possibly both, but even apart from a conscious intention for the latter, the reality of the situation was that he was making common use of extremely holy objects, an attack on God himself.

Blasphemy is the act of dishonoring God through speech or actions, and Belshazzar does both here, by misusing objects associated with the worship of God and, in doing so, praising false gods (see next section on "Idolatry"). To be sure, it is not simply the fact that these goblets are holding alcohol, because the Bible is clear that there is nothing inherently evil about alcohol. But these goblets were only to be used in the worship of God, not for state banquets. Apparently even Nebuchadnezzar understood that. In essence, Belshazzar spit in the face of God.

(3) *Idolatry.* In regard to Belshazzar's blasphemous actions, we must remember that this Babylonian king would have acknowledged the existence and divine status of the Israelites' God. His action would not have been performed with a modern belief that the worship of God was a primitive superstition. No, Belshazzar would have acknowledged Yahweh as a legitimate deity, probably a minor deity of a minor and now disgraced people. But he also surely believed that his own native deities were much more powerful. After all, Babylonia had conquered Judah. Clearly Marduk, Sin, and the other chief Babylonian deities dominated Yahweh in the pantheon.

We see a similar attitude expressed by the Philistines during the childhood of Samuel. In 1 Samuel 4 we read about the Philistine defeat of the Israelite army under the leadership of Eli's two wicked sons, Hophni and Phinehas. These latter two men had thought to stem the military success of the Philistines by bringing the ark into the war camp. From their actions and speech, it is clear that they did not do this out of actual faith, but were treating the ark as a kind of magical box or relic.

As a result of their lack of faith, God allowed the Philistines to defeat the Israelites and capture the ark. It was now time for the Philistines to learn their lesson about the power of Yahweh. In 1 Samuel 5 the Philistines act like any other Near Eastern victor (including Nebuchadnezzar in Dan. 1) by taking the ark and placing it in the temple of their chief god, Dagon. This process acknowledges Yahweh's divine status while demonstrating his subservient position to Dagon.

Daniel 5:1–31

The next day, however, the Philistines enter the temple to discover Dagon's statue fallen flat on its face before the ark. It is as if Dagon was worshiping Yahweh! They then hoist the idol back on its feet, but when they return the next day, Dagon has fallen again, this time with a broken head and hands (like a dismembered military casualty). Then after an outbreak of tumors on the people of Ashdod, they get the message and make plans to return the ark to Israel.

It is true that the ark of the covenant was a more potent symbol of God's presence and military might than the vessels, but it is also not clear whether the ark was in existence at the time of Nebuchadnezzar. In any case, the vessels of the temple were capable of serving as symbols of God's presence. Like the Philistines, Belshazzar too promoted his gods at the expense of the true God. He drank toasts to Marduk, Sin, and the others with the goblets reserved for the worship of the only true God. Belshazzar was indeed an idolater—following in the footsteps of his father, who was also an idolater (cf. Dan. 2 and 3).

The repetition of earlier sins does lead us to ask the question: Why is Belshazzar's fate different from that of Nebuchadnezzar? The episode, while not explicitly answering our question, does lead us to an answer as we read the gaps.

Judgment and repentance. We must understand the fate that differentiates Belshazzar in Daniel 5 from Nebuchadnezzar in Daniel 4. Though a proud man and an idolater, Nebuchadnezzar fares well in the book of Daniel. He is treated with respect by the prophet, and though put in his place, survives to tell about it. Belshazzar, on the other hand, does not fare as well. Indeed, he suffers a humiliating defeat and dies at the hands of his enemies. When the hand begins writing on the wall, Belshazzar's fate is sealed. He is synonymous with God's sure and quick judgment in this book. He offends God; God sentences him. The prophet confronts him with God's sentence of death, and it is immediately carried out.

But what is the difference between Nebuchadnezzar and Belshazzar? Why does one live and one die? In the final analysis, the answer lies in the sovereign decision of God. Nebuchadnezzar offended God as deeply as Belshazzar, but the prophet was there rooting for him to turn back. When he did, God restored him. Daniel does not hold out hope for Belshazzar; he delivers an unconditional message of judgment. Thus, there is no repentance and no restoration.

In a word, here we have the interplay of divine sovereignty and human responsibility presented in such a way that we cannot easily sort them out. Surely, Belshazzar should have repented, but Daniel, speaking for God, does not give him a chance. Why? Were his sins, for some unexplainable reason, so much greater? Was the example of history, that is, the previous experience

Daniel 5:1–31

of Nebuchadnezzar, sufficient to leave Belshazzar without excuse? The latter has enough of a textual justification to lead us to further exploration.

Hearing the Word of God. Daniel's judgment speech begins with a reminiscence of Nebuchadnezzar (5:18–21). He was proud indeed, but when confronted by God, he acknowledged his subservience to him. In a word, he repented when confronted by God's word and action. In verse 22, Daniel turns his attention to Belshazzar by proclaiming, "But you his son, O Belshazzar, have not humbled yourself, though you knew all this." It is the last clause that is telling here—Belshazzar knew what he was supposed to do, but failed to do so. It was not as if this was all new to him.

To be honest, we do not know how Belshazzar knew these things. It could have been the talk of the court for decades afterward. Perhaps the queen mother had talked to him before about Daniel and his God. Whatever the means of communication, Daniel tells us that Belshazzar heard in such a way that he was fully responsible for his present rebellious actions. He had not heeded the warnings, and now he was doomed.

Please notice, however, that even this strong textual clue does not resolve the issue of the relationship between divine sovereignty and human responsibility. Nebuchadnezzar is described as having more than one conversion experience in the preceding chapters. He praises Yahweh at the end of chapter 3 only to find himself rebelling against God in chapter 4, but nonetheless getting a second chance, so to speak. Why does Nebuchadnezzar get a second chance whereas Belshazzar does not even get a first? Again, the ultimate answer is bound up with our understanding of God's sovereignty, as we will see in certain New Testament passages in the next section.

"YOUR DAYS ARE numbered!"

"The handwriting is on the wall!"

These expressions are commonly used in twentieth-century English and are a modern legacy of Daniel 5. They both relate to what we have identified as the unique emphasis of the chapter, which is the awareness of the approach of certain judgment for one's offenses.

Of course, as used today, the expressions often express a belief, not in God, but in the certain hand of fate. Checking the bleak financial papers of a failing institution might elicit such a remark, or perhaps looking at the face of a terminally ill patient approaching the last few days of life. These sentences express the certainty of a bleak end.

In the Bible, of course, it is not fate that writes MENE MENE TEKEL PARSIN on the wall, it is God himself. Our story connects God with a gruesome judgment on a sinful individual. It raises the issue of God's judgment in one's life and beyond.

Where is the judgment of God? To what extent can we look at the failures and deaths of people around us today and say with confidence, "There is the judgment of God"? Does God judge people today as he judged Belshazzar in the story of Daniel 5?

The Germans are defeated in 1945 and Hitler kills himself in a bunker in Berlin. Is this the judgment of God? An atom bomb is dropped on Hiroshima. Is this the judgment of God? An epidemic rips through the gay community. Is this the judgment of God? An abortion clinic is bombed in Atlanta. Is this the judgment of God? A child molester is beaten up in New Jersey. Is this the judgment of God? A country singer's plane crashes off the coast of California. Is this the judgment of God? A Christian missionary dies in Pakistan at a young age. Surely this can't be the judgment of God, can it?

Is there a contrast between an Old Testament God of judgment and condemnation and a New Testament God of grace and mercy? By no means, the New Testament teaches that God, in Jesus, judges evil and condemns the wicked (John 8:26; 12:31). God is still judge in the New Testament (2 Tim. 4:8).[28]

But there is also clear and strong teaching that God's followers are not in a position to judge others. Perhaps the most well-known teaching in this regard is found in Matthew 7:1–2: "Do not judge, or you too will be judged. For in the same way you judge others, you will be judged, and with the measure you use, it will be measured to you." Paul echoes this understanding as he also emphasizes God's role as judge in Romans 2:1–4:

> You, therefore, have no excuse, you who pass judgment on someone else, for at whatever point you judge the other, you are condemning yourself, because you who pass judgment do the same things. Now we know that God's judgment against those who do such things is based on truth. So when you, a mere man, pass judgment on them and yet do the same things, do you think you will escape God's judgment? Or do you show contempt for the riches of his kindness, tolerance and patience, not realizing that God's kindness leads you toward repentance?

God judges, indeed, but we cannot know with certainty when suffering and death is God's judgment and when it is not. Therefore, we must keep our

---

28. We should also bring into view the culmination of God's judgment. Though we cannot see his judgment displayed consistently in the present world—the wicked sometimes prosper and the righteous sometimes perish—we know that an ultimate day of reckoning is coming. The Bible clearly teaches that those who rebel will receive what they deserve if they do not turn to Christ. This will become clearer in the last part of the book of Daniel, so we will develop the theme of judgment later.

mouths shut. We must never point to a person who suffers and say, "Behold God's judgment!"

What is the difference between Daniel and us, or for that matter between Daniel's condemnation of Belshazzar and the three friends' condemnation of Job? The difference is that Daniel was a recipient of divine revelation and as a result his words are not his own interpretation of the situation, but rather God's own words. Daniel is a mouthpiece for God's sentence on Belshazzar's life. No one today plays the same role as Daniel did in the Babylonian court. No one today has a direct pipeline to God's mind. Even Paul, in connection with the present status of the Jewish people, could state, "How unsearchable his judgments, and his paths beyond tracing out!" (Rom. 11:33).

As the book of Job teaches, not all suffering is the result of an individual's sin. That was the mistake made by his three friends. They knew that sin had its consequences and godly living had its consequences. Sin led to suffering and righteousness led to success in life. But they believed that that was the whole equation. Thus, if you observed a person suffering, that person must be under God's judgment for his or her sins. The reader knows better than any of the three friends. Because of the first two chapters, we know with certainty that Job was right in his assertions that he was innocent. He was not suffering for his sins.

Certainly the disciples of Jesus were quick to judge. As they looked at a blind man, they gave the knee-jerk reaction, "Rabbi, who sinned, this man or his parents that he was born blind?" (John 9:2). Jesus responded, "Neither this man nor his parents sinned ... but this happened so that the work of God might be displayed in his life" (v. 3).

The disciples' question seems so cruel today. How could they see God's judgment so automatically and dogmatically in this man's blindness? But are we any different today? How many look at a person infected with AIDS and don't even ask the question as they mutter quietly, "The judgment of God." Is this any less cruel or any less deserving of Christ's anger? AIDS is no more or less God's judgment for sins than cancer or the common cold. Of course, they are the result of sin. There would be no disease at all without it, but that a person has AIDS is not the special judgment of God for his or her sins, even if one contracted that disease through intravenous drug use or homosexual activity.

Our role is not to judge. Rather, it is to offer the good news of repentance and restoration. Daniel, a recipient of God's direct revelation, had the authority to withhold the good news of repentance and restoration from Belshazzar, but not so us. Today we do not say to anyone, "You are condemned; you are beyond God's mercy." If we do, we condemn ourselves, because our sin is no better than anyone else's from God's perspective. Note James 2:8–11:

Daniel 5:1–31

If you really keep the royal law found in Scripture, "Love your neighbor as yourself," you are doing right. But if you show favoritism, you sin and are convicted by the law as lawbreakers. For whoever keeps the whole law and yet stumbles at just one point is guilty of breaking all of it. For he who said, "Do not commit adultery," also said, "Do not murder." If you do not commit adultery but do commit murder, you have become a lawbreaker.

If our role is not to judge, then what is it? The world is full of trouble, evil, chaos. What are we to do about it? We are to offer words of life, not condemnation. We are to play the role of Daniel before Nebuchadnezzar, not Daniel before Belshazzar.

Of course, Daniel before Nebuchadnezzar was not morally neutral. God did not direct him to let the king go along his own merry way of rebellion and arrogance. Daniel called him to task, but with a note of deep sadness at the suffering Nebuchadnezzar experienced as well as great hope of restoration.

Neither are we to be morally neutral as we live in a world of injustice, oppression, and licentiousness. We do not seek the destruction of godless people, rather, their redemption. After all, every one of us who today call ourselves Christians were without God. And even after becoming Christians, we still sin. We must never, ever condemn any other person without a full acknowledgment of the darkness of our own hearts and the destructive nature of many of our actions. We must take the log out of our own eyes before we can remove the speck from someone else's (Matt. 7:5).

Unfortunately, I would hazard to guess that the Christian community, in the Western world at least, would be characterized by the watching world as narrow, intolerant, judgmental, and self-righteous rather than forgiving, compassionate, gracious, and redemptive. All of us who call on the name of Christ must do some serious soul-searching and repenting as we reach out to transform the world in our Lord's name.

The sin of blasphemy. The world does need transformation. The arrogance, blasphemy, and idolatry that incarnated in the actions of Belshazzar can be found in abundance in our culture today. Previous chapters have given us the opportunity to describe contemporary manifestations of pride and idolatry, so we will use this section to speak briefly about blasphemy.

Above, we described blasphemy as an act of dishonoring God through speech or actions. Specifically we observed Belshazzar's committing blasphemy through the misuse of objects associated with the worship of God—drinking from the holy temple vessels.

Today, it is true, we have no equivalent to the holy temple vessels. In Old Testament times God chose to make his presence known in special ways in certain locations. These special places—like the tabernacle and the temple—were symbolic of the great gulf that exists between a holy God and a sinful humanity. It was not possible to gain easy access into the temple. The holy place was supervised by a consecrated people, the priests, and certain rites and rituals, notably sacrifices, had to be observed in order to gain entrance into the presence of God.

In a word, there was a sharp and definite division between the holy and the profane. The temple vessels were associated with a sacred place and therefore were part of the realm of the sacred. Their profane use was therefore an abomination.

What parallels do we have today? At first sight, there appears to be none. After all, with the coming of Christ the division between holy and profane is completely done away with. This fact was anticipated in Zechariah's prophecy in Zechariah 14:20–21:

> On that day HOLY TO THE LORD will be inscribed on the bells of the horses, and the cooking pots in the LORD's house will be like the sacred bowls in front of the altar. Every pot in Jerusalem and Judah will be holy to the LORD Almighty, and all who come to sacrifice will take some of the pots and cook in them. And on that day there will no longer be a Canaanite in the house of the LORD Almighty.

Its fulfillment is vividly illustrated by the rending of the temple curtain that separated the Most Holy Place from the Holy Place (Matt. 27:51). Christ's death and resurrection, it appears, moves us into a new era. No longer is anything holy. . . .

Or is it the other way around? Indeed, that is what the Zechariah passage indicates. It is not that there is nothing holy, but that *everything is holy*. This makes sense, does it not, as we consider the difference with the Old Testament era? Whereas before Christ God made his presence known in a special way in a certain location, today we can meet God anywhere—in a church, a street, a car, our homes, a bar.

Such an understanding intensifies the concept of blasphemy. Blasphemy is not just defacing a church or a cross. It is a misuse of any part of God's creation. An assault against a fellow human being is an act of blasphemy. After all, we are all created in the image of God (Gen. 1:27; James 3:9). An angry word spoken against a fellow believer is an act of blasphemy. After all, Christians are all temples of the Holy Spirit (1 Cor. 3:16). The destruction of the environment for selfish purposes is an act of blasphemy. The land, the air, the seas are each the creation of our holy God.

Again, when we fully understand blasphemy, we are staggered by the extent to which each and every one of us is implicated. The implication, however, should not come as a surprise. Like Belshazzar we "know all this." Belshazzar knew from the example of his great predecessor Nebuchadnezzar. But where have we been told?

The world today is far better informed than in the days of Belshazzar. We have been warned and given clear directions about a proper relationship with God. God himself has given the people of the world a direct message through his Word.

This is a major component of the teaching of the parable of Lazarus and the rich man (Luke 16:19–31). The parable presents the plight of an unnamed rich man, suffering for his sins in hell. Lazarus, a beggar who suffered in life, was enjoying the afterlife in heaven. In response to the rich man's request, Abraham does not allow Lazarus to slake his thirst. The rich man's suffering incites him to beseech Abraham to allow Lazarus to go warn his still living brothers of the coming judgment. The ensuing interchange between Abraham and the rich man is revealing (Luke 16:29–31):

> Abraham replied, "They have Moses and the Prophets; let them listen to them."
> "No, father Abraham," he said, "but if someone from the dead goes to them, they will repent."
> He said to him, "If they do not listen to Moses and the Prophets, they will not be convinced even if someone rises from the dead."

The message to the rich man concerning his brothers is essentially the same as Daniel's to Belshazzar: "They should have known!" They have the Word of God at their fingertips. They need to read and respond. And, of course, the message of the parable goes beyond the rich man and his brothers to us today. We should know.... We have no excuse.

However, we do not have to look too far to see contemporary misuses of God's Word that look eerily similar to Belshazzar's profanation of the holy vessels. Not everyone who practices a postmodern approach to the Bible is guilty of profanation; indeed, Christian scholars need to think through the implications of postmodernism for reading the Bible.[29] Most exegesis, whether by evangelicals or others, simply operate with a modern-scientific worldview that is no more biblical than a postmodern one. However, it is wrong simply to assume the validity of the culture that we happen to live in without submitting it to a biblical critique.[30] Unfortunately, there are too many examples of the reverse, submitting the Bible to a postmodern critique.

---

29. I have tried to take a first step in this regard in "Reading the Bible Postmodernly," *Mars Hill Review* (forthcoming in Fall, 1998).
30. As done recently by C. Bartholomew, "Reading the Old Testament in Postmodern Times," *TynBul* 49 (1998): 91–114.

Daniel 5:1–31

One glaring example may be found in a recent interpretation of Psalm 24.[31] This essay's purpose is to demonstrate an approach to the text as well as to discuss Psalm 24. The author proclaims the postmodern dictum that texts have no determinate meaning. There is no presence, divine or authorial, to rein in our interpretation. We, as readers, can ascribe whatever meaning we like to the text. He promotes the idea that biblical interpreters should simply cut the cloth of the text to fit the needs of the audience who is paying for our skills. Nonetheless, with a move that seems to fit uneasily with his idea that the text itself has no meaning, he argues that Psalm 24 presents a view of God and war that he finds repulsive and argues that we must read "against the grain" of the apparent meaning of this text. Belshazzar takes the holy vessels of God and mocks God by drinking and toasting his idols; is Clines's treatment of the Bible far removed from this act?

---

31. D. J. A. Clines, "A World Established on Water (Psalm 24): Reader-Response, Deconstruction and Bespoke Criticism," in *The New Literary Criticism*, ed. J. Cheryl Exum and D. J. A. Clines (Valley Forge, Pa.: Trinity Press International, 1993), 79–90.

Daniel 6:1-28

IT PLEASED DARIUS to appoint 120 satraps to rule throughout the kingdom, ²with three administrators over them, one of whom was Daniel. The satraps were made accountable to them so that the king might not suffer loss. ³Now Daniel so distinguished himself among the administrators and the satraps by his exceptional qualities that the king planned to set him over the whole kingdom. ⁴At this, the administrators and the satraps tried to find grounds for charges against Daniel in his conduct of government affairs, but they were unable to do so. They could find no corruption in him, because he was trustworthy and neither corrupt nor negligent. ⁵Finally these men said, "We will never find any basis for charges against this man Daniel unless it has something to do with the law of his God."

⁶So the administrators and the satraps went as a group to the king and said: "O King Darius, live forever! ⁷The royal administrators, prefects, satraps, advisers and governors have all agreed that the king should issue an edict and enforce the decree that anyone who prays to any god or man during the next thirty days, except to you, O king, shall be thrown into the lions' den. ⁸Now, O king, issue the decree and put it in writing so that it cannot be altered—in accordance with the laws of the Medes and Persians, which cannot be repealed." ⁹So King Darius put the decree in writing.

¹⁰Now when Daniel learned that the decree had been published, he went home to his upstairs room where the windows opened toward Jerusalem. Three times a day he got down on his knees and prayed, giving thanks to his God, just as he had done before. ¹¹Then these men went as a group and found Daniel praying and asking God for help. ¹²So they went to the king and spoke to him about his royal decree: "Did you not publish a decree that during the next thirty days anyone who prays to any god or man except to you, O king, would be thrown into the lions' den?"

The king answered, "The decree stands—in accordance with the laws of the Medes and Persians, which cannot be repealed."

Daniel 6:1–28

¹³Then they said to the king, "Daniel, who is one of the exiles from Judah, pays no attention to you, O king, or to the decree you put in writing. He still prays three times a day." ¹⁴When the king heard this, he was greatly distressed; he was determined to rescue Daniel and made every effort until sundown to save him.

¹⁵Then the men went as a group to the king and said to him, "Remember, O king, that according to the law of the Medes and Persians no decree or edict that the king issues can be changed."

¹⁶So the king gave the order, and they brought Daniel and threw him into the lions' den. The king said to Daniel, "May your God, whom you serve continually, rescue you!"

¹⁷A stone was brought and placed over the mouth of the den, and the king sealed it with his own signet ring and with the rings of his nobles, so that Daniel's situation might not be changed. ¹⁸Then the king returned to his palace and spent the night without eating and without any entertainment being brought to him. And he could not sleep.

¹⁹At the first light of dawn, the king got up and hurried to the lions' den. ²⁰When he came near the den, he called to Daniel in an anguished voice, "Daniel, servant of the living God, has your God, whom you serve continually, been able to rescue you from the lions?"

²¹Daniel answered, "O king, live forever! ²²My God sent his angel, and he shut the mouths of the lions. They have not hurt me, because I was found innocent in his sight. Nor have I ever done any wrong before you, O king."

²³The king was overjoyed and gave orders to lift Daniel out of the den. And when Daniel was lifted from the den, no wound was found on him, because he had trusted in his God.

²⁴At the king's command, the men who had falsely accused Daniel were brought in and thrown into the lions' den, along with their wives and children. And before they reached the floor of the den, the lions overpowered them and crushed all their bones.

²⁵Then King Darius wrote to all the peoples, nations and men of every language throughout the land:

"May you prosper greatly!

²⁶"I issue a decree that in every part of my kingdom people must fear and reverence the God of Daniel.

Daniel 6:1–28

> "For he is the living God
>   and he endures forever;
> his kingdom will not be destroyed,
>   his dominion will never end.
> ²⁷ He rescues and he saves;
>   he performs signs and wonders
>   in the heavens and on the earth.
> He has rescued Daniel
>   from the power of the lions."

²⁸ So Daniel prospered during the reign of Darius and the reign of Cyrus the Persian.

Original Meaning

DANIEL 6 BRINGS to a close the stories concerning Daniel's activities in the foreign court. He has not changed location; he is still in the city of Babylon. However, a new empire rules the roost as Persia has replaced Babylon. Belshazzar is dead and Darius the Mede is in control.

The identity of Darius the Mede is a vexing question. This commentary is not the place for an extended discussion,[1] but we will present the problem in its broad outlines. In brief, Cyrus was the king of Persia at the time of the fall of Babylon. No Darius is mentioned in the tablets from this time period. We begin by reminding the reader of the situation just a century ago with Belshazzar. At that time, no figure named Belshazzar was associated with the end of Babylonian history. Now, however, he is a well-documented person (see comments on ch. 5).

Darius is a well-known Persian royal name but not until long after the death of Cyrus and the rule of Cyrus's son Cambyses. Darius I (522–486 B.C.) was the king who instituted a system whereby his far-flung empire was ruled by twenty satraps. Because Darius I is associated with the institution of a new system of satrapies, many scholars feel that Daniel, writing later (see Introduction), confused Darius I with the conqueror of Babylon. However, this type of confusion seems extraordinary even at a remove of several centuries. It is more likely that Darius is a throne name for someone ruling in Babylon at the behest of Cyrus.

Recent scholars have attempted to associate Darius the Mede with particular individuals whom we know played important roles at the time Persia

---

[1]. For a detailed discussion of the issue and a presentation of the preferred solution, see R. B. Dillard and T. Longman III, *An Introduction to the Old Testament* (Grand Rapids: Zondervan, 1994), 334–37.

Daniel 6:1–28

incorporated Babylon into its empire. J. Whitcomb has argued that Darius the Mede is actually Gubaru, known from the Akkadian texts as governor of Babylon.[2] The eminent Assyriologist D. J. Wiseman, on the other hand, has argued that Darius the Mede is the Babylonian throne name of none other than Cyrus himself.[3] Perhaps the most persuasive of all attempts at identification is that of W. Shea: Darius the Mede is Gu/Ugbaru, the general to whom the Nabonidus Chronicle attributes the conquest of Babylon.[4] He would be ruling as a sub-king at the whim of the ultimate ruler, Cyrus himself.

Short of a document identifying one of these figures as Darius, we cannot be certain. The identification of Darius the Mede is an important problem for those of us who believe that Daniel gives us accurate historical information, but it does not affect our interpretation. Harmonizations are possible, as we have seen from the suggestions of Whitcomb, Wiseman, and Shea, but not provable. With this brief explanation for those who are troubled by the issue, we pass on now to a consideration of the content of the passage.

The story is easily identified as a court narrative of conflict.[5] The plot is propelled by the jealousy that Daniel's peers and subordinates in the Persian government feel toward his rapid rise to the top of the political hierarchy. They seek to undermine his position by pitting his loyalty to God over against his loyalty to the Persian government, which he serves. Boogaart is correct to see the conflict ultimately as one between two empires:

> On the one hand we have Darius, ruler of all the peoples, nations, and languages that dwell in all the earth (cf. verse 25) and enforcer of the law of the Medes and Persians. On the other hand we have the God of Daniel, working signs and wonders in heaven and on earth (cf. verse 27) and enforcer of Jewish law (cf. verse 5). The kingdoms overlap and the question of sovereignty has to be resolved.[6]

As the chapter explores this conflict, it again emphasizes the overarching theme of the whole book: *In spite of present appearances God is in control.* God will be victorious over the seemingly powerful forces ranged

---

2. J. C. Whitcomb, *Darius the Mede: A Study in Historical Identification* (Grand Rapids: Eerdmans, 1959).

3. D. J. Wiseman, et al. *Notes on Some Problems in the Book of Daniel* (London: Tyndale, 1965), 12–16.

4. W. H. Shea, "An Unrecognized Vassal King of Babylon in the Early Achaemenid Period," *AUSS* 9 (1971): 51–67, 99–128; 10 (1972): 88–117.

5. Goldingay, *Daniel*, 122; Fewell, *Circle of Sovereignty*, 143.

6. T. A. Boogaart, "Daniel 6: A Tale of Two Empires," *The Reformed Review* 39–40 (1985–1987): 107.

against him and his people. Thus, this story, like those that preceded it, provides comfort for God's people, who find themselves in situations that seem beyond their control.

Daniel 6 finds its closest parallel with Daniel 3. Notice, though, a subtle difference that makes Daniel 6 more than a mere repetition. While the story of the three friends of Daniel in the fiery furnace shows how the faithful refuse to participate in idolatrous religious practices, the present chapter shows how they refuse to refrain from proper worship of God. Daniel is told not to pray to Yahweh, but he does so nonetheless. Daniel obeys God's law, not the immutable law of the Medes and Persians.

The chapter may be divided into four parts: (1) the plot against Daniel (6:1–9); (2) the trap and reluctant punishment (6:10–18); (3) Daniel's rescue and the accusers' demise (6:19–24); (4) Darius's decree (6:25–28).

The Plot Against Daniel (6:1–9)

THE STORY OPENS with the new king setting up his personal form of government for Babylonia. Over him is Cyrus, the king of Persia, so we are to understand this story as concerned only with Babylonia. While it is true that at a later date Darius will divide the entire empire into twenty satrapies, the present division involved much smaller units.[7] Darius thus pushes the governance of Babylonia in the direction of decentralization, which may help explain his later quick acceptance of the proposal to make him the chief mediator of prayer. In other words, this suggestion assures[8] him of his continued central place in the government while at the same time delegating authority to others.

By now, we are not surprised that Daniel distinguishes himself from all the other authorities whom Darius has placed in important positions throughout his kingdom. After all, we already know he is the wisest of the wise and the most capable of everyone in the land. The king's intention to promote him above everyone else is apparently leaked to the others, who for obviously selfish reasons want to block his swift rise. Unfortunately for them, Daniel's behavior conforms to his spotless reputation. They will have to manufacture a fault in his personality.

Their twisted minds come up with the ideal plan. They know that Daniel's religion is the fundamental guiding principle of his life. He would betray the king before he would betray his religion. Thus they lay their trap to trip him up.

---

7. For evidence that "satrap" can be used on a smaller scale, see Collins, *Daniel*, 264, though Collins himself still believes there is a confusion here with the later Darius.
8. At least symbolically, since it lasts only thirty days.

Their approach to the king is a masterpiece of political deception to achieve their illicit ends. The Aramaic verb (*rgs*) behind the NIV translation "went as a group" (v. 6) is ambiguous as to their attitude. As Fewell explains, the word has a semantic range that moves from "the rather innocent connotation of 'in company,' to the idea of 'conspiracy,' to the notion of 'rage.'"[9] She rightly believes that all senses of the word echo in the context. She also describes how this verb's combination with the preposition *'al* can also be interpreted in different senses from the point of view of the king himself, who thinks they are making a fuss "over" him, or from the vantage point of the conspirators themselves, who are actually working "against" him.[10]

In any case, these "administrators and satraps" are clearly lying to the king, since they claim that the proposal they are presenting has been unanimously approved by all of his subordinates. Of course, Daniel, the king's favorite, does not even know about it.

The proposal itself is strange. It definitely appeals to the vanity of the king, especially if the king is feeling any insecurity about his popularity or power. Perhaps this explains his ready acceptance of such a bizarre suggestion. On the surface, it appears to suggest to the king that he be sole deity of the realm for thirty days. While it is easy to imagine someone's overweening pride allowing him to believe he is a god, it is hard to see someone putting such a short time period on his divinity.

Questions like this have led John Walton to make the plausible suggestion that the decree does not actually "deify the king but designates him as the only legitimate representative of deity for the stated time."[11] Whichever it is, Daniel will find himself in an impossible situation from a human point of view, for the decree may not be repealed according to the custom of the Persians and Medes.[12]

The Trap and Reluctant Punishment (6:10–18)

THE NARRATIVE NOW shifts scene. We move from the court to Daniel's home where he hears of the king's decree to forbid prayer toward anything or anyone but the king himself. His response is simple: He goes upstairs and prays with the windows open toward Jerusalem. There is no speech or inner turmoil

---

9. Fewell, *Circle of Sovereignty*, 145.
10. Ibid., 146.
11. J. Walton, "The Decree of Darius the Mede in Daniel 6," *JETS* 31 (1988): 280.
12. The statement that the law of the Persians and Medes was unable to be repealed has been debated and discussed, but the same theme may be found in the book of Esther (1:19; 8:8) as well as the Greek historian Diodorus Siculus (17.30). Further, paragraph 5 of Hammurapi's law code indicates that it was a crime for a judge to change his decision (cf. Hartman and DiLella, *The Book of Daniel*, 199).

recorded in the narrative. The impression the narrative intends to impart is Daniel's unflinching obedience. He does not question, doubt, or worry; he acts. He does not bow toward Darius, but toward Jerusalem. Darius is neither the object nor the mediator of his prayers. That role is taken by Yahweh.

Why does Daniel bow toward Jerusalem? Essentially, his act is motivated by 1 Kings 8:35–36 (italics added):

> When the heavens are shut up and there is no rain because your people have sinned against you, and when they pray *toward this place* and confess your name and turn from their sin because you have afflicted them, then hear from heaven and forgive the sin of your servants, your people Israel. Teach them the right way to live, and send rain on the land you gave your people for an inheritance.

The context of these verses is Solomon's prayer of dedication of the temple in Jerusalem. God had made his presence known in a special way in the temple. As Solomon made clear, the temple did not contain God, but was the place God himself chose as the place where his people would come to worship him.

Of course, at the time of Daniel's prayer the temple was in ruins. God had abandoned his earthly home (Ezek. 9–11) because of the presumption of the people (Jer. 7) and had allowed the Babylonians to tear down the temple (book of Lamentations). Nonetheless, Judeans in exile, such as Daniel, turned regularly to the city with longing in their hearts and hope for the future.

According to the passage, Daniel did this three times a day. This practice is not mandated anywhere in Scripture, but is perhaps suggested by passages such as Psalm 55:17:[13]

> Evening, morning and noon
>   I cry out in distress,
>   and he hears my voice.

The mention of the "three times a day" indicates that Daniel's prayer on this occasion is not stirred on by the decree; it is part of his regular habit. He is not flaunting his rebellion in the face of the king's orders; it is business as usual. Indeed, the description of his prayer is a statement that he is neither flaunting nor hiding his religious practice. After all, he is praying in an upper room, and with the windows open. He is not on public display, but neither is he hiding from determined spies.

And determined spies there were. The officials who precipitated the crisis see Daniel's actions and report them to the king (vv. 12, 15). As we have

---

13. Collins, *Daniel*, 268.

seen above (cf. comments on v. 6), the verb used is *rgs*, indicating not only that they act as a group but also with malicious intent. From their description, we learn something of the content of Daniel's prayer. He is "asking God for help" (v. 11). Likely, he is turning to God for aid because he anticipates trouble from the decree. As the story continues, we discover how God answers his prayer.

The conspirators present news of Daniel's actions craftily. They know where the king's sympathies lie, so before they accuse Daniel, they remind the king of his earlier decision and its binding character. They then confront the king with the news that indicts Daniel.

The king reacts with extreme dismay. The contrast with Nebuchadnezzar's reaction to the three friends in Daniel 3 could not be stronger. While the latter responded with increasing anger to the friends' refusal to participate in the pagan rite, Darius wants to save the aged Judean counselor. However, he is trapped by his own unchangeable words and must carry out the punishment.

"So the king gave the order" (v. 16). As decreed, Daniel is thrown into the lions' den. No comparable form of punishment is known from the ancient Near East, but then powerful yet insecure nations from time immemorial have devised tortures and deaths with incredible imagination. The conception is simple enough: Develop a pit and put lions in it. The victim, in this case Daniel, could be thrown in; a stone blocked the point of entry, and the lions would be allowed to do their work. Since the punishment in this case is the execution of a royal decree, the king seals the entrance with his seal. This act does not lock the door as much as prevent tampering with it. If someone were to open the door before the next morning, it would be noticed because the seal would be broken.

The king's concern for Daniel continues through the night. He cannot eat or sleep. As he discovers the next morning to his surprise, his evening has been much more difficult than Daniel's!

Daniel's Rescue and the Accusers' Demise (6:19–24)

THE COMING DAWN finds Darius rushing to the lions' den in order to discover the fate of Daniel. Contrary to some interpreters,[14] Darius must have had at least a glimmer of hope that Daniel would survive the night. After all, he had commended Daniel into the hands of the prophet's God and called out to him the moment he reached the den.

Perhaps it is best to consider the lions' den a trial by ordeal rather than an execution per se. An execution, after all, would not have a time limit. The

---

14. Cf. Fewell, *Circle of Sovereignty*, 150.

understanding of the scene as an ordeal also explains some of the language found in the chapter. What was an ordeal? An individual was subjected to an ordeal when he was suspected of a crime, but there was some uncertainty as to his guilt. Daniel's guilt in relationship to Darius's decree appears clear, but as he emerges from the den, he claims that the lions have not hurt him "because I was found innocent in [God's] sight. Nor have I ever done any wrong before you, O king" (v. 22). Daniel's survival attests to his innocence.

Ordeals are broadly known in the ancient Near East.[15] They take many forms, but perhaps the most well known is the water ordeal. An individual suspected of a crime is thrown into a river. If he or she dies, they are guilty. But if they survive, they are innocent and set free. Biblical law contains only one possible instance of ordeal: the case of a woman suspected of adultery (Num. 5:11–31).[16]

The theology behind an ordeal is that God, who knows the heart in a way that human judges do not, will see the verdict through. Daniel's survival, then, is God's judgment of innocence on Daniel. In this judgment, Darius rejoices.

Daniel further attests to God's involvement in his survival when he informs Darius that during the night God sent his angel to shut the mouths of the lions. The angel plays the same role as the "fourth man" in the blazing furnace in Daniel 3. Furthermore, just as the three friends do not even have the smell of smoke on their clothes as they are brought out of the furnace, so Daniel doesn't have a scratch on his body when he is lifted out of the den, even though he spent the night with lions.

But perhaps the lions weren't hungry that night. Or perhaps someone sympathetic to Daniel, say Darius, had had the lions fed to the full or even drugged beforehand. Any such doubts are dispelled in the following verses when Daniel's accusers and their families are thrown into the den. The viciousness and hunger of the lions are vividly displayed by the fact they were attacked and killed before "they reached the floor of the den" (v. 24).

The accusers set a trap for Daniel, but in the end they were caught in their own trap—and not only the accusers themselves, but also their families. Modern commentators, for obvious reasons, have felt uncomfortable imagining the prophet standing by as wives and children are thrown into the den. Moreover, even though it was the Persian king's decision (after all, those children might well grow up with ideas of revenge in mind), the narrator

---

15. Tikva Frymer-Kensky, "The Judicial Ordeal in the Ancient Near East" (Ph.D. dissertation: New Haven, Conn.: Yale University, 1977).

16. Though it is possible to understand events like the Flood or the crossing of the Red Sea as an ordeal in which the innocent survive and the guilty are killed.

Daniel 6:1–28

seems to have taken some pleasure in the scene. We must remember, however, that this scene is presented to a generation of God's people who felt helpless in the grips of their oppressors. Their own families were impotent in the face of exploitation and worse. They were daily being manipulated for purposes other than their own.

Darius's Decree (6:25–28)

THE PLOT OF Daniel 6 was set in motion by Darius's issuing a decree that prayers could only be directed toward himself either as a divine figure or, as is more likely, the only mediator with the divine realm. The chapter ends with a second decree, this time promoting Daniel's God throughout his vast empire.

Has the thirty-day period of the first decree passed? If not, how could that unchangeable law be changed and replaced with this one? We cannot answer that question with certainty since we do not know the timing. In any case, God takes the place of Darius, at Darius's own urging, at the end of the chapter. What a wonderful testimony to the people of God that God truly is in control in spite of present appearances!

Darius proclaims the God of Daniel "the living God." This indicates that he not only exists, but is active in the world. Certainly the prophet's rescue shows that in a dramatic fashion. God and his kingdom will never end, and he rescues his people in astounding ways. Specifically, his rescue of Daniel from the lions' den demonstrates that "he rescues and he saves" (v. 27).

After Darius's speech, the chapter, which brings to a close the court narrative part of the book, concludes with the narrative statement that "Daniel prospered during the reign of Darius and the reign of Cyrus the Persian" (v. 28). Indeed he did. He prospered throughout his entire lifetime in the court. Fewell summarizes his progression well:

> We have seen the Hebrew sage climb the political ladder from captive prisoner to initiate to sage (ch. 1) to chief sage (ch. 2) to administrator over the province of Babylon (chs. 2–3) to the king's personal adviser (ch. 4) to third ruler in the kingdom (ch. 5) to the prime minister that the king himself intends, at the beginning of ch. 6, to set over the entire kingdom and does implicitly set over the kingdom at the end of ch. 6.[17]

Though the story of Daniel's political career thus draws to a close, even more exciting material follows in the second half of the book.

---

17. Fewell, *Circle of Sovereignty*, 154.

Daniel 6:1-28

Bridging Contexts

DANIEL 6 IS the last of six historical narratives featuring Daniel in a foreign court. Thus, we have already had ample opportunity to spell out the hermeneutical principles that allow us to move from the original context of the story to a contemporary setting. We have argued as early as chapter 1[18] that the historical narrative of the Old Testament was written not simply for remembrance, but also to serve as a paradigm for future behavior. The narratives of Daniel, in particular, are shaped to serve as life examples for later generations of God's people.

We have also confronted the issue of bringing this Old Testament text to bear on a New Testament audience.[19] Acknowledging Christ's climactic role in the history of God's story of redemption leads modern interpreters to recognize the possibility of discontinuity as well as continuity between ourselves and the ancient audience. We have also seen how Jesus himself instructed his followers to read the Old Testament in the light of his coming (Luke 24:25–27, 44). We will keep these principles in mind as we work through the contents of chapter 6.

Basic truths repeated. Although I do not want to be overly repetitive, I must nonetheless point out that Daniel 6, like the preceding five chapters, illustrates the basic themes of the book of Daniel. Despite present appearances, God is indeed in control. Regardless of the fact that powerful political forces move against Daniel, God preserves him from their clutches. In spite of the fact that the law of the Medes and Persians has condemned him to death, God preserves his life. Regardless of the fact that the lions are hungry, God does not allow them to even scratch Daniel's skin. God indeed is in control!

But Daniel not only survives in spite of his faith; he prospers. At the beginning of the chapter, he already has a position of great importance in Darius's court. The plot against him was motivated by the other leaders' jealousy of his power. As the chapter ends, the narrator drives this point home with the comment: "So Daniel prospered during the reign of Darius and the reign of Cyrus the Persian" (6:28). What an example and encouragement to God's people, who later faced similar threats and challenges! The basic message of this chapter to later readers is simple: "Remain faithful! God will take care of you."

Of course, the threats and obstacles in life can be incredibly imposing. Daniel and his three friends have already testified to that truth. In Daniel 6, we have a story where the faith of Daniel alone is tested. In many ways, this chapter parallels Daniel 3, which recorded the depth of the three friends'

---

18. Cf. pp.57–61.
19. Cf. pp. 26–27.

Daniel 6:1–28

faith, with no mention of Daniel. Here we have Daniel without the three friends. The text does not allow us any basis to speculate concerning the whereabouts or actions of the three friends here, any more than we could be certain about Daniel's absence from the earlier story.

The conflict of laws. The focus on Daniel, of course, results from the fact that he has drawn the envy of his colleagues because of his meteoric rise in Darius's estimation. They cannot find anything in his behavior or character to use in order to undermine his position, so they resort to framing him. They manipulate the king to create a law that they know Daniel will not keep. The law prohibits prayer to any god or human except Darius himself for a period of thirty days. Whether the law sets Darius on a divine pedestal or imagines him to be the conduit to the gods is irrelevant; in either case, the surface intention of the law is to create a means by which extreme loyalty to the king can be measured. The irony of the situation is that the administrators who urged the king to create this law were actually disloyal to Darius, working against his own desires and intentions, whereas Daniel, who finds himself under judgment of the law, is actually the most true of his subordinates.

Nonetheless, the law created by Darius became one of the "laws of the Medes and Persians, which cannot be repealed" (v. 8). The irony here is that the law cannot even be repealed by the king himself! A law that has as its ostensible purpose the intention to set the king up as an ultimate authority actually imprisons him to its own authority.

Even more significantly, it brings the king and his law into a fundamental conflict with God and his law. Daniel knows that God's law requires that he pray to the ultimate authority of the universe, not to a human king. The basic tension in Daniel 6 is the conflict between God's law and the law of the Medes and Persians. Daniel must choose between the two laws, and he does not hesitate for a moment. He chooses to obey God's law.

Before continuing, we should note the difference between God's relationship with his law and Darius's relationship with his. The law in both cases reflects the will and desires of the one who creates the law. Darius's law reflects what he wants, and God's law reflects what God wants. We have seen, however, that Darius's law ultimately binds him to a course of action he did not want. When he saw the consequences of his actions, he would have loved to change his mind, but he could not. He was not above the law.

Is God above his law? This is a difficult question. In one sense, we want to say, yes. God is above everything. He is not bound by his own laws. He can do whatever he wants. However, to go down that road is misleading and wrong. As opposed to Darius's relationship to the law he creates, God's law is always the perfect expression of his character. The difference between Darius and God is that the latter knows himself perfectly and knows the consequences of his acts and pronouncements perfectly. This is why the psalmist in Psalm 19:7–11 can speak of God's law in a way that would be illegitimate about any human law:

> The law of the LORD is perfect,
> > reviving the soul.
> The statutes of the LORD are trustworthy,
> > making wise the simple.
> The precepts of the LORD are right,
> > giving joy to the heart.
> The commands of the LORD are radiant,
> > giving light to the eyes.
> The fear of the LORD is pure,
> > enduring forever.
> The ordinances of the LORD are sure
> > and altogether righteous.
> They are more precious than gold,
> > than much pure gold;
> they are sweeter than honey,
> > than honey from the comb.
> By them is your servant warned;
> > in keeping them there is great reward.

The cost of discipleship. Daniel kept the law of the Lord, but at first it did not seem like reward would be the result of his obedience. Darius, bound by his own law, threw him into the lions' den. Daniel's obedience flowed from his realization that he would sin if he did not practice his own religion. In this way, it is the flip side of Daniel 3, where the three friends illustrated the realization that they would sin if they participated in the false religious practices of their idolatrous oppressors. The two chapters together thus encourage later readers to avoid false religion and to pursue legitimate religion, no matter what the cost.

And the cost was great. Daniel does not articulate it as blatantly as the three friends in their speech before Nebuchadnezzar, but we are surely to understand Daniel's attitude to affirm the belief that "the God we serve is able to save us from it [the death penalty], and he will rescue us from your hand, O king. But even if he does not, we want you to know, O king, that we will not serve your gods . . ." (3:17–18; or in the case of Daniel, he will not desist from worshiping his God). In a word, Daniel would rather be eaten by lions than stop praying to God.

Even so, notice the quiet faithfulness of Daniel. Here we revisit a theme encountered for the first time in chapter 1. Daniel does not grandstand for

Daniel 6:1–28

the faith, but neither does he try to hide his love of the Lord. He did not go to the public square or the court to flaunt his rejection of Darius's decree; rather, he went as usual to his "upstairs room" (v. 10). Yet he did not close the windows so no one could observe his prayers. It may take some effort, like that exerted by the conspirators, but Daniel was not taking any extraordinary measures to hide his lack of compliance to Darius's decree. No, he will obey the law of God, not the law of the Medes and Persians with which it conflicts.

For his obedience, he is condemned to the lions' den. Again, Darius's law no longer reflects the king's will, but he has no other choice. In the world in which he lives and helped to create, not even the king can circumvent the law. He can hope, but he cannot stop the wheels that he set in motion.

God's redemptive power. In other words, Darius, the most powerful human being in the world, has no power to save Daniel. But Daniel's faith is founded on a person who is more powerful than the king, God himself. As events unfold, we observe another important biblical theme in operation: God overrules the evil intentions of human beings to bring about great salvation.

God is not only not bound by his own law as Darius is; he can deliver his people from the evil intentions of their enemies. We have seen this important redemptive principle at work frequently in previous Scripture, but I will only use one story to illustrate it. In previous chapters we had occasion to note similarities between Daniel and Joseph. As we read the Joseph story with this principle in mind, we see again and again how God delivered him from the evil intentions of human beings. Jealous brothers wanted him dead, so they threw him in a pit. God saved Joseph from death at that point when they saw an opportunity to turn their rage into a commercial venture by selling him into slavery to the Midianites. He ended up in Egypt, where he distinguished himself in the service of the high Egyptian official Potiphar.

There, however, he eventually ran into trouble because of the evil intentions of Potiphar's wife, who framed him for attempted rape. Joseph ended up in jail. This is where he met two other high Egyptian officials, the chief baker and the chief cupbearer, whose acquaintance ultimately brought him into contact with the pharaoh himself. His new high office placed him in a position from which he could save his family from certain death by starvation during an intense famine.

Joseph's was no ordinary family. It was the seed of the promise, the promise given to Abraham in Genesis 12:1–3. Joseph himself articulated the principle we are applying to the story in Daniel 6. After the death of Jacob, Joseph's brothers thought the time of their punishment for mistreating their now powerful brother had come. In response to their pleas for mercy, however, Joseph expressed his certainty concerning God's purposes in his suffering

Daniel 6:1–28

over the years: "You intended to harm me, but God intended it for good to accomplish what is now being done, the saving of many lives" (Gen. 50:20).

In this story in Daniel, God overruled the evil intentions of the conspirators and the powerlessness of Darius in order to illustrate to countless generations of his people that he is able to save his people in the midst of the most dire circumstances. We must ask what we face that surpasses the danger Daniel faced. Moreover, as we will see, we have a much stronger basis for faith in the midst of suffering and the threat of death than Daniel did.

To take it one step further, just as God saves, he also judges. Daniel lived through the night with the hungry lions. But the next morning the conspirators meet the fate they had planned for Daniel. The lions weren't sleepy or full during the night, for the bodies of the enemies of God's people did not even hit the ground before they were gobbled up. Daniel 6 thus illustrates the principle expressed in Proverbs 28:10:[20]

> He who leads the upright along an evil path
>   will fall into his own trap,
>   but the blameless will receive a good inheritance.

Thus, Daniel 6 ends with Daniel alive and promoted and his enemies dead. To cap it all off, Darius celebrates Daniel's rescue by giving praise to an authority and a kingdom greater than his own. His decree in verses 26–27 is an implicit admission that his own power is limited, while the "living God" and his kingdom is above all.

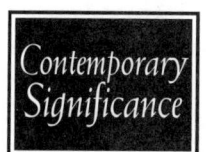

IN DANIEL 6, God calls his followers to persist in faithfulness in spite of opposition and the threat of death. He shows himself able to take care of his people in the most dire of circumstances. Daniel, his faithful servant, not only survives the lion ordeal, but he prospers to the end in the foreign court. Hebrews 11:33–34 alludes to this episode as a prime example of faith and its results. Today, Daniel is presented to us as an example of faith under duress.

Further, though Daniel 6 is not cited, surely our chapter helped provide justification for the behavior of Peter and the other apostles in Acts 5. They had just been imprisoned on the charge of preaching the gospel in Jerusalem. What do they do immediately upon their release? They preach again. When confronted, they respond, "We must obey God rather than men!" (Acts 5:29). Whether it is the law of God versus the law of the Medes and Persians, or

---

20. See P. D. Miller Jr., *Sin and Judgment in the Prophets* (Chico, Calif.: Scholars, 1982).

Daniel 6:1–28

versus the law of the Sanhedrin—or the law of the Romans, or the laws of the United States of America—God's faithful followers must always side with God's law.

Americans and most other Western Christians are spoiled, however. The democracies in which we live allow considerable room for the free exercise of religion. We may openly go to church, form our own schools, raise our children in our beliefs. If our religious conscience compels us, we can plead our case for noninvolvement in the military. We can openly protest trends in our society that are opposed to our religious values.

Private versus public situations. At times, however, Western Christians misapply the examples of Daniel and Peter. A prime example is the complaint about the lack of prayer in our public schools. Our present law prohibits a teacher from offering a prayer in our state-run schools. This bothers some Christians, who believe that Daniel 6 provides the motivation for objection. They argue that Daniel was told he could not pray, but he persisted in prayer. If we, then, are told we cannot pray, we must not cave in to the "law of the Medes and Persians." A similar kind of argument is presented in the analogous cases of Christmas displays on government property or the hanging of the Ten Commandments in a judge's courtroom.

But are these situations really analogous to Daniel 6? I suggest they are not. Daniel was not prohibited from praying in a certain location like the court; he was forbidden to pray to God at all, even in private! Indeed, it is preposterous to even imagine Daniel during his early years in Babylon insisting on prayer before the opening of his Akkadian class or the class on divination.

The confusion in the United States and probably other Western democracies arises because some Christians insist that their country is the modern equivalent of Israel. However, it cannot be urged too strongly that there are and can be no modern equivalents of Israel. There is no such thing as a "Christian nation," except in the sense of a nation where most of the inhabitants happen to be Christian at that particular historical moment.

In other words, the nation is not the church. The modern equivalent of Israel is not a political entity but rather the church. Christians should be working to keep prayer out of public schools, manger scenes off the front yard of city hall, and the Ten Commandments out of the local magistrates' offices. When the church has state backing, it grows complacent, or even worse, coercive in its witness. Indeed, study has shown that when the church gets an entrée into the power structures of the state (whether the government per se or public educational institutions), it has hurt, not helped, the cause of the kingdom. I believe we can see this in a country like Korea, where the church exercises enormous influence on the public sector and also has significant wealth and power. The power struggles within Korean ecclesiastical structures are notorious. No, the quiet faithfulness of Daniel in the privacy of his upper room has nothing to do with trying to practice public prayer in a state-run institution.

The modern parallels to Daniel 6 in Western democracies take place not in the arena of culture wars, but rather in more local situations. A librarian is fired because she refuses to work on a Sunday morning during worship services. A young teenager is told by his parents that he may not meet with the neighborhood church's youth group for prayer because they do not want him involved in "all that superstition." A wife is told that she can be a Christian, but must not act like it around the house. Where we today most often encounter conflict analogous to Daniel 6 is the law of God versus the law of an employer, a parent, a spouse.

Preparation and vigilance. Western Christians, however, must be vigilant. Their present freedom of religion could change over time. To be vigilant, however, does not mean to prepare for war or to fight for our rights. Again, the example of Daniel 6, as well as that of the disciples in the New Testament, not to speak of Jesus himself, is to prepare to risk all, even our lives. When Daniel heard about the law forbidding his prayer, he did not rally the troops for a strike or armed resistance, he prepared himself for death. The same may be said concerning the three friends in Daniel 3. Christians do not fight for their beliefs by assaulting or killing, but by dying.

The principle for this attitude comes from the Bible. We get stirring examples of this principle as it is worked on in the lives of Daniel, Shadrach, Meshach, Abednego, Peter, and many others in the pages of Scripture. But we also see examples today in the lives and deaths of our brothers and sisters who live in more coercive societies. Let me share with you the story of one of my students and his wife, Bob and Heidi Fu.

When Bob was a non-Christian, he was a leader in the protest in Tiananmen Square, which resulted in a massacre on June 4, 1989. After the protest, he became the object of intense scrutiny by the Public Security Bureau Police, but what really devastated him were betrayals by several of his colleagues. In his own words, Bob said he felt like "there was no hope, no future."

At this critical juncture in his life, one of his fellow students passed him the biography of Mr. Xi Xiong Mo, a former drug addict who converted to Christianity. Bob and his wife became Christians in that fateful year of 1989. God used them and others so that a number of his fellow students became Christians as well. Bob soon found he was again the object of the attention of the Communist Party, but now for a different reason—his Christian faith and ministry. He and his wife were both arrested in 1996 and spent two months in a Chinese jail, where they were viciously interrogated and lived in horrible conditions, but their faith grew strong.

Daniel 6:1–28

They were suddenly released from prison, but told they could be reincarcerated at any time. Bob speculates they were released in order to see who else was in their movement. Around the same time, Heidi got pregnant without obtaining the necessary quota approval slip from the police. Rearrest and forced abortion were a real possibility in her life, so they fled from Beijing to Hong Kong and finally, after being interviewed on *ABC World News Tonight*, got the attention of influential people in the United States, resulting in permission to seek asylum here.[21]

Where did Daniel find the courage to face the lions' den? His courage came from his faith in "the living God." As we saw in the previous section, this God is a God who can overrule evil to bring about good, to bring salvation. Where did Bob and Heidi Fu and countless other Christians who have faced imprisonment and death for their faith find courage to persevere? They, and we, have an even stronger basis for our faith than Daniel. Why? Because since the time of Daniel, the hope of Israel has come. Jesus Christ himself has fulfilled the prophetic anticipation of a suffering and raised Savior. The Messiah is no longer a hope for the future, but a hope based on a past event. We do not look forward to the incarnation of God's Son, but we look back to the cross.

As we look back to the cross, we see that Jesus himself faced the same threat as Daniel in the lions' den. As early Christian art attests,[22] Daniel's emergence from the lions' den is typological of Jesus death and resurrection. Towner and Goldingay explain the comparison most clearly among modern commentators.[23] As Daniel was framed on a false charge by the Persian administrators, so Jesus was framed by the jealous religious leaders of his day. They reported to the Roman authorities that he was claiming political authority with the title "king of the Jews" (Matt. 27:11). Jesus, like Daniel, was arrested while at prayer in a private location, the Garden of Gethsemane. Pilate, like Darius, worked for his release. But in the end, both Daniel and Jesus are turned over to be executed. As Towner emphasizes, however, the big difference between the two is that Daniel emerges without a scratch, while Jesus dies. Yet that difference is what underlines the superiority of the reality to its foreshadow. Jesus dies, yet he emerges from the tomb!

We have noted how Daniel in the lions' den demonstrates God's ability to overrule the evil intentions of men and women in order to bring about something good. With Joseph, we observed that God overruled the evil

---

21. Taken from personal conversations with Bob Fu and an article summarizing Bob and Heidi's story in C. Jones, "House Church Leader Granted Asylum in the USA," *China Prayer Letter and Ministry Report* 144 (November-December 1997): 1–5.

22. Towner, *Daniel*, 85.

23. Towner, *Daniel*, 84–85; Goldingay, *Daniel*, 136.

intentions of those who persecuted him to bring about salvation. Peter understands the death and resurrection of Jesus Christ as the ultimate fulfillment of this principle when he preaches at Pentecost (Acts 2:22–24):

> Men of Israel, listen to this: Jesus of Nazareth was a man accredited by God to you by miracles, wonders and signs, which God did among you through him, as you yourselves know. This man was handed over to you by God's set purpose and foreknowledge; and you, with the help of wicked men, put him to death by nailing him to the cross. But God raised him from the dead, freeing him from the agony of death, because it was impossible for death to keep its hold on him.

Now we can see the power that allows us to risk all for our faith. Jesus has not only gone into the lions' den and emerged unscathed, but he has died and been raised again. And, as Paul reminds us, his death and resurrection are the "firstfruits of those who have fallen asleep" (1 Cor. 15:20). Because of Jesus, death cannot hold us either. "Death has been swallowed up in victory. Where, O death, is your victory? Where, O death, is your sting? The sting of death is sin, and the power of sin is the law. But thanks be to God! He gives us the victory through our Lord Jesus Christ" (15:54–56).

Our faith gives us the courage to risk all, even death. Christians living in the West have not been tested to risk all. Often we act as if we are unwilling to risk anything. We need to pray for our brothers and sisters who today risk much, and we must ask the Lord to make us ready when our day of testing comes.

Our willingness to risk even our lives is what will turn the heads of the secular culture that surrounds us. Our complaints, our legislative efforts, our attempts to compel people to live according to our standards of morality will only close their ears. The power of quiet faithfulness is impressed upon us in the closing words of Darius in 6:26–27:

> For he is the living God
>   and he endures forever;
> his kingdom will not be destroyed,
>   his dominion will never end.
> He rescues and he saves;
>   he performs signs and wonders
>   in the heavens and on the earth.
> He has rescued Daniel
>   from the power of the lions.

Daniel 7:1–28

IN THE FIRST year of Belshazzar king of Babylon, Daniel had a dream, and visions passed through his mind as he was lying on his bed. He wrote down the substance of his dream.

²Daniel said: "In my vision at night I looked, and there before me were the four winds of heaven churning up the great sea. ³Four great beasts, each different from the others, came up out of the sea.

⁴"The first was like a lion, and it had the wings of an eagle. I watched until its wings were torn off and it was lifted from the ground so that it stood on two feet like a man, and the heart of a man was given to it.

⁵"And there before me was a second beast, which looked like a bear. It was raised up on one of its sides, and it had three ribs in its mouth between its teeth. It was told, 'Get up and eat your fill of flesh!'

⁶"After that, I looked, and there before me was another beast, one that looked like a leopard. And on its back it had four wings like those of a bird. This beast had four heads, and it was given authority to rule.

⁷"After that, in my vision at night I looked, and there before me was a fourth beast—terrifying and frightening and very powerful. It had large iron teeth; it crushed and devoured its victims and trampled underfoot whatever was left. It was different from all the former beasts, and it had ten horns.

⁸"While I was thinking about the horns, there before me was another horn, a little one, which came up among them; and three of the first horns were uprooted before it. This horn had eyes like the eyes of a man and a mouth that spoke boastfully.

⁹"As I looked,

"thrones were set in place,
    and the Ancient of Days took his seat.
His clothing was as white as snow;
    the hair of his head was white like wool.
His throne was flaming with fire,
    and its wheels were all ablaze.

¹⁰ A river of fire was flowing,
>   coming out from before him.
> Thousands upon thousands attended him;
>   ten thousand times ten thousand stood before him.
> The court was seated,
>   and the books were opened.

¹¹"Then I continued to watch because of the boastful words the horn was speaking. I kept looking until the beast was slain and its body destroyed and thrown into the blazing fire. ¹²(The other beasts had been stripped of their authority, but were allowed to live for a period of time.)

¹³"In my vision at night I looked, and there before me was one like a son of man, coming with the clouds of heaven. He approached the Ancient of Days and was led into his presence. ¹⁴He was given authority, glory and sovereign power; all peoples, nations and men of every language worshiped him. His dominion is an everlasting dominion that will not pass away, and his kingdom is one that will never be destroyed.

¹⁵"I, Daniel, was troubled in spirit, and the visions that passed through my mind disturbed me. ¹⁶I approached one of those standing there and asked him the true meaning of all this.

"So he told me and gave me the interpretation of these things: ¹⁷'The four great beasts are four kingdoms that will rise from the earth. ¹⁸But the saints of the Most High will receive the kingdom and will possess it forever—yes, for ever and ever.'

¹⁹"Then I wanted to know the true meaning of the fourth beast, which was different from all the others and most terrifying, with its iron teeth and bronze claws—the beast that crushed and devoured its victims and trampled underfoot whatever was left. ²⁰I also wanted to know about the ten horns on its head and about the other horn that came up, before which three of them fell—the horn that looked more imposing than the others and that had eyes and a mouth that spoke boastfully. ²¹As I watched, this horn was waging war against the saints and defeating them, ²²until the Ancient of Days came and pronounced judgment in favor of the saints of the Most High, and the time came when they possessed the kingdom.

²³"He gave me this explanation: 'The fourth beast is a fourth kingdom that will appear on earth. It will be different

Daniel 7:1–28

from all the other kingdoms and will devour the whole earth, trampling it down and crushing it. ²⁴The ten horns are ten kings who will come from this kingdom. After them another king will arise, different from the earlier ones; he will subdue three kings. ²⁵He will speak against the Most High and oppress his saints and try to change the set times and the laws. The saints will be handed over to him for a time, times and half a time.

²⁶"But the court will sit, and his power will be taken away and completely destroyed forever. ²⁷Then the sovereignty, power and greatness of the kingdoms under the whole heaven will be handed over to the saints, the people of the Most High. His kingdom will be an everlasting kingdom, and all rulers will worship and obey him.'

²⁸"This is the end of the matter. I, Daniel, was deeply troubled by my thoughts, and my face turned pale, but I kept the matter to myself."

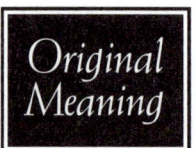

Original Meaning

CHAPTER 7 SIGNALS a major transition in the book of Daniel. The first half of the book told stories about Daniel and his three friends; we learned about their faith and courage before pagan kings from Nebuchadnezzar to Cyrus. The second half of the book, beginning with chapter 7, reports Daniel's visions of the future. Accordingly, we move from the relatively straightforward narratives of chapters 1–6 to the often enigmatic images of Daniel's prophetic vision.[1]

The Nature of Apocalyptic Literature

IN A WORD, we change genres from the first half of the book to the second. Apocalyptic replaces court narrative, demanding that we change reading strategy. Before launching into an interpretation of this and the following chapters, it is important, though we must necessarily be brief,[2] to discuss the

---

1. We should note, however, that certain characteristics link the two sections (see Introduction). For instance, chapter 7 is in the Aramaic language as are chapters 2–6. Hebrew begins again with chapter 8. Also, the four-kingdom scheme of Daniel's vision in the present chapter reminds us of Nebuchadnezzar's dream of the statue in chapter 2.

2. For more on apocalyptic literature in the Bible, see T. Longman III, *Reading the Bible with Heart and Mind* (Colorado Springs: NavPress, 1997), 213–26; *Fictional Akkadian Autobiography* (Winona Lake, Ind.: Eisenbrauns, 1991), 166–90.

nature and intention of apocalyptic literature. At this point, we will only examine the genre in terms of its original meaning; in the Bridging Context section, we will explore the legitimate appropriation of apocalyptic into our contemporary world.

The term *apocalyptic* comes from the Greek word *apokalypsis* and simply means "revelation." Indeed, the genre label is taken from the first verse of the New Testament book Revelation (also, not surprisingly, known as the Apocalypse of Saint John) and is applied to other books, both in the Bible and outside, that have similar characteristics.

Daniel is clearly such a book, and we will have recourse to connections between Daniel and Revelation as we interpret the second half of the book. But to say that Daniel and Revelation are a "revelation" is not that illuminating. After all, every book of the Bible is a revelation, in the sense that God is uncovering some aspect of his truth to his people. What is so special about sections like Daniel 7–12?

Ironically, we may get a better insight into the book from its common usage in English than we do from its Greek etymology. Some of us remember that the 1960s and early 1970s were called an apocalyptic moment in history. Political instability and the threat of nuclear extinction, still with us but not felt so imminently, led to an uncertainty about the continuance of the human race itself. Apocalyptic, then, in common parlance communicates an impending sense of doom, a feeling that existence might come to an end at any moment.

With this popular understanding of the term we are getting closer to the biblical idea, but we are not quite there yet. A violent end to history is in the ultimate purview of biblical apocalyptic. However, far from imparting a sense of doom and pessimism, books like Daniel and Revelation radiate with joy and optimism. Why? Because the end is the end of human corruption and the oppression of God's people and is brought about by the audience's warring God. Apocalyptic celebrates God's victory over the enemies of the godly.

Immediately, we note how the apocalyptic chapters of Daniel continue the theme we discovered in the first six chapters. The stories of the first half of the book illustrated how, in spite of present appearances, God is in control and will overcome the seemingly invulnerable evil forces of the day. Whether it was the evil plots of the Babylonian wise men or the rage of the king himself, God protected his people and allowed them to prosper even in adversity.

Now the theme goes further. We move from the present circumstances of God's people in captivity to their ultimate liberation. We move from human evil, evident also in the scope of chapters 7–12, to the perverse spiritual forces that stand behind them. We move from deliverance out of a burning furnace and a lions' den to salvation from the power of death itself (ch. 12)!

But the essence of apocalyptic is more than the content of the message; it concerns its inner nature. Now that we have gotten used to the rather

Daniel 7:1–28

straightforward plots of Daniel 1–6 we suddenly find ourselves in a strange world, a world of hybrid beasts and riders on the clouds. Furthermore, we encounter what look like timetables, but timetables that are impossible to penetrate (see below). Whether it is the 2300 mornings and evenings of chapter 8 or the seventy weeks of chapter 9, we have no firm basis for relating these periods to time as we know it. What are we to make of these images and dreamlike numbers?

The interpretation of these specific texts await their proper moment, but some words of introduction to apocalyptic style is in order at this point. To get right to the point, apocalyptic is a metaphor-rich genre. In this regard it is like poetry. Metaphors and similes teach by analogy. They throw light on difficult concepts and things by relating them to something we know from common experience. As such, images speak truly and accurately, but not precisely. We often do not know where the analogy stops. In this way, images preserve mystery about ideas that are ultimately beyond our comprehension. It is a travesty, then, to interpret apocalyptic images too finely, to press them in their details. As we will see, this mistake is common among biblical interpreters of apocalyptic and has led to all kinds of fanciful interpretations and outlandish claims. Caution and reserve are virtues in the interpretation of apocalyptic.

Interestingly, however, the images of Daniel are stranger to us than they were to their original audience. In what follows, we will point out that much of the stuff of the imagery comes from previous biblical revelation or from common motifs found in broader ancient Near Eastern literature. Observing these connections certainly makes the imagery more understandable, but does not erase the intentional ambiguity and sense of mystery.

We would also be remiss in our discussion of the images of apocalyptic if we simply talked about what they meant in terms of their references in the "real" world. Images evoke powerful feelings in readers. Again, because the original readers had a more immediate understanding of these images, the feelings would be more potent and natural in them. We will make the attempt, through our description, to recover these emotions for the modern reader.

Thus, the rest of this commentary is dedicated to the exposition of Daniel's apocalyptic visions. Even chapter 9, which in large part is a prayer, concludes with an apocalyptic timetable. The result is that, just as in chapters 1–6, many of the themes of chapter 7 will be repeated in chapters 8–12. Here are the major themes that reverberate in this section:

- the horror of human evil, particularly as it is concentrated in the state
- the announcement of a specific time of deliverance
- repentance that leads to deliverance

- the revelation that a cosmic war stands behind human conflict
- judgment as certain for those who resist God and oppress his people
- the equally certain truth that God's people, downtrodden in the present, will experience new life in the fullest sense.

To state it again, each of these themes appear, more or less, in each of the concluding chapters. However, in order to avoid undue repetition especially in the sections on Contemporary Significance, I plan to emphasize one of these themes in each of the following six chapters. Chapter 7, with its vision of four hybrid sea beasts, underlines the horror of human evil. Chapter 8, with its prophecy of the 2300 mornings and evenings, will stress the announcement of a specific time of deliverance. Chapter 9, Daniel's prayer requesting forgiveness for past sins, concerns repentance and restoration. Chapter 10, which pushes back the veil that keeps human beings from observing spiritual realities, will reveal the spiritual battle behind the physical one. Chapter 11, with its prophetic description of history, narrating events of the last few centuries B.C., will show how human evil leads inexorably to judgment. Finally, chapter 12 (treated with chapter 11) will conclude the book on a note of victory and resurrection for God's people.

Daniel 7 begins the apocalyptic section of this book. With its striking imagery of four hybrid beasts arising out of a chaotic sea and its ultimate encounter with the cloud-riding figure who looks like a son of man, this chapter is arguably the best known in the second half of the book. Certainly it is the one most frequently quoted and alluded to in the New Testament. Nonetheless, it is also one of the most enigmatic sections of the Old Testament.

In spite of this, the central message of the chapter is clear: God is in control. He will defeat the seemingly unconquerable powers that oppress his people. The intended effect of this message is also obvious: comfort for the faithful. Evil may seem as if it has the upper hand, but that is a temporary deception. Better to stay faithful and suffer than to fall in with evil and experience God's ultimate judgment.

The chapter may be divided into three parts: (1) horror by the sea (7:1–8); (2) heavenly power (7:9–14); (3) divine victory (7:15–28). The third part also serves as the divinely inspired interpretation of the first two parts, which are different scenes of the same vision.

Horror by the Sea (7:1–8)

THE COURT NARRATIVES ended in the Persian period during the time of Darius the Mede. Chapter 7 scrolls back to the time of Belshazzar, certainly before the event of chapter 5 (which records the last day of Belshazzar's

Daniel 7:1–28

reign and life). The chronological notice in 7:1 indicates that the vision came to Daniel during Belshazzar's first year. Miller suggests that this king's coregency began in 553 B.C.,[3] while Goldingay argues for 550/549 B.C.[4] While nothing crucial is at stake here, Goldingay points out the provocative significance of 550/549 B.C., for that was the year that Cyrus the Persian defeated Astyages, his Median overlord. In other words, the process that ultimately led to the demise of Babylonia as the center of human power had begun, and as we will see, one of the main lessons of this chapter is that, although oppressive human power seems unconquerable particularly to the vanquished, human power is in reality temporal. One evil power succeeds another in a cycle of oppression, which will be broken by only divine intervention.

Daniel's vision comes about by means of a dream, and with this note we get an indication of another difference between the closely related genres of prophecy and apocalyptic. Indeed, prophecy and apocalyptic are cousins of one another; they share many similarities, most notably that both at times concern the future. Besides some of the characteristics (content and nature of the message) noted in the section "The Nature of Apocalyptic Literature," apocalyptic is slightly different in terms of the mode of revelation. Whereas the classic prophetic mode of communication is direct from God to the seer, apocalyptic literature reports a more indirect mode of communication.

When God spoke to a prophet like Jeremiah, he spoke directly to him and then told him to speak his message to the people of Judah. When the people responded, the prophet then went back to God for further instructions (Jer. 12). The prophet is God's spokesperson; he brings God's word to the people. A different dynamic is at work in apocalyptic. God speaks to Daniel through a dream (as in Dan. 7) or through a mediator—usually an angel (e.g., Dan. 12:5–13). He is not commissioned to speak to the people but rather to write it down. Significantly, in Daniel 12 the prophet is not commanded to publish his literary revelation broadly, but rather to "close up and seal the words of the scroll until the time of the end" (12:4). The implications of this will be spelled out later in the commentary.

Daniel's report of the vision begins with the setting. He is on the coast of the sea, where the winds are whipping the waves into a frenzy. That Daniel is not giving a scientific description is immediately apparent since he attributes the wildness of the sea to the "four winds of heaven" (v. 2). They are all blowing at once. We are not to simply imagine huge waves crashing into the shore, but rather turbulent, chaotic waters moving in all directions.

---

3. Miller, *Daniel*, 195.
4. Goldingay, *Daniel*, 139, supported by G. Hasel, "The First and Third Years of Belshazzar (Dan. 7:1; 8:1)," *AUSS* 15 (1976): 153–68.

Daniel 7:1–28

On a simple psychological level, this forebodes danger. But reading this description with a broader literary background reveals that even more is at stake here. By the time of Daniel, the sea was already a potent symbol of chaos, indeed of destructive evil.[5] Here and elsewhere in the second half of Daniel the imagery of the visions may be associated with the mythology of the broader Near East. We may illustrate this with reference to the great creation myths of the Babylonians and the Canaanites.

Let me preface my remarks by pointing out that Daniel's (ultimately God's) use of these images does not mean that the Bible buys into the creation myths themselves. The best understanding of this imagery is that the biblical author evokes well-known mythological motifs to evoke a mood and communicate a message. In the end, as we will observe after we paint the full picture, we will see that, far from mindlessly borrowing this language, the Bible undermines the false religion of its idolatrous neighbors through the use of their imagery.

The most well-known creation story[6] of the Babylonians is the *Enuma Elish*. This tale begins with an account of the creation of the gods. At the beginning stands primordial Tiamat with her consort Apsu. Both of these deities represent different aspects of the waters. Indeed, Tiamat's name, when translated from the Akkadian, means "the Sea." She is the mother of the next generation of deities, including Enlil and Ea. The generation after Enlil and Ea includes Marduk. The story told in *Enuma Elish* is about how Marduk becomes the head of the pantheon.

The plot gets underway when Apsu, the father, grows angry with his noisy divine children and purposes to get rid of them. Tiamat, the mother, protests, but does not thwart Apsu's intention. However, Ea, the god of wisdom, catches wind of his intentions and succeeds in doing away with Apsu. Far from solving the problem, however, Tiamat is now enraged and turns her more potent forces against her children. Ea and the other gods stand powerless before her. Marduk comes to the rescue and agrees to fight Tiamat, the Sea, with the proviso that if he succeeds, he will be recognized as chief among the gods.

---

5. See J. Day, *God's Conflict with the Dragon and the Sea* (Cambridge: Cambridge Univ. Press, 1975); C. Kloos, *Yhwh's Combat with the Sea: A Canaanite Tradition in the Religion of Ancient Israel* (Leiden: Brill, 1986); M. K. Wakeman, *God's Battle with the Monster: A Study in Biblical Imagery* (Leiden: Brill, 1973).

6. W. G. Lambert, "A New Look at the Babylonian Background of Genesis," *JTS* 16 (1968): 287–300, warns that Mesopotamian conceptions of creation probably changed over the period of more than a millennium, in which Akkadian was the *lingua franca* of the Near East; but the *Enuma Elish* certainly reflects the majority opinion of Marduk priesthood, which was dominant during those times when the city of Babylon was the central power of the region.

This is not the place to justify what to us in the twentieth century seems a silly theology. The point is that the myth in all seriousness now relates the creation of the world in the light of the struggle between the Creator and the Sea. The fight is between Marduk, the one who brings order in the world, and Tiamat, the one who by her very nature as water desires to abolish order and boundaries.

The story is dramatically told,[7] but I will relate just its conclusion. Marduk destroys Tiamat, the Sea, and from her body creates the universe as we know it (including humankind). Nonetheless, somehow the sea continues to threaten to abolish the creation, so that Marduk must set up boundaries and guards to keep the world from reverting to its former formless state. In other words, the sea is a force ranged against God and creation in Mesopotamian theology.

The Canaanites have a similar story to tell,[8] but in place of Marduk and Tiamat stand their gods Baal and Yam (whose name also means "the Sea").[9] Yam attempts to take over the leadership of the gods and wants to put Baal in custody. Baal will have nothing to do with it and resists Yam. To make a long story short, he defeats Sea and becomes the head of the pantheon.[10]

Again, we should not get lost in the details of these stories. The point is that deep in the psyche of the people of the ancient Near East the sea was more than a dangerous place. It was a threatening force that was ranged against the beneficial forces of creation.

Daniel was not the first one to use sea imagery in this way. Elsewhere in the Old Testament, Yahweh's struggle and victory over evil is recounted as a fight against the sea and its monsters. God blasts the sea with his rebuke (Ps. 18:15); he sets a guard over the sea (Job 7:12; Jer. 5:22); he causes the sea to dry up (Nah. 1:4); he treads on the sea (Hab. 3:15); and he fights the sea monsters (Isa. 27:1).[11]

The bottom line of this lengthy but important discussion is that the description of the sea at the beginning of Daniel's vision evokes horror and an anticipation of evil. The following verses do not disappoint this expectation.

---

7. The text may be found most conveniently in *ANET*, 60–72. For more recent translations, consult B. R. Foster, *Before the Muses* (Bethesda, Md.: CDL Press, 1993), 354–402; W. W. Hallo, ed., *The Context of Scripture* (Leiden: Brill, 1997), 390–402.

8. It may be found in *ANET*, 129–42; also M. D. Coogan, *Stories from Ancient Canaan* (Philadelphia: Westminster, 1978), 75–115.

9. T. Jacobsen, "The Battle Between Marduk and Tiamat," *JAOS* 88 (1968): 104–8, has persuasively argued that the myth originated among Northwest Semites like the Canaanites and then was adopted by the Mesopotamians.

10. The text is broken after the defeat of Yam, but most scholars believe that the lost portion may have recounted creation.

11. See T. Longman III and D. Reid, *God Is a Warrior* (Grand Rapids: Zondervan, 1995), 64–69.

Daniel 7:1–28

The scene is thus set. It already evokes horror, but the story is just beginning. Out of the chaotic sea arises four great beasts, one after the other. Before commenting on the beasts individually, I need to make several general observations. (1) The beasts (with the exception of the second) are like none to be found in God's creation. That is the point—they are symbols of forces ranged against God and his creation order. These beasts are bizarre; they are mutants, perversions of what God intended by his creation. As such, they evoke not only horror in the original reader, but also revulsion.

Two lines of evidence indicate to us the Israelite reader's strong reaction to the mixed character of these beasts. (a) The first is the creation story. Here God made the various components of his creation "according to their ... kinds" (lᵉmino: Gen. 1:11–12, 21, 24, 25); the different parts of creation were created to be unique and separate. (b) The Israelite concern with separation of species was embedded in their laws, which indicated that the original creation order was to be preserved through history. A series of laws in Deuteronomy 22:9–11 is a case in point. "Do not plant two kinds of seed in your vineyard; if you do, not only the crops you plant but also the fruit of the vineyard will be defiled. Do not plow with an ox and a donkey yoked together. Do not wear clothes of wool and linen woven together." Thus, the four beasts that arise from the chaotic sea are images of grotesque horror to the original Israelite readers.

(2) We cannot be certain where the specific imagery of the beasts originates. There have been many suggestions. For instance, attention has been drawn to the hybrid beasts of Mesopotamian art.[12] P. A. Porter has read the description of the beasts of Daniel 7 in the light of the description of anomalous births in Babylonian divination texts[13] and argued that the symbolism derives from those texts.[14] Perhaps the imagery does derive from one or more of these sources; we cannot be sure. In any case, even without the knowledge of the origin of the imagery, the horrific impact of the beasts does not escape us.

(3) An obvious similarity exists between the four-kingdom scheme in the present chapter and the four-kingdom scheme of Nebuchadnezzar's vision in chapter 2. In that chapter we described the conflict between those (mostly conservative) commentators who identified the four successive kingdoms as Babylon, Medo-Persia, Greece, and Rome,[15] and those who argued for the

---

12. M. Roaf, *Cultural Atlas of Mesopotamia and the Ancient Near East* (New York: Facts on File, 1990), provides a picture of a Mesopotamian winged bull with a human head (163) and a winged lion with eagles' feet and horns (196–97).

13. We saw in ch. 1 how Daniel would have been aware of these texts.

14. P. A. Porter, *Metaphors and Monsters: A Literary-Critical Study of Daniel 7 and 8* (ConBOT 20; Lund: CWK Gleerup, 1983).

15. Such as E. J. Young, *The Prophecy of Daniel* (Grand Rapids: Eerdmans, 1949), 275–94.

Daniel 7:1–28

pattern Babylon, Media, Persia, and Greece.[16] The same debate rages in the interpretation of Daniel 7 as well.

In my opinion there are strengths and weaknesses with both approaches.[17] Perhaps the greatest problem is that chapter 7 goes on to describe the climax of the vision as the complete destruction of human evil power at the hands of the "one like a son of man" (v. 13) and "the saints of the Most High" (v. 18). Even today, more than two and a half millennia after Daniel, we still look to the future for this to happen (see Contemporary Significance section). Ancient Greece is no more; ancient Rome is no more. And contrary to some special pleading on the part of contemporary sensationalist interpretation, there are no modern descendants of the Roman empire today.[18] We will argue that, though the vision begins with the Babylonian empire, its multivalent imagery intends to prohibit definite historical identifications with the remaining three beasts. Rather, the fourfold pattern simply informs us that evil kingdoms will succeed one another (at least seemingly) until the end of time. The people of God must recognize that this is God's plan and prepare for persecution.

(4) These beasts represent "four kingdoms that will rise from the earth" (v. 17), and this from no less an authority than the interpreting angel of the second half of this chapter. We import this divinely imparted insight into our present discussion for economy of discussion, for here we will comment on the meaning and significance of the first three beasts. We will reserve our comments about the fourth beast primarily for the last section of this chapter, since that is where the interpreting angel focuses our attention in verses 15–28.

The beasts come out of the chaotic sea one after the other. The first is described as "like a lion, and it had the wings of an eagle. I watched until its wings were torn off and it was lifted from the ground so that it stood on two feet like a man, and the heart of a man was given to it" (v. 4). As with the statue in chapter 2, we begin in the present. There the head of gold was explicitly identified as Nebuchadnezzar (i.e., the Babylonian empire). Here, in the waning years of that same empire, the most natural interpretation of the symbolism is that it stands for Babylonia. Perhaps the clearest key to this iden-

---

16. For the classic exposition of a "critical" approach to this imagery, see H. H. Rowley, *Darius the Mede and the Four World Empires in the Book of Daniel* (San Diego, Calif.: Cardiff, 1935). But two evangelicals have also made a persuasive case for this approach as well: R. J. M. Gurney, *God in Control: An Exposition of the Prophecies of Daniel* (Worthing: Walter, 1980); J. H. Walton, "The Four Kingdoms of Daniel," *JETS* 29 (1986): 25–36.

17. See pp. 81–83 for arguments for and against both of these approaches.

18. Cf. the convoluted arguments of someone like Hal Lindsey, *The Late Great Planet Earth* (Grand Rapids: Zondervan, 1970), who sees in the European Common Market (now the European Union) as the fulfillment of the ten horns of Daniel 7.

tification is the fact that the hybrid animal becomes human-like, reminiscent of Nebuchadnezzar's own experience as recorded in chapter 4.

The lion and the eagle are both proud animals; they are both animals of prey. They strike fear in the hearts of the other animals, who are their food. Because of these characteristics, many great empires choose one or both animals as their national symbol. There is nothing in particular that relates them to Babylonia.

The same may be said for the second beast that rises out of the sea, the bear. For whatever reason this beast is not a hybrid but it still is a ferocious animal of prey. Indeed, the picture drawn of this particular bear has it gnawing three ribs while it is raised up on one of its sides. Its voracious appetite is encouraged by a voice that cries out, "Get up and eat your fill of flesh!"

It is with this second beast that the classic debate begins. Is the bear Medo-Persia or Media? Historically, we know Persia became a great empire by first acquiring the formerly dominant Medes into its empire. True, it was Cyrus the Persian whose forces defeated the Babylonians in 539 B.C., but it was through the agency (according to the book of Daniel) of Darius the Mede.

The imagery can be pressed to argue either position. The Medo-Persian identification argues that Media never existed as an independent world empire and that the three ribs can be identified with the three great victories of the Medo-Persian alliance: Lydia, Babylon, and Egypt. Gurney, an evangelical who argues for an identification with Media alone, cites Jeremiah 51:27–29, which lists Ararat, Minni, and Ashkenaz as Media's three allies as they go against Babylon.[19] Walton clarifies this passage by stating that the three "represent respectively Urartu, which was subdued by the Medes in 605 B.C.; Mannaea, an ally of Assyria in its final days, which fell to the Medes shortly after the collapse of Assyria; and the Scythians, who were repulsed by the Medes, probably in the reign of Cyaxares II."[20] Thus, we already find ourselves on slippery ground when it comes to specific and concrete historical identifications of the imagery of the four beasts. It is my argument that this is an intentional effect of the imagery of the vision. The purpose is not so much writing history in advance as making a theological statement about the conflict between human evil and God.

The intentional ambiguity continues with the third beast. The beast looks like a leopard, but it has four wings and four heads. As we look for the point of the imagery, we are drawn immediately to the characteristic of speed. Leopards are fast cats, and with the addition of wings, we are to imagine blazing speed. Is the significance of this imagery the blazing speed of the

---

19. R. J. M. Gurney, "The Four Kingdoms of Daniel 2 and 7," *Themelios* 2 (1977): 43.
20. Walton, "The Four Kingdoms of Daniel," 30.

Persian army and are the four heads to be associated with four kings of Persia,[21] or does it point to Alexander's *Blitzkrieg* through the Orient and the four generals who divided his vast empire after his early death?

The fourth kingdom is the most enigmatic of all. "It was different from all the former beasts" (v. 7). It appears to be only vaguely animal-like. Later, its description will be expanded to having "iron teeth and bronze claws" (v. 19). Someone like myself who enjoys science fiction is tempted to label this fourth "Robo-beast." But of course, it is not a robot. The metallic composition of its weapons (teeth and claws) simply highlights its destructive power and ruthlessness. There is little concrete description here by which we may argue for a specific identification, so the classic approaches to this text have recourse to simple historical sequence. If one has already identified the first three as Babylon, Media, and Persia, then the fourth must be Greek. If, on the other hand, one has combined Media and Persia and identified the third as Greece, then the fourth kingdom must be Roman. We will return to this question and the function of the horns in the last section of this chapter.

Heavenly Power (7:9–14)

VERSE 9 IS an abrupt transition from the scene by the sea to a courtroom. From its description, we know this is no ordinary courtroom, but again, the vision speaks in images. Note first of all that we no longer have descriptions of animal-like creatures. The two main characters are described in human-like terms: "the Ancient of Days" and the "one like a son of man."

In essence, we have gone up the chain of being. Evil human kingdoms were described as horrifying hybrid animals; the divine realm is imaged as human beings. The association is perfectly appropriate in a broader biblical view because, after all, Genesis 1:27 tells us that God created men and women in his own image.

While it is not clear from the description whether the scene takes place in heaven or on earth,[22] the imagery makes it clear that the two main participants are divine and that the attendants are celestial and not human creatures. Much of the imagery is not uncommonly associated with God's appearance (theophany) and signals his wisdom (his white hair), his righteousness (his white clothing), and his power in judgment (fire).

The first figure is called the "Ancient of Days." He is God, specifically in his role as judge. As such, he is imaged as an old and presumably wise human judge sitting in his courtroom. The second figure, "one like a son of man," is

---

21. So Gurney, "Kingdoms," 43–44.
22. Goldingay, *Daniel*, 164–65; Collins, *Daniel*, 303.

Daniel 7:1–28

more startling in his Old Testament context. He is riding the cloud chariot, which is the prerogative of God alone.

Like the image of the sea, the image of the cloud rider is an ancient one by the time we come to Daniel 7:13. Cloud imagery associated with the Lord's appearance is as old as the Exodus and the pillar of cloud by day and the fire by night (Ex. 13:21). During the climactic theophany on Sinai, the mountain was covered by a cloud (19:16). In the tabernacle, God appeared in the cloud that was present in the Most Holy Place (Lev. 16:2).

We learn of the vehicular cloud, however, in the Psalms and Prophets. God is the cloud rider in Psalm 68:4:

> Sing to God, sing praise to his name,
>> extol him who rides on the clouds—
> his name is the LORD—
>> and rejoice before him.

In Psalm 104:3–4 we read:

> He makes the clouds his chariot
>> and rides on the wings of the wind.
> He makes winds his messengers,
>> flames of fire his servants.

The Old Testament prophets also use the cloud-riding image in clear judgment/war contexts. Note Isaiah 19:1 and Nahum 1:3:

> See, the LORD rides on a swift cloud
>> and is coming to Egypt.
> The idols of Egypt tremble before him,
>> and the hearts of the Egyptians melt within them.
>
> The LORD is slow to anger and great in power;
>> the LORD will not leave the guilty unpunished.
> His way is in the whirlwind and the storm,
>> and clouds are the dust of his feet.

Like the sea image, the motif of God riding clouds also has an ancient Near Eastern background. This connection may be most closely observed in the literature from Ugarit. Baal, the chief deity and primary divine warrior of that culture, is often called the "Rider on the Clouds." Indeed it is one of his most common epithets:

> "Hearken, O Puissant Baal:
> Give heed, O Rider on the Clouds."[23]

---

23. See *ANET*, 134.

This example could be multiplied many times. Baal was the god of the thunderstorm in the Ugaritic pantheon. His cloud-riding was appropriate to his function.

Thus, Daniel 7:1–14 presents the reader with two image clusters. On the one hand, we have four beasts and horns, which represent depraved human kingdoms; on the other hand, we see two human figures, the Ancient of Days and one like a son of man, who image the divine realm. The identity of the "one like a son of man" has been a difficult one through the history of interpretation. We will reserve discussion of this critical issue for the section on Contemporary Significance.

The vision is more than descriptive of these two realms: human evil and divine judgment. It also narrates a conflict between the two, with a certain and clear conclusion. "The beast," presumably the boastful horn, was destroyed, while the one like the son of man was exalted and given an eternal kingdom. In a word, though human evil thrives in the present, God is in control and will have the final victory. The implicit message to God's people is: "Remain faithful in spite of appearances." The interpretation of the vision that follows bears this message out.

Divine Victory (7:15–28)

DANIEL REACTS TO the vision with fear and confusion. His fear signals to us later readers the overwhelming force of the revelation. Daniel looks into the abyss of human evil and into the very throne room of God. No wonder he is shaken by the experience. His confusion drives him to an angel who is present to assist him with the interpretation of these marvelous things.

The angel's initial response is short and sweet: "The four great beasts are four kingdoms that will rise from the earth. But the saints of the Most High will receive the kingdom and will possess it forever—yes, for ever and ever" (vv. 17–18). As simply stated as this answer is, an ambiguity remains that is not directly addressed in what follows, namely, the identity of the "saints of the Most High." Those who read this expression in modern English translations today most naturally think of "saints" as human and take it as a reference to God's oppressed people. However, in the Aramaic (*qaddise 'elyonim*) and in the context of its use in the Dead Sea scrolls and elsewhere in Daniel (4:13; 8:13), the phrase refers to angelic beings.

The debate on this issue has raged, but the angelic interpretation is by far the most dominant today.[24] Certainly, it paints a powerful picture that will be further expanded in chapter 10. Behind the earthly struggle stands a cos-

---

24. For an excellent concise discussion of the issue, see Collins, *Daniel*, 313–17.

mic struggle. The exiled Israelites are not just engaged in an earthly battle, but one with heavenly significance. That God and his angels will "receive the kingdom" is good news to those who are on God's side on earth.

Nonetheless, the phrase can refer to human beings as well,[25] and perhaps it is best understood to imply both God's human and angelic creatures. Whether it refers directly to God's people or indirectly to them through their spiritual representatives, the message is the same: God will win this great cosmic battle. This is good news for all of those who follow God, especially those who feel the cruel hand of their evil oppressors.

But Daniel's confusion and fear have not yet subsided, so he follows up his question with another, this time focusing on the nature of the fourth beast. The significance of the fourth beast is its climactic place in the future. It intensifies the evil of its predecessors and produces pernicious offspring in the form of eleven horns. The eleventh horn is the most rebellious: "He will speak against the Most High and oppress his saints and try to change the set times and the laws. The saints will be handed over to him for a time, times and half a time" (v. 25).

The image of a horn is well known from other biblical references. Pride and honor, whether godly (1 Sam. 2:1; Ps. 89:17[18], 24[25]; 112:9) or ungodly (Ps. 75:5), is often described by the image of a lifted-up horn, stemming from the idea of a powerful animal lifting its head high. In our present passage, the connotation is that of uncalled-for pride. It is a rebellious refusal to submit to God.

As already indicated, much energy has been exerted as to the identity of the fourth beast and the associated horns. A strong case can be made (based especially on the clear meaning of ch. 8) that the fourth beast is Greece and the ten horns are the kings that followed Alexander (though working that out is difficult), with the climactic horn being associated with the insidious figure of Antiochus IV Epiphanes, who oppressed God's faithful people in the middle of the second century B.C.

Critics, however, have pointed out that although Antiochus himself died and passed from the scene, his death could hardly be said to be followed by the incoming of God's kingdom.[26] For this reason, other scholars have argued that the fourth kingdom must be Rome and the ten horns should be identified as ten kingdoms that arise from that political entity, to be followed by

---

25. Cf. V. S. Poythress, "The Holy Ones of the Most High in Daniel vii," *VT* 26 (1976): 208–13.

26. Of course, most advocates of this approach argue that this is failed prophecy, which leads to later reinterpretation. See R. P. Carroll, *When Prophecy Failed: Cognitive Dissonance in the Prophetic Traditions of the Old Testament* (New York: Seabury, 1979). Such a view is unacceptable to those who believe that Daniel is a divinely inspired prophet.

Daniel 7:1–28

a climactic rebel to be identified as the Antichrist in the New Testament. We will say more about the latter in the Contemporary Significance section. But for now let it suffice to say that there is much to commend this approach in the light of later, fuller biblical revelation. The little horn will be defeated at the conclusion of the great cosmic struggle, a point to which the world has not yet arrived.

The only criticism to be made is the insistence that the fourth kingdom be specifically identified with Rome. Rome exists no more; it cannot be revived except perhaps in political propaganda. There are no Roman people, for instance. To think of the ten horns and the little horn as future manifestations of the Roman empire is bizarre. The best way to view the imagery of Daniel 7 is not in terms of four specific evil empires, but as four kingdoms symbolically representing the fact that evil kingdoms (of an unspecified number)[27] will succeed one another from the time of the Exile to the time of the climax of history, when God will intervene and once and for all judge all evil and bring into existence his kingdom.

It remains to comment on the enigmatic phrase "a time, times and half a time." This chronological reference is in answer to the implicit question of how long the little horn will be allowed to flaunt his power against God and his "saints." This expression is often taken to mean "one year, two years, and half a year," that is, three and a half years. The claim is then made that later chronological references give roughly the same time period.[28] Those who believe the little horn is Antiochus Epiphanes cite the period of time as roughly equal to the time that king wreaked havoc with the religion of the Jewish people in 168–165 B.C.[29] Some of those who believe the reference is to the future time of the Antichrist prefer to speak of three and a half years of tribulation for God's people at the time of the second coming of Christ.

However, questions must be raised about attempts to make this symbolic number so specific. After all, the second phrase is "times," not "two times" (i.e., it is plural, not dual). It is not impossible that the noun can stand for years (if so, it should be understood as "year, years, and half a year"), though it is not clear that it does in this context. It is better to understand this reference to be as vague as it sounds on first reading. Keil is on firmer ground when he argues that the force of the expression is symbolic. That is, the rebellion

---

27. Note the highly symbolic nature of the numbers in this section, "four" and "ten"; cf. *The Dictionary of Biblical Imagery* (Downers Grove, Ill.: InterVarsity, 1998).

28. Miller, *Daniel*, p. 215, for instance, comments "the Hebrew equivalent of this phrase occurs in 12:7 and is taken to approximate the 1,290 days of 12:11 and the 1,335 days of 12:12, both of which are just over three and a half years." But the point is that they are "over" not the same.

29. So Lacocque, *The Book of Daniel*, 153–54.

Daniel 7:1–28

of the little horn will get off to a fast start and seem like it is going to last forever, but then is suddenly cut off.[30]

At the end, Daniel remains troubled by the vision. Though it ends well from the perspective of the godly, it does paint a picture of continued and difficult oppression. The divine victory does not come easily, but through a cosmic struggle. But God had more in store for Daniel, as the next chapter immediately demonstrates.

WE HAVE MOVED from historical narration, stories rooted in real events, to apocalyptic visions. In the first half of the book, we have dealt with stories about the past and their relevance for our present at the end of the twentieth century. In the second half of the book, beginning with the present chapter, the question concerns the relevance of Daniel's visions of the future for us many centuries later.

Apocalyptic frenzy is rearing its head once again, according to "Dark Prophecies," a recent *US News and World Report* article.[31] In the magazine's poll of Americans, 66 percent, including a third of those who say they never attend church, admit that they believe Jesus Christ will return to earth some day. Unfortunately, interest in apocalyptic literature does not necessarily add up to competence in interpretation.

I have already stated that Daniel, living in the sixth century B.C., saw things beyond even his immediate future. Indeed, most would agree that Daniel's vision here and in the following chapter culminates at the climax of history, when God will come and rid the world of its evil oppressors and set up his own eternal kingdom. When stated in this way, we begin to see the continuing relevance of the apocalyptic chapters of the book of Daniel. We still live in, as Paul puts it, a "present evil age" (Gal. 1:4), from which we look to God for deliverance. In the next section, we will describe this age a little more closely as well as God's further revelation concerning our deliverance, but for now we need to pause and explore the principles for applying the lessons of ancient apocalyptic to our modern age and also bring to the fore the dominant themes of this particular chapter.

Principles for applying ancient apocalyptic. (1) The first principle for applying ancient apocalyptic is this: "Be reserved." That is, we must exercise caution in our interpretation of these highly metaphoric visions. This caution is particularly relevant on the eve of the end of the second millennium A.D.

---

30. See C. F. Keil, *Ezekiel, Daniel* (Grand Rapids: Eerdmans, 1975 [reprint]), 242–45.
31. December 15, 1997 (pp. 62–71).

Daniel 7:1–28

At different times and in different places, the church has found its attention riveted on the apocalyptic texts of the Bible. Don't misunderstand, the pictures of the end that apocalyptic gives us are always relevant to the church, but occasionally God's people become obsessed with them.

Typically, these times are times of persecution or great distress for the church or society. It is not surprising that perhaps one of the best-selling books of all time, Hal Lindsey's *The Late Great Planet Earth*,[32] a sensationalist book dealing with biblical apocalyptic, was published during the socially turbulent 1960s or that the recent Gulf War saw the publication and excessive sales of other books, cashing in on supposed connections between modern events and biblical apocalyptic.[33] While the interpretations of these books cannot be defended, they do demonstrate the original intention of apocalyptic: to provide comfort to God's people during times of trouble.

But what makes apocalyptic particularly relevant for today? In some countries around the world, Christians find themselves in deep distress, experiencing persecution. For them, the message of apocalyptic is relevant in the same way that we just described. In the West, however, even though this is a time of relative peace and economic security, apocalyptic has captured the attention of many because of the turn of the millennium. The same phenomenon could be seen a thousand years ago in Europe, the last time the millennium changed. Medieval Europe was a culture saturated in Christian theology, so the impact of apocalyptic speculation was more widespread; but even today, everyone knows the significance of Waco and many of the unsettling apocalyptic pronouncements of Harold Camping.[34] Others have seen the tract "Eighty-Eight Reasons for 1988" by Mr. Edgar Whisenant, and other claims that we live in the time of the end.

In chapter 8 we will deal more specifically with the (mis)use of apocalyptic materials to try to determine whether we are living on the eve of the end of time, but for now let this serve as a signal that as we deal with these materials, we do so with reserve and caution.

(2) We do this first by remembering that we are dealing with a type of literature that uses images with high frequency. Images communicate truth, to be sure, but not with precision. An image brings together two things that are essentially not alike in order to cast light on some aspect of the object of teaching. God is an "Ancient of Days," sitting as a judge on a throne. Literally, of course, God is not an old man, nor does he sit on a physical throne.

---

32. Lindsey, *The Late Great Planet Earth* (Grand Rapids: Zondervan, 1970).
33. J. Walvoord, *Armageddon, Oil, and the Mid-East Crisis* (Grand Rapids: Zondervan, 1974 [revised 1991]); C. Dyer, *The Rise of Babylon* (Wheaton: Tyndale, 1991).
34. H. Camping, *1994?* (New York: Vantage, 1992).

Evil human kingdoms are hybrid beasts. Yes, but not literally. To approach this material as if it demands or even invites a literal interpretation is wrongheaded. Thus, a crucial principle to reading apocalyptic literature according to its original intention is to expect images. It is wrong to say that we interpret apocalyptic literally except when it is absurd to do so.

Now, the key to the interpretation of images is to find the point of connection and not push the peripheral elements of the comparison. This means we will be left with a gray area in our interpretation. Some of the points of comparison will be obvious, but others will not be. At such points we need to hold back and not insist on our interpretation.

(3) A further important point that will prevent us from typical misunderstanding is that numbers are especially used in a symbolic manner in apocalyptic. Whether it is the "time, times, and half a time" of Daniel 7 or the "seventy weeks" of Daniel 9 or the one thousand years of Revelation 20, we must expect that we are dealing with symbolic numbers because that is the nature of apocalyptic as a genre.[35]

(4) One important way we can guard ourselves against misinterpreting these powerful images is by imagining ourselves as among those who heard these things at the time of Daniel. In the earlier discussion, I noted the ancient Near Eastern background of many of the images of Daniel 7—the sea and cloud-riding in particular. It is an important principle to read all Scripture in its original setting, especially apocalyptic. This principle, of course, calls for some work as we interpret, but the fact that you are reading this commentary indicates that you are willing to engage in the necessary task of research for proper biblical interpretation.

I want to qualify this last point by saying that the basic message of apocalyptic is communicated even to modern readers without extensive research. One cannot help but understand that the vision teaches God's people that, although it looks as if the world is under the power of human evil running rampant and is not under God's control, in this case looks are deceiving. God is in control, and there is no question concerning who is going to win this struggle. Stay faithful. Yet to prevent the outlandish and speculative interpretation of this material that is only too common, we must remember that the images and language come from antiquity.

Dominant themes of Daniel 7. To conclude by way of summary, Daniel 7 is a vision of two parts. The first part reveals that the world at present is under the sway of evil and cruel human power. The second part shows us that God is in control and will ultimately judge the rebels and establish his

---

35. For a fuller description of my approach to apocalyptic, see "What I Mean by Historical-Grammatical Exegesis—Why I Am Not a Literalist," *GTJ* 11 (1990): 37–55.

Daniel 7:1–28

kingdom among us. At present there is conflict—indeed, a cosmic war, about which we will learn more particularly in chapter 10—between the evil forces of this world and God and his faithful creatures. These, then, are the important apocalyptic themes to explore in the Contemporary Significance section: the nature of human evil, the warring activity of God, and the certainty of ultimate victory.

THE NATURE OF **human evil.** Daniel 7 paints a horrifying picture of human evil. The hybrid beasts represent powerful, destructive forces that intend to harm others. The metal teeth and the iron claws of the fourth beast intend to rip into its prey, and the godly know that they are the beast's intended meal.

Many Christians around the world today immediately understand this image. Christians in many countries know and experience the harsh rule of regimes that hate Christianity and will expend great efforts to squash its practice. In the present day, Christians in China, Indonesia, Iraq, Iran, to name just a few, live in daily fear of losing their freedom, if not their lives. In other countries—one thinks of Israeli citizens who choose to follow Christ—the threat is not physical torture, but extreme prejudice against their religious practice (not to speak of the far more numerous Palestinian Christians who live under foreign oppression). These brothers and sisters have no trouble recognizing the beast-like nature of the world in which they live.

Most Christians in the West, however, enjoy a freedom from religious harassment that may not be total, but is certainly nearly unprecedented in human history. We often forget this as we bitterly rail against the loss of "blue laws," threats against our churches' tax-free status, or our government's support of the right to abortion. Where is the beast gnawing on the bones of the people of God in the United States? After all, we see pleasant neighborhoods with our nice neighbors and flourishing churches. We wonder: "What is all this talk about superhuman power of destructive human evil?"

Of course, this experience and attitude are not shared by all Christians in America. Some of our neighborhoods, particularly in our large urban centers, are the scene of daily violence and fear. The harm is not directed especially toward the church, but Christian people find themselves in near war zones because of the actions of the renegades of our society, whether those renegades are the criminal element or crooked police. These brothers and sisters in Christ also resonate immediately with the picture of life as a battleground with life-and-death consequences—a battleground from which they desire deliverance.

Daniel 7:1–28

However, deep down, if not on the surface, those Christians who are fortunate enough not to live in a literal battle zone understand that life is a struggle, sometimes just annoying but at least occasionally a battle of nearly epic proportions. We know that whatever "peace" we experience now in our life is just a lull in the midst of a storm.

The Bible, after all, teaches that all human beings are sinners. The picture of the beasts in Daniel 7 is consistent with this lesson we learn throughout the Bible—every man and woman at heart is a self-seeking rebel against God, and we would crawl over the bodies of our fellow human beings in order to seek some small advantage for ourselves.

In a classic statement on the scope and depth of sin in the human heart, Paul collects a series of quotations from the Old Testament and strings them together in a universal condemnation of humanity (Rom. 3:10–18):

> There is no one righteous, not even one;
>> there is no one who understands,
>> no one who seeks God.
> All have turned away,
>> they have together become worthless;
> there is no one who does good,
>> not even one.
> Their throats are open graves;
>> their tongues practice deceit.
> The poison of vipers is on their lips.
>> Their mouths are full of cursing and bitterness.
> Their feet are swift to shed blood;
>> ruin and misery mark their ways,
> and the way of peace they do not know.
>> There is no fear of God before their eyes.

No one escapes this judgment—not the ruthless dictator, the benevolent president, the hard-working mayor, our law-abiding neighbor, our children and spouse, and especially not ourselves. Everyone is a sinner, "swift to shed blood." The beast is in the heart of each one of us.

Cornelius Plantinga has written an insightful analysis of the biblical view of sin, in which he defines sin as a breaking of "shalom," the Hebrew word for "wholeness, health, peace." In his words, "shalom is God's design for creation and redemption; sin is blamable human vandalism of these great realities and therefore an affront to their architect and builder."[36]

---

36. C. Plantinga Jr, *Not the Way It's Supposed to Be: A Breviary of Sin* (Grand Rapids: Eerdmans, 1995), 16.

Daniel 7:1–28

We should be quick to point out that God did not create us as "vandals." He created us in his image. The Garden of Eden was a picture of shalom until the appearance of the serpent. The serpent's identity in the Garden is obscure, though later biblical reflection makes it clear that this is Satan (cf. Rev. 12:9), the supernatural rebel. This creature introduced disharmony into the peace of the Garden, but human sin was not his responsibility. As I was driving the other day, I saw a bumper sticker that simply said, "Eve was framed." That is not the biblical story. Eve was neither framed nor coerced, nor was Adam. The disobedience of Adam and Eve broke the shalom of the Garden when they took the side of the serpent against God.

We know this first sin as the Fall (Gen. 3). Adam and Eve were ejected from the Garden into a harsh land of their own making. We are the heirs of our primordial parents. We are born sinners, but not in the sense that we are tagged with the guilt of our ancestors. No, we weren't framed either. The point is that we would have acted in the same way as Adam and Eve if we were in their place. And indeed we act in the same way from birth. We are born rebels, vandals, breakers of shalom.

But the beasts are more than individual sinners. The beasts represent corporate rebellion as well.[37] Yet it is important to realize that corporate rebellion is a product that flows from individual sin, not vice versa. Otherwise, individuals may flee responsibility for corporate harm.

The beasts represent "kingdoms," not just one sinner but an organized plurality of sinners. I remember the wise words of my former teacher, Jay Adams, when he warned his young students about an overly romantic view of marriage. He alerted us that marriage would not be the answer to all our loneliness or problems. He said that our current problems flowed from the fact that we, like all human beings, are sinners. He then reminded us that marriage was a union of two sinners and challenged us by saying, "What do you think happens when two sinners are brought together?" His warning was wise because it prevented us from being shocked when, after marriage, we had our first disagreement or argument.

Adams was talking about a marriage of two Christians. Imagine the union of thousands, millions, and today even billions of sinners? Imagine further that a handful of these sinners are given the power of decision, even the power of incredible destructive forces. Can we really be surprised at the callousness

---

37. See the works by W. Wink, *Engaging the Powers: Discernment and Resistance in a World of Domination* (Minneapolis: Augsburg Fortress, 1992); *Naming the Powers: The Language of Power in the New Testament* (Philadelphia: Fortress, 1984); *Unmasking the Powers: The Invisible Forces That Determine Human Existence* (Philadelphia: Fortress, 1986); *When the Powers Fall: Reconciliation in the Healing of Nations* (Minneapolis: Augsburg Fortress, 1998); R. Mouw, *Politics and the Biblical Drama* (Grand Rapids: Eerdmans, 1976).

Daniel 7:1–28

of an oriental despot, a Caesar, a medieval king, a Führer, an Ayatollah, or a president?

Individual sinners are harmful, sometimes deeply. But sinners bound together behind a group cause can cause great devastation. Nationalism, racism, sexism, denominationalism, factionalism—great evil can arise when sinners come together with a common purpose against someone outside of the group, the "other." We can depersonalize the other; they aren't quite human, and so to harm the other is not quite the same as hurting one of our own. George Steiner reminds modern sophisticated culture that such attitudes reside in the breasts of all people:

> It would be fantastically arrogant to suppose that we know that we have evolved into a kind of creature that likes living with those that smell different, look different, sound different. Sit in a railway carriage or bus in a land where you don't speak a single word of the language. Have you ever noticed the panic that starts growing in your civilized soul, the sense that something is hideously wrong, that your very identity may soon be torn apart? It could be that autonomy is the natural form of the social unit, and that those who would thrust others together may be doing so in the name of a transcendent vision of justice, hope, human fairness, but that they may also be hurrying something very complicated. We don't know. Human beings do tend to be with their own. Not all. Not the exceptional. But most human beings.[38]

Of course, not every nation or its ruler is a repository of evil. We must also account for common grace as well as the work of the Holy Spirit. But the phrase "power corrupts" rings true for a reason. The point is that the power of the beast image is as true today as it was at the time of Daniel, when God's people were oppressed by Babylon, in the middle of the second century B.C., when they were oppressed by the Seleucid king Antiochus IV Epiphanes, or at the time of Jesus, when the Romans held sway in Palestine.

The warring activity of God. Ultimately, the battle is "not against flesh and blood, but against the rulers, against the authorities, against the powers of this dark world and against the spiritual forces of evil in the heavenly realms" (Eph. 6:12). This ultimate spiritual battle behind our earthly struggles was anticipated in the Old Testament (see esp. the comments in ch. 10), but the New Testament rips away the curtain so that we see the heart of the battle.

---

38. G. Steiner, *No Passion Spent* (New Haven, Conn.: Yale Univ. Press, 1996), 235. For a Christian assessment, see the powerful work by M. Volf, *Exclusion and Embrace: A Theological Exploration of Identity, Otherness, and Reconciliation* (Nashville: Abingdon, 1996).

Daniel 7:1–28

This battle will continue until the final day. When we turn to Revelation 13, what do we encounter? A beast, indeed, a beast emerging from the sea. Revelation's imagery derives most immediately from the book of Daniel.[39] This insight reminds us of our continuity with the fears and struggles of Daniel's generation. We too find ourselves in a struggle that threatens to overwhelm us.

But Daniel did not just paint a picture of horrifying and seemingly invulnerable evil. We will reserve discussion for the chapters to follow, but we cannot leave Daniel 7 without attention to the picture of hope in the midst of the chaos. A "son of man" rides a cloud to the rescue of those who are oppressed by the beastly human kingdoms. We have already commented that the cloud signals the divine status of this human-like figure. Only God rides the ethereal war chariot.

But the more precise identity of this figure awaits the fuller revelation of the New Testament. In Revelation 1:7 and in the so-called "little apocalypses" of the Gospels (cf. Mark 13:26), Jesus himself is the One who rides the cloud chariot into the final battle. Jesus is the divine warrior, who will defeat the beast, the forces of evil at the end of time.

The certainty of ultimate victory. How can we be sure of victory? What makes us think that Jesus will conquer rather than the serpent? The cross is our guarantee. Jesus defeated Satan on the cross. This is the testimony of Paul, who wrote concerning the removal of our sin: "He took it away, nailing it to the cross. And having disarmed the powers and authorities, he made a public spectacle of them, triumphing over them by the cross" (Col. 2:14–15).

Paul's use of military language is not accidental, but is part and parcel of the canon-wide theme of divine warfare. From the beginning of the canon (Ex. 15:3) to its end in Revelation, God's people are told that their Lord fights for them against the evil that oppresses them—both external enemies and the sin that remains in their own hearts.[40] This is the comfort that the Bible presents to God's people today, whether a Christian in an Iranian jail or one in America feeling the ridicule of a "toxic culture"[41] in the West. God has won the victory on the cross, and history's victorious denouement is certain.

Daniel 7 gives us a glimpse of the warfare that explains conflict in the world today, and chapters 10–12 will take us even further into these divine mysteries.

---

39. G. K. Beale, *The Use of Daniel in Jewish Apocalyptic Literature and in the Revelation of St. John* (Washington, D.C.: Univ. Press of America, 1984).

40. M. Kreft, "The Influence of the 'Holy War' Motif on Pauline Theology" (Th.M. thesis: Westminster Theological Seminary, 1985); D. Allender and T. Longman III, *Bold Love* (Colorado Springs: NavPress, 1991).

41. See comments on Daniel 1.

Daniel 8:1–27

IN THE THIRD year of King Belshazzar's reign, I, Daniel, had a vision, after the one that had already appeared to me. ²In my vision I saw myself in the citadel of Susa in the province of Elam; in the vision I was beside the Ulai Canal. ³I looked up, and there before me was a ram with two horns, standing beside the canal, and the horns were long. One of the horns was longer than the other but grew up later. ⁴I watched the ram as he charged toward the west and the north and the south. No animal could stand against him, and none could rescue from his power. He did as he pleased and became great.

⁵As I was thinking about this, suddenly a goat with a prominent horn between his eyes came from the west, crossing the whole earth without touching the ground. ⁶He came toward the two-horned ram I had seen standing beside the canal and charged at him in great rage. ⁷I saw him attack the ram furiously, striking the ram and shattering his two horns. The ram was powerless to stand against him; the goat knocked him to the ground and trampled on him, and none could rescue the ram from his power. ⁸The goat became very great, but at the height of his power his large horn was broken off, and in its place four prominent horns grew up toward the four winds of heaven.

⁹Out of one of them came another horn, which started small but grew in power to the south and to the east and toward the Beautiful Land. ¹⁰It grew until it reached the host of the heavens, and it threw some of the starry host down to the earth and trampled on them. ¹¹It set itself up to be as great as the Prince of the host; it took away the daily sacrifice from him, and the place of his sanctuary was brought low. ¹²Because of rebellion, the host ⌊of the saints⌋ and the daily sacrifice were given over to it. It prospered in everything it did, and truth was thrown to the ground.

¹³Then I heard a holy one speaking, and another holy one said to him, "How long will it take for the vision to be fulfilled—the vision concerning the daily sacrifice, the rebellion

Daniel 8:1–27

that causes desolation, and the surrender of the sanctuary and of the host that will be trampled underfoot?"

¹⁴He said to me, "It will take 2,300 evenings and mornings; then the sanctuary will be reconsecrated."

¹⁵While I, Daniel, was watching the vision and trying to understand it, there before me stood one who looked like a man. ¹⁶And I heard a man's voice from the Ulai calling, "Gabriel, tell this man the meaning of the vision."

¹⁷As he came near the place where I was standing, I was terrified and fell prostrate. "Son of man," he said to me, "understand that the vision concerns the time of the end."

¹⁸While he was speaking to me, I was in a deep sleep, with my face to the ground. Then he touched me and raised me to my feet.

¹⁹He said: "I am going to tell you what will happen later in the time of wrath, because the vision concerns the appointed time of the end. ²⁰The two-horned ram that you saw represents the kings of Media and Persia. ²¹The shaggy goat is the king of Greece, and the large horn between his eyes is the first king. ²²The four horns that replaced the one that was broken off represent four kingdoms that will emerge from his nation but will not have the same power.

²³ "In the latter part of their reign, when rebels have become completely wicked, a stern-faced king, a master of intrigue, will arise. ²⁴He will become very strong, but not by his own power. He will cause astounding devastation and will succeed in whatever he does. He will destroy the mighty men and the holy people. ²⁵He will cause deceit to prosper, and he will consider himself superior. When they feel secure, he will destroy many and take his stand against the Prince of princes. Yet he will be destroyed, but not by human power.

²⁶"The vision of the evenings and mornings that has been given you is true, but seal up the vision, for it concerns the distant future."

²⁷I, Daniel, was exhausted and lay ill for several days. Then I got up and went about the king's business. I was appalled by the vision; it was beyond understanding.

Daniel 8:1–27

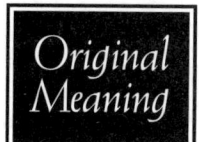

THE CONNECTION OF Daniel 8 with chapter 7 is obvious. The first verse associates the two by introducing the second vision as occurring "after the one that had already appeared to me." It comes from approximately the same time period, Belshazzar's third year, two years after chapter 7. In addition, the actors in the prophetic visions of both chapters are animals, and we soon see that these animals represent kingdoms, that is, political entities. In both cases, there is a concluding focus on a horn that emanates from these animals. Finally, both chapters concern hostility between the animal kingdoms and the divine realm.

But closer examination forces us to recognize differences between the chapters as well. Some appear relatively incidental to the meaning of the text. For instance, the prophecy in chapter 7 is called a dream, whereas the prophecy in eight is termed a "vision." From the description of the two, the distinction is not so much in terms of content or form, but rather in terms of the way the prophecy is mediated to Daniel (see comment below on v. 1).

Another difference between the prophecies of the two chapters has to do with the nature of the animals and the transparency of the imagery. In chapter 7, we encountered hybrid animals of grotesque appearance, while in chapter 8, the animals seem normal (with the possible exception of the horns). In our description below, we will see the ease with which we can associate these animals and their horns with particular and well-known political entities. This fact explains why commentators over the years have registered little of the interpretive disagreement that we saw in chapter 7.[1]

The similarities between these two chapters mean that the themes of the two are closely related. Indeed, we have already indicated that chapters 7–12 focus on six important themes:

- the horror of human evil, particularly as it is concentrated in the state
- the announcement of a specific time of deliverance
- repentance that leads to deliverance
- the revelation that a cosmic war stands behind human conflict
- judgment as certain for those who resist God and oppress his people
- the equally certain truth that God's people, downtrodden in the present, will experience new life in the fullest sense.

---

1. In an interesting study contributing to the history of interpretation of the apocalyptic portions of Daniel, S. Nunez (*The Vision of Daniel 8: Interpretations from 1700 to 1800* [Berrien Springs, Mich.: Andrews Univ. Press, 1987]), in his description of a host of interpreters in the period covered by his research, demonstrates the wide-ranging agreement on the interpretation of the imagery of chapter 8. This is not without exception, however, as our comments on the 2300 evenings and mornings will show.

Daniel 8:1–27

While we will have occasion to comment on each of these themes in this chapter, in keeping with our intention to focus on one of these themes in each of chapters 7–12 (see comments in "The Nature of Apocalyptic Literature" in the Original Meaning section of chapter 7), we will pay particular attention here to the issue of the announcement of a specific time of deliverance. Furthermore, we would be remiss if we did not point out that the overarching theme of this chapter supports the major theme of the book as a whole: *In spite of present circumstances, God will win in the end.*

However, Daniel 8 not only has connections within the book of Daniel. As we read this chapter, we cannot help but think of Ezekiel. Daniel finds himself at the Ulai canal outside of Susa when he receives his vision (1:2), reminiscent of Ezekiel beside the Kebar River (Ezek. 1:1). Ezekiel too symbolically represented people through the use of animal and shepherd imagery (Ezek. 34).[2] This connection with Ezekiel will help us to understand the nature of Daniel's vision.

With chapter 8 the book reverts to Hebrew (Aramaic being the language of chs. 2–7). No explanation for the switch back is given in the text, and no scholarly argument has yet achieved a consensus of opinion.

The vision of Daniel in this chapter has, generally speaking, a two-part structure: (1) the vision of a ram and a goat (8:1–14), and (2) the interpretation of the vision (8:15–27).

The Vision of a Ram and a Goat (8:1–14)

DANIEL'S VISION TAKES place in the third year of Belshazzar's reign. If Hasel is correct, this situates the vision in 548/547 B.C.[3] In the vision, Daniel is located near the city of Susa (in the province of Elam) on the Ulai Canal. Some think that Daniel was literally present in this location,[4] and as a high official in the realm, he certainly could have traveled this distance.[5] However, the connections noted above with the book of Ezekiel suggests that Daniel, like Ezekiel, was carried to the Ulai by means of his prophetic vision, not physically.

When Daniel had his vision, Susa was already an ancient city and was the leading city of Elam. Later, however, it would become the winter residence of the Persian kings. The significance of the location is probably that it was

---

2. Collins, *Daniel*, 329–30, reminds us that animals also represent leaders and nations in the Animal Apocalypse of 1 Enoch.
3. G. Hasel, "The First and Third Years of Belshazzar (Dan. 7:1; 8:1)," *AUSS* 15 (1976): 153ff.
4. Josephus, *Antiquities*, 10.11.7; G. Archer, "Daniel," *EBC* (Grand Rapids: Zondervan, 1985), 101.
5. Susa was a little over two hundred miles east of Babylon.

outside of the Babylonian empire and near the center of future power. According to Collins, the Ulai Canal was a human-made waterway that was called the Eulaeus in later classical writings.[6] Towner is wrong to deny the existence of this waterway or the fact that Susa was an active city during Belshazzar's reign.[7]

The first thing that presents itself to Daniel in the vision is a ram. This ram has two horns and charges with great success in three directions: west, north, and south.

Then a second animal interrupts his vision of the ram. It is a goat, coming from the west. Notable about the goat is a single large horn. This goat attacks the ram ferociously and succeeds in knocking off its horns. The goat utterly overwhelms the ram. It has great speed, indicated by its racing across the landscape "without touching the ground" (v. 5). However, the goat's power does not last forever, perhaps only a very short time. There is no slow decline of its power, but it is suddenly cut off. The prominent horn is broken and in its place grow four others, spreading out in four directions.

The description of the success and travail of the ram and the goat are simply a prelude to the focus of the passage, which centers on a small horn that grows out of one of the four. Already, we know that the symbol of the horn points to a king or a kingdom.[8] This small horn takes on large proportions as it grows to the south, to the east, and toward the Beautiful Land. The latter can be none other than Israel itself, the land of milk and honey (cf. Ezek. 20:6, 15), the land considered most attractive by virtue of a divine perspective appreciated by Daniel.

But the growth of this small horn reaches beyond human dimensions. It grows until it attains the "host of the heavens" (v. 10) and enters into a conflict with this heavenly army. Strikingly, the text reports that the small horn achieves some measure of success against its rivals in the sky. Then, climactically, the horn challenges "the Prince of the host" (v. 11). Significantly, its incursion against the Prince is described as harm done to the formal worship of Israel: "It took away the daily sacrifice." This sacrifice may refer specifically to the morning and evening sacrifices at the temple (Ex. 29:39–41; Num. 28:3–8),[9] or it may refer to a disruption of the entire temple ritual.[10] The latter

---

6. Collins, *Daniel*, 329.
7. Towner, *Daniel*, 116, cf. the comments of E. Yamauchi, *Persia and the Bible* (Grand Rapids: Baker, 1990), 292–93, relevant to the existence of Susa during the neo-Babylonian period. Indeed, he states that "Susa was occupied continuously from 3500 B.C. to the thirteenth century A.D." (283).
8. See discussion on p. 189.
9. So Miller, *Daniel*, 227.
10. So Young, *The Prophecy of Daniel*, 172.

interpretation may be supported by the line that "the place of his [the Prince's] sanctuary was brought low" (v. 11).

Verse 12 is difficult and its interpretation uncertain: "Because of rebellion, the host ⌐of the saints¬ and the daily sacrifice were given over to it." The NIV indicates by the half brackets that the genitive phrase "of the saints" is added and suggests in a footnote that the "host" can be taken as "the armies." Indeed, the Hebrew word for "host" usually has military connotations.[11] The problem of the verse surrounds the reference to "rebellion" and "host/armies." We reserve full discussion of the latter when we come to the more illuminating interpretation section in the second half of the chapter, but our conclusion will be that the primary reference is to the heavenly armies of God. Associated with them are faithful Israelites, who fight against the incursions of the small horn (8:9, also to be identified below).

In a word, it is clear that God's side will take some blows during the struggle "because of the rebellion." Is this the rebellion of the little horn or of God's people. Arguments can be given for either side of this debate, but within this chapter little evidence exists for the latter view. True, in chapter 9 responsibility for the plight of the Israelites in the Babylonian exile rests squarely on the shoulders of the rebellious people. Here, however, we are not talking about the condition of God's people in the sixth century; rather, as we will soon see, we are hearing about the struggles of God's faithful people in the middle of the second century. While it is true that the reference could be to those Jewish people who drifted from God's way at that time, that is doubtful. The meaning of the passage appears to be that God's people suffer at the hands of a power that rebels against God and seeks to take his place.

Again, the astounding fact is that this little horn succeeds at least for a while and that the "truth" was thrown to the ground. Our identification of the historical circumstance in view here awaits the next section, but we will anticipate that discussion by saying that this statement finds its fulfillment in the burning of Torah scrolls by the little horn, as recorded in 1 Maccabees 1:56–57, which describes events in the middle of the second century B.C.: "The books of the law that they found they tore to pieces and burned with fire. Anyone found possessing the book of the covenant, or anyone who adhered to the law, was condemned to death by the decree of the king" (NRSV).

At this point, the action of the vision of Daniel 8 stops. Note that throughout the vision there is no indication of a reversal, a victory of the forces of God over the power of the small horn. The first half of chapter 8 concludes rather with a discussion between two celestial creatures about "how long" these horrible events will last. That "how long" is reminiscent of a frequent lament in the Psalms (cf. 6:3; 13:1–2; 35:17).

---

11. P. J. Els. "צבא," NIDOTTE, 3:733–35.

How long will the sanctuary and its ritual be disrupted? While the one celestial being directs his question to the other, it is notable that the answer is addressed not to the celestial being, but rather to Daniel (v. 14): "It will take 2,300 evenings and mornings; then the sanctuary will be reconsecrated."

It is with the interpretation of this chronological statement that we encounter the most disagreement about the interpretation of the symbolism of the chapter. Literally, the phrase translates "evening, morning—two thousand, three hundred." Does this mean 2300 days, reflecting the language of Genesis 1 ("there was evening, and there was morning—the [Xth] day")? Or does it mean 1150 days, with the reference to evening and morning being to the daily sacrifices? In other words, were there 1150 morning sacrifices and 1150 evening sacrifices, totaling 2300 sacrifices but 1150 days? Our answer to this question also awaits the interpretation that follows.

The Interpretation of the Vision (8:15–27)

THE VISION HAS come to an end and Daniel struggles to understand its significance. Suddenly, a humanlike figure appears before him, and he hears the voice of another person "from the Ulai." The text suggests[12] that the voice is disembodied and seems to hover over the waterway. The first figure is named; he is Gabriel (meaning "God's hero"), a leading angel in God's heavenly army.[13] The source of the voice is not named, but we are surely to believe that it is the voice of God himself, who, after all, commands this powerful angelic being to reveal to Daniel the meaning of the vision that he has been watching.

Gabriel approaches Daniel, and Daniel, overwhelmed by the spiritual power that stands before him, drops to his face. The first words from Gabriel announces the interpretation of the vision under a general heading: It "concerns the time of the end" (v. 17). Later, he will describe the scope of the vision as "what will happen later in the time of wrath, because the vision concerns the appointed time of the end" (v. 19).

This general introduction might at first lead us to believe that the vision concerns the end of history, the consummation, what Christians now refer to as "the Second Coming." Indeed, this phrase can have that sense (cf. 12:4). Some scholars opt for this meaning in this passage.[14] But the clear interpretation of the context of the vision's climax places it squarely in the middle of the second century B.C. In light of that context, we believe that the phrase

---

12. The Hebrew literally says that the voice came from "between the Ulai" (v. 16).
13. Gabriel is the first angel to be named in the Bible. He appears again in the New Testament to announce ahead of time the great acts of redemption about to take place (cf. Luke 1:19, 26).
14. Wood, *A Commentary on Daniel*, 223–24.

indicates the end of the persecution initiated by the little horn, identified below with the Seleucid king Antiochus IV.[15]

Gabriel interprets the animal symbolism given earlier in the chapter in a precise manner. Unlike chapter 7, where the animals are said to be "four kingdoms," here they are identified with particular and well-known political entities.[16] The ram with the two horns represents the "kings of Media and Persia" (v. 20). In the vision itself, one horn grew larger than the other, which is surely a reference to the fact that the Persian part of this empire soon swallowed the Median part and assumed dominance.

The goat with the single horn that speedily devastated the ram is "Greece," the single horn being its first king—Alexander the Great. He achieved an unprecedented domination from Italy to India in unbelievable time; but he died suddenly at age 33 in 323 B.C., leaving behind two young sons, Alexander and Herakles.[17] These boys were ultimately murdered, and the world was carved up between Alexander's powerful generals, the Diadochi. The Diadochi are the "four prominent horns" (v. 8; cf. v. 22).

The vision then skips over about two centuries of history (later detailed in the vision of ch. 11). For now the focus goes immediately to one particular horn. Scholars almost universally agree that the horn that grew out of one of the four is the second century B.C. Seleucid ruler, Antiochus IV Epiphanes. We know much about this king from intertestamental writings like the Maccabees. He started out small and grew large. He was not actually the first in line to succeed his older brother Seleucus IV, but through the political manipulation for which he became famous (he was a "master of intrigue" [v. 23]), he managed to push his nephew out of the way and gain the throne. He grew large through military success, pushing his influence into Egypt as well as east into Persian, Parthia, and Armenia, not to speak of his domination of Palestine.

Antiochus IV, however, established himself as a "completely wicked" and "stern-faced king" (v. 23) through his incredible intrusion and disruption of

---

15. In the words of Keil, "'Time of the end' is the general prophetic expression for the time which, as the period of fulfillment, lies at the end of the existing prophetic horizon—in the present case the time of Antiochus," quoted in Miller, *Daniel*, 231.

16. The argument has been made by many scholars that the specific symbolism of the ram and the goat originate in the zodiac. The argument is primarily based on the writings of a first century A.D. author named Teucer, who places Persia under the sign of the ram and Syria under the sign of the goat. Collins, *Daniel*, 330, raises doubts about the approach, however, by pointing to the late date of this information (even assuming a middle second century B.C. date for the prophecy as he does) and also by the fact that the goat is the sign for Syria, not Greece.

17. Actually, Alexander was not born until two months after Alexander the Great's death. Herakles's claim to the throne was likely a hoax.

the Jewish ritual. Jewish religion and practice stood in the way of his policy of Hellenization, and among other atrocities, he ordered the cessation of temple sacrifice in 167 B.C. and profaned the temple by introducing a holy object sacred to the god Zeus, to which he sacrificed a pig, abhorrent to Jewish religion. This holy object has been suggested to be a meteorite that became a cult object that the Jews referred to as "an abomination that causes desolation" (9:27).

Such actions against the formal worship of God's people was far more than an affront against the people; it was an attack against heaven itself. Antiochus indeed took a stand against the "Prince of princes," that is, against God. But such arrogance can only lead to one conclusion: utter defeat. The defeat of the small horn is announced simply and definitively: "Yet he will be destroyed, but not by human power" (v. 25). The latter clause should not be taken to mean that no human agency was involved in the downfall of Antiochus, but rather that the ultimate power behind the Maccabean freedom fighters was God himself, who gave them the victory and allowed them to restore the temple to its former function as a center for worship of the true God.

Finally, the angelic interpreter reaffirms the time frame of the suffering and its end: "The vision of the evenings and mornings that has been given you is true, but seal up the vision, for it concerns the distant future" (v. 26). Interestingly, even in historical retrospect we cannot be dogmatic about the meaning of the 2300 evenings and mornings. Above we have commented that there are at least two equally plausible ways to interpret this number: 2300 days (its most natural reading) or 2300 morning and evening sacrifices (i.e., 1150 days). The second interpretation can be supported by the context and a knowledge of the sacrificial system in Israel.

It is also possible to fit both numbers, approximately, into the time of its fulfillment in the middle of the second century B.C. After all, when does the period start, with the prohibition of sacrifice in late 167 or earlier with the removal of Onias III from the high priesthood in 171? And when does it end, with the reconsecration of the high priesthood in 164 or in 163 when Antiochus died? Or, contrary to both of these literalistic interpretations, is the number symbolic?[18]

In the final analysis, we cannot be dogmatic. The number is given not so much so that those who read Daniel's sixth-century prognostications in the second century could compute when the suffering would stop as much as to assure them that God had things under control. Furthermore, the number indicates with certainty that there would be a stopping point to the persecution, even if that number could not be computed into a definite date in the

---

18. As argued by Goldingay, *Daniel*, 213.

calendar as they knew it. As we will comment in the next sections, this number is typical of chronological numbers throughout the book of Daniel. They may not be used for date settings or for establishing apocalyptic calendars. Moreover, if we cannot be certain of numbers used in prophecies that have already been fulfilled, how likely can we figure out the numbers that point to times in the far distant future?

The prophecy ends with Daniel "exhausted" and confused. Though clear in many regards, the vision would have astounded someone living in the sixth century B.C., where Media, Persia, and Greece were relatively small points on the map. Not only that, but we have seen in regard to the 2300 days that even today, centuries after the fulfillment, certain elements are still not clear to us.

IF WE HAVE been reading through the book of Daniel, by now its major theme is well ingrained in our minds: In spite of present appearances, God is in control and will triumph against the forces of evil. After reading chapter 8, we can readily see how this is the case here. We will spell it out more clearly in the light of the six important points that we anticipated were present to some degree in each of the last six chapters of the book.[19]

(1) The horror of human evil is especially concentrated in the state. Like chapter 7, Daniel 8 paints a picture of world history using animal imagery. A goat fights a ram. The goat's single horn is broken and is replaced by four horns. From one of the four a small horn sprouts and assumes god-like proportions. These images clearly represent political entities, nation states that will, from Daniel's sixth-century perspective, rise up in the future. They are all characterized by violence. The ram dominates other unspecified animals; the goat tramples the ram. Its horn is broken off, and the cycle of violence goes on and on.

The focus, however, is on the violence of the small horn, which is directed against God and his hosts. The small horn attacks the formal worship of God's people, and thus this violence is a new level of horror that cannot go unanswered.

(2) A specific time of deliverance is announced. Daniel 8 gives a limit to the time in which the small horn can work its devastation: 2300 evenings and mornings. We noted above the difficulty of determining the precise length of time this represents. In Daniel's words, "it was beyond understanding"

---

19. See pages 178–79.

(v. 27). It is this theme we will explore in greater detail in the Contemporary Significance section, so we reserve further discussion until that time.

(3) Repentance leads to deliverance. This theme is absent or at least subdued in this chapter. There is ambiguity in the sentence in verse 12, "Because of rebellion, the host ⌊of the saints⌋ and the daily sacrifice were given over to it [the horn]." Is the rebellion that causes the turmoil the rebellion of the people who are thus punished by the small horn, who would then be God's unknowing tool of judgment? Or is the rebellion the assault of the small horn on God, which has evil consequences for his people? We cannot know for sure, but even if the former (which I think is less likely) is true, it is still the case that the present chapter (as opposed esp. to ch. 9) focuses more on the atrocities directed against God and his hosts than on any sin that holds God's people culpable for their suffering.

(4) A cosmic war stands behind human conflict. In historical retrospect, we can assert with great certainty that the climactic battle described in this chapter as instigated by the small horn is the persecution of the Seleucid king Antiochus IV against observant Jewish people in the mid-second century B.C. However, the prophetic description of this future event makes it clear that more is going on behind the scenes. We await chapter 10 for an even more dramatic disclosure, but we already get an overture to the theme that a spiritual conflict stands behind the earthly one. It is not Antiochus versus the Maccabees alone, but it is a little horn who presumes to be a god who fights against the Prince of princes and his starry hosts. A cosmic battle is ultimately at issue here. A fuller discussion of this theme is found in chapter 10.

With the god-like pretension of Antiochus, we also see how readily he can become a symbol for all those who in their overweening pride seek to replace God on the throne of the universe. Of course, Satan was the first to attempt this rebellion against his Creator, but Christians know that someone is coming who will seek to replace God and will help instigate the events that lead to God's final redemptive intrusion into human events. Later, we will explore how Antiochus becomes an apt symbol for the one Christians know as the Antichrist.

(5) Judgment is certain for those who resist God and oppress his people. The vision itself ends with a rather subdued statement of the downfall of the small horn. The bulk of the description of the small horn's career is on its seeming successes. It is only in answer to the question "how long" this wicked devastation will be allowed to continue that the angel says simply, "It will take 2,300 evenings and mornings; then the sanctuary will be reconsecrated" (v. 14).

As already noted, the statement is forceful, but still not greatly developed. The small horn, Antiochus and all he represents, will be certainly and

Daniel 8:1–27

definitively destroyed, but "not by human power" (v. 25). That is, God himself will ultimately bring Antiochus down.

(6) God's people, downtrodden in the present, will experience new life in the fullest sense. "The sanctuary will be reconsecrated" (v. 14)—stated as a simple statement. When God defeats the forces of evil represented in Antiochus, it will result in a restoration of the temple.

The temple was more than a building; it was a symbol of God's presence with his people, hence a source of life and hope. Its desecration at the hands of Antiochus was an assault against God and cause for despair among the faithful. But the restoration of the temple meant a new life, the possibility of intense fellowship with God once again. We will see in chapter 12 that this too anticipates even greater realities than temple worship. There we learn that the faithful can hope for resurrection and a blessed eternal life in the presence of God beyond death itself.

OUR STRATEGY FOR treating the major themes that echo throughout the second half of Daniel calls on us to treat the second one ("the announcement of a specific time of deliverance") here. For a treatment of the other five themes, consult the Contemporary Significance sections of chapters 7, 9, 10, 11, and 12.

Each unit in the apocalyptic section of Daniel contains some kind of chronological notice. In chapter 7, we learn that the saints will be handed over to the climactic king for "a time, times and half a time" (7:25). In chapter 9, we get the infamous "seventy weeks of years" (9:25–27). In chapter 12 (chs. 10–12 is a single unit), we read the enigmatic statement that the time between the abolishment of the sacrifice and the setting up of the abomination of desolation will be "1,290 days," followed by the even more enigmatic statement, "Blessed is the one who waits for and reaches the end of the 1,335 days" (12:11–12). While each of these passages will be treated in its own contexts, here we discuss the general issue of how these passages apply to us today.

Numbers in apocalyptic literature. Daniel is not the only apocalyptic book that contains provocative calendrical numbers. Most notable is the controversial reference in Revelation 20:3 to the thousand-year binding of Satan. The debate over this passage has caused debate among sincere Christians for many years. Is it to be understood as a literal millennium to begin at some date in the future, or is it a symbolic number standing for the period of time between the first and second coming of Christ? These two camps are known as amillennialism and premillennialism.

Daniel 8:1–27

Our comments will have ramifications for this debate, though we will not address it directly. Our concern here is to inquire what effect Daniel's chronological statements are supposed to have on us living on the eve of the third millennium A.D.? Are they pointers to the date of the return of Christ or do they intend to communicate another message to us?

Date-setting the Return. It is important to address this issue at the present time because the press is filled with reports that apocalyptic speculation is on the rise because of the shift of millennium. Further, the church is constantly bombarded with claims that someone has finally figured out the difficult apocalyptic numbers and has determined that we are living in the period of the end. We hear often that there is only a limited amount of time before Christ returns and history will come to a dramatic end, which is usually characterized as a period of violence.

In early 1994, I debated Harold Camping of Family Radio. Mr. Camping had faithfully been teaching the Bible virtually every night for the past thirty years. He had built up a faithful following over those years by offering biblical teaching on many important theological and practical issues. While his teaching could be characterized as overly dogmatic on certain controversial issues like divorce, he did not have a reputation for the sensational. In addition, he was an advocate of Reformed theology, from which school of thought usually emanated rather reserved teaching about the end times. Thus, when he published a book in 1993 in which he claimed to be able to unseal (Dan. 8:26; 12:9) the apocalyptic teaching about the time of the return of Christ, it generated a furor in churches not used to such speculation.[20]

At the time I was teaching a seminar on "How to Interpret Prophecy" with Ray Dillard, my colleague at Westminster Theological Seminary. After the publication of Camping's book, we started to get a lot of anxious questions about the validity of his claims. Moreover, people in my own church became intrigued and a few even were persuaded by his arguments that Christ was going to return in September 1994.

It quickly became obvious to me that this was more than an interpretive debate. It had a dramatic effect on people's lives. One person I know drove his credit card balance to the max and got into serious financial trouble. His response? "Who cares! In a few months, Christ is coming again, so I don't have to worry about not paying my bills." Another friend was having serious marital problems. His wife had left him and the children. When I went on a pastoral call to visit him, I asked him if he had made any attempts to speak to his wife about their problems. His response? "No, I don't need to. In a matter of months, Christ is coming again and my problems will disappear." These

---

20. H. Camping, *1994?* (New York: Vantage, 1993).

are just two of the horror stories that I heard over the months preceding September 1994 from those who were persuaded that Mr. Camping had found the key to the difficult chronological notices in the apocalyptic teaching of the Bible, including Daniel.

When I debated Mr. Camping, it was May 1994, about four months from the date he had put forward as the time Christ would return. When I arrived at the location for the debate, I was completely floored. I was used to doing seminars on the Bible and getting good-sized groups of people interested to learn more about principles for interpreting prophecy, but I was not prepared for the huge group that had assembled to hear a discussion with the man who said that he had the date for the return of Christ figured out.

Of course, I could understand that Christians would be vitally interested in when their Lord was going to return again to "wipe away every tear" (Rev. 7:17; cf. 21:4), but didn't they know that the Jesus they were expecting also taught clearly, "No one knows about that day or hour, not even the angels in heaven, not the Son, but only the Father" (Mark 13:32)? How could some man or woman claim to know what Jesus himself said was hidden from him?

In one sense I was surprised, but in another I was not. I am, of course, using Mr. Camping as an example of a phenomenon that has happened again and again throughout church history. Countless claims have been made that someone has figured out that the Bible teaches an exact time for Christ's return. As a matter of fact, one scholar's research has numbered over two hundred such claims since 1945 alone![21] Thus, my anecdote must not be taken as a critique of Mr. Camping alone but of the whole enterprise of using apocalyptic as a tool for figuring out when Christ is coming again. Date-setting is not an appropriate contemporary use of apocalyptic literature. That is the burden of my argument in this section.

Misuses of apocalyptic. Before continuing with my argument, let me point out that there are two misuses of apocalyptic in this way. (1) Mr. Camping represents the claim that one can use the Bible's apocalyptic chronology as a calendar to argue for a precise date for Christ's return. In answer to my challenge based on Mark 13:32, Mr. Camping coolly responded, "I don't know the day or the hour, I know the month and the year." This statement, of course, is a complete misunderstanding of Jesus' intention in that verse.

Now we might wrongly believe that this approach to the issue takes care of itself in the long run, and indeed it sometimes does—eventually. When I spoke to the group in May (which was mostly made up of his already convinced followers), I began by saying, "I know that I can't convince most of

---

21. See S. D. O'Leary, *Arguing the Apocalypse: A Theory of Millennial Rhetoric* (New York: Oxford Univ. Press, 1994).

you today, but I want you to have something to think about in October." But when October came, Mr. Camping, in his radio broadcasts, while shaken, held out for the calendar year. When 1994 turned into 1995, he suddenly had the insight that the Bible meant the "Jewish year," which ended in the spring of 1995. When the second half of 1995 came, he cited the example of Jonah, who announced the demise of Nineveh only to have God spare that city. In other words, he wasn't wrong; God in his compassion for the lost just delayed his return.

Similar strategies of reinterpretation may be seen throughout history, perhaps most notably after the apparent failure of William Miller's prediction of Christ's return sometime during the Jewish year that ran from March 21, 1843 to March 21, 1844. When this date passed, a slight miscalculation was discovered, which led to a new date, October 22, 1844. There was tremendous disappointment when that date passed, but Miller's influence did not. Instead, a whole new movement developed from this Baptist minister's predictions. A group withdrew from the mainstream church to form another denomination, which we know today as the Adventist movement. Even today Adventist theologians argue that something important happened in 1843, a kind of anticipatory fulfillment of Daniel's prophecy in chapter 9.[22]

(2) But there is another type of misuse of these materials that must also be addressed. Only rarely does someone pick a precise date for the fulfillment of these chronological statements in Daniel and Revelation. The more typical pattern is the claim that the Bible teaches that, while we cannot pick a date, all the signs are pointing to the end within our lifetime. In our own time, the most well-known advocate of this reading of apocalyptic literature is Hal Lindsey.

As a senior in high school and not yet a believer, the first Christian book I ever read was Lindsey's *The Late Great Planet Earth*. Nowhere does the author pick a date. He wisely listens to Christ's teaching on that point. However, one cannot read his book without thinking that Christ must return before the mid–1970s. Everything was poised for the end of existence. Nuclear arsenals were just waiting for the button to be pressed. World food resources could not last more than a few more years. The environment would kill us before a few years were out. The end was near; the signs of the time were in full play.

This leads to an important issue. The Jesus who told us we could not know the day or the hour also told us to look for the signs of the time (cf.

---

22. See the argument by J. Doukhan, *Daniel: The Vision of the End* (Berrien Springs, Mich.: Andrews Univ. Press, 1987). In the midst of my critical comment on Adventist origins I want to be quick to point out that there is much of great value in the teachings of the Adventist church and that some of the best Old Testament scholars today are Adventist.

Daniel 8:1–27

Mark 13). The latter days will be marked by earthquakes, wars and rumors of wars, false messiahs, and the appearance of the antichrist. When the gospel has been preached to all the nations, then we will be on the edge of the consummation. Such indications will alert us to the fact that Christ is about to return.

Perhaps of all the events in recent history that most make us think that our time is that special time has been the rebirth of the nation of Israel, the location of so many great redemptive events. I vividly remember my first visit to Israel in 1976, overlooking the Megiddo Valley (biblical Armageddon). The tour guide pointed out the military airfield below and commented on the fact that before the first generation of the new nation passed, the great final conflagration would take place right there in the valley below us. It is significant for me to think that the year I am writing these comments is the fiftieth anniversary of the birth of the nation of Israel, and most have understood the reference to a generation as being no more than fifty years.

But should the signs of the times be understood in this way? If so, what sense did it make for Jesus in the same breath to tell his followers (Mark 13:33–36):

> Be on guard! Be alert! You do not know when that time will come. It's like a man going away: He leaves his house and puts his servants in charge, each with his assigned task, and tells the one at the door to keep watch.
>
> Therefore keep watch because you do not know when the owner of the house will come back—whether in the evening, or at midnight, or when the rooster crows, or at dawn. If he comes suddenly, do not let him find you sleeping. What I say to you, I say to everyone: "Watch!"

To put it bluntly, why should they—why should we—watch unless we see the signs of the time?

But note that every generation has seen the signs of the time. This is why we are tempted, particularly when we have not listened to Jesus' clear teaching about not knowing the precise time, to think that our time is that special time.

I will not address every one of those signs,[23] but what age has not experienced earthquakes, wars, and rumors of wars? If there seem to be more wars and more earthquakes, could that not be because global communication is now possible and more immediate? What age has not recognized the

---

23. See the insightful comments of A. Hoekema, *The Bible and the Future* (Grand Rapids: Eerdmans, 1979).

Antichrist among them? After all, there are a lot of people, some of them satanically evil and powerful, who are "against Christ."[24] And what is the criterion for reaching every nation (or, as some argue, "people group")? Is it when one person, or more than 50 percent, or everyone in a nation/people group has heard? These are unanswerable questions.

The signs of the time do not intend to tell us that we are living in the shadow of Christ's return, but rather to remind us that we live in the last days, the days between the first and second coming of Christ. When we hear of an earthquake, we are not to say, "The time is nigh." Rather, we are to remind ourselves that we are still on this side of the consummation. We are to remind ourselves to be prepared, because Christ will appear "like a thief in the night" (1 Thess. 5:2).

That leads us back to the function of the highly symbolic numbers in Daniel and elsewhere, which are so difficult to figure out. Their purpose is not for date-setting but for comfort. They remind us that God knows what he is doing. God is sovereign and has set a limit on how long the present evil world will oppress us. These facts should comfort us by reminding us that God is in control of the situation.

I submit for our consideration that the misuse of these apocalyptic dates is an attempt to wrest control from God and place it firmly in our own sinful grasp. But the result is disruption in the church and in our lives. Such vain speculation leads, as in the case of the people I mentioned above, to a complete disregard for present realities. God calls us to live in the present while waiting with hope for the future.

---

24. A surprising number of them whose name in some fashion spells out 666, from Nero on.

Daniel 9:1–27

IN THE FIRST year of Darius son of Xerxes (a Mede by descent), who was made ruler over the Babylonian kingdom—²in the first year of his reign, I, Daniel, understood from the Scriptures, according to the word of the LORD given to Jeremiah the prophet, that the desolation of Jerusalem would last seventy years. ³So I turned to the Lord God and pleaded with him in prayer and petition, in fasting, and in sackcloth and ashes.

⁴I prayed to the LORD my God and confessed:

"O Lord, the great and awesome God, who keeps his covenant of love with all who love him and obey his commands, ⁵we have sinned and done wrong. We have been wicked and have rebelled; we have turned away from your commands and laws. ⁶We have not listened to your servants the prophets, who spoke in your name to our kings, our princes and our fathers, and to all the people of the land.

⁷"Lord, you are righteous, but this day we are covered with shame—the men of Judah and people of Jerusalem and all Israel, both near and far, in all the countries where you have scattered us because of our unfaithfulness to you. ⁸O LORD, we and our kings, our princes and our fathers are covered with shame because we have sinned against you. ⁹The Lord our God is merciful and forgiving, even though we have rebelled against him; ¹⁰we have not obeyed the LORD our God or kept the laws he gave us through his servants the prophets. ¹¹All Israel has transgressed your law and turned away, refusing to obey you.

"Therefore the curses and sworn judgments written in the Law of Moses, the servant of God, have been poured out on us, because we have sinned against you. ¹²You have fulfilled the words spoken against us and against our rulers by bringing upon us great disaster. Under the whole heaven nothing has ever been done like what has been done to Jerusalem. ¹³Just as it is written in the Law of Moses, all this disaster has come upon us, yet we have not sought the favor of the LORD our God by turning from our sins and giving attention to your truth. ¹⁴The LORD did not hesitate to bring the disaster upon

Daniel 9:1–27

us, for the LORD our God is righteous in everything he does; yet we have not obeyed him.

[15]"Now, O Lord our God, who brought your people out of Egypt with a mighty hand and who made for yourself a name that endures to this day, we have sinned, we have done wrong. [16]O Lord, in keeping with all your righteous acts, turn away your anger and your wrath from Jerusalem, your city, your holy hill. Our sins and the iniquities of our fathers have made Jerusalem and your people an object of scorn to all those around us.

[17]"Now, our God, hear the prayers and petitions of your servant. For your sake, O Lord, look with favor on your desolate sanctuary. [18]Give ear, O God, and hear; open your eyes and see the desolation of the city that bears your Name. We do not make requests of you because we are righteous, but because of your great mercy. [19]O Lord, listen! O Lord, forgive! O Lord, hear and act! For your sake, O my God, do not delay, because your city and your people bear your Name."

[20]While I was speaking and praying, confessing my sin and the sin of my people Israel and making my request to the LORD my God for his holy hill—[21]while I was still in prayer, Gabriel, the man I had seen in the earlier vision, came to me in swift flight about the time of the evening sacrifice. [22]He instructed me and said to me, "Daniel, I have now come to give you insight and understanding. [23]As soon as you began to pray, an answer was given, which I have come to tell you, for you are highly esteemed. Therefore, consider the message and understand the vision:

[24]"Seventy 'sevens' are decreed for your people and your holy city to finish transgression, to put an end to sin, to atone for wickedness, to bring in everlasting righteousness, to seal up vision and prophecy and to anoint the most holy.

[25]"Know and understand this: From the issuing of the decree to restore and rebuild Jerusalem until the Anointed One, the ruler, comes, there will be seven 'sevens,' and sixty-two 'sevens.' It will be rebuilt with streets and a trench, but in times of trouble. [26]After the sixty-two 'sevens,' the Anointed One will be cut off and will have nothing. The people of the ruler who will come will destroy the city and the sanctuary. The end will come like a flood: War will continue until the end, and desolations have been decreed. [27]He will confirm a

Daniel 9:1–27

covenant with many for one 'seven.' In the middle of the 'seven' he will put an end to sacrifice and offering. And on a wing of the temple he will set up an abomination that causes desolation, until the end that is decreed is poured out on him."

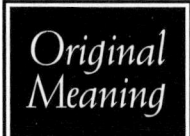

Original Meaning

DANIEL 9 BEGINS like the other chapters in its immediate context by announcing the time when the events described in it take place. It is the first year of Darius the Mede, the one whom we understand to be the ruler of Babylonia after the Persians defeated the native dynasty represented by Belshazzar.[1] The year, then, is 539 B.C.

While the introduction to the chapter is familiar, its contents are unusual for the book. The immediate context is full of apocalyptic visions, yet here we encounter a prayer stimulated by Daniel's reading of Scripture. The prophet is reading the letter of Jeremiah and notes his declaration that the Exile will last seventy years. This insight leads him to turn to God with a prayer of confession.

Some scholars feel that the prayer fits awkwardly in its context.[2] However, such concerns arise only when one has a rigid view of the composition of a biblical book. That the apocalyptic visions are interrupted by a prayer is not at all illogical to the context. In fact, note that Daniel's prayer leads to the appearance of Gabriel, who answers his prayer with an explanation of the seventy years (vv. 20–27), which is a typical way in which numbers are treated in apocalyptic.

Some scholars insist, however, that the context, in which Daniel is struggling with the interpretation of Scripture, demands not the prayer of confession that appears in the chapter, but rather a prayer of illumination. After all, that is what Gabriel provides, an explanation of the Jeremiah passage. But again, Daniel knows that the end of the Exile does not come automatically; it requires confession and repentance. That is the intention of his prayer.

Other scholars feel that Daniel's confession represents a view of the suffering of the exiles that is alien to the book. It is true that the book in the main deals with the tribulations that the foreign oppressors were pressing on God's people. But a faithful Israelite like Daniel would know where the true blame of the Exile rested—not on Babylon, but on the rebellious people of God themselves. Indeed, we observed in the first few verses of the book that this

---

1. See the discussion on pages 157–59. If Darius is not the Babylonian throne name for Cyrus, he is likely ruling at the behest of this Persian emperor.
2. As in Hartman and DiLella, *The Book of Daniel*, 245–46.

Daniel 9:1–27

Exile was not an autonomous act on the part of the godless Babylonians. God was behind the process that brought the Israelites under their control. This strongly implies an understanding that the Exile was the result of Israel's sin. Furthermore, Daniel is reading Jeremiah, the prophet who made it clear why the Babylonians won the day—Israel's breaking of the covenant.

Scholars often refer to the theology expressed in Daniel's prayer as Deuteronomic, that is, as reflecting the theology of Deuteronomy.[3] This Old Testament book is in the form of a report about the covenant relationship between God and his people. A covenant is similar to a treaty.[4] In simple terms, God makes certain promises to his people, and in response they are to obey the laws he announces to them. Essential to a covenant are the blessings and curses: If God's people obey the laws God gives them, he will bless them with security, fertility, and prosperity (Deut. 28:1–14); but if they disobey the law—in particular, if they depart from the worship of the true God—they will be cursed with (among other things) oppression by enemies and exile. Typical is the curse in 28:64–68, a passage that clearly anticipates the Babylonian Exile:

> Then the LORD will scatter you among all nations, from one end of the earth to the other. There you will worship other gods—gods of wood and stone, which neither you nor your fathers have known. Among those nations you will find no repose, no resting place for the sole of your foot. There the LORD will give you an anxious mind, eyes weary with longing, and a despairing heart. You will live in constant suspense, filled with dread both night and day, never sure of your life. In the morning you will say, "If only it were evening!" and in the evening, "If only it were morning!"—because of the terror that will fill your hearts and the sights that your eyes will see. The LORD will send you back in ships to Egypt on a journey I said you should never make again. There you will offer yourselves for sale to your enemies as male and female slaves, but no one will buy you.

From Daniel's perspective, centuries after the writing of Deuteronomy Israel suffered for having broken the covenant and were now experiencing the curses of the covenant.

But Daniel also realized that this was not the end of the story. God is merciful and forgiving. Indeed, in another relevant passage of Scripture, the formula for restoration is clearly put forth. First Kings 8 narrates the dedication

---

3. Towner, *Daniel*, 129–39.
4. M. Kline, *Treaty of the Great King* (Grand Rapids: Eerdmans, 1963); J. Niehaus, *God at Sinai* (Grand Rapids: Zondervan, 1995).

Daniel 9:1–27

of the newly built temple. At that time, Solomon offered a prayer in which he recognized that a time might come when Israel's sin would lead to their defeat at the hands of an enemy (1 Kings 8:33–34, 46–51):

> When your people Israel have been defeated by an enemy because they have sinned against you, and when they turn back to you and confess your name, praying and making supplication to you in this temple, then hear from heaven and forgive the sin of your people Israel and bring them back to the land you gave to their fathers....
>
> When they sin against you—for there is no one who does not sin—and you become angry with them and give them over to the enemy, who takes them captive to his own land, far away or near; and if they have a change of heart in the land where they are held captive, and repent and plead with you in the land of their conquerors and say, "We have sinned, we have done wrong, we have acted wickedly"; and if they turn back to you with all their heart and soul in the land of their enemies who took them captive, and pray to you toward the land you gave their fathers, toward the city you have chosen and the temple I have built for your Name; then from heaven, your dwelling place, hear their prayer and their pleas, and uphold their cause. And forgive your people, who have sinned against you; forgive all the offenses they have committed against you, and cause their conquerors to show them mercy; for they are your people and your inheritance, whom you brought out of Egypt, out of that iron-smelting furnace.

Solomon is here reflecting the theology of Deuteronomy. Daniel does not cite Solomon's prayer; he may not even be thinking of it, but he certainly reflects its theology. In this sense, Daniel represents a Deuteronomic theology. And what else would we expect? Daniel's thinking is founded on God's revelation, which includes Deuteronomy, Kings, and Jeremiah.

Interest in this chapter has usually bypassed the prayer for the more enigmatic prophecy of the seventy weeks. This is unfortunate, for the prayer contains much rich theology and important practical application to those of us reading it today. The seventy weeks has amassed an incredible bibliography and a bewildering array of interpretations. We will do our best to cut through the maze to get at the heart of the teaching of that passage without getting bogged down in esoterica.

Our discussion of the chapter will be divided into five parts: (1) Preparation for prayer (9:1–4a); (2) invocation and confession (9:4b–10); (3) God's punishment (9:11–14); (4) appeal for mercy (9:15–19); (5) the prophecy of the seventy weeks (9:20–27).

Daniel 9:1–27

Preparation for Prayer (9:1–4a)

AS IS TYPICAL of the book of Daniel, the chapter begins with a chronological notice. It is the first year of Darius, "who was made ruler over the Babylonian kingdom" (v. 1). This Darius had forcibly replaced Belshazzar (coregent of Nabonidus) on the throne and was likely a subordinate ruler of Cyrus of Persia (for an extended discussion of the question of the identity of Darius the Mede, see comments on ch. 6).

The significance of the mention of Darius's first year (539 B.C.) was that this was the year in which the Persians defeated the Babylonians, whose empire, under Nebuchadnezzar, had defeated and exiled Judah some decades before. Darius's first year as king of Babylon would have coincided with the first year of Cyrus as the great king of the Persian empire—also the year, therefore, that witnessed the decree to allow some Judeans to return to their homeland.

Daniel's prayer seems to have taken place in anticipation of this decree. His witness to the fall of Babylon may have caused him to turn to the Scriptures with new eyes.

Rarely do we see such an explicit reference from one biblical book to another as we see here with Daniel's appeal to Jeremiah. Some scholars are unwilling to speak of a closed prophetic canon or an authoritative Scripture at this point,[5] but it is certainly hard to avoid the implication of the latter. What Jeremiah has written, after all, is referred to as the "word of the LORD." Here we see the equation between the prophet's words and the word of the one who commissioned him. Reading Jeremiah's words sets off Daniel's passionate appeal in verses 4–19.

But what did Daniel read in Jeremiah? Though verse numbers are not given, Daniel certainly had passages like Jeremiah 25:11–12; 29:10 in mind:

> This whole country will become a desolate wasteland, and these nations will serve the king of Babylon seventy years.
>
> "But when the seventy years are fulfilled, I will punish the king of Babylon and his nation, the land of the Babylonians, for their guilt," declares the LORD, "and will make it desolate forever."
>
> This is what the LORD says, "When seventy years are completed for Babylon, I will come to you and fulfill my gracious promise to bring you back to this place."

In essence these passages teach that the king of Babylon will dominate the ancient Near East (including Judah) for seventy years, after which time

---

5. For instance, Collins, *Daniel*, 348.

Daniel 9:1–27

Babylon itself will come to an end. In the first year of Darius, Babylon has come to an end as a world power, being replaced by Persia. Daniel recognizes this as the time when the Exile may come to an end.

Note that seventy years, counting backward from 539, is 609 B.C. What happened in 609? As far as Judah and the Exile is concerned—nothing.[6] The first incursion we know about is the one mentioned in Daniel 1:1–2, dated to around 605 B.C. Is seventy years a round number for the period of 605 to 539? Perhaps. However, seventy also suggests a symbolic number being seven multiplied by ten, two numbers of completeness.[7] Seventy may also be seen as the approximate or symbolic number for a lifetime.[8]

The interpretation of this number becomes even more complex, however, when we examine two later biblical books as they reflect on Jeremiah's prophecy of seventy years of exile. (1) Second Chronicles 36:20–22 also refers to Jeremiah's seventy years. The Chronicler draws an interesting connection to the Sabbath rests of the land. Leviticus 25:1–7 and 26:31–35, 43 command the Israelites to allow their land to rest every seven years, which apparently they rarely, if ever, did. He then interprets the Exile as a divinely imposed period to make up for the seventy missed sabbatical years. But more telling for our interpretation of Daniel 9, it appears as if the Chronicler understood the seventy years to begin in 586 B.C., the year in which Nebuchadnezzar destroyed the temple and completed the deportation process. He also understood the Exile to end in 539 B.C. with Cyrus's decree, thus clearly taking the number symbolically.

(2) The other relevant passage is Zechariah 1:12, where the prophet reports the plaintive cry of an angel who asks: "How long will you withhold mercy from Jerusalem and from the towns of Judah, which you have been angry with these seventy years?" According to Zechariah the seventy years are apparently still in process in 519 B.C. (the second year of a later Darius).

When we compare these passages and reflect on the number itself, we reach the conclusion that the number is not literal, nor even referring to one specific period of time. This should not concern us; it is the predominant way in which numbers are used in apocalyptic. The recognition of this fact should also prepare us for the even more extravagant use of numbers later in the chapter.

---

6. R. E. Winkle, "Jeremiah's Seventy Weeks for Babylon: A Reassessment, Part II: The Historical Data," *AUSS* 25 (1987): 289–99, is an unsuccessful attempt to place the start at events in 609 B.C.

7. "Numbers," in *The Dictionary of Biblical Imagery* (Downers Grove, Ill.: InterVarsity, 1998).

8. W. L. Holladay, *Jeremiah I: A Commentary on the Book of the Prophet Jeremiah* (Hermeneia; Philadelphia: Fortress, 1985), 668–69.

Daniel 9:1–27

In any case, it is with a scripturally inspired sense that the Exile is coming to a close that Daniel turns to the Lord in prayer. It is significant that only in the context of this prayer is the covenant name Yahweh ("LORD" in NIV) used. This is appropriate in a prayer that appeals to God's covenant promises to forgive and restore his people on the basis of their confession.

Daniel's preparation for prayer indicates the kind of prayer that will follow. He fasts and puts on sackcloth and ashes, all of which are actions that indicate his deep sorrow and grief. Towner is right to identify the following prayer as a "prose prayer of penitence" and to cite its close connections with prayers found in Ezra 9:6–15; Nehemiah 1:5–11 and 9:6–37. They are "all penitential in character and all containing elements of ascription, confession, and petition."[9]

Invocation and Confession (9:4b–10)

THE PRAYER BEGINS by calling on God's name. Indeed, it paints a powerful picture of the Lord, especially in contrast to his people. Daniel acknowledges him as "great and awesome" as well as faithful to the covenant. The latter is most to the point of the prayer. As explained above, the theology of this chapter is based on the theology of the covenant, particularly the Mosaic covenant as recorded in Deuteronomy. Daniel appeals to God as the one who keeps his covenant with all who obey the laws associated with that covenant. He characterizes the covenant as a "covenant of love." The word here translated "love" is the rich term *hesed*, which is the affection that leads to covenant faithfulness on God's part. He does not quickly punish his people, and he stands ready to bless them when they obey his laws.

However, Daniel confesses that God's people have not obeyed his commands, but have rebelled against him instead. They have not listened to the warnings of the prophets who were sent to God's people to get them to change their attitudes and behavior to conform to God's will. The prophets are like the lawyers of the covenant. When the covenant is broken, they appear in order to accuse the people with the ultimate intention of restoring their love and fidelity to God. Isaiah, Jeremiah, Ezekiel, and many others were used by God to carry the message of warning and repentance, but they went largely unheeded.

The prophets were sent, according to Daniel, to all strata of society—from kings to common people. None of them, however, responded. Rather, they persisted in their foolish and dangerous rebellion. In the next few verses of the confession, Daniel marks a contrast between the sin of the people and the mercy of God. God is faithful; his people are rebellious. The prophet is brutally honest in his acknowledgment of the responsibility of God's people

---

9. Towner, *Daniel*, 130.

for their present dire condition. They are in exile because they have rebelled against the covenant God made with them through Moses.

God's Punishment (9:11–14)

IN THE NEXT section of his prayer, Daniel draws a direct connection between the sin of the people and their present suffering. We cited above two of the curses Daniel has in mind, but there are more (see Deut. 27–28). Between the Law of Moses and the Prophets, God's people had no excuse. They knew what the consequences of their actions would be. But somehow they rationalized it. Perhaps they grew presumptuous because of God's long patience with them. They would sin without immediate punishment, so they began to doubt that God would really follow through with his threats. Jeremiah 7:1–29, the so-called "temple sermon" of Jeremiah, charges Israel with presumption because of the presence of the temple in the city. They wrongly reasoned that if God's residence was the temple, there would be no way that an enemy, even one as mighty as Babylon, could defeat their city. They were safe as long as God lived in Jerusalem, and since the temple was immovable, they were safe forever.

What they did not consider was the possibility that God would abandon his temple (Ezek. 9–11). They further did not reckon with the possibility God himself would turn against them and lead the Babylonian army into the streets of Jerusalem (Jer. 21:3–7). Indeed, the horror of the resulting destruction of Jerusalem reverberates through the biblical literature of the exilic period, as seen in Lamentations 2:2–5:

> Without pity the Lord has swallowed up
>   all the dwellings of Jacob;
> in his wrath he has torn down
>   the strongholds of the Daughter of Judah.
> He has brought her kingdom and its princes
>   down to the ground in dishonor.
> In fierce anger he has cut off
>   every horn of Israel.
> He has withdrawn his right hand
>   at the approach of the enemy.
> He has burned in Jacob like a flaming fire
>   that consumes everything around it.
> Like an enemy he has strung his bow;
>   his right hand is ready.
> Like a foe he has slain
>   all who were pleasing to the eye;
> he has poured out his wrath like fire
>   on the tent of the Daughter of Zion.

> The Lord is like an enemy;
>   he has swallowed up Israel.
> He has swallowed up all her palaces
>   and destroyed her strongholds.
> He has multiplied mourning and lamentation
>   for the Daughter of Judah.

The description in Lamentations goes on and on; we cannot fathom the horror that the faithful felt at the destruction of their beloved city and their temple.

Though horrible, however, Daniel does acknowledge again that God was right in what he had done. The destruction of Jerusalem and the Exile of Judah were not acts of an arbitrary God, but rather the consequences of the sinful attitudes and actions of God's people, about which they were repeatedly warned.

Appeal for Mercy (9:15–19)

DANIEL HAS BEEN praying not just on his own behalf, but as the representative of the people. He has not confessed his own sins, but rather the sins of the nation. From that foundation, he now asks God to show mercy to his people and restore the destroyed city. We noted above from 1 Kings 8 that restoration was possible after divine punishment, but it required this kind of acknowledgment of responsibility on the part of the people.

Here the prophet calls on God as the One who delivered his people out of Egypt. The Exodus was a pivotal event in the life of God's people. It defined them as a nation. Through it, God freed them from slavery and brought them into the Promised Land. The prophets before Daniel saw an analogy between the Exodus and the future deliverance that would free them from the shackles of the Exile (cf. Isa. 40:3–5; Hos. 2:14–15). In essence, the return from the Exile would be a sort of second Exodus.

Though the plea for God's mercy follows the confession and could not proceed without it, it is wrong to think that the confession is the basis of God's restoration. Daniel knows that the people are still sinful and if there is any hope for them, it is in God's righteousness and not their own (vv. 16, 18). Daniel's appeal is ultimately based not on the people's plight but on the reputation of God himself.

The Prophecy of the Seventy Weeks (9:20–27)

DANIEL'S PRAYER GIVES the impression of completeness, ending as it does with an impassioned plea for God to hear the prayer and forgive his people without delay (v. 19). The prophet is still in a prayerful frame of mind, perhaps

Daniel 9:1–27

continuing with urgent appeals to God to answer the prayer, when he is suddenly interrupted by Gabriel, the angel who interpreted the vision of the previous chapter. Gabriel may well have had the task of interpreter among the angels of the Lord.

We must remember that Daniel's prayer for forgiveness and restoration was motivated by his reading of Jeremiah's prophecy that the Exile would last seventy years. Gabriel's answer to Daniel's prayer is an interpretation of the seventy years in a way that seems to extend its purview. Gabriel apparently suggests that the end of the seventy-year exile begins a process, one that will last for seventy "sevens," or weeks of years—usually understood as 490 years.

We will begin our exploration of Gabriel's speech by paraphrasing it without attempting to relate it to the future or historical events. Daniel has prayed for forgiveness and restoration, and Gabriel now communicates the heavenly answer by reinterpreting the seventy years as seventy "sevens."[10] During this period six actions will be completed: (1) the finishing of transgression, (2) the end of sin, (3) the atonement of the wicked, (4) the bringing in of everlasting righteousness, (5) the sealing up of vision and prophecy, and (6) the anointing of the most holy (v. 24). The accomplishment of these six actions certainly sounds like an answer to Daniel's prayer, but they are being pushed off to the future (the force of the seventy "sevens" to be explained below). They are, in the words of J. J. Collins, an "eschatological ideal."[11]

The first two actions describe the end of sin, presumably on the part of God's people; after all, that was what Daniel's prayer called for. However, it may also encompass the sins of all people, including the sins of the nations described as beasts in chapters 7 and 8. The third action, "to atone for wickedness," emphasizes the theme of the first two, the eradication of sin. But whereas the first two simply describe the cessation of sinful activity, this third action implies that God removes the consequences of already committed sinful behavior.

While the first three actions describe the eradication of the negative, the next three are more positive in focus. The first is clearly positive, though of a general nature and hard to specify: The completion of the seventy sevens will see the introduction of "everlasting righteousness." The second, the sealing of vision and prophecy, is sometimes misunderstood as a sealing away. But sealing in its ancient context is better understood as a mark of approval, an authentication of the prophetic word. Perhaps in this context it implies the act of authentication, that is, the ultimate fulfillment of Jeremiah's

---

10. Or perhaps, as suggested in the previous paragraph, the seventy "sevens" are seen as prolonging the just completed seventy-year Exile.

11. Collins, *Daniel*, 353.

Daniel 9:1–27

prophecy. The last, and perhaps the culmination of the six actions, is the anointing of "the most holy." Some take the reference as pointing to the temple and its cleansing by the Maccabean rebels after being profaned by Antiochus Epiphanes in the middle of the second century B.C. Another ancient tradition, however, takes the reference not to a place but to a person—the Messiah.

These six actions take place during the entire period of seventy "sevens." They describe the eradication of evil and the establishment of righteousness. In the present, Daniel and his companions know an imperfect world, but in the future things will be wonderful.

Far from concluding his speech, Gabriel continues by taking a more nuanced look at the seventy "sevens." He divides the period into parts, charting a kind of forward-looking history of the seventy "sevens." In essence, he divides the entire period into three parts (vv. 25–27). (1) The first seven "sevens" and (2) the next sixty-two "sevens" are in one sense treated as a single unit—though in another obvious way as two—and encompass the period between the decree to restore and rebuild Jerusalem and the coming of "the Anointed One."[12] We are already used to this enigmatic way of referring to future time periods, so we are not surprised at the questions that arise from these numbers. Why exactly is the first seven "sevens" separated from the next sixty-two? Apparently, we are to think of that shorter period as having a kind of integrity of its own, but what marks its ending point? Which decree of many that we know about is in Gabriel's mind? Who is "the Anointed One"? We will address these questions below.

With the phrase "streets and a trench" (v. 25a) the passage intends to communicate that Jerusalem will be completely restored and that this restoration will take place in an atmosphere of "trouble" (v. 25b).

The end of the sixty-nine "seven's" (the combination of the two first periods) marks a turbulent time. Again, the language is enigmatic. The Anointed One will be cut off, and the "people of the ruler" will destroy the "city and the sanctuary" (v. 26). The devastation will be complete and perhaps quick since it is compared to a flood. It will be a time of war and desolation.

(3) The last "seven," the seventieth, is itself divided in the middle and, far from clearing things up, continues the enigma. In the first place, the action of the seventieth week emanates from a single individual, who is simply

---

12. A close reading shows an ambiguous relationship between the first seven "sevens" and the next sixty-two. The NIV (see also the NJB and NLT) reads the two periods together as stretching from the decree to the appearance of the Anointed One, motivated no doubt in part by a desire to associate the Anointed One with Christ. Other versions and interpreters understand the two periods as separate, with the Anointed One appearing after the first seven "sevens'" (cf. NRSV; REB; NAB).

referred to as "he." The closest antecedent is the "ruler" (*nagid*) of verse 26. The latter's relationship to the Anointed One is unclear and, as we will see, debated. Are they the same? After all, in verse 25 it is clear that the "Anointed One" is called the ruler (*nagid*), but the ruler in verse 26 is associated with destructive actions; and most Christian interpretations understand the Anointed One in a positive manner.

Nevertheless, it is clear that the actions of the seventieth week are the work of a destructive force. The unspecified "he" confirms a covenant for one "seven," presumably the seventieth, but in the middle of it he cuts off sacrifice and offering. While it may be possible to construe the latter in some way as positive, the erection of "an abomination that causes desolation" clearly is not. The period of the prophecy ends with the end of this disruptive person. In the next section, we will delve further, but with great caution, into the morass of interpretations of this enigmatic oracle.

DANIEL 9 BEGINS with Scripture reading, which leads to prayer that results in divine revelation. Daniel's reading of Jeremiah's letter moves him to acknowledge and ask forgiveness for the sins of God's people. The prayer, in turn, brings Gabriel to Daniel with a message from God.

The relationship between God's Word and prayer. Before turning our focus to the content of the prayer and revelation, let's pause for a moment on the dynamic of Daniel's communication with God. We get a rare Old Testament glimpse of Scripture reading in relationship to prayer. How do human beings communicate with God? Daniel 9 provides an illustration. God speaks to us through the words of his representatives, the prophets—in this case the writings of Jeremiah. Though dead and gone by this time, Jeremiah's written word still speaks God's word to his people. Daniel hears God's words in Jeremiah and responds through prayer. God then sends Gabriel with yet further revelation.

The principle is clear, though its contemporary application awaits the next section: God speaks to his people in his written and spoken Word. This principle is simple on the surface, but is really at the heart of biblical religion and contrasts with modern ideas of Christianity. Since the nineteenth-century philosophers Feuerbach and Nietzsche, it has commonly been believed that the God of Christianity is the product of human imagination. Human beings desire a God, so they have constructed him in their own image. The Bible, however, claims to be the revelation of God to human beings. God uses human language to make his existence and nature known to us. In the Bible,

Daniel 9:1–27

he makes his will known to his people. Daniel understands this as he meditates on Jeremiah's letter.

The six themes of Daniel 7–12, reviewed. While the form of Daniel 9— a prayer of repentance—is unique to its context, the surrounding chapters focus on apocalyptic visions of the future, whose content, especially when the divine revelation at the end is taken into account, shares themes with the preceding and following chapters. In the section "The Nature of Apocalyptic Literature" in the Original Meaning section of chapter 7, we identified the six themes that reverberate throughout the second half of the book of Daniel, together supporting the overarching thesis of the book of Daniel: *In spite of present appearances, God is in control and will win the victory.*

(1) Human evil is horrible, particularly as it is concentrated in the state. This theme has certainly been in the forefront of the previous two chapters. Chapter 9 sees a shift of focus that has attracted the attention of previous interpreters. Throughout Daniel, the pagan nations, like Babylonia and Persia, have been seen as renegades from God. In Daniel's prayer, Israel too is named as rebel and transgressor. The suffering of God's people is ultimately the result of their own sin.

(2) A specific time of deliverance is announced. Gabriel's response to Daniel's prayer is an extended announcement of the time of deliverance. As we discussed at length in the previous chapter, the numbers given in reference to the time of the fulfillment of prophecy or the end are wrongly understood as a kind of apocalyptic calendar. They rather give the sense of a definite end to suffering, a time known and determined by God himself and not revealed to human beings. The numbers are ultimately symbolic and impossible of conversion to an absolute date.

In our interpretation of the "seventy 'sevens'" in the preceding section, we noted the futile search for an interpretation of these numbers to fit with our understanding of history. Attempts to correlate these years, understood as 490 years, with the date of Antiochus Epiphanes, Jesus Christ's first coming, his second coming, or any of the countless other special redemptive events that have caught interpreters' attention, have been unpersuasive to any but a few devoted followers. Such futile efforts work against the purpose of these texts, which is to point to God's determined timing of the end of sin and suffering without revealing the exact timing.

(3) Repentance leads to deliverance. Evil is the result of resisting the way of God. Sin produces suffering. God is revealed as a holy God in this book, who judges those who sin. But he is also a gracious God, who forgives those who come to him and confess their sins. Acknowledgment of sin and confession—in a word, repentance—leads to deliverance or restoration. This theme has been earmarked for special discussion in this chapter; we will reserve further comment until we finish our survey of the six themes.

(4) A cosmic war stands behind human conflict. This theme takes on major proportions in Daniel 10, but even here we get a glimpse of the supernatural universe that lies behind human history. Daniel prays to God, who in response sends an angel with his answer. In the next chapter we will see that these angels, even as they come with answers to prayer, are involved in a conflict with other supernatural powers (see comments on ch. 10).

(5) Judgment is certain for those who resist God and oppress his people. Even though the evil of God's people is stressed in Daniel 9, the evil power that oppresses them does not escape condemnation and judgment. As we have commented above, the language of the "seventy 'sevens'" is difficult, and at times even the basic characters of the prophecy are unclear. However, no doubt attends the revelation that the period of time culminates in the destruction of the final embodiment of evil, who sets up "an abomination that causes desolation" (9:27). God wins out in the end.

(6) Equally true is the fact that God's people, downtrodden in the present, will experience new life in the fullest sense. Daniel's prayer describes the covenant people as sinful and distant from God. Their sin has resulted in the judgment of the Exile. His prayer, however, is motivated by the hope of restoration that Jeremiah's prophecy instilled in his heart. He longs for that time of deliverance. It is with a message of life that Gabriel comes to Daniel. We have seen under the previous point that the message includes punishment for those who resist God to the end, but it also talks about the restoration of God's people. The "seventy 'sevens,'" after all, have as their purpose "to finish transgression, to put an end to sin, to atone for wickedness, to bring in everlasting righteousness, to seal up vision and prophecy and to anoint the most holy."

Repentance and forgiveness. We have reserved chapter 9 for a fuller discussion of the third important theme of the last half of Daniel: repentance that leads to deliverance. Daniel prays a prayer of confession that apologizes for the past sins of his people, with the hope that God will hear his prayer and begin the process of forgiveness and reconciliation. In this section, we will explore more deeply the theological dynamics that fueled Daniel's hope.

At the heart of Daniel's prayer stands one of the most potent and pervasive theological themes of the Old Testament: the covenant. Its sudden appearance in Daniel 9 has led some commentators, as we have seen, to question whether Daniel's prayer is a foreign intrusion into the book. However, the covenant is such an important concept among the Old Testament people of God of whatever period that it is more surprising when it is absent. It is so pervasive an idea that it often lurks in the background, surfacing only at strategic moments. Daniel 9 is such a strategic moment.

Daniel 9:1–27

The apocalyptic visions of the latter half of this book envision a deliverance for God's people from the oppression that began with Nebuchadnezzar's incursion into Judah (see 1:1–2). Israel's culpability for this turn of events is strongly implied in the language used there for the process of domination and exile that began at that moment "the Lord delivered Jehoiakim king of Judah into his hand." Behind this simple statement stands the judgment of God, based on the curses of the covenant.

We will first explain the concept of *covenant* more carefully—an English word often used to translate the Hebrew word b^{e}rit. This word is not a part of our everyday vocabulary, but it still has a vital life as a legal term. It is a legal expression for a relationship where commitments are made and sanctioned by law, which have the force of penalties for noncompliance. In many ways, *covenant* is a good translation equivalent for the biblical idea. More recent evidence from the ancient Near East, however, allows us to understand this legal term more precisely. The legal relationship is best recognized as a political treaty. In other words, in the covenant/treaty God is the Great King, who enters into a political treaty with his servant people Israel.

This understanding was reached by the awareness that certain key texts describing the covenant relationship between God and Israel bear a similar structure and reveal similar content to ancient Near Eastern treaties, particularly those found in the Hittite capital of Boghazkoi.[13] This structure illuminates the theological principle at work in Daniel 9. As we describe the six parts of a covenant/treaty document, we will illustrate them from the book of Deuteronomy. Deuteronomy is not a treaty per se, but rather a sermon that describes the treaty relationship. Thus, it follows the outline only roughly, yet close enough to see that the concept is fairly applied to Deuteronomy. Using this biblical book as our paradigm covenant has the further advantage that the Mosaic covenant is the one that lies most directly behind Daniel's prayer.

The book of Deuteronomy follows the typical pattern of a treaty between the king of a powerful nation and the king of a relatively modest nation. This type of relationship is called a vassal treaty (as opposed to a treaty of equals, called a parity treaty) and has at least six standard elements:

- *Introduction.* An ancient Near Eastern vassal treaty began with the introduction of the two parties involved. In Deuteronomy 1 we do not have the actual treaty document, but we have an account of the ritual that affirms it. Clearly the two parties are God, who is the Great King, and the people of Israel, who are his servant people (Deut. 1:1–5).

---

13. Several ancient Near Eastern treaties may be found in English translation in *ANET*, 201–6, 529–35.

Daniel 9:1–27

- *Historical review.* An ancient treaty often began with a review of the history of the relationship between the two parties. In secular treaties, the great king would lay it on thick by telling the vassal king how wonderful he had been to the weaker nation and how ungrateful the other king had been to him. In Deuteronomy, of course, the historical remembrance is more than manipulative political ideology. It is the truth. God has been overwhelmingly gracious to Israel. From the Red Sea crossing to the moment forty years later when they stand poised to enter the Promised Land, God has taken care of his people (Deut. 1:9–3:27).
- *Law-giving.* After the gracious relationship between God and Israel has been firmly established, God gives them the law. This, too, follows the pattern of the ancient Near Eastern treaties, in which the present obligations of the law sprang from the relationship of the past. In Deuteronomy, though not in all biblical covenants, the law takes up the lion's share of the content (Deut. 4:1–26:19). Perhaps the reason for this is Moses' concern that Israel has been so disobedient in the desert.

The important theological point is that God delivers the law only after he has established his relationship with Israel. His law is not the cause of the relationship but the way in which the relationship will be continued and enriched. This is what we mean by saying the laws come in the context of grace. To make sure that Israel gets its priorities straight, the Ten Commandments begin with this reminder, "I am the LORD your God, who brought you out of Egypt, out of the land of slavery" (Deut. 5:6; cf. Ex. 20:2). God has graciously acted on their behalf, prior to anything they can do to earn his benevolence.

- *Rewards and consequences.* Next Deuteronomy stipulates consequences for disobedience. In ancient Near Eastern treaties, the great king would inform the vassal that wonderful rewards would follow obedience to his laws, while punishment would surely reach the one who disobeyed. In a similar manner, conditions are attached to Israel's response—either blessings or curses (Deut. 27:1–28:68). These blessings and curses make their presence felt throughout the canon of the Old Testament. Samuel and Kings in particular view the Exile as a result of breaking the laws of Deuteronomy, which has thus brought on the dreaded curses. Deuteronomy 28:64 is an ominous anticipation of that horrible period of Israel's history when God promises disobedient Israel that he will "scatter [them] among all nations."
- *Witnesses.* A treaty, being at heart a legal document, needs witnesses. In the ancient Near Eastern treaties, the gods and goddesses of the

respective nations often served in this capacity. For Israel, the witness is God's creation, heaven and earth itself (Deut. 30:19–20).

- *Review and succession.* To complete the picture of the treaty or covenant in Old Testament times, we must mention the concern for the treaty text itself (e.g., where it should be placed) and for a regular reading of the document, as well as the provision for the succession of kings, especially in the vassal country. Treaties looked beyond the present to the future. Scribes made two copies of the treaty and usually placed them in the most important temples of the two nations entering the relationship.

This procedure wasn't necessary in the divine-human covenant, though it has been suggested that the two tablets of the law are actually two copies. In either case, the law is written and placed in the most sacred spot possible—the ark of the covenant. Every seven years, during the Feast of the Tabernacles, the priests are to read the law so the people can reaffirm their allegiance to it (Deut. 31:9–13).

In other words, the covenant provides the reason why the Israelites are suffering at the hands of the Babylonians. They have broken the law and are suffering the consequences of the curses, which includes removal from the Promised Land and exile to a foreign land. A prime example from the curse section of the book of Deuteronomy (28:64–68) is quoted above. But that is not the end of the story. Also quoted above is 1 Kings 8:46–51, which talks about the possibility of restoration. This hope also grows from the book of Deuteronomy, which envisions in 30:1–10 a time when the sins of the people have triggered the curses of the covenant. However, thanks to God's grace, the story does not end for God's people at that point:

> When all these blessings and curses I have set before you come upon you and you take them to heart wherever the LORD your God disperses you among the nations, and when you and your children return to the LORD your God and obey him with all your heart and with all your soul according to everything I command you today, then the LORD your God will restore your fortunes and have compassion on you and gather you again from all the nations where he scattered you. Even if you have been banished to the most distant land under the heavens, from there the LORD your God will gather you and bring you back. He will bring you to the land that belonged to your fathers, and you will take possession of it. He will make you more prosperous and numerous than your fathers. The LORD your God will circumcise your hearts and the hearts of your descendants, so that you may love him with all your heart and with all your soul, and live. The LORD

Daniel 9:1–27

your God will put all these curses on your enemies who hate and persecute you. You will again obey the LORD and follow all his commands I am giving you today. Then the LORD your God will make you most prosperous in all the work of your hands and in the fruit of your womb, the young of your livestock and the crops of your land. The LORD will again delight in you and make you prosperous, just as he delighted in your fathers, if you obey the LORD your God and keep his commands and decrees that are written in this Book of the Law and turn to the LORD your God with all your heart and with all your soul.

Daniel's prayer is founded on the Deuteronomic covenant. He understands the present situation as the result of the breaking of the law and the consequent curses. But he also understands that the road to recovery is through repentance, which involves full acknowledgment of past transgression. There is no "forgive and forget" without confession here or anywhere in the Bible. Notice too that nowhere do we get the slightest evidence that Daniel has personally participated in the sins that led to the people's present condition. Yet he does not say, "Forgive them, Lord." Rather, he identifies with the people and cries out, "We have sinned and done wrong. We have been wicked and have rebelled; we have turned away from your commands and laws" (Dan. 9:5).

On the basis of a covenant relationship, Daniel turns to the Lord and confesses the sins of the people and includes himself among them. He acknowledges God's righteousness in the Exile, but also turns to the Lord with the hope of repentance. Repentance is the road to reconciliation.

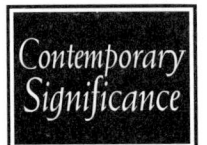

HEARING GOD'S VOICE **today**. Daniel turned to the writings of Jeremiah to hear the voice of God. Here he heard God speak to him and the nation, and it motivated his response of prayer and repentance. God then spoke to him further through the agency of Gabriel, an angel. Where do we go to hear God speak today? Where does God reveal himself to us? The opening verses of the book of Hebrews (1:1–4) points us in the right direction:

> In the past God spoke to our forefathers through the prophets at many times and in various ways, but in these last days he has spoken to us by his Son, whom he appointed heir of all things, and through whom he made the universe. The Son is the radiance of God's glory and the exact representation of his being, sustaining all things by his powerful word. After he had provided purification for sins, he sat

down at the right hand of the Majesty in heaven. So he became as much superior to the angels as the name he has inherited is superior to theirs.

Jesus is God's fullest revelation of himself to us. He is God in human form. Where do we meet God in Jesus today? Most directly in the Bible. We should listen to Paul's well-known advice to Timothy (2 Tim. 3:14–16):

> Continue in what you have learned and have become convinced of, because you know those from whom you learned it, and how from infancy you have known the holy Scriptures, which are able to make you wise for salvation through faith in Christ Jesus. All Scripture is God-breathed and is useful for teaching, rebuking, correcting and training in righteousness, so that the man of God may be thoroughly equipped for every good work.

The difference between the time of Daniel and our own time is that we have a completed canon, Old and New Testament, which reveals God to us. We can see the pattern of God's progressive revelation as it tells the story of redemption that culminates in Jesus Christ. That is why we insist on ultimately reading the Old Testament through the light of the New Testament. It is one Word of God, which culminates in the New. The brighter light of the New Testament often helps us see the Old Testament more clearly.

However, as we have done in this commentary, it is essential first to consider the teaching of the Old Testament on its own grounds first. We must ask the question what the original audience understood before we can legitimately push forward to the New Testament. Otherwise, we risk the danger of reading into the Old Testament what is not there or missing important elements of its teaching.

The new covenant in Jesus. As we bridge the horizon to the fuller revelation of the New Testament in Daniel 9, we first of all notice that the foundational concept of the covenant reaches its culmination in the teaching of Jesus. Daniel looked back to the Mosaic covenant, while Jesus speaks of a new covenant.

At the end of his life, just before going to the cross, Jesus shared a last meal with his disciples, at which he introduced a ritual we know as the "Lord's Supper" or "communion." This ritual is described in the following words in Matthew 26:26–30:

> While they were eating, Jesus took bread, gave thanks and broke it, and gave it to his disciples, saying, "Take and eat; this is my body."
> Then he took the cup, gave thanks and offered it to them, saying, "Drink from it, all of you. This is my blood of the covenant, which is

poured out for many for the forgiveness of sins. I tell you, I will not drink of this fruit of the vine from now on until that day when I drink it anew with you in my Father's kingdom."

When they had sung a hymn, they went out to the Mount of Olives.

Jesus thus seals a covenant with his twelve disciples. This should remind us of God's covenant dealings in the Old Testament. As a matter of fact, Luke adds the word "new" before "covenant" (Luke 22:20), making an explicit connection with Jeremiah 31:31–33. Jesus' language signifies continuity and discontinuity in the idea of the covenant as we move from the Old to the New Testament, and Jeremiah's prophecy is an important transitional statement.

Jeremiah, as we have already seen, not only told the people about their coming punishment based on their breaking of the covenant law, but he also gave them the hope that their punishment would lead to their repentance and to the rescue of the remnant. The most notable instance of this is in the so-called Book of Consolation. Jeremiah 31:31–34 is at the heart of God's message of hope:

"The time is coming," declares the LORD,
   "when I will make a new covenant
with the house of Israel
   and with the house of Judah.
It will not be like the covenant
   I made with their forefathers
when I took them by the hand
   to lead them out of Egypt,
because they broke my covenant,
   though I was a husband to them,"
                                 declares the LORD.
"This is the covenant I will make with the house of Israel
   after that time," declares the LORD.
"I will put my law in their minds
   and write it on their hearts.
I will be their God
   and they will be my people.
No longer will a man teach his neighbor,
   or a man his brother, saying, "Know the LORD,"
because they will all know me,
   from the least of them to the greatest,"
                                 declares the LORD.

Here we see a bridge between the Old Testament and the New, but one that suggests that there is both continuity and discontinuity. It is a covenant that has its foundations in the Old Testament covenants, but in some sense it is new.

What is new (i.e., what discontinuity is there) between the old covenant and the new? O. P. Robertson is correct to locate the necessity of discontinuity in the failure not of God or his covenant, but with the people. "The expulsion of the people of God from the land of promise at the time of the exile dramatizes their massive failure under the old covenant."[14] According to Jeremiah, the new covenant is internal, immediate, and intimate in comparison to the old covenant. These differences are not a difference in kind as much as in degree. It is perhaps more precise to say that the new covenant is *more* internal, immediate, and intimate than the old.

The passage from Jeremiah 31 just quoted indicates that the new covenant "boasts a unique feature in its power to transform its participants from within their hearts."[15] Further, there is no need for a teacher in the new covenant. Christians, as new covenant believers, know by experience that this promise does not imply that we know everything or that everything concerning God and his Word is clear to us. Nor does it mean that teachers and ministers should seek employment elsewhere. What it does mean is that no longer are human mediators of the covenant relationship needed. In the Old Testament, Moses, David, and many other leaders were the immediate recipients of the covenant relationship, and they in turn mediated it to the people. According to the New Testament, there is only one mediator and he is not merely human, he is Jesus Christ, Son of God (1 Tim. 2:5).

However, "new" in this case does not imply a complete break with the old. Robertson recognizes this and names the new covenant, the covenant of consummation. This highlights the fact that Jesus Christ does not abrogate or ignore the old covenants but rather fulfills them.

Space and time do not permit full justification of this point. Robertson does an excellent job showing how the new covenant relates to the old. He utilizes what we, his former students, used to call the "lazy V" diagram to indicate that the covenants are a function of progressive revelation, each building on the previous ones until they are consummated in Christ (see diagram on the following page).

The diagram visually represents the fact that Jesus fulfills the covenant with Abraham with its promises of descendants, land, and blessing for the nations (Gen. 12:1–3). Jesus Christ fulfills the covenant of law mediated by

---

14. O. P. Robertson, *The Christ of the Covenants* (Phillipsburg, N.J.: Presbyterian and Reformed, 1980), 271.
15. Ibid., 276.

Daniel 9:1–27

The Covenant Structure of Scripture[16]

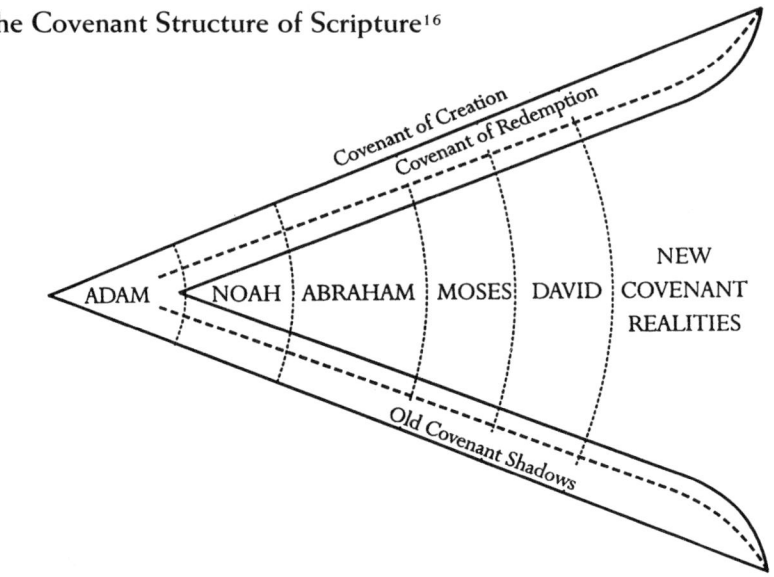

Moses, since he is the one who fulfills the conditions of the law. He also fulfills the covenant of the kingdom of David (2 Sam. 7), since he is David's greater Son who sits on the throne of the heavenly kingdom, which was merely reflected by David's political kingdom.

But what is the role of the law in the new covenant? This is a complex and highly debated subject, which we neither can nor need to solve here except in general outline.[17] Obeying the law has never been the route to establish a relationship with God. In the Old Testament, this is recognized by the fact that God rescued the Israelites from Egypt before giving them the law on Mount Sinai. The New Testament, particularly Paul, is clear that our salvation does not result from our obedience to the law (Gal. 3:10–11):

> All who rely on observing the law are under a curse, for it is written: "Cursed is everyone who does not continue to do everything written in the Book of the Law." Clearly no one is justified before God by the law, because, "The righteous will live by faith."

However, the New Testament also indicates a continuing role for the law in such passages as James 1:22–25:

---

16. From O. P. Robertson, *The Christ of the Covenants* (Grand Rapids: Baker, 1980), 62.
17. For further discussion, see T. Longman III, *Reading the Bible with Heart and Mind* (Colorado Springs: NavPress, 1997), 113–28.

> Do not merely listen to the word, and so deceive yourselves. Do what it says. Anyone who listens to the word but does not do what it says is like a man who looks at his face in a mirror and, after looking at himself, goes away and immediately forgets what he looks like. But the man who looks intently into the perfect law that gives freedom, and continues to do this, not forgetting what he has heard, but doing it—he will be blessed in what he does.

This language is reminiscent of the Old Testament teaching that those who keep the law will be blessed and those who do not will be cursed.

Again, this subject is complicated and the danger of a superficial understanding is great. For one thing, there is the question of how the Old Testament law functions in the New Testament. A full discussion would show that there is a continuity in principle, but not in the application found in the case law or in the penalties.[18] Moreover, we need to remember that though there is strong teaching in Deuteronomy, the Prophets, Proverbs, and elsewhere that living a godly life leads to good results, there is also the teaching of Job, Ecclesiastes, and other books that keep us from reducing this to a facile formula. Good people do suffer in this life; bad people sometimes prosper. The New Testament indeed tells us that ultimate retribution does not take place in this life, but the next. However, to use one example, it is much more likely that you will have a good marriage if you do not commit adultery than if you do.

Jesus himself tells us that the law continues to play a crucial role in the new covenant (Matt. 5:17–20):

> Do not think that I have come to abolish the Law or the Prophets; I have not come to abolish them but to fulfill them. I tell you the truth, until heaven and earth disappear, not the smallest letter, not the least stroke of a pen, will by any means disappear from the Law until everything is accomplished. Anyone who breaks one of the least of these commandments and teaches others to do the same will be called least in the kingdom of heaven, but whoever practices and teaches these commands will be called great in the kingdom of heaven. For I tell you that unless your righteousness surpasses that of the Pharisees and the teachers of the law, you will certainly not enter the kingdom of heaven.

The need for repentance. Yet as we all know, not only from the Bible but from our own experience, no one keeps the law perfectly. We have all broken

---

18. A helpful discussion may be found in B. K. Waltke, "Theonomy in Relation to Dispensational and Covenant Theologies," *Theonomy: A Reformed Critique* ed. W. Barker and R. Godfrey (Grand Rapids: Zondervan, 1990), 59–87.

Daniel 9:1–27

the law. Breaking God's law leads to rupture in relationships—both in our relationship with God and often in human relationships. Through our sin, we strain our ties with those who are close with us: spouse, friends, coworkers, Christian brothers and sisters.

We can see how this works in Daniel 9. Daniel recognized that Israel's sin has ruptured its relationship with God. Historically, this break in relationship is represented by the Exile. Daniel prays to restore that relationship through a prayer of confession, apology, and repentance.

At the heart of the Christian religion stands repentance. It is not that our faith results from repentance, but repentance flows from faith in a God who forgives. Theologically, we may want to talk about how God initiates the movement toward repentance in our heart,[19] but then we do not want to lose sight of the fact that our relationship with God, once broken, is restored through an act of repentance: "The time has come.... The kingdom of God is near. Repent and believe the good news" (Mark 1:15).

God requires acknowledgment of our sin in the context of restoring a relationship with us. And repentance does not stop after someone becomes a Christian. We must continue to acknowledge our inadequacies and rebellion in our relationship with God.

Before we go any further, we must square this point with a fundamental teaching of the New Testament. While we must repent of our sins, again our relationship with God is not based on our ability either to keep the law or even to keep up with our daily repentance. Why? Because our faith is not built on our good works or obedience, but rather on the work of Jesus Christ. He is the perfect lawkeeper. He is the only one who never broke the law, but he is also the one who died on the cross because of sin. In fulfillment of Old Testament sacrificial practice, Jesus is our substitute.

In the Old Testament period, an animal sacrifice accompanied the act of repentance. By sacrificing an animal, the Israelites acknowledged the depth of their sin. The animal died in their place. The New Testament teaches us that our repentance does not need an animal sacrifice because Jesus our high priest offered "one sacrifice for sins," and by this one sacrifice "he has made perfect forever those who are being made holy" (Heb. 10:12–14).

Jesus' death and resurrection is the foundation of our faith, not our repentance; but God calls us to repent of our sins to maintain a good relationship with him. As Paul states it, "godly sorrow [over some infraction] brings repentance that leads to salvation" (2 Cor. 7:10). Daniel displayed this sorrow in the light of the sin of God's people, which moved him to repentance and

---

19. As Wink, *When the Powers Fall*, 18, puts it: "We can repent, in fact, precisely *because* God has already forgiven us."

restoration with God. Paul describes the same principle to the Corinthians and through them to us.

Repentance not only restores the divine-human relationship, but it is also at the heart of reconciliation among God's human creatures. Let's pause again before expanding on this thought to make explicit why we treated the role of repentance in the divine-human relationship first. The Bible teaches time and again that human relationships can only be truly restored on the basis of a restored relationship with God. We see the two intertwined as early as the Garden of Eden (Gen. 2–3). Adam and Eve enjoyed a perfectly intimate relationship with one another in the Garden as long as they worshiped God. However, the story of the Fall is the story of mistrust and rebellion against God, which resulted not only in estrangement from God but also alienation from one another.

David demonstrates how distance from God produces a break in human relationships. In David's sin with Bathsheba, he violently tore human relationships as he slept with a married woman and then saw to it that her husband died in battle (2 Sam. 11). David tried to cover up his sin, but God sent Nathan the prophet to confront him with it. Psalm 51 is David's prayer of repentance (and indeed is one of a number of model prayers of repentance found in the Psalter). Here is how that psalm begins (Ps. 51:1–4):

> Have mercy on me, O God,
>   according to your unfailing love;
> according to your great compassion
>   blot out my transgressions.
> Wash away all my iniquity
>   and cleanse me from my sin.
> For I know my transgressions,
>   and my sin is always before me.
> Against you, you only, have I sinned
>   and done what is evil in your sight. . . .

Taken on its own, these verses are shocking. What could David mean that he sinned only against God? Tell that to Uriah in his grave. But in an important sense David is right. Our sins against other human beings are first and foremost sins against God, in whose image all human beings have been created.

Nonetheless, our acts and statements of repentance must go beyond a prayer, to the offended person. To restore a broken relationship often requires first a broken and humble heart. Jack Miller tells a powerful story of repentance in his book *Come Back, Barbara*.[20] It is the story of a daughter who rebels

---

20. J. Miller and B. Miller Juliani, *Come Back, Barbara*, 2d ed. (Phillipsburg, N.J.: Presbyterian and Reformed, 1997).

against her upbringing by disowning God and rejecting her parents. Jack describes Barbara as turning her back on her spiritual heritage by pursuing a glamorous lifestyle of money, pleasure, and drugs. The story of the return of this prodigal daughter is a stirring one, one that climaxes with Barbara's acknowledgment of her rebellion and a return to God and family through faith and repentance.

Today, Barbara is a leader in New Life Church in Philadelphia, the church her now-deceased father founded a couple of decades ago. Jack Miller was my pastor for a number of years before his death, and his ministry had as one of its major themes the need for daily repentance in our relationship with God and with one another. His prescription for Christian living did not devolve to become a formulaic asking of forgiveness for every little offense against another. Indeed, overt repentance can at times be a bigger offense than the original offense. I remember a friend of mine becoming convinced that she had to ask the forgiveness of everyone she had ever sinned against in the past twenty years of her life. She dutifully called her parents, her friends, former boyfriends, and acquaintances. By doing this, she brought herself some measure of relief, but she succeeded in dredging up old emotions that had been resolved long before. Wisdom is needed to know how to proceed in the matter of past offenses.

But repentance goes even further than just between individuals. Walter Wink's recent contribution to his "Powers" series emphasizes that whole societies may find it necessary to repent in order to achieve some measure of reconciliation. As he strongly states it, "human societies could not exist without forgiveness and the public acts of contrition and confession that make reconciliation possible."[21]

Perhaps the most dramatic example that Wink provides is the process happening in South Africa at the time of this writing. South Africa witnessed for many decades the brutal oppression of the black majority at the hands of the white minority in the form of the insidious institution of apartheid. Now, however, South Africa has achieved a large measure of democracy, and the black majority finds itself in positions of power. One might expect (and justice might insist) in such a situation that the powers of vengeance would immediately engulf the society in a bloodbath, but that is not what has happened. On the contrary, grace is being displayed in such institutions as the Truth and Reconciliation Commission, established in 1995. This commission announced a period of time during which individuals who committed atrocities can come forward and make a full disclosure of their crimes with the promise of amnesty in most cases and in the court of law.

---

21. Wink, *When the Powers Fall*, 14.

The principle is biblical. There is no reconciliation without confession. After the set period of time, the offenders who do not come forward will be prosecuted to the full extent of the law, but repentance brings restoration. True, the commission is not God. Its work is imperfect. For one thing, some who seek amnesty come forward and disclose without contrition. And certainly the commission cannot insist that the families of victims embrace those who even sincerely repent of their crimes of hate. But it is a promising sign, this measure of societal repentance, which, as Wink's narrative illustrates, has produced many moving individual stories.

Daniel 10:1–11:1

IN THE THIRD year of Cyrus king of Persia, a revelation was given to Daniel (who was called Belteshazzar). Its message was true and it concerned a great war. The understanding of the message came to him in a vision.

²At that time I, Daniel, mourned for three weeks. ³I ate no choice food; no meat or wine touched my lips; and I used no lotions at all until the three weeks were over.

⁴On the twenty-fourth day of the first month, as I was standing on the bank of the great river, the Tigris, ⁵I looked up and there before me was a man dressed in linen, with a belt of the finest gold around his waist. ⁶His body was like chrysolite, his face like lightning, his eyes like flaming torches, his arms and legs like the gleam of burnished bronze, and his voice like the sound of a multitude.

⁷I, Daniel, was the only one who saw the vision; the men with me did not see it, but such terror overwhelmed them that they fled and hid themselves. ⁸So I was left alone, gazing at this great vision; I had no strength left, my face turned deathly pale and I was helpless. ⁹Then I heard him speaking, and as I listened to him, I fell into a deep sleep, my face to the ground.

¹⁰A hand touched me and set me trembling on my hands and knees. ¹¹He said, "Daniel, you who are highly esteemed, consider carefully the words I am about to speak to you, and stand up, for I have now been sent to you." And when he said this to me, I stood up trembling.

¹²Then he continued, "Do not be afraid, Daniel. Since the first day that you set your mind to gain understanding and to humble yourself before your God, your words were heard, and I have come in response to them. ¹³But the prince of the Persian kingdom resisted me twenty-one days. Then Michael, one of the chief princes, came to help me, because I was detained there with the king of Persia. ¹⁴Now I have come to explain to you what will happen to your people in the future, for the vision concerns a time yet to come."

¹⁵While he was saying this to me, I bowed with my face toward the ground and was speechless. ¹⁶Then one who looked like a man touched my lips, and I opened my mouth

Daniel 10:1–11:1

and began to speak. I said to the one standing before me, "I am overcome with anguish because of the vision, my lord, and I am helpless. [17]How can I, your servant, talk with you, my lord? My strength is gone and I can hardly breathe."

[18]Again the one who looked like a man touched me and gave me strength. [19]"Do not be afraid, O man highly esteemed," he said. "Peace! Be strong now; be strong."

When he spoke to me, I was strengthened and said, "Speak, my lord, since you have given me strength."

[20]So he said, "Do you know why I have come to you? Soon I will return to fight against the prince of Persia, and when I go, the prince of Greece will come; [21]but first I will tell you what is written in the Book of Truth. (No one supports me against them except Michael, your prince. [11:1]And in the first year of Darius the Mede, I took my stand to support and protect him.)

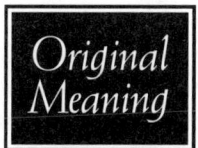

IN DANIEL 10 we see the curtain pulled back a bit further so that we get an intriguing, yet mysterious glimpse of the heavenly realities that stand behind human conflict. This chapter is the first part of the final vision of the book of Daniel (which includes chs. 10–12). In general outline, this vision may be structured as follows:

1. Introduction to the Vision (10:1–11:1)
2. The Vision (11:2–12:3)
3. God's Instructions to Daniel (12:4–13)

This three-chapter unit is the third major vision concerning future realities in the second half of Daniel. It supplements the visions found in chapters 7–8. Chapter 9, we have seen, is a prayer, but even that chapter ends with the prophecy of the seventy weeks of years. Thus, we are again reminded that the focus of the second part of the book is on the future. But even though this is true, God's passion is to provide comfort to Daniel, and through him the faithful of his generation, in the midst of their suffering, alienation, and oppression.

To know that such a great salvation is coming in spite of the present circumstances cannot help but deeply encourage the godly. The passage continues to function with this intention to those who are living faithfully at a time far removed from that of Daniel. As we will observe, the prophecy continues to veil its revelation. It is more like a provocative glimpse at the future

Daniel 10:1–11:1

than anything a later reader can use to predict dates or specific events, but it is enough to serve its purpose: comfort and encouragement in spite of present suffering. Once again, therefore, for this entire section the purpose continues to be that of the whole book: *In spite of present appearances, God is in control and will win the victory.*

Daniel 10:1–11:1 serves as an introduction to the vision. It describes Daniel's distraught state of mind, leading to intense prayer. In response to that prayer God sends a messenger. Below we will discuss the ambiguity concerning the supernatural appearance described in this chapter. Is one being or two beings standing before Daniel? The answer to this question, however, does not affect our understanding of the whole. God, at some cost, sends a messenger through to Daniel with a striking revelation concerning the future (cf. 11:2–12:3).

Before we get too far ahead of ourselves, however, let us turn our attention to 10:1–11:1 and examine the introduction to the vision under two headings: (1) a heavenly vision (10:1–9), and (2) a conversation with a supernatural being (10:10–11:1).

A Heavenly Vision (10:1–9)

CHAPTER 10 BEGINS similarly to the previous three chapters, with a date that sets when the events of the chapter occur: in the third year of Cyrus.[1] Cyrus was the Persian emperor who conquered Babylon in 539 B.C., leaving Darius the Mede in charge. This date is surely to be understood as three years after he became king of Babylon, thus inheriting authority over the Jewish population there. The date is probably 536/35 B.C. Already some of God's people have returned home under Sheshbazzar and Zerubbabel (Ezra 1–2). Many, however, decide to stay in exile, including Daniel. We are not given any reasons, but perhaps his advanced age plays into the decision. We know that God has further use for him in Babylon.

In any case, this was the year that Daniel receives his final and climactic vision, described in chapters 10–12. Interestingly, in a parenthetical comment, Daniel's Babylonian name, Belteshazzar, is cited.[2] He has not been referred to by this name since chapter 5, and here is the only occurrence in the second half of the book. The reasons for this particular use escape us, but certainly it reminds us of Daniel's life in the foreign court. Perhaps it is to remind us that even at the end of his life Daniel is still in exile.

---

1. For a brief discussion of the potential conflict between this date and the note that Daniel remained in Babylon until the first year of Cyrus, see comments on 1:21. It is true that the LXX has "first year of Cyrus," but as Hartman and DiLella point out (*The Book of Daniel*, 262), this is likely an attempt to harmonize the two references.

2. For discussion of the meaning and significance of this name, see comments on chapter 1.

The introduction to the appearance of the supernatural being(s) (v. 1b) describes the message's major topic and asserts that it is "true" and understandable. The topic is war—"a great war" that is coming in the future.

Daniel then describes for us, the readers, what he was doing at the time of the reception of the vision. For three weeks up to that moment, he has been in mourning. From the later words of the supernatural being we understand that this period of mourning was accompanied by prayer for understanding (v. 12). During this three-week period he had abstained from meat and wine. This reference indicates that Daniel's earlier abstention from choice food in favor of vegetables (ch. 1) was for a special short-term purpose and was not part of his long-term lifestyle. He denies himself in this case to gain a special hearing from the Lord.

Daniel also informs us that he did not use lotions during this time. The climate of the ancient Near East was hot and dry during much of the year and oils helped soothe the skin. But during a period of mourning such attention to personal comfort and even cleanliness was inappropriate and naturally neglected. Daniel was in a state of prayerful turmoil.

Then, on the twenty-fourth day of the first month,[3] Daniel, standing on the banks of the Tigris River,[4] receives a vision of a heavenly being that terrifies him. He has a human appearance, dressed like a priest in linen (Lev. 6:10) and wearing a belt of gold. His physical description looks more like a statue than an actual human being. His body is "like chrysolite, his face like lightning, his eyes like flaming torches, his arms and legs like the gleam of burnished bronze" (v. 6a). Furthermore, his voice booms "like the sound of a multitude" (v. 6b).

As many commentators have pointed out, the language that describes this heavenly being bears many similarities with descriptions of heavenly realities found in Ezekiel (esp. Ezek. 1). Christopher Rowland gives an excellent summary of the connections:

> The first four words of Daniel 10:5 reveal very close contact with Ezekiel 9:2, though the overall impression given by the vision is of a closer connection with the first chapter of Ezekiel. The phrase "his loins" is found in Ezekiel 1.27 to describe the human figure, and the

---

3. It is interesting to note that this time overlaps the observance of Passover and the Feast of the Unleavened Bread, which took place from the fourteenth day to the twenty-first day of the first month (Num. 28:16–25).

4. The "great river" in the Bible was usually the Euphrates, which marked the lower boundary of Mesopotamia (cf. Gen. 15:18; Deut. 1:7; Josh. 1:4, etc.). The Tigris, marking the upper boundary of Mesopotamia, is mentioned twice in the Bible (cf. also Gen. 2:14), only here being described as "the great river." Daniel's exact location on the Tigris is not given, but the general location situates him away from the city of Babylon (which is on the Euphrates).

more explicit references to the different parts of the angel's body in Daniel 10.6 seems to be a development of the more reserved outlook of Ezekiel. In the same verse the eyes of the angel are said to be "like flaming torches." A similar phenomenon is said to be in the middle of the living creatures in Ezekiel 1.13. Whereas in Ezekiel 1.16 the wheels of the chariot are said to be "like the gleaming of a chrysolite," in Daniel the word *tarshish* (chrysolite) is now transferred to the description of the body of the angel. The body and feet can be paralleled in Ezekiel 1.23 and 1.7 respectively, and the voice of the angel (Dan. 10:6) bears some resemblance to the phrase "a sound of tumult like the sound of a host" in Ezekiel 1.24. The phrase "like the gleam of burnished bronze" is quoted verbatim from Ezekiel 1.7, where it is used of the legs of the living creatures.[5]

Those around Daniel do not see the vision, but somehow they sense some great power because they immediately flee the scene and hide. The situation is reminiscent of Paul's Damascus road experience (see Acts 9), where Paul's companions also saw nothing, though they heard a sound and stood speechless. Daniel, however, sees and hears, and in response, he staggers and collapses. Indeed, he apparently faints with his face buried in the ground.

Full discussion of the identity of the heavenly appearance awaits the next section. However, our first thought may be that this is a theophany. After all, the language, though sometimes indirectly connected to God, has already been associated with the great throne/chariot theophany of Ezekiel 1. Later, we will develop a connection between Daniel 10 and Revelation's description of Christ (cf. Rev. 1:15). Both the antecedent reference to Ezekiel and the later use of the imagery for Christ might lead us to the conclusion that the supernatural being standing before Daniel is divine. However, before we can conclusively assert that this is correct, we must proceed to the next section, where we hear a heavenly being speak.

A Conversation With a Supernatural Being (10:10–11:1)

VERSE 9, WHICH closed the previous section, reported that Daniel heard the figure dressed in linen speaking, but the content of his speech was not given there. Daniel's response to the vision and the voice was to faint dead away. The present section opens with the first of three supernatural ministrations (see also vv. 16, 18). Towner aptly calls these three angelic touches "celestial first aid."[6] The first is the touch of a hand, which gives Daniel the strength to get up from

---

5. C. Rowland, *The Open Heaven* (New York: Crossroad, 1982), 99.
6. Towner, *Daniel*, 152.

the ground to all fours. He then addresses the prophet with words of encouragement, beginning with "you who are highly esteemed." The Hebrew for this English phrase is really two words, ʿis-ḥᵃmudot, the first noun being the common word for "man" and the second a noun derived from the verbal root ḥmd (best known as the main verb of the tenth commandment, "to covet"). Daniel is a highly desired, precious man, coveted by God.[7] Indeed, this angelic visitation is for Daniel, so he should take encouragement.

With these words, Daniel receives courage enough to stand, though he is still trembling. The verb "trembling" in verse 11 is the hiphil participle of the verb rʿd. Earlier (v. 7), the men with Daniel were said to be overwhelmed with terror. Literally, the phrase used there should be rendered "great trembling [the noun ḥᵃradah] fell on them." Trembling (whether described by the verb rʿd or the noun ḥᵃradah) characterizes those who come into contact with the supernatural realm.[8]

As the supernatural figure continues to speak with Daniel in verse 12, he again encourages the waning prophet. He begins with the straightforward command, "Do not be afraid." We see this comment at the beginning of a number of such speeches in the Bible (Gen. 15:1; 26:24; Judg. 6:23; Luke 1:13; Rev. 1:17). He then explains that, though the divine realm heard and began responding immediately to Daniel's prayers three weeks earlier, there was a delay because of a conflict, an obstacle in the form of the "prince of the Persian kingdom" (v. 13).

The supernatural speaker almost casually mentions the "prince of the Persian kingdom," but questions immediately rise in our minds. Who is this "prince" who can resist a heavenly being? What is the nature of the conflict of which we get this tantalizing glimpse? And, once again, what is the identity of the supernatural being who addresses Daniel and his connection with the vision of the figure dressed in linen (vv. 5–6)?

Perhaps we should start with the last question. In the previous section, we observed that the language and imagery associated with the being dressed in linen draws us to other theophanies. Our first impulse, supported by Daniel's reaction to the appearance, is to identify that figure with God himself. It is also most natural to associate this linen-clad figure with the one speaking to Daniel in the present section. Commentators like E. J. Young make this identification.[9] However, other scholars rightly question such an association. After all, what power could resist God for twenty-one days, as

---

7. Cf. also 9:23; 10:19.

8. Today, the ultraorthodox Jewish community sometimes goes by the name ḥaredi ("tremblers"), one source of their name being this chapter in Daniel. Another name for the same group is ḥasidim, from the Hebrew word ḥesed, which means "covenant lovingkindness."

9. Young, *The Prophecy of Daniel*, 225.

Daniel 10:1–11:1

the "prince of the Persian kingdom" apparently had done? Can we really imagine God being thwarted in his purposes so effectively, even if temporarily? With that in mind, Miller suggests that we are really dealing with two figures here: a theophany followed by an angelophany.[10] Thus, God is not hindered, but rather his powerful, but not omnipotent angel.

Furthermore, in verse 13 we will learn that the supernatural being speaking to Daniel was unable to overcome the obstacle provided by the "prince of the Persian kingdom" until Michael comes to his aid. Are we to think that God is unable to overcome this hindrance without the help of one of his created angels? Doubtful to say the least, Miller goes on to identify the angel as specifically Gabriel, on the speculative assumption that Gabriel is the messenger angel, a kind of Hebrew Hermes; but we know so little of the details of the angelic world that such a naming is no more than an educated guess, an unnecessary one at that.

I am attracted to Miller's suggestion that the two figures are different, the first being God and the second an angel, but I am also hesitant to be dogmatic about my affirmation of it. After all, there is no clear textual signal that tells us that a second figure has come into play with verse 10. It effectively solves a problem, but as such, we should hold it only as a possible hypothesis. In any case, we have a clear case of spiritual conflict. On the one side stands God's powerful angelic army and on the other "the prince of the Persian kingdom."

Who is this "prince of the Persian kingdom"? Calvin said that this was a reference to the human prince Cambyses.[11] But how likely is it that Daniel sees God's angels detained by a skirmish with Cambyses? No, these verses give us a hint at the cosmic battle that parallels the earthly struggles of God's people. The "prince of the Persian kingdom" is a supernatural being who fights on behalf of that human kingdom. The Old Testament knows of such spiritual entities and events in other books besides Daniel, perhaps most notably in Deuteronomy 32:8–9:

> When the Most High gave the nations their inheritance,
>   when he divided all mankind,
> he set up boundaries for the peoples
>   according to the number of the sons of God.[12]
> For the LORD's portion is his people,
>   Jacob his allotted inheritance.

---

10. Miller, Daniel, 281–82.
11. Calvin, Daniel 7–12, 252; cf. W. H. Shea, "Wrestling With the Prince of Persia: A Study on Daniel 10," AUSS 21 (1983): 235.
12. Here we side, as do the majority of modern scholars, with the reading found in the Dead Sea Scrolls and the LXX (the NIV footnote). The Hebrew Masoretic text, represented

The Bible here, we would argue, refers to God's angelic creatures who make up his heavenly council as "the sons of God." There are angels, in other words, "assigned" to different nation states. Such might also be implied in the warning found in Deuteronomy 4:19: "And when you look up to the sky and see the sun, the moon and the stars—all the heavenly array—do not be enticed into bowing down to them and worshiping things the LORD your God has apportioned to all the nations under heaven." The same connection between rebellious human power represented in the state and evil cosmic powers may be seen in Isaiah 24:21–23:

> In that day the LORD will punish
> > the powers in the heavens above
> > and the kings on the earth below.
> They will be herded together
> > like prisoners bound in a dungeon;
> they will be shut up in prison
> > and be punished after many days.
> The moon will be abashed, the sun ashamed;
> > for the LORD Almighty will reign
> on Mount Zion and in Jerusalem,
> > and before its elders, gloriously.

We must be careful not to speculate on the hints the Bible gives us, but that there are spiritual powers, good and bad, behind the various human institutions is a truth taught in the Old Testament and, as we will see in the Bridging Contexts and Contemporary Significance sections, in the New Testament as well.

In summary, the picture that emerges from Daniel 10:12–14 is that of a heavenly conflict. On the one side stands those spiritual forces that emanate from the Lord. The speaker, who is an unnamed angelic power (if not God himself) and Michael fight on God's side. Michael, whose Hebrew name means "Who is like God?" is mentioned four places in the Bible besides here (Dan. 10:21; 12:1; Jude 9; Rev. 12:7). Throughout the Bible, he plays an important leadership role in God's heavenly army. He is called "chief prince" and "archangel." In a word, he is a powerful spiritual being. On the other side stands "the prince of the Persian kingdom," who himself is powerful, but we are to understand that he is evil as well. He has tried to keep the heavenly messenger away from Daniel but has not succeeded, though (as we will see below) the fight is far from over.[13]

---

in the main text in the NIV, is likely the result of scribal nervousness over the theology represented by the original text. In other words, in the light of Israel's later repeated apostasies, the scribes may have worried that the verse sounded too close to the polytheism that so tempted Israel.

13. This also shows that the conflict is not just about the response to Daniel's prayer.

After describing the conflict that led to the delayed answer to Daniel's prayer, the heavenly messenger announces the substance of his message, which will be delivered beginning with 11:2: "Now I have come to explain to you what will happen to your people in the future, for the vision concerns a time yet to come" (10:14). Some believe that the language here suggests that the vision will at some point address the time just before the end of history as we know it.[14]

Again, Daniel is overwhelmed by the vision and bows to the ground, unable to speak. Again, a supernatural being ministers to him by touching his lips so he can speak. Though this being is referred to with a phrase similar to that found in 7:13 ("one like a son of man"), we should not be too quick to identify the two, since the phrase could be used of any humanlike appearance of God or angels. The touch of the lips reminds us of the call of Isaiah (Isa. 6:7), though here the emphasis is on the granting of strength in the midst of weakness, not on cleansing. This touch only gives Daniel the strength, it appears, to express his weakness. Thus, another touch follows in verse 18, accompanied by exhortations not to be afraid and to be strong (v. 19). Thanks to the supernatural ministrations, the prophet announces that he is ready to receive the vision.

The present chapter division obscures the flow of the section. We have already pointed out that chapters 10–12 are a unit. Granted that chapter divisions are necessary for such a long unit, the first one should have come either after 10:19 or after 11:1, not in its present place. In 10:20 the speech of the "one like a son of man" commences. In 10:20–11:1, the figure, probably an angel, gives a general overview of what is to come before outlining the details (the bulk of ch. 11). He is going to tell Daniel "what is written in the Book of Truth." Collins is surely right that, from what follows, we are to understand that book as containing the course of future history as shaped by God. He is also correct to note that the concept of such a book, followed by a detailed reading of centuries that follow Daniel, has a strong deterministic flavor.

How one reacts to that idea depends to some extent on one's attitude toward God, but within the world of the text, which we are invited to share, this is nothing short of gloriously good news. Remember that the people

---

14. As Miller, *Daniel*, 286–87, points out: "'In the future' is a translation of the Hebrew *be'aharit hayyamim*, usually rendered 'in the latter days.' Normally the phrase describes events that will recur just prior to and including the coming of the kingdom of God upon the earth...." If this were clearly the case, it would provide a strong argument supporting the argument that the latter parts of chapter 11 refer to the future Antichrist. However, as Collins points out (*Daniel*, 161), that is not clearly the case, since the Hebrew phrase can refer to "a definitive change in the future but not to an end of history."

contemporary with this book and throughout most periods of history are the oppressed people of God, who see no human escape from their oppression. The fact that God has scripted history and that the rescue of his people is the punch line is cause for great optimism and celebration (see the Contemporary Significance sections of chs. 11–12).

The angel tells us that he will soon return to the fray. The conflict with the prince of Persia, whom we have argued is the spiritual evil that supports the human kingdom oppressing God's people, goes on. After a while, it is implied, another spiritual power, the prince of Greece, will come. To use the language of chapters 7–8, another beast will come along. The fight will continue. But before the prophecy of the future goes on, the angel, perhaps here identifying himself as Gabriel (by allusion to Dan. 9:1), says that he has been fighting, with Michael, the prince of Persia since the very beginning (i.e., the first year of Darius the Mede). This reminds us, who tend to think of the Persians (who allowed God's people to return to Judah) as much better than the Babylonians, that these new oppressors are also evil and need to be overcome. God and his angels announce that they will fight on behalf of their people.

IN "THE NATURE of Apocalyptic Literature" in the Original Meaning section of chapter 7, we identified six major themes that run throughout Daniel 7–12. By way of review, these are:

- the horror of human evil, particularly as it is concentrated in the state
- the announcement of a specific time of deliverance
- repentance that leads to deliverance
- the revelation that a cosmic war stands behind human conflict
- judgment as certain for those who resist God and oppress his people
- the equally certain truth that God's people, downtrodden in the present, will experience new life in the fullest sense.

We have already established the fact that Daniel 10–12 stands as a single unit. Thus, we need not expect all six themes to be present in chapter 10. According to our announced schedule, here we will discuss the fourth theme concerning the cosmic war, which, of course, is the heart of our chapter. Before we do, however, I should mention that the first theme is clearly present in the chapter as well. Heavenly powers fight evil spiritual powers that are associated with the state, specifically Persia and Greece. In other words, Persia and Greece are revealed as more than just human evil, as horrible as that is, for the veil is pushed back a bit to see the spiritual horrors that stand behind their power.

Holy war in the Old Testament. To more fully understand the cosmic war that lies behind this human conflict, we must situate the content of this chapter in the broader story of holy war in the Old Testament. This will also provide the basis on which we grasp the connections with the spiritual warfare of the New Testament. Only a brief description of this incredibly pervasive and significant biblical theme can be given here,[15] but we can at least sketch out a basic skeleton outline that will help us build a bridge from the ancient world of the Old Testament to the New Testament and ultimately our own situation.

Holy war is a term never found in the Old Testament itself.[16] However, the term is useful because it describes the character of warfare found there. At the center of holy war is Yahweh, the divine warrior. God fights on his people's behalf to give them the victory. Another way of stating the same truth is to say that God uses his people as a tool of his judgment against the evil of the world. We can see this impulse at work at the Red Sea (Ex. 15), the battle of Jericho (Josh. 6), the defeat of the Midianites at the hands of Deborah and Barak (Judg. 5), and the anticipation of the defeat of Nineveh (Nahum), to name just a few. It is not that Israel does not fight, but they know that their victory is not a result of their own power and strategy, but because of God's fighting on their behalf.

The presence of Yahweh as the divine warrior explains many of the distinctive features of Old Testament holy war. Before a battle, Israel had to be sure that the conflict was God's will (Josh. 5:13–15; 1 Sam. 23:1–6). They were not given carte blanche for warfare. This explains why the ark of the covenant was often taken along into the battle. The ark was the mobile symbol of God's presence on earth. It explains too why the act of warfare took on the aura of worship, requiring the troops to be a cultically clean state. A soldier had to be as spiritually prepared to enter battle as he would to enter the holy precincts of the sanctuary. Warfare was an act of worship in the Old Testament.

After the battle, Israel's response was to praise the Lord (Ex. 15). After all, they knew that God had won the victory. In those cases where Israel actually had the upper hand in terms of numbers or weapons technology, God insisted that they divest themselves of these advantages before they entered the battle for fear that afterwards they would praise themselves, not God. Many psalms found their original purpose in the celebration of holy war victory (Ps. 24; 98).[17]

---

15. For a much fuller discussion, see T. Longman III and D. Reid, *God Is a Warrior* (Grand Rapids: Zondervan, 1995).

16. For this reason, some, like R. Smend (*Yahweh War and Tribal Confederation* [Nashville: Abingdon, 1970]), prefer the term "Yahweh war."

17. T. Longman III, "Psalm 98: A Divine Warrior Victory Song," *JETS* 27 (1984): 267–74.

But there was a flip side to this idea of holy war. Israel was not always the tool of God's judgment; at times it was the object. W. Moran coined the term *unholy war* to describe those times when God turned his warring activity against Israel.[18] This term is not felicitous, however, since any war with which God is involved is by definition holy. Moran also used the phrase *reverse holy war*; this is better, since Israel found itself, because of its disobedience, in a reversed situation, feeling the brunt of Yahweh's anger. While anticipations can be noted (e.g., 1 Sam. 4–5), the most striking example of reverse holy war is the destruction of Jerusalem in 586 B.C. and is recorded by the author of Lamentations, who cries out (Lam. 2:4–5):

Like an enemy he [God] has strung his bow;
    his right hand is ready.
Like a foe he has slain
    all who were pleasing to the eye;
he has poured out his wrath like fire
    on the tent of the Daughter of Zion.
The Lord is like an enemy;
    he has swallowed up Israel.
He has swallowed up all her palaces
    and destroyed her strongholds.
He has multiplied mourning and lamentation
    for the Daughter of Judah.

These are just a few examples, both positive and negative from Israel's point of view, where God pictures himself as a warrior in the Old Testament. Prior to Daniel 10, though, we should point out, Israel's most recent experience was the latter—God as an enemy. Israel had been carried off into captivity, not as a historical accident, but rather at the command of Yahweh as the divine warrior.

Holy war in Daniel. The book of Daniel is written with this as a background. Yahweh in the distant past fought on Israel's side when they were obedient. However, he also fought against them when they strayed. Where do they go from here? It is Daniel's repentance on behalf of the people that triggers the divine response: "I am fighting on your behalf and will indeed be victorious! Your freedom from oppression will indeed be won once and for all." We have seen this in Daniel 7, with the vision of the victory of the one like the son of man over the power represented by the beasts. We have seen this subtly asserted in the interpretation of the vision of Daniel 8, when it is said of the "master of intrigue" that "he will be destroyed, but not by human power" (8:25), as well as at the end of the prophecy of the "seventy 'sevens'"

---

18. W. Moran, "The End of the Unholy War and the Anti-Exodus," *Bib* 44 (1963): 333–42.

(9:20–27), which states concerning the one who sets up an abomination of desolation that the end has been decreed for him (9:27).

In chapters 11–12, Daniel will describe this victory more clearly. But chapter 10 serves an important purpose by exposing the spiritual realities behind the wars of Yahweh up to this point. In the description of the historical battles throughout most of the Old Testament, the concentration is on the earthly. Certainly the heavenly forces that have supported Israel have been revealed, but not the spiritual powers on the other side.

But we should not be surprised. At its origin the spiritual nature of the conflict is clear. Genesis 3 introduces conflict into the world. Behind the rebellious decision for which Adam and Eve were responsible stands the instigation of the serpent. The serpent, as later Scripture (Rev. 12:9) makes clear, was not an ordinary animal, but rather an incarnation of the evil one, Satan himself. The conflict that emanates from Genesis 3 to the consummation anticipated in the book of Revelation is understood in spiritual terms according to the curse God places on the serpent (Gen. 3:14–15):

> Cursed are you above all the livestock
>   and all the wild animals!
> You will crawl on your belly
>   and you will eat dust
>   all the days of your life.
> And I will put enmity
>   between you and the woman,
>   and between your offspring and hers;
> he will crush your head,
>   and you will strike his heel.

The redemptive history that follows describes a conflict that flows from this curse between those who follow God and those who side with the serpent.[19]

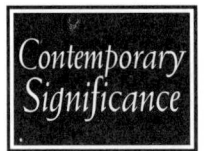

IN DANIEL 10 the veil is pulled back slightly, and we see the divine realities behind human conflict. As we situated the chapter in the context of the Old Testament as a whole in the previous section, we noted how deeply involved God has been in warfare. Here we are at the heart of one of the deepest difficulties that contemporary readers have

---

19. Genesis 3 and Daniel 10 are not the only texts in the Old Testament where the cosmic battle is described. In many of the texts where God is seen locked in combat with the sea or Leviathan (see comments on Dan. 7:2), we may well have allusion to spiritual realities (cf. Ps. 18:14–15; 24:1–2; 29:10; 74:12–17; Isa. 27:1; Nah. 1:4a). For more, consult chapter 5, "God Wars Against the Forces of Chaos," in Reid and Longman, *God Is a Warrior* (72–82).

Daniel 10:1—11:1

with the Old Testament: How can God be so centrally involved in something so gruesome as warfare?

In addition, there is the sad fact that through the history of the church these texts have been used to justify warfare. How many lives have been lost in the name of a "holy cause"? From Constantine through the Crusades to modern American wars, the holy wars of Joshua and others have been used as justifications for violence against "godless heathens" or those with dangerous theologies. Perhaps most despicably we see certain fringe individuals and groups that claim the name of Christ to utilize violence in the name of defending "Christian" values in the midst of the culture wars. We need only cite the murder of an abortion doctor in Pensacola by an evangelical or the tactics of the Christian Identity Movement.

For most contemporary Bible readers, the holy wars of the Old Testament are an embarrassment. How can they have any contemporary relevance at all?

Holy war and the New Testament. Daniel's picture of the warrior God in chapters 7–12 pointed to the future. God was fighting on behalf of his people to be sure, but there was also a strong message that the decisive battle was yet to come; that is the note on which the Old Testament concluded and which reverberated through the prophetic silence of the intertestamental period. When that silence was broken with John the Baptist, he was simply continuing the hope expressed in Daniel for the coming intervention of the divine warrior who would bring evil to a violent justice (Matt. 3:11–12):

> I baptize you with water for repentance. But after me will come one who is more powerful than I, whose sandals I am not fit to carry. He will baptize you with the Holy Spirit and with fire. His winnowing fork is in his hand, and he will clear his threshing floor, gathering his wheat into the barn and burning up the chaff with unquenchable fire.

Jesus came to the Jordan, and John recognized him as the one about whom he had been talking. He baptized Jesus and soon thereafter was imprisoned by Herod. While in prison John began to hear reports about the ministry of Jesus, and these reports distressed him greatly. He did not hear of burning and threshing, but rather of healing, exorcisms, and preaching the good news. Where was the divine warrior? John responded to these reports by sending his disciples to interrogate Jesus: "Are you the one who was to come, or should we expect someone else?" (Matt. 11:3). Jesus took these visitors out with him while he did more of the same—healing, exorcising, and preaching. In doing so he was telling them that indeed he was the one John was anticipating. He is the divine warrior. However, he has come to intensify and heighten the battle. No longer will the battle be waged against the flesh and blood enemies of God's people, but rather he will fight Satan himself.

Daniel 10:1–11:1

Daniel 10 indicates in a way rarely addressed in the Old Testament that there was already a cosmic-spiritual dimension to the warfare of old. Now we see that Satan has become the clear object of divine battle. The irony of the gospel is that that battle is won, not through killing, but rather by dying. Jesus, the warrior, accomplished his great victory by dying on the cross.

Jesus put away human weapons of violence and commanded his followers to do the same when he rebuked Peter for using a sword to attempt to prevent his arrest on the eve of his crucifixion: "Put your sword back in its place ... for all who draw the sword will die by the sword. Do you think I cannot call on my Father, and he will at once put at my disposal more than twelve legions of angels? But how then would the Scriptures be fulfilled that say it must happen in this way?" (Matt. 26:52–54).

Paul too understood the warlike character of the cross and reflected on Christ's death by using military language. On the cross, Jesus "disarmed the powers and authorities" and "made a public spectacle of them, triumphing over them" (Col. 2:15). In Ephesians 4:7–8, he spoke of the ascension by quoting an Old Testament divine warrior hymn (Ps. 68) to the effect that Jesus was leading a victory parade to heaven.

Jesus has completed and won the great conflict about which we read throughout the Old Testament, the battle begun in Genesis 3:15 and provocatively described in Daniel 10. But the victory is an already/not yet event. That is, the victory has been secured on the cross, but it still awaits its final denouement. Some scholars have likened the victory of the cross to the defeat of Germany at the battle of Normandy. After D-Day, the back of German power was broken in Europe and there was no doubt about the conclusion of the war. Nonetheless, battles still had to be fought and lives lost before the war would end.

We live spiritually between D-Day and V-Day. The victory has been won, but the fight is still real. The New Testament continues its use of military language to communicate both important truths: (1) We are in the midst of a tremendous battle with the forces of evil, and (2) the final victory is in sight.

The Christian's holy war manifesto. Let us explore the first of these truths by citing what I call the Christian's holy war manifesto, Ephesians 6:10–18:

> Finally, be strong in the Lord and in his mighty power. Put on the full armor of God so that you can take your stand against the devil's schemes. For our struggle is not against flesh and blood, but against the rulers, against the authorities, against the powers of this dark world and against the spiritual forces of evil in the heavenly realms. Therefore put on the full armor of God, so that when the day of evil comes,

Daniel 10:1—11:1

you may be able to stand your ground, and after you have done everything, to stand. Stand firm then, with the belt of truth buckled around your waist, with the breastplate of righteousness in place, and with your feet fitted with the readiness that comes from the gospel of peace. In addition to all this, take up the shield of faith, with which you can extinguish all the flaming arrows of the evil one. Take the helmet of salvation and the sword of the Spirit, which is the word of God. And pray in the Spirit on all occasions with all kinds of prayers and requests. With this in mind, be alert and always keep on praying for all the saints.

Many Christians neglect reading this passage on the basis of the Old Testament theme of the divine warrior, and our neglect can cause us to lose hope during the fury of the battle. When my boys were small, sometimes we would wrestle. They loved beating on their father until the tide turned and the old man suddenly experienced a surge of energy and overthrew all three attackers. The swing from victory to defeat brought a cry of consternation: "Dad, let us up! Let's quit! Let's play something else!"

The same is true when we stand dressed in our well-starched armor, Bible under our arm, ready to pounce on a problem. When the mud and blood begin to mingle together in an unearthly hue, it is important to know that God is still the divine warrior, who has already secured victory, no matter how tragically defeating this particular battle may appear.

We are to fight, just as Israel was to fight. But also like Israel, we need to recognize that we will have victory only as we allow God to use us. We are not to be passive; we are to "stand firm." But our strength to do this comes only as we put on the "armor of God."

Who is the enemy Paul is referring to in Ephesians 6? Our ultimate enemy is Satan and his demonic powers. Our struggle against him encompasses three fronts, and we should not underestimate our enemy's strength. To do so will lead to the temptation to fight our battles in our own strength, and our own strength will lead to our quick and easy defeat. When we realize that we have no power to ourselves to fight the battles of life, we are driven to Jesus, our divine warrior. He is the One who provides us with the spiritual weapons we need to fight—truth, righteousness, the gospel of peace, faith, salvation, the Spirit, and prayer.

(1) The first front is the battle against evil "out there." Most Christians do not need to be convinced that there is a lot of sin and evil in the world. Wickedness emanates from institutions and people (unfortunately from Christians as well as non-Christians), from ourselves (as we will discover in the third front), as well as from others. The following is just the tip of the iceberg.

Many Christians from Roman times to today have suffered at the hands of a wicked government. Christian martyrs through the ages testify to the potential wickedness of political institutions. One of many contemporary situations is the plight of a Ugandan Christian named Kefa Sempangi. I went to seminary with Kefa and heard his account firsthand. He has since published a book, *A Distant Grief*,[20] in which he remembers his near death at the hands of one of then-president Idi Amin's death squads and his subsequent flight to the Netherlands and the United States. But even after his return to Uganda in the post-Amin era, his life as a minister and a politician has been beset by further persecutions.

The medical industry, the heart of so much mercy and healing, is also one of the perpetuators of the abortion industry, and, as such, is an institution, like all other human institutions, tainted by the hand of the Evil One. One woman confided in me that as a teenager she turned to her doctor for help when she discovered she was pregnant. The doctor advised her that she needed an abortion and calmed her fears with the assurance that there was nothing wrong with the procedure. She has struggled with guilt-induced insomnia ever since.

My wife and I will never forget the call we got from the Yale University student clinic where we went to find out whether she was pregnant with our second child. The nurse told her, "You're pregnant," but before we had time to rejoice, the nurse asked my wife if she wanted an abortion. In this world torn by conflict, the human institution most dedicated to preserving human life finds itself destroying it.

Many, indeed all, other human institutions are similarly affected by the conflict between the divine and the demonic. I have been active in sports through the years. I have derived enjoyment and a healthier body because of it. But I can also testify on some levels there is a sports ethos that allows, and even encourages, the use of pain-deadening and muscle-enhancing drugs, which are ultimately life-threatening. My wife and I both sport bad knees, the direct result of coaches insisting that we start playing too soon after a minor injury. They were more interested in winning than in health.

Even the church as an institution has been the source of much pain and evil. It doesn't take the obvious cases like the Spanish Inquisition to illustrate this point. We have all experienced the hardness of a dysfunctional church family at some point in our Christian life. One of the saddest moments of my life was when I was up for ordination. The denomination I belonged to had a liberal tendency, but I did not know much better since I was still a young Christian at the time. It was the denomination in which I grew up, and I felt

---

20. K. Sempangi, *A Distant Grief* (Glendale, Calif.: Regal Books, 1979).

attached to it. However, I was wise enough to go to an evangelical seminary because I knew I had to be taught by people who respected the Bible as God's Word, something not true of this denomination's seminaries.

About a year into my work, the ordination council called me to a meeting and told me that they would not ordain me because I attended an evangelical seminary and because I held certain biblical doctrines. What hurt me more than anything was the conversation I had with another person my age while I was waiting for the committee to meet with me. This man ridiculed me for my trust in the Bible and then proceeded to deny every doctrine I considered important to Christianity—the historicity of Jesus, the role of the Holy Spirit, the trustworthiness of Scripture, and the Second Coming. He, too, was meeting with the church council that day, but for a reason different from my own. He was being ordained on Sunday, and they were setting up the service for him! I felt like someone kicked me in the face.

These are just a few of the examples of societal forces and institutions that are the source of evil against which we should battle. But we all know that institutions are not abstract entities that exist independent of human involvement. Institutions are made up of people. We are talking about a spiritual battle with real people on either side.

(2) Another front is the fight to "win souls." Opinions may differ, but I cringe every time I hear someone say, "I won a soul for Christ." Perhaps it's the arrogant voice that usually goes along with the claim. But I must admit that there is some truth to this old Christian expression. When we share the gospel with others, we are involved in warfare, just as real as, and indeed with longer lasting implications than, the battle of the Israelites against Jericho.

A careful study of the entire Bible indicates that evangelism replaces warfare as we move from the Old to the New Testament. That is, in the Old Testament, the predominant way of relating to the outsider (the non-Israelite) was to fight with real weapons. In the New Testament, the way we are to relate to the non-Christian is defined by Jesus in the Great Commission: "Therefore go and make disciples of all nations, baptizing them in the name of the Father and of the Son and of the Holy Spirit, and teaching them to obey everything I have commanded you" (Matt. 28:19–20).

Does not experience teach us that evangelism is often like a war? Some of our experiences are more explicitly warlike than others. There are plenty of Christians who can tell horrifying stories of real abuse as a result of evangelism. The main reason for this is that when we share the gospel with a stranger or friend, we are not just involved in a quiet clash of ideas with another rational human being. We are sharing the news of sin and redemption with someone who is on Satan's side, whether that person is conscious of it or not.

If a person is not devoted to Christ, there is only one other alternative—he or she is devoted to Christ's enemy. That is why Paul talks about baptism as a symbol of death. It is warfare. If a person becomes a Christian, one dies to the old self and puts on the new by "having been buried with him [Christ] in baptism and raised with him through your faith in the power of God, who raised him from the dead" (Col. 2:12).

(3) The battle on the third front is that between the "new self" and the "old self." Jesus instructed us to take the beam out of our own eye before we take the speck out of our brother's eye (Matt. 7:5). In this way, he was telling us that the battle is not only against others, it is also within ourselves. Facing the deeply embedded evil of our own hearts is where the most bitter fighting occurs. It's like a civil war. Your enemy, your old self, is a dearly loved friend you really don't want to kill. The apostle Paul perceptively shared the struggle that went on in his own heart, knowing that it is a struggle we all go through (Rom. 7:21–24a):

> So I find this law at work: When I want to do good, evil is right there with me. For in my inner being I delight in God's law; but I see another law at work in the members of my body, waging war against the law of my mind and making me a prisoner of the law of sin at work within my members. What a wretched man I am!

Once we become Christians, we are no longer in Satan's army; we are in Christ's. We fight for the gospel, taking on Satan, our former commander-in-chief. However, there is a part of us that still acts as if we are part of this world rather than pilgrims looking forward to the realities of heaven. The Bible names this tendency the "old self" (Eph. 4:22; Col. 3:9) and tells us to cast it off and put on the "new self." Theologians call this the process of "sanctification," but that is just another way of saying that Christians should become more like Christ every day.

Whatever you call it, our Christian growth is a battle against Satan in our own hearts. This front, for most of us, is the hardest. It's not easy to fight evil in another person. It may be tough for some of us to share the gospel with others. But it is grueling to face the dark, cold reality that we have to battle against our own vicious and destructive thoughts, emotions, and actions.

This is because deep down we really enjoy our sin and find any way we can to justify it in our eyes. I am not often emotionally down, but when I am depressed I need to have a scapegoat—God has given me too much work, my wife is ignoring me, my children are brats, my Little League team is uncommitted. I would much rather be happy than depressed, but at times like this, I would rather be depressed than to think that I have overcommitted myself to writing projects, been cold toward my wife, not disciplined my children sufficiently, and not taught my Little Leaguers how to hit or field.

As we engage in battle on this final front, we must remember that it is ultimately God against whom we struggle. It is not merely the new us that takes on the old us in our own power. The battle of the cosmos—the struggle between God and Satan—is waged in our very hearts, and the message of the Bible is absolutely clear: Nothing can stand before God in defiance and survive. This is the reason why the battle always goes to the advantage of the new self; it is God who fights for us. The Bible confirms that life is a battle. This is why God has revealed so much throughout its pages about his nature as a warrior and our participation in his army.

Our weapons. However, it is important to remember, especially as we focus in this commentary on an Old Testament book, that as we move from the Old Testament to the New Testament period, the warfare has shifted from a physical to a spiritual battle. It is one we must fight with spiritual weapons, not physical ones. That is, the teachings of Jesus do not allow us to hit an abortionist or bomb a clinic. We are not permitted to kidnap a potential convert and force him or her to listen to the gospel. And we should not whip ourselves (physically as some monks did in the Middle Ages) to discourage our sinning. Our weapons are prayer, faith, and bold love.

(1) Most of us think of prayer as a retreat from the action, not as an offensive weapon with which we attack the enemy. After all, when we want to pray, we usually seek out a quiet spot. We also hear and use the expression "let me pray about it" when we are not sure we want to do something we are asked to do.

In reaction against this, we must cultivate a mindset that sees prayer as a powerful tool by which to foil Satan's schemes and destroy his handiwork. We are to see prayer as our principal means of communication with our divine war Commander.

In the war between Iraq and the allied forces who came to the aid of Kuwait, one of the largest of many discrepancies between the two sides was in the area of communication. The allies were in constant touch with each other and knew the enemy positions through the use of highly sophisticated technology. On their part, the front lines of the Iraqi armies knew little about their enemy's positions and could not even communicate with their commanders in Baghdad. The result was a lopsided victory for the Allies.

We need to use prayer to ask our spiritual Commander to open our eyes to the conflict so we may see where the Enemy is located, and then to provide us with the strength to carry on the battle.

The curses of the psalms are a model of using prayer as a weapon. The psalmist in Psalm 69:24–25, 27 made some strong statements as he spoke to God about his enemies:

> Pour out your wrath on them;
>> let your fierce anger overtake them.
> May their place be deserted;
>> let there be no one to dwell in their tents....
> Charge them with crime upon crime;
>> do not let them share in your salvation.

While these psalms are models to us for prayer, they must be wisely used in the knowledge that the object of our warfare has shifted from flesh and blood enemies to spiritual ones. Our weapons must be spiritual, too. One concrete way the Christian can use prayer as a weapon against an abuser is to pray for his or her repentance.

(2) A second weapon of spiritual warfare is faith, a deep trust in the One who is our commander-in-Chief, Jesus Christ. Faith is multifaceted. One of the ways to think of faith is as a willingness to let go, to relax in the presence of someone who is good. A small child squeals with anticipation as her father lifts her above his head and gently tosses her into the air, catching her as she tumbles toward the ground. Such a child could scream and cry at being lifted and turn her little body into a stone-like, inflexible dead weight. Such a response would indicate a lack of trust. Faith may not take away all our fear or doubt, but it will enable us to know, at some deep level, that our Father is good and his purpose consistent with his character.

Faith, then, is an assertion of trust, even when our circumstances point in a direction that seems to call into question God's goodness. Faith is vision of what cannot be seen, a knowing of something that is beyond verifiable human knowledge. It is an assent to the inner witness of the Spirit that continues to keep a flame alive in us after all our efforts to snuff it out have failed. Fundamentally, we know that he is capable and willing to bring the battle to a successful completion. Indeed, the Scriptures tell us that he has already accomplished the victory on the cross, and we have a preview of the final day in the book of Revelation.

One of the many lessons of the Vietnam War was the disastrous consequences of a lack of trust between soldiers and their commanding officers. Soldiers often did not trust the abilities of their officers, and there were even alarming reports of soldiers putting a bullet in the back of their officers during battles. A firm trust in God is incredibly important if we are to endure the day-to-day battles of life. We need to know that God is there in his power to encourage us to face the angry boss at work, our unrepentant spouse, or our disobedient children.

These are just two of the spiritual weapons which Ephesians 6 mentions. In closing I want to emphasize that the spiritual nature of our weapons does not mean that they are intangible. We are not to be passive. We are not called to love people, even those who hurt us, from a distance, but we are required to move into their lives to open the door to their repentance.

Territorial demons? Before shutting the door on our discussion of spiritual warfare, we must address the issue of engagement with supernatural enemies, specifically territorial demons. Is this a fourth front of our warfare? There is a growing call in some sectors of the church worldwide and in America today to engage in battle with demons that control specific geographical regions.[21] The foundational text for such a strategy is Daniel 10, so it is vital for us at least to speak to the issue, if only briefly.

I must confess, as I discuss this volatile issue, that my experience in this area has not been extensive or encouraging. Biblically, I affirm the existence of the world of supernatural evil forces, and Daniel 10 in particular witnesses to the association in some sense of demonic powers with specific geographical regions. However, as I have emphasized above, this chapter gives us just the merest of glimpses, and it seems to me that advocates of spiritual mapping take the concept far beyond the limits of biblical revelation. Fortunately, much of their research into the demonic activity of a city really does help them uncover the ethos of a geographical area. They can see the sinful tendencies and atmosphere of an area as they move in to evangelize, but to seek to name and exorcize demons should not and, as far as I can tell from their writings, does not deflect from the task of moral persuasion as they present the gospel as a challenge to a particular culture.

Clinton Arnold has written an excellent analysis of the phenomenon known as "strategic-level spiritual warfare," associated with C. Peter Wagner and others. In his book *Three Crucial Questions About Spiritual Warfare*,[22] he both affirms and criticizes the practices of people who engage in a deliverance and spiritual-mapping ministry. He speaks from deep knowledge of Scripture, having written a number of scholarly studies of the biblical material as well as dialogued closely with Wagner and other practitioners. I recommend his book heartily for those who wish to probe this issue more deeply.

Perhaps the two most important conclusions that Arnold reaches in regard to the issue before us are these: (1) The Bible affirms demonic activity and the relationship between demons and specific geographical locations; (2) "of even greater significance ... is the fact that the Bible nowhere narrates, describes, or instructs us on how, or even whether, we are to engage these

---

21. Differences abound among those who advocate this brand of spiritual warfare. A helpful introduction to the topic, written by supporters like George Otis Jr., Cindy Jacobs, Kjell Sjoberg, and Victor Lorenzo, has been edited by C. P. Wagner, *Breaking Strongholds in Your City: How to Use Spiritual Mapping to Make Your Prayers More Strategic, Effective and Targeted* (Ventura, Calif.: Regal, 1993).

22. C. Arnold, *Three Crucial Questions About Spiritual Warfare* (Grand Rapids: Baker, 1997).

high-ranking territorial spirits."[23] In regard to the second point, we should note that Daniel never engages or prays against the spiritual enemies about which the celestial beings speak. He leaves those matters to God.

In the midst of a controversial issue, we must not forget the central teaching of Daniel 10: the amazing truth that God's people are not in the conflict alone. The Bible as a whole calls us to the life of a warrior in a world of conflict. But God does not send us out to fight on our own or even to pool our resources with other Christians. No, he sent his Son to first win the battle. He defeated evil by dying on the cross. He shows us that the way of victory is through love and sacrifice, not hate and greed. He gives us confidence to face abuse today because "our present sufferings are not worth comparing with the glory that will be revealed in us," when he comes to rescue us for the last time (Rom. 8:18).

---

23. Ibid., 161.

Daniel 11:2–12:13

NOW THEN, I tell you the truth: Three more kings will appear in Persia, and then a fourth, who will be far richer than all the others. When he has gained power by his wealth, he will stir up everyone against the kingdom of Greece. ³Then a mighty king will appear, who will rule with great power and do as he pleases. ⁴After he has appeared, his empire will be broken up and parceled out toward the four winds of heaven. It will not go to his descendants, nor will it have the power he exercised, because his empire will be uprooted and given to others.

⁵"The king of the South will become strong, but one of his commanders will become even stronger than he and will rule his own kingdom with great power. ⁶After some years, they will become allies. The daughter of the king of the South will go to the king of the North to make an alliance, but she will not retain her power, and he and his power will not last. In those days she will be handed over, together with her royal escort and her father and the one who supported her.

⁷"One from her family line will arise to take her place. He will attack the forces of the king of the North and enter his fortress; he will fight against them and be victorious. ⁸He will also seize their gods, their metal images and their valuable articles of silver and gold and carry them off to Egypt. For some years he will leave the king of the North alone. ⁹Then the king of the North will invade the realm of the king of the South but will retreat to his own country. ¹⁰His sons will prepare for war and assemble a great army, which will sweep on like an irresistible flood and carry the battle as far as his fortress.

¹¹"Then the king of the South will march out in a rage and fight against the king of the North, who will raise a large army, but it will be defeated. ¹²When the army is carried off, the king of the South will be filled with pride and will slaughter many thousands, yet he will not remain triumphant. ¹³For the king of the North will muster another army, larger than the first; and after several years, he will advance with a huge army fully equipped.

¹⁴"In those times many will rise against the king of the South. The violent men among your own people will rebel in fulfillment of the vision, but without success. ¹⁵Then the king of the North will come and build up siege ramps and will capture a fortified city. The forces of the South will be powerless to resist; even their best troops will not have the strength to stand. ¹⁶The invader will do as he pleases; no one will be able to stand against him. He will establish himself in the Beautiful Land and will have the power to destroy it. ¹⁷He will determine to come with the might of his entire kingdom and will make an alliance with the king of the South. And he will give him a daughter in marriage in order to overthrow the kingdom, but his plans will not succeed or help him. ¹⁸Then he will turn his attention to the coastlands and will take many of them, but a commander will put an end to his insolence and will turn his insolence back upon him. ¹⁹After this, he will turn back toward the fortresses of his own country but will stumble and fall, to be seen no more.

²⁰"His successor will send out a tax collector to maintain the royal splendor. In a few years, however, he will be destroyed, yet not in anger or in battle.

²¹"He will be succeeded by a contemptible person who has not been given the honor of royalty. He will invade the kingdom when its people feel secure, and he will seize it through intrigue. ²²Then an overwhelming army will be swept away before him; both it and a prince of the covenant will be destroyed. ²³After coming to an agreement with him, he will act deceitfully, and with only a few people he will rise to power. ²⁴When the richest provinces feel secure, he will invade them and will achieve what neither his fathers nor his forefathers did. He will distribute plunder, loot and wealth among his followers. He will plot the overthrow of fortresses—but only for a time.

²⁵"With a large army he will stir up his strength and courage against the king of the South. The king of the South will wage war with a large and very powerful army, but he will not be able to stand because of the plots devised against him. ²⁶Those who eat from the king's provisions will try to destroy him; his army will be swept away, and many will fall in battle. ²⁷The two kings, with their hearts bent on evil, will sit at the same table and lie to each other, but to no avail, because an

Daniel 11:2—12:13

end will still come at the appointed time. ²⁸The king of the North will return to his own country with great wealth, but his heart will be set against the holy covenant. He will take action against it and then return to his own country.

²⁹"At the appointed time he will invade the South again, but this time the outcome will be different from what it was before. ³⁰Ships of the western coastlands will oppose him, and he will lose heart. Then he will turn back and vent his fury against the holy covenant. He will return and show favor to those who forsake the holy covenant.

³¹"His armed forces will rise up to desecrate the temple fortress and will abolish the daily sacrifice. Then they will set up the abomination that causes desolation. ³²With flattery he will corrupt those who have violated the covenant, but the people who know their God will firmly resist him.

³³"Those who are wise will instruct many, though for a time they will fall by the sword or be burned or captured or plundered. ³⁴When they fall, they will receive a little help, and many who are not sincere will join them. ³⁵Some of the wise will stumble, so that they may be refined, purified and made spotless until the time of the end, for it will still come at the appointed time.

³⁶"The king will do as he pleases. He will exalt and magnify himself above every god and will say unheard-of things against the God of gods. He will be successful until the time of wrath is completed, for what has been determined must take place. ³⁷He will show no regard for the gods of his fathers or for the one desired by women, nor will he regard any god, but will exalt himself above them all. ³⁸Instead of them, he will honor a god of fortresses; a god unknown to his fathers he will honor with gold and silver, with precious stones and costly gifts. ³⁹He will attack the mightiest fortresses with the help of a foreign god and will greatly honor those who acknowledge him. He will make them rulers over many people and will distribute the land at a price.

⁴⁰"At the time of the end the king of the South will engage him in battle, and the king of the North will storm out against him with chariots and cavalry and a great fleet of ships. He will invade many countries and sweep through them like a flood. ⁴¹He will also invade the Beautiful Land. Many countries will fall, but Edom, Moab and the leaders of Ammon will

be delivered from his hand. ⁴²He will extend his power over many countries; Egypt will not escape. ⁴³He will gain control of the treasures of gold and silver and all the riches of Egypt, with the Libyans and Nubians in submission. ⁴⁴But reports from the east and the north will alarm him, and he will set out in a great rage to destroy and annihilate many. ⁴⁵He will pitch his royal tents between the seas at the beautiful holy mountain. Yet he will come to his end, and no one will help him.

¹²:¹"At that time Michael, the great prince who protects your people, will arise. There will be a time of distress such as has not happened from the beginning of nations until then. But at that time your people—everyone whose name is found written in the book—will be delivered. ²Multitudes who sleep in the dust of the earth will awake: some to everlasting life, others to shame and everlasting contempt. ³Those who are wise will shine like the brightness of the heavens, and those who lead many to righteousness, like the stars for ever and ever. ⁴But you, Daniel, close up and seal the words of the scroll until the time of the end. Many will go here and there to increase knowledge."

⁵Then I, Daniel, looked, and there before me stood two others, one on this bank of the river and one on the opposite bank. ⁶One of them said to the man clothed in linen, who was above the waters of the river, "How long will it be before these astonishing things are fulfilled?"

⁷The man clothed in linen, who was above the waters of the river, lifted his right hand and his left hand toward heaven, and I heard him swear by him who lives forever, saying, "It will be for a time, times and half a time. When the power of the holy people has been finally broken, all these things will be completed."

⁸I heard, but I did not understand. So I asked, "My lord, what will the outcome of all this be?"

⁹He replied, "Go your way, Daniel, because the words are closed up and sealed until the time of the end. ¹⁰Many will be purified, made spotless and refined, but the wicked will continue to be wicked. None of the wicked will understand, but those who are wise will understand.

¹¹"From the time that the daily sacrifice is abolished and the abomination that causes desolation is set up, there will be

1,290 days. ¹²Blessed is the one who waits for and reaches the end of the 1,335 days.

¹³"As for you, go your way till the end. You will rest, and then at the end of the days you will rise to receive your allotted inheritance."

DANIEL 11:2–12:13 CONTAINS the second and third parts of the larger unit begun in Daniel 10:1 (i.e., 10:1–12:13, which concludes the book of Daniel). Chapter 10 introduced the circumstances surrounding the vision; these next two sections contain the contents of that message and a concluding dialogue between Daniel and two heavenly beings.

The vision of part 2 (11:2–12:4) is unlike any that have preceded it in Daniel. It begins with a lengthy prophecy about unnamed kings and their actions. While there is nothing similar to this prophecy in the Old Testament, we have examples from the broader ancient Near East, the most notable parallel being the so-called Dynastic Prophecy.[1] This genre of prophecy, not using personal names, reads the details of history closely. Daniel 11 covers a period from the Persian period to the time of Antiochus Epiphanes. From what we know about the period we can affirm that the prophet writes with the accuracy of a historian. As a matter of fact, that is what many scholars feel is going on in this passage.[2] That is, Daniel 11 is not a forward-looking prophecy from the standpoint of the sixth century B.C., but rather a backward-looking history cast in the literary form of prophecy.

The arguments in favor of the latter view are strong. As we will see in our exposition, one reading of the chapter understands 11:40–45 to apply to the same king, Antiochus Epiphanes IV, as described in verses 21–39. The only problem is that, while we can confirm the historical accuracy of the description of this king in the first part, verses 40–45 appear to be an attempt at actual prophecy rather than history in prophetic form. The point made is that we can tell actual prophecy from quasi-prophecy because the former fails.

Even though the prophecy fails, many scholars who have a high regard for the Bible provide rationale for why such literature exists in the Word of God.[3]

---

1. Cf. A. K. Grayson, *Babylonian Historical-Literary Texts* (Toronto: Univ. of Toronto Press, 1975). For the fullest discussion of this text (and other similar Akkadian texts) and its connections to Daniel, see T. Longman III, *Fictional Akkadian Autobiography* (Winona Lake, Ind.: Eisenbrauns, 1991), 131–95.
2. See Goldingay, *Daniel*, 282–86, who uses the term *quasi-prophecy* to describe this literary phenomenon.
3. Ibid., 310–12.

These scholars represent one legitimate attempt to deal with a difficult exegetical problem. One of the foundations of a typical defense of the presence of "prophecy after the fact" in the Bible is that it is a well-known genre of literature in the ancient Near East. It is precisely with this argument that I have found myself unable to follow and accept this line of reasoning. It is indeed true that this genre of literature is well known in the ancient Near East, if we mean by this that it is well attested. However, for this type of literature to work—that is, if it is to achieve its intended effect on an audience—they cannot know that it is quasi-prophecy. In order to build up the reader's confidence that God controls history and that he is sovereign over the future, the reader must believe that the prophecy is precisely that.[4]

The reading below assumes that Daniel 11 is actual prophecy. However, I admit up front that the explanation given for the transition from Antiochus IV to a future antichrist figure is not a particularly strong one. In short, there are no clear textual signals that there is a change of referent as we move from verse 39 to verse 40. There are subtle indicators, such as the mention of the "time of the end" and the increased use of mythical materials, but we must be aware of the tenuousness of our interpretation and allow room for difference of opinion on this point of interpretation among those who affirm the truth of the Word of God.

Part 2 ends on a strong note of hope, at least for those who agree with Daniel. As we will see, we get the first and only Old Testament reference to double resurrection in 12:2–3. Not only will the righteous rise to their reward, but the wicked will meet their punishment.

Part 3 functions as a kind of appendix and could be given a separate entry in the commentary. However, for reasons of convenience, we will treat 12:5–13 with what immediately precedes it. It is linked with chapters 10–12 by bringing us back to the scene at the river, with the heavenly being's hovering over the middle of the river. Now there are clearly two other angelic beings, and the book concludes with a final dialogue between Daniel and these supernatural beings.

We will study this unit of Daniel guided by the following outline: (1) Persia and Greece (11:2–4); (2) struggles between the kings of the North and the kings of the South (11:5–20); (3) the climactic king of the North (11:21–35); (4) the king who will do as he pleases (11:36–45); (5) the salvation of God's people (12:1–4); (6) final words (12:5–13).

---

4. Goldingay strengthens his argument with an appeal to the work of S. Niditch, "The Visionary," in *Ideal Figures in Ancient Judaism*, ed. by J. J. Collins and G. W. Nickelsburg (Chicago: Scholars, 1980), 153–79, who asserts, on the basis of comparative anthropological evidence, that the author of the book of Daniel actually had an experience through which he identified with that historical character.

Daniel 11:2–12:13

Persia and Greece (11:2–4)

IT MAY SEEM odd that the angel begins by asserting that what he says is true. Would Daniel have expected anything else? Of course not, but the statement reminds us that we are to imagine Daniel in the sixth century hearing detailed events that cover the next few centuries. As we look back with our *Cambridge Ancient History*[5] or its equivalent, we do not need much convincing. In our commentary we will supply names and specific events for the prophecies as they move from the time of Daniel to the time of Antiochus IV Epiphanes. The specific events are so well documented that we will not footnote the connections we make between the prophecies and the actual events. Such may be found in any reputable history of the period.

The angel begins with the assertion that three more kings will appear in Persia, and then a fourth. Now, unless we are willing to admit that Daniel knew the history of the Seleucid period perfectly but the Persian period inadequately, we must not understand this statement to mean that only four Persian kings ruled after the first, namely, Cyrus.[6] Conceivably, the four kings include Cyrus and refer to the only four Persian kings mentioned in the Bible (Cyrus, Darius, Xerxes, and Artaxerxes, cf. Ezra 4:5–7), but this is doubtful. After all, the reference suggests four kings besides Cyrus.

We are not certain either who the fourth king is, the one who "will be far richer than all the others" (v. 2). He is also characterized as the one who will "stir up everyone against the kingdom of Greece." Our first thought, and perhaps the best guess, is Xerxes I (486–465 B.C.). This Persian was a great and powerful king, and it is arguable that he set off the chain of events that over a century later led to the downfall of Persia at the hands of the Greeks, for he chose to invade areas controlled by Greeks. He failed at this attempt, being defeated at Salamis in 480 B.C., but his actions led to a Greek-Persian conflict that ended with Alexander.

The other candidate for the fourth Persian king is the last Persian emperor, Darius III (336–330 B.C.), who was the one who fell to Alexander. He was not the richest, but he was the one to fall. Miller puts forward an attractive hypothesis, though again not provable because it does not take us even close to the fall of Persia, that the three kings are those that follow Cyrus in succession (Cambyses, Smerdis, and Darius I Hystaspes) and that the fourth is Xerxes I.[7]

---

5. Especially vol. 7, part 1, *The Hellenistic World*, ed. F. W. Walbank; A. E. Astin, et al. (Cambridge: Cambridge Univ. Press, 1984).

6. There were thirteen rulers (a few of which, like Smerdis [522], Xerxes III [424], Sogianos [424–423], ruled only a very short time) of Persia in all; cf. E. M. Yamauchi, *Persia and the Bible* (Grand Rapids: Baker, 1990) for a helpful survey of the period.

7. Miller, *Daniel*, 291.

Daniel 11:2–12:13

To be frank, however, we cannot be sure how to construe the mind of the author at this stage.

This verse is one of the few ambiguities in the chapter. We know with certainty the identity of the "mighty king" of verse 3—none other than Alexander, whom we call "the Great." But as soon as he came on the scene, he disappeared from it. Alexander was king of Macedon, succeeding his father Philip, in 336 B.C., and by 330 he had conquered Persia. He continued his conquests and reached the Indus, but died in 323, leaving his mentally challenged half brother Philip III and his son Alexander IV in charge. These two were under the guidance of Perdiccas. All three were eventually murdered: Perdiccas in 321, Philip III in 317, and Alexander IV in 311. Power passed into the hands of Alexander's four leading generals—thus the reference in verse 4 to the "four winds of heaven."

Since Daniel is concerned with the people of God, focus immediately shifts to two of the Diadochoi (or "Successors," as the four were known), those who had their power base in Syria (the kings of the north) and those who had their power base in Egypt (the kings of the south). In the north, the rulers eventually became known as the Seleucid dynasty, and in the south ruled the Ptolemies. Judah was right in the middle, and the story of the third and second centuries B.C. is an account of how Judah passed back and forth between the Ptolemies and the Seleucids.

Struggles Between the Kings of the North and the Kings of the South (11:5–20)

THE STORY OF the Ptolemies and Seleucids begins in earnest in verse 5. To start, the king of the south is Ptolemy I. He had taken Egypt from the point of Alexander's death. The king of the north was Seleucus I. Upon Perdiccas's assassination (421 B.C.), he was given the satrapy of Babylon, but in 316 had sought refuge with Ptolemy in Egypt to avoid conflict with another powerful Diadochi, Antigonus. When Ptolemy and Seleucus defeated Antigonus in Gaza in 312, Seleucus returned to Babylon. In 301 B.C. at the Battle of Ipsus the struggles between the various Diadochi were resolved when the elderly Antigonus and his son Demetrius were defeated. It was at this time that Syria-Palestine was assigned to Seleucus. However, his long-standing ally Ptolemy moved against his holdings and occupied Palestine. Seleucus and his successors never gave up claim to this area, however, so there was now tension between the two that would play itself out to the end of the period.[8]

---

8. See S. Mandell and J. Hayes, *A History of the Jews From the Hellenistic Through the Early Roman Eras (333 BCE–135 CE)* (Louisville, Ky.: Westminster/John Knox, 1998), 30.

Some years later (ca. 250 B.C.) a dynastic marriage was planned, presumably to soothe matters between the two royal houses (cf. v. 6). Ptolemy II Philadelphus gave his daughter Berenice in marriage to Antiochus II Theos, who was the grandson of Seleucus. Antiochus II had divorced his first wife, Laodice, to marry Berenice. A son, whose name we do not know, was born of the second union, but then Antiochus reconciled with Laodice, who promptly had her husband, Berenice, and her son poisoned; thus, "she will not retain her power" (v. 6).

Needless to say, these actions did not help the relationship between the Seleucids and the Ptolemies. In verse 7 we have an allusion to the fact that Ptolemy III Euergetes, Berenice's brother, came to the throne in 246 B.C. and waged war against the son of Laodice, Seleucus II Callinicus, who had inherited the northern throne. In the process of the successful campaign, Ptolemy III stole the images of the gods and returned them to Egypt. However, his success was not long-lived for Seleucus II attacked the south and, though he did not take Egypt, recovered his land. The battles continued.

The sons of Seleucus II Callinicus, alluded to in verse 10, are Seleucus III Cerannus, who ruled from 227–223 B.C., and one of the most famous of all the Seleucid rulers, Antiochus III the Great, who had a long reign from 223–187. In the south Ptolemy IV Philopator took the throne but was not up to the task; thus, Antiochus III got back large tracts of his land. Daniel 11:10 says that he was successful "as far as his fortress." We cannot be certain about this reference. Driver claimed this is a playful reference to Gaza, which is on the doorstep to Egypt, while Montgomery argued that the phrase means that he was hostile toward the fortress, which would make it a reference to Egypt itself.[9]

The story of Antiochus III the Great's reign continues through verse 19. The significance given to his reign likely has much to do with the fact that it was through his agency that Palestine finally shifted from Ptolomaic control to Seleucid control, thus setting the scene for the horrors of his son's reign (cf. below on vv. 21ff.).

Verse 11 describes what has come to be known as the battle of Raphia in 217 B.C., between Antiochus III and Ptolemy IV.[10] In 218 Antiochus was steadily advancing in Coele-Syria and in the winter set up his headquarters in the city of Ptolemais. The next summer (June 22, 217 B.C., to be exact), Ptolemy IV and Antiochus III met in Raphia in the most southern part of

---

9. See S. R. Driver, *The Book of Daniel* (Cambridge: Cambridge Univ. Press, 1900), 170, and J. S. Montgomery, *A Critical and Exegetical Commentary on the Book of Daniel* (ICC; Edinburgh: T. & T. Clark, 1927), 437, plus discussion in Collins, *Daniel*, 379.

10. H. Heinen, "The Syrian-Egyptian Wars and the New Kingdoms of Asia Minor," *The Cambridge Ancient History*, vol. 7, part 1, 436–39.

Daniel 11:2—12:13

Palestine. The Ptolemaic side had the advantage in numbers and won the day. Antiochus retreated to his capital in Antioch.

Ptolemy won the battle, but it would be relatively short-lived. He did not follow up his victory, but allowed Antiochus to lick his wounds. Of course, it may not have been logistically possible for Ptolemy to do any more than that. Furthermore, for the first time the Ptolemies used native Egyptian troops for the war, and not long afterward the native Egyptians were exercising their newfound sense of power and rebelling against the ruling foreign house. These revolts added an element of internal instability to the picture for the Ptolemies.

Antiochus began to recover a few years later, and he exerted his efforts to the eastern part of his empire and recovered land that had been lost on that front. That kept him occupied from 212–205 B.C. In 204 suddenly Ptolemy IV and his queen died. Ptolemy IV was only thirty-five at the time of his death and his son and heir, Ptolemy V (who would receive the cognomen Epiphanes) was about six years old. Antiochus felt that the time was right to press the advantage against his old enemy in Egypt. While Ptolemy V was young, the real power was a high official named Agathocles, who was not popular in Egypt because of his heavy-handed policies.

The first engagement did not go well for Antiochus III; Scopas, the Ptolomaic general, beat him back. But in 200 B.C. at the battle of Panium (later called Caesarea Philippi), Antiochus won a decisive victory. After a century of Ptolemaic rule, Syria-Palestine came under the control of the Seleucids.

Verse 14 is obscure in detail, but acknowledges that these great events caused turmoil among the Jewish people. We are not sure to whom the "violent men" refer, but we do know there were political power plays going on at the time in Jerusalem. The Oniads controlled the high priesthood and supported Egyptian rule, but the Tobiads, a politically powerful family related by marriage to the Oniads, leaned in the opposite direction. Again, we are not even sure about what is meant by "vision." It may even be that some took heart at the prophecies of Daniel, giving them courage to think they were at the time when the end of foreign oppression was to arrive. They may have taken matters into their own hands, but failed. We cannot be certain.

Whereas Ptolemy IV did not follow up his victory at Raphia with Antiochus III, Antiochus pursued Scopas to Sidon; this is likely the reference in verse 15. Collins suggests that the "best troops" indicates Scopas's Aetolian mercenary troops.[11]

In verse 16 Daniel notes that the victor began to get heady and perhaps overconfident. Earlier we heard this about Alexander just before his death

---

11. Collins, *Daniel*, 380.

(v. 3), and later we will hear it about another king (v. 36). Soon we will observe that, like Alexander, Antiochus III's rule would not last forever either, and he would have a terrible end.

But in the meantime he set himself up in the "Beautiful Land," which of course is Palestine (Dan. 8:9; 11:41; cf. Jer. 3:19). Antiochus then decided on an age-old strategy to keep his opponents in line—the institution of dynastic marriage. He gave his daughter Cleopatra to Ptolemy V in marriage with the hopes that she would incline his heart toward his father-in-law and serve as a kind of ambassador-spy in the potentially hostile empire of Egypt. However, as our verse seems to indicate, the plot did not come to fruition as Antiochus had hoped. Cleopatra, as sometimes happened in these dynastic marriages, placed, if not her affections, at least her self-interest with her husband. Indeed, she became the leading power in Egypt after the death of her husband in 182, and her son Ptolemy VI Philometer succeeded her eight years later.

Antiochus never tired of ambition, and in accordance with the prophecy of verse 18 started annexing parts of Asia Minor as well as some Greek islands. In 196 B.C. he encroached on Thrace. All of this began to arouse the attention of the new power in that part of the world, Rome. He did not obey Roman warnings, so the Roman senate sent the consul Lucius Cornelius Scipio against him. Antiochus was defeated at Thermopylae in 191 and Magnesia in 190. He then had to retreat to the core of his empire. He had been reduced to stealing precious materials from the temple of Bel at Elymais, and he died in 187.

His son Seleucus IV Philopator (187–175) succeeded him, but he was not popular because of the burden he put on the people to raise the tribute to keep the Romans off his back. One of his ministers was a man named Heliodorus. According to 2 Maccabees 3 he was the one who tried to sack the temple in Jerusalem. Seleucus IV died under mysterious circumstances just as his younger brother, who had been made a hostage in Rome after the battle of Magnesia, was returning to his homeland. That younger brother's name was Antiochus IV, who got the nickname Epiphanes. The attention of the text turns now to this highly significant figure.

The Climactic King of the North (11:21–35)

ACCORDING TO DANIEL, the struggles between the south (Ptolemaic Egypt) and the north (Seleucid Syria) culminated with one ruler, a "contemptible person" (v. 21). The prophecy's assessment of his importance and his character is based exclusively on the turmoil that his rule created in Jerusalem. This man greatly offended the orthodox Jewish sensibilities of his time. For this, he became paradigmatic of human power that exalts itself with disregard for God himself. We will see that his actions are considered paradigmatic with ultimate wickedness toward the end of the chapter.

We left the story in verse 20, with the mysterious death of Seleucus IV in 175 B.C., while Antiochus was en route to Syria after being a hostage in Rome. When Antiochus IV was allowed to leave Rome, he was replaced by Demetrius, his nephew, who would have been his father's successor. Antiochus received the news of his brother's death while in Athens. He also heard that Heliodorus, perhaps behind the death of Seleucus, was plotting to seize power. Antiochus rushed home to come to the aid of another nephew, who was also named Antiochus. On the way back, he received the support of Eumenes, the king of Pergamum, who wanted to support the native dynasty over a pretender like Heliodorus. Antiochus, with this help, reached Antioch and ruled for the next five years as coregent with young Antiochus. In 170 B.C., the latter died and Antiochus IV ruled alone.

There is some disagreement among commentators over the sequence of verses 22–24. Collins believes that verse 22 is a general statement about Antiochus IV's reign with a dischronologized reference to the deposition of Onias III from the high priesthood (see below), then verses 23–24 go back to describing Antiochus's initial takeover of Seleucia from his nephew.[12] Miller, on the other hand, feels that verses 22–24 are chronological and discuss the first phase of the Syrian-Egyptian war. He thus asserts that Ptolemy VI is the "prince of the covenant" mentioned in verse 22.[13] I find the latter improbable and so side with Collins.

It is also unclear exactly what is in view in verse 23. The ambiguous language does not allow us to be dogmatic as to whether it is still referring to Antiochus's coming to power in Syria with the help of a "few people" (Eumenes being the most notable as well as his brother Attalus, so Collins) or his gaining influence in Jerusalem.[14] The story behind the latter is as follows.

Onias III was high priest, not only the most important religious position in Jerusalem at the time but also the highest political office. He was, however, pro-Egyptian. The Tobiad family was an extremely powerful force in the city. They were not native, having emigrated from across the river some years before. With them, in a pro-Syrian (and thus pro-Antiochus IV) party, was Jason, Onias's brother and thus a member of the priestly family. The pro-Syrian party wanted to turn Jerusalem into a Greek city.[15] Antiochus was much better off with Jason rather than Onias in the high priesthood

---

12. Ibid., 382.
13. Miller, *Daniel*, 298–99, following Calvin.
14. So Goldingay, *Daniel*, 299–300.
15. See Mandell and Hayes, *A History of the Jews*, 51–54.

Daniel 11:2—12:13

and manipulated the situation so that Jason assumed that position. Such manipulation of that sacred office brought on the displeasure of the faithful and was really just the beginning. Such a reward for Jason and the Tobiads was probably in the mind of the prophet when he spoke of Antiochus's beneficence in verse 24.

Verse 25 turns our attention now to Antiochus's actions against the south. Polybius tells us that it was actually the south that was the aggressor, but the pivotal first battle took place as the northern army passed into southern territory. The political situation in the south was that, after the death of Cleopatra the wife of Ptolemy V, who served as regent until 176 B.C., her young son Ptolemy VI Philometer took the throne. Two of his advisors were the real power, however, Eulaeus and Lenaeus. They were the ones who initiated a new anti-Syrian policy, and Antiochus was likely making a preemptive strike against them. The battle was joined south of Gaza near Pelusium, and Antiochus won the day. Ptolemy was a young man at the time and the defeat was probably to be blamed on the two advisors, who may be the referent to the phrase "those who eat from the king's provisions" (v. 26).

Ptolemy VI's younger brother, Ptolemy VII, declared himself king in Alexandria, while Ptolemy VI ruled from Memphis. Antiochus failed at his attempt to take Alexandria and returned to the north, leaving some troops behind just outside of Egypt proper. Those troops apparently were needed since the very next year (168 B.C.) he invaded Egypt again (v. 29). The two Ptolemy brothers had reconciled and stood as a united front. More telling against Antiochus was the intervention of Rome. The consul Popillius Laenas came and presented him with a senatorial decision that he remove himself from Egypt. According to Mandell and Hayes, he was a legate without consular imperium.[16] However, in a show of force, the Roman legate drew a circle in the sand around Antiochus and told him that he must make a decision before leaving the circle. This must have been extremely embarrassing to Antiochus, but he knew better than to disobey. So he withdrew, probably none too happy; and he, of course, returned via Judea.

I have passed over verse 28b in order to talk about Antiochus's second Egyptian campaign and for a reason. There is some confusion in the sources (e.g., 1 and 2 Maccabees) about what happened when. For our purposes, it is only important to point out that Antiochus took increasingly aggressive steps against what God's faithful people would call proper worship. For one thing he looted the temple. He also had a fortress erected (called the Akra) near the temple in order to keep an eye on the activities there. Most distressing was his stopping the daily sacrifice on the altar and placing in the temple an

---

16. Ibid., 58.

idolatrous object, probably a meteorite representing Baal Shamem (the Syrian version of Zeus). This object is called "the abomination that causes desolation" in the book of Daniel. According to Mandell and Hayes, it "was constructed upon the altar of burnt offerings in the Temple courtyard. It was on this altar and similar ones outside Jerusalem that swine were said to have been offered (1 Macc. 1:44–47; *Ant.* XII 253) after the cessation of the traditional, daily *tamid* sacrifices."[17]

The people of God were split into two parties (v. 32): those who supported Antiochus and his program of Hellenization of Judea and those who did not. Jason had earlier been removed from the high priesthood and replaced by a person named Menelaus, who was not even a member of the right family to be a priest. But he was probably supported by the powerful Tobiads and simply outbid Jason for the position. However, while Antiochus was waging his second Egyptian campaign, Jason, the deposed high priest, heard a rumor that Antiochus had been killed and so he moved against Menelaus. However, Antiochus, upset about the frustrations of his plans in Egypt, was far from dead. Thus, upon his return he acted against God's people. He had many massacred and sold as slaves.

The real heroes during this time of distress are the "wise," who will instruct the "many" (v. 33). They are those who would be on Daniel's religious wavelength. There is some disagreement over how the "wise" are related to the Hasmoneans or whether the latter are referred to as the "little help," or whether there is any connection at all. The debate has to do with how the book of Daniel views an active, violent reaction to their oppression. I believe it is wrong-minded to say that the book of Daniel represents a pacifist view that waits for God the warrior to act. In the earlier historical battles of Israel, God won the war, to be sure, at places like Jericho, but that did not mean that Israel did not take action in some way. In other words, the ideology of the book has plenty of room for appreciation of armed resistance to the oppression.

The King Who Will Do As He Pleases (11:36–45)

ANYONE WHO DOES not acknowledge a difficulty here is a polemicist in the worst possible sense. That is, he or she knows better that this is a difficult passage one way or the other, and not to acknowledge the difficulty and not to allow for tolerance for the other view is simply bad faith. The issue is: Who is in mind in verses 36–45? Further complicating the issue is the question of whose "mind" are we referring to, the human author or the divine author? It is our understanding of the nature of revelation (cf. 1 Peter 1:10–12) that the

---

17. Ibid., 65, though Mandell and Hayes think this may be an "ideological fiction," since it was not mentioned in 2 Maccabees.

human author did not fully understand the implications of what he was speaking about. In other words, it is conceivable that Daniel thought he was still describing the climactic king of the north, whom he has been speaking about since verse 21 and whom we have identified as Antiochus IV Epiphanes, but the divine intention may have been much broader.

There are several signals for a broader intention. (1) The language takes on bigger-than-life terms. As Clifford (who does not follow us in assigning an eschatological meaning to these verses) puts it, we get mythical, cosmic language here, that is, language that lifts us above mundane, earthly activity.[18] (2) We have the language of the "time of the end" (v. 40). This takes us to the edge of history, which, of course, was not achieved at the time of Antiochus Epiphanes, as horrible as his reign was. (3) Finally, we know that verses 40–45 simply do not work when applied to the life and death of Antiochus Epiphanes. Antiochus did not "extend his power over many countries; Egypt will not escape" (v. 42). Nor did he die when he "pitch[ed] his royal tents between the seas at the beautiful holy mountain" (v. 45).

The latter is what drives certain scholars, some with an indisputably orthodox view of Scripture,[19] to opt for a late date of the book of Daniel. They often do so on the grounds that a "prophecy after the fact" is a well-known ancient literary genre. That the genre is well attested is true; however, they are wrong to think it was recognized by contemporary audiences as prophecy after the fact. The comparable examples of prophecy after the fact only worked if their authors could deceive their audiences into thinking they were written ages ago. My research into this genre and this particular use of pseudonymity keeps me from going in the direction of these scholars.[20] However, it would be disingenuous of me to suggest that there are not strong arguments that support their view. Also, it is mischievous of other scholars to suggest that somehow their views are indications that they are not consistently evangelical in their approach to the Bible.

Why not assert, on the basis of the textual signals described above, that this prophecy is of the Antichrist, pure and simple? The difficulty is that there is no clear transitional statement between verses 35 and 36 or later between verses 39 and 40. In the earlier part of the chapter, there are clear signals that the narrator moves from one king to the next (cf. vv. 2, 7, 20–21), but not in the present section. Here we have the primary textual reason why we cannot simply rule out of court the argument that verses 36–45 continue the "prophecy" of Antiochus Epiphanes.

---

18. R. J. Clifford, "History and Myth in Daniel 10–12," *BASOR* 220 (1975): 23–26.
19. Most notably, Goldingay, *Daniel;* D. G. Meade, *Pseudonymity and Canon* (Tübingen: J. C. Mohr, 1986).
20. See here T. Longman III, *Fictional Akkadian Autobiography*.

There are views, of course, that are over the edge. For instance, some embrace the idea that the author of Daniel, living in the middle of the second century B.C., was intentionally working a fraud by presenting his prophecy as coming from the sixth century. In this case, the end of Daniel 11 is nothing but a failed attempt at predicting the future.

However, as mentioned above, my own opinion is that Daniel is speaking from the sixth century and is looking into the future. It is from this perspective that I will interpret the verses. The perspective followed here has found brief but articulate expression in the commentary by Baldwin.[21] She begins by reminding us that biblical prophecy often exhibited the characteristic of telescoping future events. The image conjured by this term is that of a collapsible telescope—one that looked like a short one-piece tube until extended, revealing three parts. In the same way, biblical prophecy was often presented as one event, but as we witness its fulfillment we see that it was really more complex than that.[22]

Baldwin cites the prophecy of Jesus in Mark 13 and its Synoptic parallels. Reading it in a later period of time we see that elements of it were fulfilled in an anticipatory way in the destruction of Jerusalem in A.D. 70, but that it also looked forward to the time that we are all still anticipating, the second coming of Christ. In the same way, John the Baptist's description of the one whom he would baptize was clearly fulfilled in Christ's first coming in one sense, but awaits the Second Coming for further fulfillment. John's own doubts expressed in Matthew 11:1–19 demonstrate as well that in this case the prophet spoke better than he consciously knew. Thus, in Daniel 11:36– 45 we see references to Antiochus Epiphanes taking on larger than life characteristics, which we, living in the light of the New Testament, might describe as anticipatory of a figure called the Antichrist.[23]

The pride of this king will be enormous. He will exalt himself not only above every other human being, but above the gods themselves. His pride, as well as his fall, equals that of the morning star in Isaiah 14:12–14:

> O morning star, son of the dawn! ...
> You said in your heart,
> "I will ascend to heaven;
> I will raise my throne
> above the stars of God;
> I will sit enthroned on the mount of assembly,
> on the utmost heights of the sacred mountain.

---

21. Baldwin, *Daniel*, 198–201.
22. A. Hoekema, *The Bible and the Future* (Grand Rapids: Eerdmans, 1979).
23. This word is used for the first time in the letters of John (see 1 John 2:18).

I will ascend above the tops of the clouds;
I will make myself like the Most High."[24]

As a king, the Antichrist not only has pride, but he also has power, which leads him to assert his own sovereignty so that he will "do as he pleases." As such, he attacks the gods. Interestingly, he is castigated not only for rejecting the true God, but also for disdain showed toward his own ancestral religion, perhaps mentioned because it reinforces the idea that he is a man of incredible pride. "The one desired by women" is often an epithet of Tammuz, whose cult of the dying and rising god features a prominent place for women, but is more likely the Syrian reflex that features Adonis as the object of attention.

In an apparent contradiction, however, the passage goes on to describe how this king, who exalts himself above every god, pays homage to "a god of fortresses" (v. 38)—though this may simply be a reference to the attention he pays to his own military machine and his insatiable desire to oppress others. Of course, Antiochus with his lifelong desire to subjugate the south is a suitable model for this bigger-than-life king.

Verse 40 begins with the phrase "at the time of the end," begging the question "the end of what?" Certainly it means the end of the pride and life of the king who does as he pleases. Miller is correct to point out that this "end" is followed in 12:1–3 by the resurrection of the dead, and so we should take this as a clue that the end (in its ultimate sense) is the end of time. Miller, however, I believe errs by continuing to equate the details of the following verse to specific end-time events. At this stage of biblical revelation, we are getting some of the earliest glimpses of final things. The New Testament (see below) will provide much more on the final judgment. Yet even so, we are left today with only the taste of the great realities to come. We should be extremely cautious in our treatment of these truths.

Indeed, all I feel safe asserting is the following: Verses 40–45 look forward to a violent end to history. This end will see the destruction of the pride and arrogance of the wicked. The next section goes on to talk about the other side of the coin, the great eschatological reward for those who are on God's side in the conflict.

The Salvation of God's People (12:1–4)

THE CHAPTER DIVISION obscures the fact that 12:1–4 is integrally connected with what preceded at the end of chapter 11. The king who resisted the gods and exalted himself (11:36–45) has come to a pitiful end. We have

---

24. See also Ezek. 28:1–19. This arrogance is anticipated in the horn that speaks arrogant words against God (Dan. 7:8, 11, 25; 8:9–12).

argued above that this previous section telescopes earthly and cosmic realities as well as near-future and far-future events. The king is Antiochus, but he is also something more (i.e., worse) than Antiochus. The end is in the second century, but the end is also in the still-distant future. Just as the ideal king of the Psalms was grounded in the Davidic reality but anticipated the Messianic glory, so the wicked king of the end of Daniel is grounded in the Antiochene reality but anticipated the horror of the Antichrist.

Thus, when chapter 12 begins "at that time," we find ourselves again in that flux between earthly and heavenly reality. We deal with the definitive end of Antiochus's persecution of God's people as well as their final struggle. We are, in a phrase, at "the theological climax of the book."[25]

We have been introduced to Michael already (see 10:13, 21) as God's warring angel, the "patron angel of Israel."[26] Verse 1 has military and judicial overtones. Michael judges and fights in order to protect God's people. This comes at a time of unprecedented "distress," but the distress is no sooner announced than the fact of deliverance is introduced.

This deliverance is spelled out in more detail in verse 2, a truly amazing verse about which Towner declares, "There it is, the first and only unambiguous reference to the double resurrection of the dead in the entire Old Testament!"[27] There may be others (cf. Isa. 26:19), but we agree that this is the clearest. Even so, we are left with many questions if we restrict ourselves to Daniel 12 without recourse to later New Testament teaching about the topic of the afterlife. Of course, we must not develop a whole doctrine of the afterlife from this one verse. But we can confidently affirm that it celebrates the vindication that will come both in the reward for which the righteous are destined and in the punishment for which the wicked—by which we are to understand those who have worked against the purposes and people of God—are reserved.

The righteous are described as "those who are wise" (v. 3) and may indeed have as their reference those belonging to Daniel's group or the teachers among them. They will shine "like the brightness of the heavens," presumably "like the stars," which in other contexts stand for celestial beings (Judg. 5:20; Job 38:7; 1 Enoch 104; T. Moses 10:9; 2 Apoc. Bar. 51). This hope is expressed as a metaphor, however, and we should not press the language literally.

This great hope is to be preserved through the ages, not hidden. Miller understands the force of verse 4 correctly when he states an earlier biblical analogy:

---

25. J. Lindenberger, "Daniel 12:1–4," *Interp* 39 (1985): 182.
26. G. W. E. Nickelsburg Jr., *Resurrection, Immortality, and Eternal Life in Intertestamental Judaism* (Cambridge: Cambridge Univ. Press, 1972), 11.
27. Towner, *Daniel*, 166. This view is widely held, though Goldingay (*Daniel*, 308) doubts it, asserting that it has a "this-worldly connotation."

In the ancient Near East the custom was to "seal" an important document by impressing upon it the identifying marks of the parties involved and the recording scribe. A sealed text was not to be tampered with or changed. The original document was duplicated and placed ("closed up") in a safe place where it could be preserved.[28]

Miller cites Jeremiah 32:9–12, where there are clearly two documents, one public and one preserved for posterity.

Therefore, the picture is not that of a document that becomes clearer to understand the closer we get to the end times, which will then constitute the unsealing of Daniel's prophecy. Indeed, the best understanding of the "many will go here and there to increase knowledge" is a negative one. Collins points out the allusion to Amos 8:12: "Men will stagger from sea to sea and wander from north to east, searching for the word of the LORD, but they will not find it," and comments that since the prophecy is sealed, this knowledge is unattainable.[29] That is, people will scurry about desperately trying to find knowledge in their own power, but will fail in their attempt.

Final Words (12:5–13)

SOME SCHOLARS BELIEVE that this section has the traits of a later gloss or appendix (see comments on vv. 11–12). But it is fitting, now that the message of prophecy has been delivered, to return to the scene and characters described in 10:4–21. We are back at the bank of the river, the celestial being still hovering over the water. Now, however, there are clearly two other figures (probably angelic) on each side of the river. One of the two is surely the angel who delivered the message (conceivably Gabriel, though unnamed both here and in ch. 10). The other angel is unnamed, but (and this is more of a stretch) he might be Michael, who was mentioned at the end of chapter 10 as the angel who helped fight the way to reach Daniel in the first place. These ambiguities, combined with the debate over the divine or angelic identity of the figure in linen, make the scene a bit murky, but this ambiguity does not affect the interpretation.

Daniel again finds himself in the position of overhearing a conversation between celestial beings. One of the angels on the bank addresses a climactic question to the other one, obviously the superior, hovering over the water: "How long will it be before these astonishing things are fulfilled?" (v. 6). This question, though delivered by the angel, would be of dire interest to Daniel and his spiritual heirs, who would find themselves in periods of distress. How

---

28. Miller, *Daniel*, 320.
29. Collins, *Daniel*, 399.

long would the suffering last? A term closely related to the "astonishing things" (*pᵉla'ot*) of verse 6 was used in 11:36 (*nipla'ot*, NIV, "unheard-of things"); thus, the immediate reference to the question in 12:6 may be what follows in 11:36–12:3. If so, as we have suggested, it may have a double reference to the time of Antiochus and the time of greater horror to follow.

Before answering, the hovering figure dressed in linen garments makes an unprecedented gesture (v. 7): He lifts both hands toward heaven and swears "by him who lives forever." In Deuteronomy 32:40, God lifts one hand to heaven and swears by himself who lives forever. The double-handed gesture, at least as far as we can tell, is a statement of emphasis and certainly evokes a solemn atmosphere around what is to follow.

This figure then delivers an enigmatic answer that reminds us of the answer given in 7:25: "a time, times and half a time" (12:7). As we saw there, the intention is not to give a precise time period but rather to indicate that just as wickedness seems to be gaining momentum, it will be slowed and then stopped. Such cessation will happen at a time of great distress, since it will be at the moment when "the power of the holy people has been finally broken." Deliverance comes at the most unlikely time. God seems to work that way. When human resources run out, God steps in to demonstrate his power.

But Daniel, like us, wants more information. Thus, he asks in verse 8, "My lord, what will the outcome of all this be?" The reply comes, not harshly but clearly, that now is not the time. The celestial being tells Daniel to get on with life ("Go your way," v. 9), and again he emphasizes the closed nature of the revelation (they are "closed up" and "sealed").

Nonetheless, he does expand his earlier comments on the period to follow (v. 10). We are, I believe, to take them as words that describe the period from Daniel's time to the end. The wicked will continue to be wicked and not understand, while those who are wise will understand. In the light of Daniel's own confession that he did not understand the words of the celestial being (v. 8), we should comment that the reference to lack of understanding is not to the enigmas of the end but rather to the wicked's not understanding the overall purposes of God's plan. They continue to be wicked because wickedness seems to win out. They do not see the long-term, eschatological perspective, where it is not the wicked who will have victory but the wise, the righteous, who rise to "everlasting life" (12:2). They will shine like stars, whereas the wicked will wake up to "everlasting contempt."

But the enigmas continue in verses 11–12. Two more time periods are specified. Both are impossible to pinpoint with real events or to correlate with each other. Is the reference to Antiochus, who abolished sacrifice and then set up an object that venerated Zeus in the temple? Is it to a future desecration perpetrated by the eschatological Antichrist? Is it both? All these views have been put forward.

Indeed, if the original reference of the angel's question in verse 6 was to the things described prophetically in 11:36–12:3, then perhaps we are still dealing with a conflation of Antiochus and the greater terror that follows in the future.[30] Antiochus, after all, abolished sacrifice and set up an abomination, and it was about three years before the temple was cleansed, thanks to the victory of the Maccabees. Perhaps the fact that all the numbers cited here are a little longer suggests that the text is pointing beyond that historical reference point to something still future to us. Jesus, we will see, certainly understands that to be the case (see below on his comments on the "abomination that causes desolation").[31]

What is the relationship of the 1290 days to the 1335 days (12:11–12) to the 2300 evenings and mornings (8:14) to the "time, times and half a time" (7:25; 12:7; if understood as three and one half years, the day totals are in the ballpark with these other numbers)? God alone knows—and that seems to be the point. God knows that there is an end that he has determined, but we cannot figure it out because we are not supposed to. Leave it to God, the angel says to Daniel, and through him he speaks to us. Once again to Daniel, but also to us, he says: "Go your way till the end. You will rest, and then at the end of days you will rise to receive your allotted inheritance" (12:13).

This is a fitting conclusion for Daniel and for the book. You may suffer now, but God has given you a glimpse of the coming glory. God will set things right. Your reward is coming, but for now "go your way." By these words, God gives Daniel and all of his heirs the confidence to persist in the light of continuing persecution and trouble.

---

30. Baldwin, *Daniel*, 208, adds the intriguing observation that it would be historically incorrect to say that Antiochus broke the power of the people of God (v. 7). This suggests to her that something more than the second century B.C. is hinted at here.

31. Other scholars, who adopt a second-century B.C. date for this section of Daniel, suggest that the reference is exclusively to the period of Antiochus and that we are dealing with failed prophetic expectation. They point out that since the Maccabees actually cleansed the temple within three years, even the shorter three-and-a-half-year date, meant that the "Danielic" party had something else in mind for fulfillment, perhaps the resurrection of the martyrs. When that did not happen after three and a half years, they suggested 1290 days. Then when that failed to be the period for fulfillment, they tacked on a few more days to get the 1335 days. This is ingenious given their presupposition and the fact that this is often how modern apocalyptic speculation works; but how likely is it that a written text would be updated in such a short time? Mention should also be made of the fact that there were a number of different calendars in use during the second century B.C.—a solar calendar, a lunar calendar and a luni-solar calendar (for details, see Goldingay, *Daniel*, 309–10). Such an observation does not clarify things as much as complicates them, that is, makes the references even more enigmatic to us and most likely to the original audience.

Daniel 11:2–12:13

Bridging Contexts

DANIEL 11–12 PRESENTS the visionary message of the supernatural creatures who fought their way to Daniel in chapter 10. The concluding unit (12:5–13) finds Daniel and his celestial companions in the same place as in chapter 10 and brings this final unit to completion. As we have observed above, the visionary message looks with remarkable clarity into the near and far future. Names are not used, but from our position of historical retrospect, we can provide them along with a description of many of the events of the fourth to second century B.C. We recognize the events alluded to in chapter 11 through other sources like Polybius, Josephus, and 1 and 2 Maccabees.

This narrative is presented from the vantage point of the sixth century B.C. Even if Goldingay and other scholars are correct that the prophecy was actually composed in the second century B.C.,[32] the book intends us to understand it to come from the sixth century. In either case, the book of Daniel makes a strong statement about the sovereignty of God over the historical process. If we have been reading straight through the book of Daniel, this will hardly surprise us. Every passage that we have studied has contributed to the overarching theme of the book: *In spite of present circumstances, God is in control and will win the day*.

Perhaps in no chapter is God's control displayed in such detail as in chapter 11. Indeed, for those of us living at a later time, it raises the issue of the meaning of history. If God is in such control, how can our decisions hold any meaning? Can I be held responsible for my actions if I am a mere puppet on a string held by an all-powerful being? Towner believes that the answer to the last question is no. In his often insightful commentary, he states that Daniel's theology of history means that it is "essentially meaningless.... History's only point then becomes simply to demonstrate that God's eternal decree is certain to come to pass."[33]

Before exploring this issue of divine sovereignty and human responsibility, it is important to remind ourselves of the six major themes of the second half of the book, because most of them play an important role in this climactic prophetic vision. The six are:

- the horror of human evil, particularly as it is concentrated in the state
- the announcement of a specific time of deliverance
- repentance that leads to deliverance
- the revelation that a cosmic war stands behind human conflict

---

32. Goldingay, *Daniel*, 314–16.
33. Towner, *Daniel*, 175.

- judgment as certain for those who resist God and oppress his people
- the equally certain truth that God's people, downtrodden in the present, will experience new life in the fullest sense.

With the exception of the theme of repentance, we will have occasion to see all these themes displayed prominently in these two chapters. However, to complete our plan of focusing on a theme per chapter (see comments in "The Nature of Apocalyptic Literature" in the Original Meaning section of chapter 7), we will here explore carefully the last two elements: Judgment is certain for the wicked; reward is certain for the righteous.

Divine sovereignty and human responsibility. It is in the term *certain* that we get the connection with the issue of divine sovereignty. How can Daniel say that judgment and reward are certain for the wicked and the righteous? Because God is sovereign; he is in control.

This is why the issue of divine sovereignty over history was not a problem for Daniel or his readers. He was not approaching it as a philosophical problem, but rather proclaiming good news to a captive people. In the present, the wicked are in control and prospering, whereas the godly are suffering. But that is not the end of the story. Far from rendering history meaningless, it imbues it with ultimate significance. What would be meaningless is if all the suffering faithfulness of God's people resulted only in a nameless grave. What would lead to despair is if, after treading over the godly, the wicked would be celebrated in death.

Is not this the problem that the Teacher in Ecclesiastes expressed? To him, God was not in control, or at least he didn't seem to be. "God is in heaven and you are on earth" (Eccl. 5:2). For the godly, life is one pain after another, and then they die. For the wicked—well, let's listen to the words of the Teacher: "I saw the wicked buried—those who used to come and go from the holy place and receive praise in the city where they did this. This too is meaningless" (8:10).[34]

For Daniel's audience, God's control of history was positive because it meant things would turn out right in the end. This knowledge led to joy in the present (cf. Ps. 73[35]).

However, we cannot avoid the philosophical questions in this way completely. Does divine sovereignty eradicate human responsibility? Does God's control mean that human beings have none? Are we simply acting out a script already written? Certainly that is what Daniel 11 appears to be—a script for the history of the ancient Near East in the centuries between the beginning of Persian rule and down to the time of Antiochus Epiphanes.

---

34. For Ecclesiastes, see T. Longman III, *The Book of Ecclesiastes* (NICOT; Grand Rapids: Eerdmans, 1998).
35. See the treatment of this psalm on pp. 124–26.

Daniel 11:2—12:13

Divine sovereignty and human responsibility—this is an old, old debate among theologians. And, I would be quick to add, its endurance as a point of contention warns us that the ultimate answer may be beyond our grasp. Another way to put it is, the Bible does not tell us enough to allow us to answer how these two work together in harmony.

What does the Bible teach us? It shows us, as we have seen clearly in Daniel, that God is in control. But it also informs us that human beings make decisions for which they are responsible. In the words of Philippians 2:12: "Therefore, my dear friends, as you have always obeyed—not only in my presence, but now much more in my absence—continue to work out your salvation with fear and trembling, for it is God who works in you to will and to act according to his good purpose."

God works out our salvation. We work out our salvation. God controls history; he brought Antiochus Epiphanes down and allowed the temple to be cleansed. Human beings act in history; the Hasmonean rebellion liberated the temple.

Now some people see Daniel as a quietist, as someone who would say, "God will take care of it" or "Let God. . . ." They reason that Daniel would be against the Hasmonean rebellion or any overt actions that would try to wrest control out of the hands of God and into their own. I beg to differ. It is difficult to know what Daniel would have thought of Judas Maccabeus, but in principle he would not have been against him. That is, he would not reject out of hand human efforts. Daniel understood that divine sovereignty and human responsibility formed a mystery, but he also understood that they both were operative. He emphasizes the former because God's people were relatively powerless. Thus, the news of God's sovereignty was good news.

And indeed throughout the Bible, we see that God's control over history, while not eradicating human responsibility, was something that brought joy and confidence to his people. Let's begin with the story of Joseph.

The Joseph narrative has surprisingly little God-talk in it. As it narrates Joseph's movements from Palestine to Egypt, and from the house of Potiphar to jail and finally to Pharaoh's court, the narrator does not reflect on God's agency in his life. Joseph does the best that he can and then, or so it appears, the blind forces of chance push him around. However, that is not the way Joseph understands it, and from the climactic position of Joseph's final speech, it is not the way the narrator wants us to take it. In what must be understood as a thematic statement, Joseph speaks to his brothers, who are afraid that since Jacob has died, their brother will now work his revenge: "You intended to harm me, but God intended it for good to accomplish what is now being done, the saving of many lives. So then, don't be afraid. I will provide for you and your children. And he reassured them and spoke kindly to them" (Gen.

50:20–21). They meant evil against Joseph and were responsible, and were it not for their repentance, they would be punished; but God meant it for good. He used the sinful, selfish actions of the brothers to bring about the greater purpose of helping his people survive a crushing famine.

Samson is another case in point. A close study of the Samson narrative indicates that he did nothing unless it was for his own good. He was a self-absorbed man, if ever there was one. But God overruled his sinful tendencies to use him to harass the enemy, the Philistines, and ultimately to bring a huge disaster on their leadership. He married a Philistine woman, which brought him into conflict with the enemy, and he responded by burning their fields or killing a large number of them with the jawbone of an ass. Once he actually destroyed the gate of the Philistine city of Gath—a wonderful display of power over this arrogant enemy. But why did he tear it down with his superhuman strength? Because he was caught visiting a prostitute and he was holding the gate over his head to keep from getting killed!

Even the dramatic end of Samson's story is clouded, at best, with mixed motives. After Delilah's betrayal, he found himself in Philistine custody, bereft of his strength, blinded, and made a fool. As he stood bound to a pillar, he made one final request of God: "O Sovereign LORD, remember me. O God, please strengthen me just once more, and let me with one blow get revenge on the Philistines for my two eyes" (Judg. 16:28). He then brought down the house—literally—on the heads of the Philistines, as well as his own. Again, a great victory over the enemy, but for what reason? His own eyes, not the glory of God. God controls history. He can even overrule the evil or mixed motives of others to bring about his purposes.

We get another important window on the issue of divine sovereignty and human responsibility from the theology of holy war in the Old Testament.[36] Again, we bow before a mystery. God's victory is certain; there is no doubt about the outcome of a war when Yahweh enters the battle. The Israelites can just stand back and watch as God overwhelms the enemy. But they do not. They always enter the fray in some way. At Jericho, God commands them to march around the city each day for six days and then on the seventh to march around the city seven times and then blow their trumpets (Josh. 6). This they do. They participate, though there is no doubt as to the outcome or to whom the praise belongs.

God fights for Israel also during the days of Gideon (Judg. 7). He could have defeated the Midianites alone, but he does not do so. Indeed, he commands Gideon to pare down his troops from 32,000 to 300, but the 300 troops still have a job to do.

---

36. Cf. T. Longman III and D. Reid, *God Is a Warrior*; see discussion above on pp. 254–56.

Goliath was a giant of a soldier, but no match for God. The Lord could have said to Israel, "Stand back so you don't get singed," just before he threw a lightning bolt down from the heavens to reduce the giant to a pile of ash. But that is not the way he did it (1 Sam. 17). Rather, he sends in unarmored and poorly weaponed young David, an inexperienced boy, against a hardened mercenary; but since God is on the side of David, there is again no doubt about the outcome. The head of Goliath is cut off.

Similarly, Daniel 11–12 concerns the various kingdoms that oppress Israel in the fourth and third centuries. Though we do not hear of God's direct involvement in the manner of holy war until the final conflict, we do see his guiding hand in the rise and fall of successive kingdoms (Persia succeeded by Alexander's Greece, succeeded by the Ptolemies and Seleucids). Indeed, the implicit message of this narrative is that, though they all have imperial pretensions, none of them can achieve any lasting or significant empire (in the grand scheme of things) because they keep each other in check. We particularly see this in the seesaw conflict between the Ptolemies and the Seleucids as they wrestle for control of Israel, the "Beautiful Land."

Thus, while we struggle with the harmony between the two themes of divine sovereignty and human responsibility, the Bible clearly teaches that God is sovereign and humans are responsible. We cannot provide a philosophical answer to the conundrum, but they work together. How? We cannot tell. This perspective will leave some dissatisfied. God does not ask for comprehension, but rather for humility before the mystery—the amazing mystery that God can take even sinful human actions and work things out for good.

The wicked and the godly each get their ultimate due. What is the intended effect of the foregoing on the original audience? Towner this time has it right: "The fact that the predicted course has been followed in exquisite detail leads that reader to turn about and face forward with confidence, certain that the future, too, though not yet come to pass, will be as securely in God's hand as world history has been since the seer's time."[37]

Why confidence? Because, though prospering in the present, the wicked will get their due, and, though suffering in the present, the godly will get their reward. God will see to it.

We have seen these themes from the beginning of the book. Daniel and the three friends, though put through extremely difficult times, were raised higher and higher in glory, while their enemies often were humiliated or even died. We have seen in each of the previous visions of Daniel (chs. 7, 8, 9) that the triumphant wicked end up being destroyed themselves. In chap-

---

37. Towner, *Daniel*, 148.

ters 10–12, "events unfold as a pointless sequence of invasions, battles, schemes, and frustrations."[38] Persia falls to Greece (11:3); the great kingdom of Alexander "will be broken up and parceled out toward the four winds of heaven" (11:4). Their successors will fall as well, including Antiochus and the greater evil force that he represents: "Yet he will come to his end, and no one will help him" (11:45).

But that is not enough. Our chapters go further—indeed, further than anywhere else in the Old Testament—in order to address the issue of justice and retribution. The rewards and punishments for faithfulness and rebellion go beyond death itself: "Multitudes who sleep in the dust of the earth will awake: some to everlasting life, others to shame and everlasting contempt. Those who are wise will shine like the brightness of the heavens, and those who lead many to righteousness, like the stars for ever and ever" (12:2–3).

The wicked will certainly be eternally shamed; "for the wicked to die the same death as the righteous is not enough."[39] Many places in the Old Testament struggle with the issue of divine retribution. After all, the book of Deuteronomy with its covenantal form implies, when isolated from the rest of the canon, that obedience to God will lead to blessings (Deut. 28:1–14), while disobedience will lead to suffering (28:15–68). The book of Proverbs, at least its major theme,[40] celebrates the way of the righteous over the way of the wicked:

> The house of the wicked will be destroyed,
> but the tent of the upright will flourish. (Prov. 14:11)
>
> The path of life leads upward for the wise
> to keep him from going down to the grave. (15:24)
>
> Understanding is a fountain of life to those who have it,
> but folly brings punishment to fools. (16:22)

But experience did not seem to bear this out, at least with the precision of an absolute principle. The Teacher was deeply troubled by real life when he expressed what he observed and gave advice to his listeners based on his experience (Eccl. 7:15–18):

> In this meaningless life of mine I have seen both of these:
> a righteous man perishing in his righteousness,
>   and a wicked many living long in his wickedness.

---

38. Goldingay, *Daniel*, 316.
39. Ibid., 319.
40. See R. van Leeuwen, "Wealth and Poverty: System and Contradiction in Proverbs," *Hebrew Studies* 33 (1992): 25–36, who isolates a small number of proverbs in the book that recognize the complicated nature of retribution.

Daniel 11:2–12:13

> Do not be overrighteous,
>   neither be overwise—
>   why destroy yourself?
> Do not be overwicked,
>   and do not be a fool—
>   why die before your time?
> It is good to grasp the one
>   and not let go of the other.
>   The man who fears God will avoid all extremes.

But the Teacher was looking only "under the sun."[41] Daniel, thanks to the revelation provided by the celestial beings, gets a view above the sun. If there is going to be any ultimate retribution, it must be "above the sun." Dying is not enough; there must also be eternal shame for people like Antiochus, who persecute God's people. They must be raised from the dead to experience that shame.

Similarly, on the other side, the life of the godly during the period in Daniel's purview is hardly just reward for faithfulness in the midst of persecution. The celestial revelation gives Daniel and his followers the good news: They have something wonderful to look forward to, even after death. As mentioned before, this is the clearest teaching of the afterlife in the Old Testament, but there are certainly indications that lead up to this point.

Genesis 2 describes the first man and woman in the Garden of Eden. The Garden has in its midst two trees, one being the tree of life. The implication seems to be that as long as Adam and Eve are in the Garden they will enjoy life. However, they rebelled against God and were ejected from the Garden, no longer having access to the tree of life. As such, they eventually died. It was with their rebellion against God that death entered the world.

Nonetheless, they did not die immediately, and it was possible for Adam and Eve and their descendants to enjoy a relationship with God. Still, there is little explicit talk about life after death in most of the Old Testament. At best, existence was understood to continue in a shadowy locale called Sheol, which may simply be a reference to the grave. Sheol is not presented in a positive light, nor was fellowship with God thought to continue, as we see in the plea of Psalm 6:5: "No one remembers you [God] when he is dead. Who praises you from the grave?"

Other psalms, however, hint at some kind of continuing existence beyond the grave. Perhaps Psalm 16:9–11 is just talking about healing from a near fatal sickness, but the language is certainly suggestive:

---

41. For how this passage and the overall teaching of the Teacher fits into the book of Ecclesiastes and the theology of the canon, please see the introduction in Longman, *Ecclesiastes*.

Therefore my heart is glad and my tongue rejoices;
> my body also will rest secure,
because you will not abandon me to the grave,
> nor will you let your Holy One see decay.
You have made known to me the path of life;
> you will fill me with joy in your presence,
> with eternal pleasures at your right hand.

In a similar vein are Psalm 49:15 and 73:23–26:

But God will redeem my life from the grave;
> he will surely take me to himself.

Yet I am always with you;
> you hold me by my right hand.
You guide me with your counsel,
> and afterward you will take me into glory.
Whom have I in heaven but you?
> And earth has nothing I desire besides you.
My flesh and my heart may fail,
> but God is the strength of my heart
> and my portion forever.

Other provocative passages may speak of national resurrection, but they use language that provokes thoughts of individual resurrection:

Come, let us return to the LORD.
He has torn us to pieces
> but he will heal us;
he has injured us
> but he will bind up our wounds.
After two days he will revive us;
> on the third day he will restore us,
> that we may live in his presence. (Hos. 6:1–2)

> Then he said to me: "Son of man, these bones are the whole house of Israel. They say, 'Our bones are dried up and our hope is gone; we are cut off.' Therefore prophesy and say to them: 'This is what the Sovereign LORD says: O my people, I am going to open your graves and bring you up from them; I will bring you back to the land of Israel. Then you, my people, will know that I am the LORD, when I open your graves and bring you up from them. I will put my Spirit in you and you will live, and I will settle you in your own land. Then you will know that I the LORD have spoken, and I have done it, declares the LORD.'" (Ezek. 37:11–14)

Isaiah 26:19 is as close as we get to the teaching of Daniel 12:2–3 elsewhere in the Old Testament, and like the Hosea and Ezekiel passages just quoted, it too is probably primarily focused on national restoration:[42]

> But your dead will live;
> > their bodies will rise.
> You who dwell in the dust,
> > wake up and shout for joy.
> Your dew is like the dew of the morning;
> > the earth will give birth to her dead.

Just how new the idea of the resurrection of the dead was to Daniel's original audience is difficult for us to gauge. But we reject the idea that it is a completely foreign idea brought into the Bible via Persian or Hellenistic religious ideas. This is not to deny that perhaps interaction with these and other, earlier foreign ideas about the afterlife affected the formulation and expression of the idea in the Bible, but it is an idea that is also implicit from the very beginning of biblical religion. As we read the Bible as a whole, we see that the idea of an afterlife, like that of other important biblical ideas, has a seed form early, but is more fully developed as God continues to reveal himself to his people.

With that, we turn to a consideration of contemporary significance, where we will see that these ideas are developed even further and take on even greater clarity. Indeed, in many cases we will note that the New Testament authors actually appropriate the language of the book of Daniel in order to show the certainty of the fate of both the wicked and the godly.

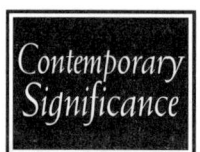

WE ARE NOW at the end of the book of Daniel, and we have heard the central theme of the book over and over again: *In spite of the present evil situation, God is in control.* In a word, God is sovereign. In order to avoid repetitiveness in the commentary, we have not fully developed the theme in each chapter, though the contents of each chapter would justify such a treatment. Rather, we raised the issue in the introduction and provided reminders throughout the commentary. However, now that we have reached the climax of the book and certainly the strongest expression of God's sovereignty not only within the world but even over death, we are justified to spend some time again reflecting on the significance of that theme

---

42. As Collins argues in his helpful excursus "On Resurrection," *Daniel*, 394–98.

Daniel 11:2–12:13

for our life today. For, you see, God is still sovereign today at the turn to the third millennium A.D., just as he was in the first millennium B.C.

God's sovereignty. That God is sovereign is true in spite of the fact that when we open the morning's newspaper or listen to the news on TV or the radio, we may have a different idea. My wife and I use a radio alarm, and we wake up every morning to a news station in our hometown of Philadelphia. Besides sports scores and weather, we hear the accounts of the latest scandals, wars, and local murders and other crimes. It is easy to be melodramatic and say that the streets of our cities are a war zone, but without resorting to hyperbole it is still obvious that social and moral chaos is evident all over the world. It is tempting to believe that when we step out into that world every morning, we are prey to incredible risk. Who knows whether, when we step out of our homes (or even before) in the morning, "our time is up" and we will find ourselves the victim of crime, disease, or accident?

The potential for harm is huge when we look at the statistics. Just last week two incidents illustrated this to me on a personal level. As I was driving my son back from school on a nice sunny day, we came to an intersection where our progress was blocked by police activity. As we sat there, a police officer pulled his gun as he walked in front of our car and set off in hot pursuit of a criminal. I did not stay around long enough to see if shots were fired, but the potential was there. In a second incident, a young university student downtown was not as fortunate. As he sat in his classroom painting a picture, a drive-by shooting occurred. Besides killing the intended victim, a stray shot went through the window of the classroom, seriously wounding the young student.

How easy it is to wander into the middle of a situation and end up dead or wounded. On one level, there is really nothing we can do to protect ourselves from these risks. We can work out, be incredibly well informed, be cautious, and still be struck down in some form. This was the conclusion of the Teacher (Eccl. 9:11–12):

> The race is not to the swift
> > or the battle to the strong,
> nor does food come to the wise
> > or wealth to the brilliant
> > or favor to the learned;
> but time and chance happen to them all.
> > Moreover, no man knows when his hour will come:
> As fish are caught in a cruel net,
> > or birds are taken in a snare,
> so men are trapped by evil times
> > that fall unexpectedly upon them.

Daniel 11:2—12:13

This was the Teacher's "under the sun" perspective. We are like fish caught in a net, prey to time and chance.[43]

In Daniel 11 we get an "above the sun" perspective on life. There we see God's hand guiding the events of history. In the words of Daniel's earlier prayer, "he sets up kings and deposes them" (2:21). The Persians fall to Alexander, and Alexander gives way to the Seleucids and the Ptolemies. God finally brings all this human pretension to an end, but even before this climactic moment we see his sovereignty at work in the affairs of human beings.

The good news is that God is no less in control today than he was in antiquity. To hear some modern Christian leaders talk, we might not believe this is the case. With a note of panic in their voice, they tell us that things have gotten out of control in the seat of our government. If we do not act immediately (often by sending in a check), our whole society will be turned over to the devil!

I am not prepared to defend the moral quality of our government, nor (as will become obvious below) do I want to argue to "let go and let God." God does expect us to work for righteousness' sake. What I object to is the shrill note, the panicky mood, the sense of loss of control. God *is* in control.

> And we know that in all things God works for the good of those who love him, who have been called according to his purpose. For those God foreknew he also predestined to be conformed to the likeness of his Son, that he might be the firstborn among many brothers. And those he predestined, he also called; those he called, he also justified; those he justified, he also glorified. (Rom. 8:28–30)

We see in the New Testament what we saw in the Old in the case of Joseph, Samson, Daniel, and the holy war tradition. While it looks as if life is going to hell, God is working behind the scenes to bring about good, often more than good—he accomplishes his people's rescue, their salvation. Think of the death of Jesus Christ in the light of Peter's sermon recorded in Acts 2:22–24:

> Men of Israel, listen to this: Jesus of Nazareth was a man accredited by God to you by miracles, wonders and signs, which God did among you through him, as you yourselves know. This man was handed over to you by God's set purpose and foreknowledge; and you, with the help of wicked men, put him to death by nailing him to the cross. But God raised him from the dead, freeing him from the agony of death, because it was impossible for death to keep its hold on him.

---

43. For an interpretation of this passage and for an explanation how such a bleak view fits into the message of the Bible as a whole, see Longman, *Ecclesiastes*, in loc.

God was in control even as the soldiers were nailing his hands and feet to the cross. The soldiers were nonetheless responsible—they were "wicked"—even though their actions fit into the overarching plan of God.

How does this have contemporary significance for us? In many ways. First of all, it is this act that provides our salvation. It is the death of Jesus that substitutes for our death, and his resurrection that anticipates our own (see below).

But it is also relevant because it provides the theological background to the Romans 8:28–30 passage cited above. God works out everything, including acts of harm against us, for our good. As we continue reading that passage, we see the effect this truth should have on us today (8:31–39):

> What, then, shall we say in response to this? If God is for us, who can be against us? He who did not spare his own Son, but gave him up for us all—how will he not also, along with him, graciously give us all things? Who will bring any charge against those whom God has chosen? It is God who justifies. Who is he that condemns? Christ Jesus, who died—more than that, who was raised to life—is at the right hand of God and is also interceding for us. Who shall separate us from the love of Christ? Shall trouble or hardship or persecution or famine or nakedness or danger or sword? As it is written:
>
> "For your sake we face death all day long;
> we are considered as sheep to be slaughtered."
>
> No, in all these things we are more than conquerors through him who loved us. For I am convinced that neither death nor life, neither angels nor demons, neither the present nor the future, nor any powers, neither height nor depth, nor anything else in all creation, will be able to separate us from the love of God that is in Christ Jesus our Lord.

God is in control in spite of present circumstances. In sixth-century Babylon it looked to the godly as if Babylon and then Persia were in control. But they weren't. In second-century Palestine it looked as if Antiochus Epiphanes was in control, but he wasn't. In the first century of Jesus and Paul, it looked as if Rome was in control, but it wasn't. To Christians living two thousand years after Jesus, it may look as if Satan is in control, but he isn't. God is in control, and because of that we can have boundless joy and optimism in the midst of our struggles.

And we do have struggles. Those struggles may be political or cultural. They may be emotional or psychological. They may be relational. But whatever the struggle, whatever the oppression, God is in control, and in spite of present appearances he will bring victory over evil and honor to those who remain faithful to him. The book of Daniel is a call to all God's people to remain steadfast in their love and obedience to him in spite of present turmoil.

Objections to God's sovereignty. What a wonderful message! Why do so many today recoil from it? One reason may be that deep inside of ourselves we would prefer to think of ourselves as free, even if our freedom meant despair. To many control implies servitude and dependency, and the spirit of our age desires autonomy, even at a cost.

Two worldviews are prevalent in secular culture today, modernism and postmodernism,[44] the latter presently in the process of displacing the former. Both have at their heart an impulse toward autonomy and a desire to avoid ultimate dependency on a higher power.

The spirit of modernism was captured by the Enlightenment, an intellectual movement originating from the Renaissance and perhaps best exemplified by its starting point, the philosopher Descartes (1596–1650), who proclaimed as the foundation to his theory of knowledge *cogito ergo sum* ("I think, therefore I am"). Existence has its foundation not in God, but in the autonomous self. Indeed, the Enlightenment may be understood as a reaction against the dogmatism of the medieval church. Modern men and women do not accept anything because of tradition or because of authority, especially church authority, but because reason proves it. Science may perhaps be possible only because of a Christian worldview, but the scientific method is often wielded in a spirit of autonomous reason. Modernism and science are an extremely optimistic approach to life, in their faith in the human mind to improve the world and to discover their world.

But that optimism has been seriously eroded since the late nineteenth century by a spirit of suspicion that detects beneath an indefatigable confidence in reason as the avenue to truth, a manipulative will-to-power and self-interest. Postmodernism casts doubt on human ability to come into direct contact with reality as well as on our pretensions to determine meaning. The modern chapter of such skepticism begins with nineteenth-century philosophers Feuerbach and Nietzsche. Their primary struggle was still against the dogmatism of Christian theology, but they also undermined any hope that one can approach reality in an unprejudiced manner and achieve truth. In perhaps one of his most famous sayings, Nietzsche wrote in his *Notebooks* (1873): "What is truth? A mobile army of metaphors, metonymns and anthropomorphisms."[45] As A. C. Thiselton goes on to comment and further quote Nietzsche:

---

44. J. Wilson, *Gospel Virtues* (Downers Grove, Ill.: InterVarsity, 1998) provides an excellent description of these two worldviews.

45. F. Nietzsche, "On Truth and Lie in the Extra-Moral Sense," in Walter Kaufmann, ed., *The Portable Nietzsche* (New York: Viking, 1968), 46.

Especially in religion, Nietzsche urges, people use "errors" for their own advantage, self-interest or power. Some promote erroneous "lies" merely from sheer personal need. In this sense, Nietzsche exclaims: "Truth is that kind of error without which a certain species of living cannot exist. The value of Life is ultimately decisive." Nietzsche goes further. He includes even "facts" here. He writes: "All that exists consists of interpretations." "Truths are illusions we have forgotten are illusions."[46]

While Nietzsche's comments here are directed specifically toward the global truth statements of theology and philosophy, they are equally relevant toward the modern spirit of science. Increasingly, scientists recognize that what they provide are not absolutely true statements about reality, but models and metaphors that explain phenomena.

It is Nietzsche's skepticism that dominates philosophy departments today in the form of postmodernism or deconstruction. A leading motif of this thought is, in the language of Nietzsche, the death of God, and in the language of Jacques Derrida, his most famous modern disciple, the denial of the Absolute Signifier. In its place stand autonomous men and women. Nietzsche hated what he called the "slave morality" of Christianity: Christians believe in an all-controlling God before whom human beings should submit even in the light of their suffering; he felt that this picture, a picture of life that we get in Daniel 11, was despicable and diminished humanity. It kept human beings in their place. Just like the caste system in India, which has served to keep the upper classes as the oppressors and the untouchables and other lower classes as the menial servants, so Christianity and biblical religion have kept humans docile in their suffering and pain.

These perspectives of postmodernism have been exacerbated by the hope for the afterlife. What better way to keep servile people down in this life than to tell them that there is a better life coming as long as they are obedient in the present? Of course, this fueled much of the criticism of Karl Marx, an older contemporary of Nietzsche, who felt that biblical religion was an "opiate" of the people. In a more popular vein, this jaundiced attitude is expressed by the commonly heard sarcastic remark directed toward Christianity, which they see as promoting a "pie in the sky by-and-by," and the jibe that Christians are so "heavenly-minded that they are no earthly good."

Descartes, Feuerbach, Nietzsche, Marx, and Derrida are just notable representatives of the thinkers who represent the currents of the worldviews known as modernism and postmodernism. How convenient it would be to

---

46. A. C. Thiselton, *Interpreting God and the Postmodern Self* (Grand Rapids: Eerdmans, 1995), 5.

say that they are just an elite with which we need have little to do. However, whether they merely express the spirit of an age or influence an age—or a combination of the two—the important point is that they articulate what drives many men and women living today. It is really unimportant how the dynamic works. It could be that these thinkers influence modern university teachers and other leaders, who then influence journalists, screen writers, musicians, ministers, and others, who in turn mediate these ideas to the mass populace. Or perhaps the thinkers are expressing their own experiences and wisdom based on their experiences along with everyone else.

Indeed, one guess why postmodernism with its denial of even the possibility of absolute truth has so captured the modern imagination is because we no longer live in an isolated society. A century ago it was much easier for a non-mobile population with unsophisticated means of communication to live in the blissful illusion that their way of life was the best one. Now we have air travel, radios, television, movies, the Internet. In America and many other places in the world we have a mixing of ethnic groups with their different beliefs and worldviews on an unprecedented scale. And in a secular democracy like ours it is wrong simply to privilege one of those worldviews above the others. Postmodernism's lack of confidence in the truth, stemming from a denial of deity, may represent a hesitation in the light of a global community.

At its heart, however, is a revulsion of the kind of claim that Daniel 11–12 makes about a sovereign God. In the interests of an autonomous self, God must be rejected. In the summer of 1998 one of the most popular movies was called *The Truman Show*, starring Jim Carey. On one level, this movie was an ironic critique of our media-saturated culture, but it actually went much deeper and illustrated the fact that the philosopher's message is in accord with the thinking of the wider population. The main character in the movie was Truman. Without his knowledge, he was born and lived his entire life in a huge television studio. For over thirty years, he did not know that everyone he came into contact with—his father, mother, wife, friends, and even the people walking their dogs down his street—were paid actors, nor did he know that he was the subject of a television show that played twenty-four hours a day, seven days a week. There were five thousand cameras in the studio, in the buttons of the actors, in street lights, in his desk at work. The weather and even the rising sun were controlled by computers. He was the center of a huge soap opera, and what caught the attention of the audience was the fact that he did not know it.

Finally, through a series of miscues, he began to realize the "truth," that he was living an illusion. His life was controlled not by his decisions, but by a director, Christophe. Once he discovered that his life was scripted, he wanted nothing more than to escape. Even though his life was good and there were uncertainties and dangers on the outside, he wanted to gain his independence and throw off the shackles of the director. His fight to achieve that independence and escape the "set" brought the dramatic tension to the story.

At the very end, when Truman had won all our affection and we all desired his escape from this benevolent control, the deeper theological intentions of the movie came out. The director, speaking from his control tower, which was in the manufactured sky (heavens) of the set, spoke with a microphone to the exhausted Truman, who had just battled his way to the edge of the set, appealing to him to stay under his control. But in an assertion of modern/postmodern autonomy and to the approval of all of us in the audience, he rejected this control and left the set.

Even though we all can applaud Truman's rejection of a human authority that was ultimately self-interested and manipulative, the movie intended for us also to desire complete autonomy even from God. The implicit message of the movie and the explicit urgings of philosophers like Nietzsche is that God's control diminishes, not enhances, our humanity.

Here is where the critique is wrong. It is wrong because the sovereignty of God does not make us puppets on a string (see Bridging Contexts section). It does not render our actions meaningless, as they did Truman's. They are a word of comfort and hope in the midst of despair and pain. Daniel 11–12 reminds us that it is not divine sovereignty that leads to oppression, but rather human autonomy. It is the king who "will do as he pleases," who "will exalt and magnify himself above every god and say unheard-of things against the God of gods" (11:36), whom we have to fear and not God.

Even so, we as Christians must be sensitive and careful. Why was there such a strong reaction against Christianity? Why did the Enlightenment throw off the shackles of church dogma? Why did Nietzsche feel that Christianity diminished humanity, when the Bible tells us the opposite? Why do people today recoil at evangelicals in the public square? Oh, how easy it is to ascribe this only to the perversity of autonomous people. But we must be honest and acknowledge that the truth has been used to manipulate, condemn, repress, restrict, and oppress others in illegitimate ways. And we do not have to go back to theological arguments of the past that led to Jewish pogroms, to people who tried to resist civil rights, or to the support of apartheid in the name of the faith. Christianity is being used in the present to promote nonbiblical models of the family, the relationship of the sexes, destructive attitudes toward people of "alternative lifestyles," and so forth.

We are so worried that our country or society will end up in social or moral chaos that the church sometimes speaks with a panicky voice and tries to impose a coercive lifestyle on those with whom we differ. We need to remind ourselves that God is in control. We can certainly voice our differences and disapproval, but we must do so with love in our voice and with open arms to embrace the other person. We can do this, even though it involves tremendous risk, because God is in control. The risk is that our society might, in one sense, go to hell and be a dangerous place to live, but in another sense, there is no risk because God is in control and there is more to life than the present.

Again, God's sovereignty and ultimate control is good, not evil like the director in the movie *The Truman Show*. Postmodern society shows the effects of postmodern philosophy. The tenor of the former is captured by Proverbs 29:18: "When people do not accept divine guidance, they run wild. But whoever obeys the law is happy" (NLT). We should rejoice in God's sovereignty, for not only is it still true that God is in control, but it is clearer to us than to Daniel's contemporaries that there is something beyond this life. It is to that subject that we will turn in closing.

The ultimate resolution. We do not need to argue a lot to convince people that life is essentially unfair. True, the wicked sometimes end up having their schemes blow up in their faces. Certainly there are some good, godly people who get the praise they deserve. But for the most part that is not the case. The wicked sometimes flourish and the godly often suffer. If this life were everything, it would be true to say that it is unfair, and, if one believes in God, it would be fair to say that God is unfair. The problem of retribution is a huge one in the Bible, particularly the Old Testament. We need only think of the books of Job and Ecclesiastes to remember how the Old Testament saints struggled with this issue.

Daniel 12, however, makes it clear that the wicked will ultimately get what they deserve—destruction and shame—while the godly will get what they deserve—honor and life. These themes are much more fully developed in the New Testament and are the basis of Christian hope in the midst of a difficult present.

In the Gospels we see Jesus Christ, God himself, subjecting himself to the suffering of the world, even enduring death. But Christ did not just die; he rose again. In 1 Corinthians 15 Paul develops the idea that Christ's death and resurrection formed a pattern we will follow. Christ suffered so that we might have hope for the future.

Death has been swallowed up in victory.

"Where, O death, is your victory?
Where, O death, is your sting?" (1 Cor. 15:55)

Death is not the end of the story, according to the New Testament.

Daniel 11:2–12:13

The themes of Daniel are developed nowhere more fully than in the book of Revelation. It has long been noted that Daniel informs much of the thinking and imagery of that book. It is therefore not surprising that it is here that we learn most fully about the end of history and the ultimate destiny of humanity and of each and every individual.

One link may be seen in the description of the glorified Christ that stands toward the beginning of the book. Note how it reminds us of the figure dressed in linen in Daniel's final vision (Rev. 1:12–16):

> I turned around to see the voice that was speaking to me. And when I turned I saw seven golden lampstands, and among the lampstands was someone "like the son of man," dressed in a robe reaching down to his feet and with a golden sash around his chest. His head and hair were white like wool, as white as snow, and his eyes were like blazing fire. His feet were like bronze flowing in a furnace, and his voice was like the sound of rushing waters. In his right hand he held seven stars, and out of his mouth came a sharp double-edged sword. His face was like the sun shining in all its brilliance.

Other descriptions of Christ in the book of Revelation also reflect not only Daniel 10–12, but also Daniel 7 and the figure of the "one like a son of man."

In Revelation we learn more about the final war with Michael at the head of the angelic warriors (Rev. 12:7). After all, the seals are being opened (5:1–4). Even some of the time sequences seem closely related to the time indicators of the book of Daniel (13:5).

Revelation gives us the picture of the end, when God's victory in Christ is secure. The victory was won on the cross, but we await the Second Coming for its ultimate resolution. When that occurs, the final judgment will take place. Everyone will rise from the dead—some to eternal shame (Rev. 20:11–15) and some to the glories of the New Jerusalem (chs. 21–22).

This is the hope with which the book of Daniel ends and which, developed further, the Bible as a whole concludes; it is a future, an eschatological hope. How is this not "pie in the sky by-and-by"? Well, in one sense it is. We have allowed the ridicule of the world to diminish our eschatological hope, and we should not because the Bible does give us hope based on future realities. But this hope is not tenuous, based on wish fulfillment; it is based on faith: "Now faith is being sure of what we hope for and certain of what we do not see" (Heb. 11:1). In other words, it is based on past realities as we have already seen in 1 Corinthians 15, the death and resurrection of Christ.

Our faith in the past event of the cross gives us a certain hope for our future, which in turn gives us confidence in the midst of a troubled present. Though we suffer now, we also can live life to its fullest. In spite of difficulty,

Daniel 11:2–12:13

we know that something better is coming in the future and so we can enjoy the present. The message of the books of Daniel and Revelation is not to just wait for the future; rather, in the angelic words to Daniel, it is to "go your way till the end. You will rest, and then at the end of the days you will rise to receive your allotted inheritance" (Dan. 12:13).

Scripture Index

Genesis

1:11–12	183
1:21, 24, 25	183
1:27	152, 186
2–3	241
2	294
2:14	247
3	196, 256
3:14–15	256
11	127
11:1–9	142
12:1–3	168, 237
12:2–3	59
15:1	249
15:18	247
26:24	247
28:10–22	77
39	58
41	73
44:5	55
50:20–21	291
50:20	169

Exodus

8:19	138
13:21	187
15	254
19:16	187
20:2	232
20:3–6	104
27:19	46
29:39–41	203
30:27	46
31:8	46
31:18	138

Leviticus

11	52
16:2	187
25:1–7	222
26:31–33, 43	222

Numbers

5:11–31	163
6:1–4	52
28:3–8	203

Deuteronomy

book	219, 220, 223, 239
1:1–5	231
1:7	247
1:9–3:27	232
4:1–26:19	232
4:19	251
4:20	102
5:6	232
11–12	292
12:23–26	52
18:14	55, 77
22:9–11	183
27–28	224, 232
28:1–14	219, 293
28:15–68	293
28:64–68	60, 219, 233
28:64	232
30:1–10	233
30:19–20	233
32:8–9	250
32:39	102

Joshua

1:4	247
5:13–15	254
6	254, 291

Judges

5	254
5:20	284
6:23	249
7	291
16:28	291

1 Samuel

2:1	189
4–5	47, 146, 255
13	141
15	141
17	292
20:30–34	52
23:1–6	254

2 Samuel

9:9–13	52
11	241
12	141
14:25	49
19:27–29	52

1 Kings

3:5	77
8	219
8:33–34	220
8:35–36	161
8:46–51	220, 233
15:15	46
18	141

2 Kings

14:14	46
20:19	81
24:1–4	43
24:1	43
24:13	47
25:13–17	47

2 Chronicles

4:16	46
36:4–8	45
36:6–7	43
36:20–22	222

Ezra

1–2	246
1:1–4	143

Scripture Index

1:9–11	47	73	126, 289	14:12–14	282	
2:62	52	73:3–12	124	19:1	187	
4:5–7	273	73:23–26	295	26:19	284, 296	
7–10	144	74:12–17	256	27:1	182, 256	
9:6–15	223	75:5	189	39:7	48	
		78	28	40–48	75	

Nehemiah

		78:1–8	29	40:3–5	225
1–7	144	89:17, 24	189	44:12–20	105
1:5–11	223	98	254	44:28	137
7:64	52	104:3–4	187	45:1	137
9:5	79	106:48	79	46:6–7	75
9:6–37	223	112:9	189	46:9–10	75
11–13	144	113:2	79	47	55
		118:22	92, 93	47:13–14	75

Esther

		127:1	128	59:3	52
book	136	145:13	118		
1:13	79			**Jeremiah**	
1:19	160	**Proverbs**		book	218, 219, 220
8:8	160	book	85, 89, 90	3:19	277

Job

		1–9	85	5:22	182
		1:7	86	7	161
book	87, 150, 239	1:8–9	85	12	180
7:12	182	1:20–33	86	31	237
12:13	79	10–31	85	31:31–34	236
38:7	284	12:11	85	31:31–33	236
		14:11	293	32:9–12	285

Psalms

		15:23	92	36	141
2	27	15:24	293	46:2	45
6:3	204	16:22	293	51:27–29	185
6:5	294	26:7, 9	92	52:17–23	47
8:3	138	28:10	169		
13:1–2	204	29:18	304	**Lamentations**	
16:9–11	204			book	'161
18:14–15	256	**Ecclesiastes**		2:4–5	255
18:15	182	book	86, 87, 239		
19:7–11	167	5:2	289	**Ezekiel**	
24	154, 254	7:15–18	293	1	247, 248
24:1–2	256	8:9–10	127	1:1	202
29:10	256	8:10	289	1:7	248
30	129	9:11–12	297	1:13	248
30:6–7	129	12:8	86	1:16	248
35:17	204	12:13–14	86	1:24	248
41:14	79			1:27	247
49:15	295	**Song of Songs**		9–11	161
51	241	4:4	49	9:2	247
51:1–4	241			17:1–10	119
55:17	161	**Isaiah**		20:6, 15	203
68:4	187	6:7	252	24:21–23	251
69:24–25, 27	263	7	27	28:1–19	283

Scripture Index

31:3–14	119	7:1	180	1:4	182, 256
34	202	7:8	283	**Habakkuk**	
37:11–14	295	7:11	283	3:15	182
Daniel		7:13	252	**Zechariah**	
1–6	19, 42, 58, 176, 178	7:25	210, 283, 286, 287	1:12	222
1	74, 89, 90, 100, 107, 133, 143, 146, 164, 167	8–12	178	14:20–21	152
		8	81, 88, 176, 178, 179, 189, 192, 255, 292	**Malachi**	
1:1–3	21	8:1–4	137	1:7, 12	52
1:1–2	123, 231	8:9–12	283	**Matthew**	
1:2	133, 202	8:9	277	2:1–12	55
1:5	76	8:13	188	3:11–12	257
1:21	21	8:14	287	5:17–20	25, 239
2–7	19, 116	8:15–20	137	7:1–2	149
2–6	176	8:25	255	7:5	151, 262
2	19, 20, 56, 96, 102, 123, 133, 140, 147, 164, 176, 183, 185	9	46, 178, 193, 210, 245, 292	10:16	67, 69
		9:1	253	10:28	111
2:11	100	9:20–27	256	11:1–19	282
2:21	298	9:25–27	210	11:3	257
2:22	54	9:27	207, 256	23:35	108
2:49	99	10–12	88, 198	26:26–30	235
3	19, 55, 83, 87, 97, 123, 133, 134, 147, 148, 159, 162, 163, 164, 165, 167, 171	10	179, 188, 194, 210, 230	26:52–54	258
		10:1	21, 56	27:11–14	111
		10:3	53	27:11	172
		11	22, 97, 179, 210	27:51	152
3:16–18	19	12	112, 177, 179, 180, 210	28:19–20	261
3:17–18	167	12:1–3	108	**Mark**	
3:31	116	12:4	180, 205	1:15	240
4	19, 56, 133, 134, 140, 145, 147, 148, 164, 185	12:5–13	180	13	214, 282
		12:7	190	13:26	198
4:8	50	12:9	211	13:32	212
4:9	140	12:11	190	13:33–36	214
4:13	188	12:12	190	**Luke**	
4:20	102	**Hosea**		1:13	249
5	19, 21, 47, 56, 117, 164, 179	2:14–15	225	1:19, 26	205
		6:1–2	295	6:27	79
5:14	116	9:3	52	16:19–31	153
6	19, 55, 97, 133, 221	**Amos**		16:29–31	153
6:10	28	7:17	52	20:18	93
7–12	19, 22, 177, 229	8:12	285	22:20	236
7–8	245	**Nahum**		24:25–27	26, 61, 125, 165
7	19, 81, 88, 178, 179, 180, 185, 210, 255, 289, 292, 305	book	254	24:44–45	27, 61, 125
		1:3	187	24:44	165
7:1–2	22				

Scripture Index

John
8:26	149
9:2	150
12:31	149
17:14	67
17:16	67
17:18	67
17:21	67

Acts
2:22–24	173, 298
5	169
5:29	111, 169
9	248
10	61
14:8–20	83
15	61
22:3–5	87
24–26	111

Romans
1:21–22	106
2:1–4	149
3:10–18	195
7:21–24	262
8:18–27	126
8:18	266
8:28–30	298, 299
8:31–39	299
11:33	150
13:1–7	65
15:4	124

1 Corinthians
1:18–2:16	87
1:20	87
1:29	129
1:30	88
3:16	152
8	61
10:6	29, 59, 124
15	304, 305
15:20	173
15:54–56	173
15:55	304

2 Corinthians
7:10	240
10:17	129

Galatians
1:4	191
3:10–11	238

Ephesians
4:7–8	258
4:22	262
6	259, 264
6:10–18	258
6:12	197

Philippians
2:6–11	125
2:12	290
3:20	67

Colossians
1:15	111
2:3	88, 90
2:12	262
2:14–15	198
2:15	258
3:9	198

1 Thessalonians
5:2	215

2 Timothy
2:5	237
3:14–16	235
4:8	149

Titus
3:3	68

Hebrews
1:1–4	234
10:12–14	240
11:4–40	29
11:33–34	169
12:2	130
12:11–12	130

James
1:22–25	238
2:8–11	150
3:9	152
5:10–11, 16–18	29

1 Peter
1:10–12	26, 280

1 John
2:18	282

Jude
8	251

Revelation
book	128, 177, 213, 264
1:7	198
1:12–16	305
1:15	248
1:17	249
7:17	212
12:7	251
12:9	196
13	198
17:14	128
20	193, 210
20:11–15	305
21–22	305
21:4	212

Subject Index

abomination of desolation, 207, 256, 279, 286
afterlife, 108, 128, 179, 201, 210, 230, 253, 284, 289, 294–96, 301, 304–6
Akkadian, 49
Ancient of Days, 186, 188
angel, 102–3, 188, 205–6, 226, 247–53, 273, 284–87
animal imagery, 121, 183–86, 188, 194, 196, 201, 203, 206
Antichrist, 190, 214–15, 272, 281–84
Antiochus Epiphanes, 190, 197, 206–7, 209–10, 226–27, 229, 271–74, 281–84, 286, 290, 199
apocalyptic, 176–77, 180, 190–92, 205, 207, 210, 215, 222, 225–29, 253, 287
Aramaic, 49, 101, 116, 119, 139, 160, 177, 202
astrology, *see* divination

Baal, 187
Babylon, 121, 123, 284
Babylonian Chronicle, 136
blasphemy, 137, 145–46, 151–52

Christ, 26–27, 61, 67, 87–88, 90–93, 111–12, 125, 227, 266, 282, 299
chronology, 42–45, 56, 75–76, 96, 134, 157, 190, 192–93, 201–2, 205, 207–8, 210–15, 222, 246, 253, 287–88
church/state, 170
comfort, 126, 179, 198, 245–46, 249, 292, 303
confidence, 122
control, *see* God, sovereignty of
covenant, 52, 219, 223, 230–39
creation, 183
culture and Christianity, 61–69, 107–8

Daniel, the book of, date, 21–24, 117
Darius the Mede, 135, 157–58, 246, 253

death, 107–12, 116, 127
demons, *see* Satan
deliverance, 178, 201, 208–9, 225, 229
dietary laws, 52
discipleship, 167
dispensations, 83
diviners, divination, 50, 77–78, 87, 99, 116, 183
dreams, 74, 77–78, 80, 88–89, 116, 119–20, 133
dynastic prophecy, 271

Enuma Elish, 181
envy, 166
Esther, 58
ethics, 27–29, 57–58
eunuch, 51
evil, 178, 194, 201, 208, 229, 253, 288

folly, 85–86

Gabriel, 205–6, 226, 228, 234, 250
genre, 57–60, 74, 97, 117, 133, 143–44, 158, 176–77, 180, 271–72
God, as cloud rider, 187; as king, 82, 89, 92, 103; sovereignty of, 20, 45, 56, 62, 73, 75, 79, 82, 88–89, 97, 116, 118, 122–28, 134, 142, 147–48, 164–65, 172–73, 177, 179, 193, 202, 207–8, 229, 246, 252–53, 288–92, 296–306; as warrior, 179, 189, 194, 204, 209, 247, 250–51, 253–66, 284, 288, 291–92

hermeneutics, continuity/discontinuity with the NT, 24–25, 29, 124, 236–39
history, 59, 144
horn imagery, 189, 203–4, 206

idols, 52, 62, 75, 97–101, 103–12, 134, 137, 146–47
imagery, 178, 192

Subject Index

Joseph, 58, 73–74, 168, 172, 290
judgment, 143, 149–50, 169, 179, 201, 209, 253, 289, 292–96, 304–6

law, 166–67, 169–70, 236, 239–40

mantic wisdom, *see* wisdom
Michael, 251, 284–85
mystery, 78, 80

names, 50–51
narrator, 144–45
number imagery, 190, 193, 210, 215, 222, 227–28

oppression, 72
ordeal, 163
outline, 30–31

persecution, 126
postmodernism, 110–11, 153–54, 302
prayer, 78, 85, 91–92, 161, 164–65, 167, 170, 178, 220, 223, 225–26, 228–29, 240–41, 246–47
Prayer of Nabonidus, 117
pride, 47, 116, 121–30, 122–30, 134, 145, 189, 209
proverb, 92

Qumran, 117, 188

redemption, 168
relationships, 109, 240–43
repentance, 134, 147–48, 150, 178, 201, 209, 229–30, 239–43, 253
responsibility, human, 147–48, 288
revelation, 90, 150, 180

Satan and demons, 128, 256, 259, 262, 265–66
schools, 67
sea, 180–82, 184, 257
self, 110–11
Septuagint, 96
shame, 129–30
sin, 195–97, 219, 225, 240–43, 262
Son of Man, 186, 188, 198, 255
story, 58–59, 96, 101, 105, 144

temple articles, 46–47, 133, 137–38, 141, 145, 147, 151, 153
tree, 119

wisdom, 54–55, 58, 73–74, 78–79, 85–93, 101, 116, 139, 144, 242, 284
Word of God, 148, 153, 221, 228, 234–35, 237

We want to hear from you. Please send your comments about this book to us in care of the address below. Thank you.

GRAND RAPIDS, MICHIGAN 49530 USA
WWW.ZONDERVAN.COM